REIMAGINING CIVIL SOCIETY COLLABORATIONS IN DEVELOPMENT

At a time when uneven power dynamics are high on development actors' agenda, this book will be an important contribution to researchers and practitioners working on innovation in development and civil society.

While there is much discussion of localization, decolonization, and 'shifting power' in civil society collaborations in development, the debate thus far centres on the aid system. This book directs attention to CSOs as drivers of development in various contexts that we refer to as the Global South. This book takes a transformative stance, reimagining roles, relations, and processes. It does so from five complementary angles: (1) Southern CSOs reclaiming the lead, (2) displacement of the North–South dyad, (3) Southern-centred questions, (4) new roles for Northern actors, and (5) new starting points for collaboration. The book relativizes international collaboration, asking INGOs, Northern CSOs, and their donors to follow Southern CSOs' leads, recognizing their contextually geared perspectives, agendas, resources, capacities, and ways of working. Based on 19 empirically grounded chapters, the book also offers an agenda for further research, design, and experimentation.

Emphasizing the need to 'Start from the South' this book thus re-imagines and re-centres Civil Society collaborations in development, offering Southern-centred ways of understanding and developing relations, roles, and processes, in theory and practice.

Margit van Wessel is an Associate Professor at the Centre for Integrative Development, Department of Communication, Technology, and Philosophy at Wageningen University & Research, The Netherlands.

Tiina Kontinen is an Associate Professor for International Development Studies, at the University of Jyväskylä, Finland.

Justice Nyigmah Bawole is a Professor of Public Administration and Management, and Dean, at the University of Ghana Business School.

REIMAGINING CIVIL SOCIETY COLLABORATIONS IN DEVELOPMENT

Starting from the South

Edited by
Margit van Wessel, Tiina Kontinen, and Justice Nyigmah Bawole

Routledge
Taylor & Francis Group
LONDON AND NEW YORK

Designed cover image: Ryan J. Lane/ Sara Kamiloska/Juan Encalada

First published 2023
by Routledge
4 Park Square, Milton Park, Abingdon, Oxon OX14 4RN

and by Routledge
605 Third Avenue, New York, NY 10158

Routledge is an imprint of the Taylor & Francis Group, an informa business

British Library Cataloguing-in-Publication Data
A catalogue record for this book is available from the British Library

ISBN: 978-1-032-14767-3 (hbk)
ISBN: 978-1-032-14775-8 (pbk)
ISBN: 978-1-003-24100-3 (ebk)

DOI: 10.4324/9781003241003

Typeset in Bembo
by codeMantra

MIX
Paper | Supporting responsible forestry
FSC™ C013985
www.fsc.org

Printed in the United Kingdom
by Henry Ling Limited

CONTENTS

CONTRIBUTORS

Mohammed Awal Alhassan has longstanding experience as a development practitioner, currently leading Norsaac, a Ghana-based policy-influencing organization. As a partnership expert, he guided civil society organizations into sustainable partnerships for effective programming. He has interest in research and works with Marijke Priester on a transformational civil society initiative for social change.

Lyla André is a PhD candidate in International Relations at the UCLouvain, Belgium, working on European Union management of the Syrian refugee crisis in Lebanon, with a special focus on childhood education. Her research interests revolve around refugee management in the Middle East as well as European Union development and humanitarian policies in that region.

Elena Aoun is an Associate Professor and Researcher at the UCLouvain, Belgium. Her work focuses on Middle East conflict and crisis dynamics and especially on the role of international actors and powers such as the European Union, as well as the role of civil society actors.

Susan Appe is an Associate Professor at the University at Albany, SUNY, in the United States and co-editor of *Voluntas: International Journal of Voluntary and Nonprofit Organizations.*

Albert Arhin is a Research Fellow at the Bureau of Integrated Rural Development, Kwame Nkrumah University of Science and Technology, Ghana. His research focuses on civil society organizations, sustainability, and climate change.

Justice Nyigmah Bawole is a former Head of Department, the Dean, and Professor of Public Administration and Management at the University of Ghana Business School. He obtained a PhD in Development Policy and Management from the University of Manchester.

Stella Wanjiru Chege is a development practitioner from Kenya. She has an interest in social justice and believes that every voice counts. In 2018, she joined the #shiftthepower conversations calling for more equitable power sharing in international development.

Nandini Deo is an Associate Professor of Political Science at Lehigh University, United States. She is writing a book about corporate influence on civil society. Her previous books include *Postsecular Feminisms, Mobilizing Religion and Gender in India*, and *The Politics of Collective Advocacy in India* (with Duncan McDuie Ra).

Jimm Chick Fomunjong is a Cameroonian. He heads the Knowledge Management and Communication Units of the West Africa Civil Society Institute. He has a deep passion for and expertise in supporting Africans and African civil society organizations in documenting their praxis and in sharing and learning from the experiences documented by the African civil society sector.

Lena Gutheil is an anthropologist by training and is currently employed as a Researcher at the German Institute of Development and Sustainability (IDOS), where she conducts policy-relevant research. She obtained her PhD at Radboud University in the Netherlands in 2021, studying project management practices among civil society organizations.

Sarah Haaij, the Netherlands, is an international journalist who reports on globalization, human rights, and the sweet and sour of development interventions. Her articles, podcasts, and photography always start from a point of interconnectedness. Her work has appeared in international and Dutch media outlets including *The Guardian* and *The New Humanitarian*.

Runa Khan, Bangladesh, is the Founder of FRIENDSHIP, an International Social Purpose Organization established in 2002. FRIENDSHIP works for the most vulnerable and unaddressed climate-impacted communities, bringing direct services to 7 million people each year. She is an international speaker, Rolex Laureate, Ashoka fellow, Schwab Social Entrepreneur, and author of six books on pedagogy, two on children's stories, and numerous articles.

Themrise Khan is an independent development practitioner and researcher based in Pakistan, with over 25 years of experience in aid effectiveness, gender, and global migration. She has worked with several multilateral and bilateral organizations, INGOs, and local NGOs in Pakistan and South Asia and authored a number of reports, research studies, articles, and book chapters in her areas of expertise.

Njeri Kimotho is an international policy advisor and capacity builder from Kenya working in inclusive sector transformation. She is an expert and consultant with over 13 years of experience, including field experience in Africa, Latin America, and Asia. Her longstanding experience in international development intersects feminism, intersectionality, gender equality, social inclusion knowledge, and practice.

Sara Kinsbergen is an Assistant Professor in the Department of Anthropology and Development Studies at Radboud University, the Netherlands. She has a longstanding track record in studying the identity, role, and relations of small-scale, voluntary, citizen-led development organizations, as well as their partnerships and development interventions.

Tiina Kontinen is an Associate Professor in International Development Studies at the University of Jyväskylä, Finland, where she leads a research group on citizenship and civil society in development. She is the author of *Learning and Forgetting in Development NGOs: Insights from Organizational Theory* (2018).

Emmanuel Kumi is a Research Fellow at the Centre for Social Policy Studies of the University of Ghana. His research interests focus on civil society organizations, civic space, lobby and advocacy, African philanthropy, and the politics of development.

Nancy Kankam Kusi is currently the Programmes Officer of the Knowledge Management Unit at the West Africa Civil Society Institute. She is an international development researcher and practitioner interested in development initiatives that promote community philanthropy, shifting power and resources to the grassroots, and the localization of development initiatives in the global South.

Emmanuel Malisa is a Lecturer at Sokoine University of Agriculture, Tanzania. He holds a PhD (Rural Development) and BSc (Agriculture General). His main research interest is in the institutional dimensions of natural resources management and evaluation of agricultural production options. He has over ten years of experience in the planning and management of development projects.

Mieke Molthof is a Researcher in the Department of Anthropology and Development Studies at Radboud University, the Netherlands, and Policy Advisor on International Affairs at the Netherlands Ministry of Health, Welfare, and Sport.

Femke Mulder is a Researcher in the field of disaster and humanitarian studies affiliated with Vrije Universiteit Amsterdam in the Netherlands and Anglia Ruskin University in the United Kingdom. She has a background in organizational sciences and anthropology. Her area of expertise is disaster knowledge management towards societal resilience.

Alice N. Ndidde works in the Department of Adult and Community Education at Makerere University, Uganda. She is interested in education and community development, with a focus on gender issues. She authored 'Gendered citizenship in rural Uganda: localized, exclusive and active', a chapter in *Practices of Citizenship in East Africa* (edited by Holma & Kontinen, 2020).

Catherine Odenyo-Ndekera is a gender specialist from Uganda with over 15 years of experience in gender and social inclusion. She has a Master's degree in Gender Studies and Public Health. Her feminist experience spans multiple women-led organizations in the South in which she has held board memberships and executive positions.

Marijke Priester started her career as social anthropologist in the mid-1980s in Dutch academia and politics, before becoming a dedicated development practitioner, serving as manager in international advocacy and strategic partnerships. She is now an independent advisor and works with Mohammed Awal Alhassan on a transformational civil society initiative for social change.

B. Rajeshwari, based in Punjab, India, is an independent researcher and senior consultant with niti consulting pvt. ltd, working on projects related to sustainable development and monitoring and evaluation. She also works on research related to civil society collaborations, development partnerships, and gender-inclusive development.

Kibui Edwin Rwigi is a Programme Officer at the Partnership for African Social and Governance Research (PASGR), a Nairobi (Kenya)-based not-for-profit organization whose mission is to advance research excellence in governance and public policy in Africa. Rwigi has research interests in participatory democracy, social policy and urban marginality.

Alena Sander is a Research Affiliate at the UCLouvain, Belgium, where she completed her PhD in 2021 on the resistance of Jordanian women's NGOs from within at the intersection of neo-liberal development and neopatriarchy. Her research focuses on the cooperation between Northern-based donors and Southern stakeholders in development, power relations, and resistance.

Esi Eduafowa Sey is the Project Director of the Young African Leaders Initiative (YALI) Regional Leadership Center West Africa, Accra. She obtained a PhD in Public Administration and Policy Management from the University of Ghana in 2019.

Marja Spierenburg is a Professor in the Anthropology of Sustainable Development and Livelihoods at Leiden University, the Netherlands, and Research Fellow at Stellenbosch University, South Africa. Her research focuses on the role of the private sector in nature conservation and land reforms in Southern and East Africa, and the impacts on local communities' access to land and livelihood strategies.

Samantha Temple is a doctoral candidate in the School of Public Affairs at the University of Colorado Denver, United States. Her research examines third-sector issues in East Africa, West Africa, and comparatively. Temple's work history includes development work with the United States Peace Corps and fundraising for a global non-profit.

Dorothee ter Kulve, the Netherlands, is the founder and chair of FRIENDSHIP Netherlands, which was set up in 2007. Ter Kulve's academic background is in business administration and international relations. Her career took her from a multinational company to a private business before she joined FRIENDSHIP. She has worked and lived with her family in the Czech Republic, China, Singapore, the Netherlands, and the United Kingdom.

Linda van der Hoek is a graduate of Wageningen University & Research, the Netherlands. She holds a Master of Science degree in Development Studies. She is currently working as a Project Advisor at the Wilde Ganzen Foundation.

Charles Kojo Vandyck is a Ghanaian and currently serves as the Head of the Capacity Development Unit at the West Africa Civil Society Institute. He has 15 years of experience working on civil society strengthening. He is a Core Team Member of the Reimagining INGOs systems change initiative and an IFC-Learning and Performance Institute Trainer.

Naomi van Stapele is a Professor of Inclusive Education at the Centre of Expertise for Global and Inclusive Learning, The Hague University of Applied Sciences, the Netherlands. She researches inclusion and exclusion mechanisms in education with members of marginalized groups as fellow researchers to counteract dominant power relations.

Margit van Wessel is an Associate Professor in the Strategic Communication Chair Group at Wageningen University & Research, the Netherlands. Civil society advocacy and civil society collaborations in the context of development and the environment are her main research interests, with a special focus on questions of voice, representation, inclusion, and power.

Anna Vellinga is a graduate of Radboud University, the Netherlands. She holds a Master of Science degree in Anthropology and Development Studies, as well as a Bachelor of Science degree in Political Science. She works in employee customer service at Evangelische Omroep, Dutch faith-based broadcasting association.

Janna Visser is an independent (research) consultant from the Netherlands with strong expertise in the fields of gender equality, women's empowerment, and social inclusion. She holds a Master's degree in Gender Studies and Public Administration and has multiple years of professional experience in the international development sector and academia.

Lise Woensdregt, a PhD candidate in the Sociology Department at Vrije Universiteit Amsterdam, the Netherlands, uses ethnographic methods and works with members of marginalized communities to study sex work, community organizing, and the international development aid system. She is committed to developing alternative methods of knowledge production, including community-led research and action.

Thomas Yeboah is a Ghanaian and a Research Fellow at the Bureau of Integrated Rural Development of the Kwame Nkrumah University of Science and Technology, Ghana. His research focuses on migration and development, children/young people and work, gender, rural livelihoods, and development interventions.

Selma Zijlstra is a PhD researcher in the Department of Anthropology and Development Studies at Radboud University Nijmegen, the Netherlands. Her research focuses on the interactions among civil society, communities, government, and the private sector. Before pursuing her PhD, she was an editor and journalist for *Vice Versa*, a magazine about international development.

Sandy Zook is an Assistant Professor in the School of Public Affairs at the University of Colorado Denver, United States. Her research examines civil society, non-profit/NGO financial management, and governance.

ACKNOWLEDGEMENTS

We thank all the civil society organizations, their leaders, staff members, activists and volunteers, and others who have shared their thoughts and experiences. They have made this book possible. We thank Jennifer B. Barrett and Rebekka Flam for their excellent editorial support. We also thank the Dutch Research Council (NWO) and Partos for the financial support needed to make this book open access.

1

INTRODUCTION

Towards reimagining civil society collaborations in development

Margit van Wessel, Tiina Kontinen and Justice Nyigmah Bawole

Introduction

Collaborations between civil society organizations (CSOs) in development are a subject of ongoing critical debate. Questions such as how to advance transformative change, make development inclusive, deal with changing civic space, and localize civil society action are central to current critical explorations of collaborations between CSOs from the Global South and those from the Global North.

In this chapter, we contextualize this edited volume as a contribution to these discussions, combining ideas from research literature with CSOs' own reflection papers, guidelines, and studies. As illustrated by the book's title, *Reimagining Civil Society Collaborations in Development: Starting from the South*, this volume is a collection of contributions that present imaginings of practical ways in which change can take place, supported by empirical analyses of collaborations. The authors of the chapters in this volume come from different locations in the Global North and the Global South. Both academics and practitioners are represented among the authors, who thus combine theory-based analyses with reflections on long-term lived experiences of collaboration, each providing a unique voice and contribution to the ongoing debate.

In this book, we conceive of 'development' broadly, as actors involved in this debate address not only development but also humanitarian work and peacebuilding. The resulting insights are often shared across these domains; therefore, in this book, approaches from each of the three overlapping domains of development, humanitarian aid, and peacebuilding are included. Many academic publications on CSO collaborations in each of these domains reveal and problematize the dominance of Northern CSOs and donors. Furthermore, organizations and practitioners in the sector have recently begun to produce (self-)critical discussions and attempts to change practices.

DOI: 10.4324/9781003241003-1

The main aim of the book is to contribute to ongoing discussions concerning civil society collaborations by providing conceptually grounded and empirically embedded examples to support a reimagination of the nature of these collaborations. The contributions draw on diverse locations, experiences, and fields of development. However, each contribution shares the starting points of focusing on local contexts, questioning current understandings and practices, and providing new ideas on how to transform CSO collaborations to advance Southern leadership. The overall narrative of the book is built around the idea of 'starting from the South', which refers to the exploration of Southern actors' vantage points, situated within their contexts, and their engagements with relevant others in shaping and contributing to development as potential starting points for rethinking CSO collaborations.

Thus far, discussions concerning the need to transform relations among CSOs largely begin from the North–South dyadic relations rooted in Northern control over funding and the imposition, through that control, of understandings, knowledges, priorities, and ways of working that are mostly based on the overall paradigm of managerialism (Aagaard & Trykker, 2019; Banks et al., 2015; De Almagro, 2018; Jalali, 2013). This literature thus generally focuses on the role of international non-governmental organizations (INGOs) and other Northern CSOs as key actors in a system that disadvantages CSOs in the Global South. Problems are widely understood to be structural and systemic and thus in need of system-level changes rather than small improvements. Such changes would require that Southern CSOs be at the centre and in the lead, rather than playing the role of implementation partners.

Despite the commitments to change towards the localization of development, as expressed in the Grand Bargain commitment for humanitarian action, for instance, and the broader discussions on shifts towards 'equal partnership', funding continues to be largely controlled by INGOs, Northern CSOs, and, often, their back donors. Research shows that it is still the case that only a small percentage of international development funds go directly to local- or national-level CSOs (see e.g. Development Initiatives, 2020). Many donors that provide funding for civil society initiatives emphasize contextualization and local ownership of programmes; however, they continue to support programming by Northern development CSOs and channel funds through them as 'fundermediaries' that pass funds to other actors as a main function (Sriskandarajah, 2015), rather than allocating these funds directly to organizations in the Global South. In a recent book, Mitchell and colleagues (2020) argue that INGOs have developed into organizations set up to manage programmes, arguably compromising their capacity to advance transformation. In practice, Northern development INGOs maintain positions of leadership and control, often working through programmes that are supposed to operate across countries. These programmes often involve programme-level Theories of Change that they seek to implement (sometimes in adapted form) through their partners in diverse contexts, contracted based on their fit with the INGOs' or Northern CSOs' ambitions, agreements with back donors, and ways of working that are legitimate within the development sector. Themes like local ownership, sustainability, and empowerment are fundamental elements of legitimate ways of working.

At the same time, organizational requirements for collaboration continue to favour professionalized and formalized organizations, with governance, programmatic requirements, and accountability structures set up to meet the needs of INGOs or Northern CSOs and their funders rather than those of country-level CSOs or the people with whom they work (Choudry & Kapoor, 2013; cf. van Zyl & Claeyé, 2019). The expertise of INGOs and Northern CSOs is valued more than the contextual, experiential, and otherwise different expertise of CSOs in the Global South (Hayman et al., 2016). Through these structural conditions, civil society collaborations continue to impose understandings, agendas, and approaches on CSOs in the Global South. In these collaborations, such understandings, agendas, and approaches are commonly prioritized over others, with support going to organizations that are ready to work in line with these perspectives, while other voices are often depoliticized and silenced through organizational policies (see e.g. Banks et al., 2015; De Almagro, 2018; Seay, 2015; Stroup & Wong, 2017). Disagreements around what constitutes 'the local', with INGOs' offices in the Global South being accused of displacing 'really' local organizations and reproducing unequal power relations at country level, have added to the complexity of the matter in recent years (Khan & Kontinen, 2021). INGOs' readiness to engage with the dynamics and challenges they face has also been debated (Mitchell et al., 2020), with some publications suggesting that INGOs' resistance to change is at least partly rooted in threats to their self-preservation posed by calls and ideas for sector transformation (Bond, 2021a; Fowler, 2016).

What needs to change? Recent reflections in the development system

Although academic research does not yet offer much direction in terms of how to transform civil society collaboration in practical terms, numerous initiatives from within civil society have sought to contribute on this front in recent years. Some of these initiatives have taken the forms of seminars, conferences, and studies that result in publicly available reports calling for action. These initiatives are mostly organized by INGOs, or associations or consortia of INGOs, while sometimes prominently involving the voices of Southern CSOs and experts (e.g., Baguios et al., 2021; Barbelet et al., 2021; Bond, 2021a, 2021b). Other initiatives are more Southern-led or seek to integrate voices from North and South, such as the work of WACSI (see e.g. WACSI, 2021), a report by Moyo and Imafidon (2021), the RINGO initiative (RINGO, 2021a, 2021b), and the work of the Global Fund for Community Foundations (e.g. Hodgson et al., 2017).

The discussion within and about the development sector has been ongoing for years now. Control over resources, engrained organizational practices, and mental models appear to combine to create a situation where change can only come through system transformation (see e.g. Bond, 2021a; Partos, 2022; Roesdahl et al., 2021). At the same time, in publications, the multiple changes sought are not necessarily identified or discussed in relation to other changes. Discussions primarily culminate in identifications of principles that should ground behaviour, along with descriptions and propagation of desired behaviours.

The changes that are propagated involve multiple actors (INGOs/Northern CSOs, funders, and country-level actors) and conditions structuring these actors' behaviours. Conditions that have been addressed in these discussions include power relations, norms, standards, values, practices, understandings, and discourses. In the following paragraphs, we introduce six main issues that actors from within the development sector – again, broadly conceived – have identified as themes and normative goals that should be pursued in transforming civil society collaborations. Some reflections are firmly embedded in the aid system, others put themselves more outside of it, presenting what those involved consider alternatives to a broken system. However, although arguments differ in approach and emphasis, many of the publications overlap in their analysis and envisioning of steps to move forward. The six main themes and goals represent common understandings about what should change in collaborations between CSOs.

First, a prominent and central argument is that control should shift to Southern CSOs and that collaboration with Southern CSOs should be geared towards providing support – rather than direction – to people and organizations well aware of their support needs. Shifting control over funding to Southern CSOs (see e.g. Bond, 2021a) and provision of core funding (Humentum, 2022) and 'quality funding' that is flexible, predictable, and multi-year (Metcalfe-Hough et al., 2021; Willitts-King & Metcalfe-Hough, 2021) should be part of the change. Also direct funding of Southern CSOs is a theme, with publications indicating some increases of this, while also indicating barriers such as eligibility criteria and promoting alternative approaches to overcome these (AWID & Mama Cash, 2020; OECD, 2020; Ismail, 2019). Notably, there is almost no literature that addresses Southern CSOs as agents who can themselves do more to obtain funding directly. Meanwhile, the leadership of communities as actors with agency in their own right, and as rightful owners of their own development is often propagated, speaking often of 'locally-led' (Bond, 2021a) or 'community-led' (Hodgson et al., 2017) development, arguing for this in terms of legitimacy and effectiveness. With regard to attitudes and the roles emerging from these, 'How can we help?' should be the motto for INGOs and Northern CSOs, as they deploy their comparative strengths (e.g. in fundraising, technical capacities, or convening power) and play facilitating and bridging roles, accepting Southern ownership and leadership (Bond, 2021a; Oxfam, 2020; Partos, 2022; RINGO, 2021a; Roesdahl et al., 2021; Schmalenbach et al., 2019). Relatedly, working with existing networks rather than setting up collaborations anew is also sometimes proposed – to replace the practice of INGOs and Northern CSOs selecting partners based on their predefined programme needs (Hodgson et al., 2017; Partos, 2022; van Wessel et al., 2019).

Second, a reorientation around capacity and capacity strengthening is needed. Programmes should be rooted in capacities in the Global South, helping to develop these while also acknowledging already-existing capacities (Baguios et al., 2021; Partos, 2022; RINGO, 2021b; van Wessel, 2021). CSO publications also problematize the common practice of designing 'capacity building' based on observed capacity deficits vis-á-vis standards imposed by the North and argue for more mutual capacity development (Lijfering et al., 2022; Patel & van Brabant, 2017; Peace Direct, 2020). There are also calls for strengthening capacity to build leadership and sustainability rather than to serve project needs and compliance (Moyo & Imafidon, 2021). Some publications also stress that the COVID-19 crisis has brought to the fore the capacities and key roles of local CSOs (e.g. Stopping as Success, 2022).

Third, accountability structures should be created that centre on the people with whom CSOs work, accepting their criteria for success while giving more space to political roles for Southern actors and working against the push towards compliance with donor requirements as a key preoccupation for CSOs receiving funding. Programmes should build in sustainability and transition to local control by shifting resources and responsibilities over time through exit strategies and business models that match these ambitions (Bond, 2021a; Paige et al., 2021; Partos, 2022; Peace Direct, 2021; Stephen & Martini, 2019; van Brabant & Patel, 2018).

Fourth, the setup of collaborations must be representative of the people involved, rather than privilege the voices of (mostly Northern-based) INGO/Northern CSO staff and 'experts'. Through changes in governance structures, e.g. inclusion of Southern actors in boards and advisory committees, Southern actors can more effectively ensure that their perspectives shape interventions (Partos, 2022). A recent report focusing on the topic presented the governance of humanitarian INGOs as non-representative of affected populations or countries and as prioritizing management and fundraising competencies over subject matter expertise. The report advised improving representation 'on metrics such as gender, race/ethnicity, background, geography, and age at the strategic level', also including the 'participation of aid recipients not only at the program level where accountability can often be treated as a box to tick, but also in governance' (Worden & Saez, 2021, p. 11).

Fifth, rather than falling back on well-known approaches to minimize risk, there should be openness to experimentation and a readiness to try alternatives. Instead of seeking out partners that mirror leading CSOs' own approaches and capacities, programmes should accommodate diversity in organization type, gender, cultural and ethnic group, knowledges, capacities, language, and age (Bond, 2021a; Paige et al., 2021). Trust is presented as a promising and just foundation for funding and collaboration (Dalberg, 2020; Partos, 2022).

Sixth, a broader, overarching argument is that the development sector has a colonial mentality, with inequalities sometimes also framed as being grounded in institutional racism, systematically downplaying actors in the Global South as lacking not only expertise or capacity but also trustworthiness and the 'neutrality' required to do development work properly (Bond, 2021a; House of Commons International Development Committee, 2022). A need to 'decolonize aid' (Paige et al., 2021) when it comes to CSOs has been increasingly discussed. Recent reports also suggest that racism is a common experience for people of colour working in the development sector (Bheeroo et al., 2021; Paige et al., 2021). Responding to such conditions, Arbie Baguios developed an 'anti-racist and decolonial framework' to help understand and address them (Baguios, 2022). Relatedly, there have been calls to change development language. While seemingly inclusive notions such as empowerment, partnership, and localization are now widely embraced, these and other expressions can still be experienced as colonial, with reference to, for example, 'developing countries', 'capacity building', 'beneficiaries', and even 'development' called out as such. One could add here that concepts like 'localization', 'Southern leadership', and 'local ownership' are also imposed constructs that problematically define individuals and organizations in terms of unequal relations with outsiders (cf. Bond, 2021b). Interestingly, while local ownership and local leadership are central to these discussions, Southern CSOs, rather than being seen as active agents driving change through their own initiatives, still often appear to be conceptualized as the recipients of proposed changes that are to be offered to them by well-meaning transformed INGOs and donors (cf. Kluczewska, 2019), facilitating a more leading for local actors within programmes, or equal partnership. Other, rarer contributions emphasize Southern agency and ways of being as starting points. Such work may call for decolonizing ontologies, epistemologies, types of actors, relations, and actions (see e.g. Baguios et al., 2021). More rarely still, work may also zoom in on challenges within Southern contexts and within Southern CSOs, to be addressed by Southern CSOs themselves (e.g. Moyo & Imafidon, 2021).

Recent initiatives for putting change into practice

There are also examples of diverse recent and ongoing initiatives that seek to advance some of the transformations that have been put forward in practice. The Start Network seeks to make systemic-level shifts in the way humanitarian aid is approached and delivered by shifting power and decentralizing decision making to locally-led networks and organizations.[1] The RINGO initiative operates as a network with a platform through which innovations transforming INGOs are collected, advanced, and shared (see RINGO, 2021a, 2021b). The Partos Shift the Power Lab seeks to advance transformation through co-creation of innovative solutions.[2] The Southern-centred NEAR Network is a platform of Southern CSOs seeking to advance Southern civil society leadership through innovations, knowledge sharing, and advocacy.[3]

Some donors and INGOs are also seeking transformation, at least to some degree and on some important fronts, in particular control over funding and agendas. Some foundations work to advance a more leading role for local and national civil society. An example is the Start Fund that distributes funds for humanitarian action through local committees.[4] The Netherlands Ministry of Foreign Affairs' Strengthening Civil Society programme (2021–2025), which allocates €1.364 billion to civil society collaborations, requires funded CSOs to shift control to CSOs in the Global South. Funded CSO alliances must include Southern CSOs as partners sharing control on various fronts, and Southern CSOs are eligible for leading roles (Netherlands Ministry of Foreign Affairs, 2019). INGOs and others in this programme have developed new governance arrangements geared towards more shared control, as illustrated by the example of the Just Future consortium (Just Future, 2020). Drawing on other recent INGO initiatives that are transforming INGO governance, Pritchard (2021) provides a broad set of recommendations to shift power through governance, not only embedding communities in governance structures but also dismantling unequal pay structures and building a culture of locally led leadership. Some INGOs have also redefined their strategies in more generally transformative terms, such as Oxfam GB, stressing solidarity and shifting power as principles and conceptualizing its own role as supportive to Southern actors (Oxfam GB, 2020).

The sustainability of changes achieved by programmes is a key concern in many internationally funded CSO collaborations in development. Making initiatives more locally led means placing the control of programmes in the hands of local actors over time, as well as the exit of the international actors involved – a related concern around which initiatives are being taken. Initiatives and reports focusing on the question of how to attain sustainability often pay significant attention to this process of transitioning to local leadership, as illustrated by the recent book, *What Transformation Takes* (Peace Direct, 2020), which documents and analyses these processes in various programmes (see also Stopping as Success, 2022).

However, in spite of the apparent salience of the issues around collaborations and the embracement of transformative principles for CSO collaborations in the initiatives discussed above, thus far there appears to be disappointingly limited translation into practical ways of working and actual implementation across the development sector. We also find little examination for effectiveness (Barbelet et al., 2021; Bruschini-Chaumet et al., 2019; Paige et al., 2021; Stephen and Martini, 2019; van Brabant & Patel, 2018). At the same time, there appears to be much experimentation currently that has thus far not led to publications on implementation and impact.

Meanwhile, the #Shiftthepower movement, which started out from community philanthropy (with the Global Fund for Community Foundations in a leading role), is an example of initiatives questioning the centrality of INGOs in development.[5] This movement argues for the need for and feasibility of local actors more independently shaping development. Relatedly, in recent years, innovative funding structures have also been developed, including, for example, participatory grantmaking, which involves constituencies in grantmaking.[6] Additionally, trust-based philanthropy does away with the formal risk-focused requirements of applying, reporting, and accounting, replacing them with approaches that are less demanding on such fronts, grounding collaboration in trust. This creates space for otherwise easily excluded actors, flexibility, and direct and core funding that builds organizations' longer-term capacity.[7] Country-based pooled funding provides more direct access to funding for national and local CSOs (Baguios et al., 2021).

At the same time, many Southern CSOs continue to depend on foreign funding as a lifeline, and this funding is still largely controlled by Northern NGOs and INGOs, with little sign of imminent change. In turn, many Southern CSOs continue to adapt their agendas and ways of working to requirements of Northern CSOs and INGOs, implicating them, too, in the state of affairs. The casting away of the current funding architecture centred on INGOs, Northern CSOs, and their back donors seems unlikely. However, the key question of 'Who is in control – Northern or 'local' organizations?' reduces the question of how to shape development to one of control, rooted primarily in funding relations, which still does not do much justice to the multidimensional nature of questions regarding how and with whom civil society can shape development. Although we acknowledge that many civil society collaborations involve a variety of actors such as the media, universities, governments, and corporations, this book pushes these questions further with a focus on civil society itself, focusing on the specific power relations and debates around these actors. With this focus, we seek to help shape civil society collaborations through imaginings that start from the South, with collaborations in Southern contexts with Southern CSOs in leadership roles, grounded in their contextual realities. Rather than taking a funds-centred focus on 'shifting power', this book emphasizes 'shifting perspectives' as the basis for transformation (which would also have to accompany any shift in how funds are distributed and managed).

This book's contribution: towards new roles, relations, and processes

In adopting the starting point of shifting perspectives, this book differs from many other publications on the transformation of civil society collaborations in development. Other work on this topic has tended to conceptualize and develop local ownership in terms of control, often within the boundaries of funding relations, taking a programmatic approach to development, with professional (I)NGOs collaborating with 'local' partners. Although they seek to provide more space to Southern CSOs to shape programmes and roles, such perspectives are still firmly rooted in existing understandings and approaches as to how to see and go about development. Although these works may be critical and somewhat destabilizing, they still take a great deal of usual practices for granted, maintaining a focus on such themes as 'leadership', 'capacity', 'management', financial sustainability', and 'communication'.

Rather than focusing on designed transformations in development, such as innovative financial arrangements and governance structures or their processual and relational dimensions, in this book, we take the imagination as an important route for producing new possibilities and directions that can inspire others and provide a basis for further changes, including innovations in funding. Learning to do things differently is not only rooted in structures facilitating such learning. It is also rooted in the development of imaginings of what doing things differently could look like, and from which understandings of realities and of what is possible these might be achieved. In many of the chapters in this book, formal structures, and procedures in funding relations, therefore, do not have a leading role, although we acknowledge that these elements are important for many organizations.

In a similar vein, to capture productive imaginings of how to do things differently, we explore CSOs and their collaborations from the starting point that Southern CSOs are agents seeking to act from their own agendas and understandings of what is possible and desirable. CSOs are often expert navigators of their own contexts, and they are frequently embedded in multiple relations shaping their roles. The relation with a Northern (donor) partner is just one of these. Therefore, the book aims to counteract the bias of seeing Southern CSOs mainly as 'partners', viewing them instead as organizations and groups in their own right, embedded in the social and political contexts from which they emerged and in which they navigate.

Against this backdrop, from the perspective of 'starting from the South', the book seeks to answer three general and intertwined questions around roles, relations, and processes in civil society collaborations. We use 'role' to refer to behaviours tied to normative expectations associated with a position in the collaboration (drawing on Allen & van de Vliert, 1984). A 'relation' is a tie or set of ties between actors through which roles in the collaboration are defined and reinforced. By 'process', we mean a continuous operation or series of operations through which the nature of the collaboration is defined and enacted. First, focusing on roles, we ask how to reimagine who can do what in CSO collaborations when we start from the perspectives of Southern CSOs and acknowledge their agency. Second, exploring relations, we address the question of who matters and how, attempting to distance ourselves from the North–South binary. Third, looking at processes, we ask what new collaborations would look like if 'starting from the South' were more prevalent.

To sketch a conceptual landscape for addressing these questions, in Chapter 2, 'Conceptual foundations: reimagining roles, relations, and processes', Margit van Wessel and Tiina Kontinen introduce the notion of imagination as understood in this book and reflect on what the existing research literature says about roles, relations, and processes in civil society collaborations. Beginning with Chapter 3, each chapter offers a theoretically informed and empirically grounded argument addressing certain aspects of roles, relations, and processes in CSO collaborations. These chapters are grouped into five sections focusing on diverse perspectives related to the overall theme of starting from the South. The themes – 'reclaiming the lead', 'displacing the North–South dyad', 'asking

Southern-centred questions', 'learning new roles for the North', and 'choosing new starting points for collaboration' – each provides an important angle from which to approach starting from the South. The collection is not exhaustive but offers a range of original insights from researchers and practitioners on how to explore CSO collaboration from a variety of relevant points of views that may come in with abandoning Northern dominance in conceptualizing and practicing CSO collaboration in development.

The first section focuses on the theme of reclaiming the lead. In Chapter 3, 'Reflections on using a community-led research and action (CLRA) methodology to explore alternatives in international development', Lise Woensdregt, Kibui Edwin Rwigi, and Naomi van Stapele provide ideas for doing things differently based on their experience with community-led research methodology, where local CSOs take leadership roles in research and analysis to inform the design of activities, with the Northern researchers acting as facilitators. In this chapter, the authors emphasize the processes through which Northern academics should give up power. Chapter 4, 'Reimagining development from local voices and positions – Southern feminist movements in the lead' by Njeri Kimotho, Catherine Odenyo-Ndekera, and Janna Visser, promotes new kinds of collaborations based on Southern feminist leadership and Southern feminists' understandings and practices of engaging with patriarchy. The authors of this chapter stress the role of Southern feminists as independent from Northern feminists and the processes of building the leadership of Southern feminist movements. In Chapter 5, 'Building resilient communities by growing community assets, capacities, and trust', Stella Wanjiru Chege, inspired by her long-term experience as a Southern practitioner, focuses on the roles of local CSOs as drivers of development and INGOs as investors. Discussing a particular approach, she illustrates processes that are geared towards building assets and pooling various resources, including the contributions of local actors. Finally, in Chapter 6, 'Contesting practices of aid localization in Jordan and Lebanon: Civil society organizations' mobilization of local knowledge', Elena Aoun, Lyla André and Alena Sander provide an analysis of how CSOs in Jordan and Lebanon reclaim leadership, rooted in their various kinds of knowledge, and how such agency on the part of CSOs leads to processes of Northern actors adjusting to the context-specific demands regarding the nature of collaboration.

The second section introduces ideas related to displacing the North–South dyad. In Chapter 7, 'Southern civil society organizations as practical hybrids: Dealing with legitimacy in a Ugandan gender advocacy organization', Tiina Kontinen and Alice Ndidde focus on the multiple legitimacy relations of Southern CSOs and show how legitimacy is not only negotiated vis-á-vis different actors but also diverse logics. The authors of this chapter explore the relations in which the legitimacy of Southern CSOs is negotiated and the processes of drawing from contextually relevant institutional logics. Susan Appe shows how diaspora grassroots organizations in the United States are reshaping the conventional divide between North and South in CSO collaborations in Chapter 8,

'Beyond the North–South dyad: Diaspora-led organizations in development collaborations'. Appe focuses on the roles of Northern-based Southern initiatives to support the homeland, where caring and personal relationships are central. In Chapter 9, 'Exploring mutual dependence through non-financial resource exchanges: A Tanzanian non-governmental organization network case study', Sandy Zook, Samantha Temple, and Emmanuel Malisa provide an analysis of the importance of non-financial resources in CSO networks and their power relations. The chapter investigates the roles of multiple partners providing different resources in the partnership, as well as the importance of recognizing a variety of resources in the relations and collaboration processes.

The third section, focusing on asking Southern-centred questions, continues with distancing the analysis from North–South relations and engaging with the dynamics within Southern civil society. In Chapter 10, 'Advocating for land rights in Kenya: A community-based organization's attempt to reconcile external funding with local legitimacy', Selma Zijlstra and Marja Spierenburg explore the legitimacy of Kenyan advocacy CSOs vis-á-vis the different standards stemming from Northern partners and local communities. These authors illustrate how recentring legitimacy relations to focus on communities and constituencies is essential and how a reflexive process is needed to reshape the roles of Northern CSOs. Chapter 11, 'Surreptitious symbiosis in promoting advocacy? Collaboration among non-governmental organizations, social movements, and activists in West Africa', by Emmanuel Kumi and Albert Arhin, shows how West-African CSOs find that these collaborations enhance advocacy through increased voice and impact, enhanced credibility, and visibility. The chapter also shows that transnational advocacy collaboration among NGOs, social movements, and activists is limited and runs into challenges related to power relations, and presents recommendations for addressing challenges and capitalizing on opportunities. Chapter 12, 'Moving beyond (en)forced North–South collaboration for development: Possibilities from Pakistan', by Themrise Khan, shifts the focus from Africa to Pakistan and examines the civil society initiatives drawing on the models of local charities rather than those created or supported by international funding. The chapter discusses the roles of Southern CSOs as independent from Northern CSOs, as well as the possibility of incentivizing the role of Southern actors and their potential for supporting development through existing local initiatives. Chapter 13, 'Shifting the narrative: localization and "shift the power" in the African context' by Emmanuel Kumi, Thomas Yeboah, Nancy Kankam Kusi, Jimm Chick Fomunjong, and Charles Kojo Vandyck shifts the narrative on localization and 'shift the power', exploring how African CSOs understand and contribute to changing the international aid architecture and identifying ways forward, with emphasis on changes within African contexts. In Chapter 14, 'Contrasting gifting postures in a Ghanaian local community: Are there lessons about African philanthropy?', Esi Eduafowa Sey and Justice Nyigmah Bawole identify a seemingly contrasting gifting behaviour when it comes to giving in African communities when exercised in everyday practices or in the context of an INGO project. They show how willingness to contribute is logically related to the level of trust community members have and reflect on the implications of their argument for the emerging literature on African philanthropy in development.

The fourth section of the book shifts the lens to Northern actors and discusses 'learning new roles for the North'. In Chapter 15, 'Localizing humanitarian knowledge management: A call for pragmatic robust action', Femke Mulder suggests an approach of pragmatic robust action to address power challenges in humanitarian knowledge management. The chapter views Southern CSOs as knowledge brokers in humanitarian action. She proposes a radical restructuring of North–South knowledge management relations to make it possible to put evolving local knowledges and debates at the centre of humanitarian action. She contends that this would make knowledge management more effective and improve the social justice outcomes of knowledge management data (data justice). Chapter 16, 'The journey to Southern leadership in programming: The story of a decade-long Ghanaian–Dutch Partnership', invites the reader to join a critical journey with the authors, Mohammed Awal Alhassan and Marijke Priester, practitioners coming from different sides of a Dutch–Ghanaian partnership. In this self-reflective dialogue, they retrospectively consider their collaboration, finding that Southern leadership was often absent and, even in the presence of the best of intentions, difficult to realize. They discuss how a change of mindset and a change of system, including new roles for Northern actors, will bring the goal of Southern leadership nearer. In Chapter 17, 'Starting advocacy programmes from the South: Rethinking multi-country programming', Margit van Wessel proposes turning advocacy programming upside-down. She presents avenues for building new roles for Northern CSOs working from this perspective: rethinking identity, linking up with what is there, and working with opportunities and complementarity.

The final main section of the book discusses choosing new starting points for collaboration. In Chapter 18, 'A feminist approach to collaboration: A sex workers' network in India', B. Rajeshwari, Margit van Wessel, and Nandini Deo discuss how a feminist approach may facilitate counteracting power in situations where a Southern CSO is in the role of supporting its partners and facilitating their voices. These authors show how applying feminist principles such as creating space for diversity and acknowledging intersectionality can build equality in partnerships and facilitate dialogic processes. In Chapter 19, 'Practising organizational autonomy at the community level: Evidence from advocacy projects in Uganda and Vietnam', Lena Gutheil shows the role of Southern CSOs in navigating complex relations with their partners and the government to achieve their own goals. She suggests relativizing the notion of autonomy in civil society collaborations. An empirical analysis based on a taxonomy of autonomy demonstrates, for instance, how less autonomy can sometimes mean more effectiveness. In terms of process, the chapter suggests that relational autonomy is enacted during collaborations where various limiting and enabling factors from organizations and state institutions come into play. In Chapter 20 'Beyond the

North–South dichotomy: A case study on tackling global problems starting from the South', drawing on their experience with FRIENDSHIP in Bangladesh, Runa Khan, Dorothee ter Kulve, and Sarah Haaij discuss how to build new kinds of collaborations and funding relations internationally from a position of Southern leadership. In Chapter 21, 'Shift the power? Constraints and enablers of more equitable partnerships between non-governmental organizations: The case of Dutch small-scale development initiatives in Uganda and India', Sara Kinsbergen, Mieke Molthof, Linda van der Hoek, and Anna Vellinga reflect on the role of small-scale private development initiatives in supporting CSOs in the Global South. These authors highlight the importance of personal relations, which can create a long-term bond between actors from the North and those from the South but can also make it more difficult to confront the power of Northern actors. In the process of developing such private initiatives, implicit rules concerning negotiations evolve, which could be complemented by more formal rules to enable the negotiation of power differences.

In the final chapter, Margit van Wessel, Tiina Kontinen, and Justice Nyigmah Bawole return to the questions posed in the introductory chapter, reflect on the answers to these provided by the individual chapters, and review the main insights emerging from the five sections of the book. The chapter also discusses an agenda for further exploration, research, design, and experimentation concerning reimagining civil society collaborations in development in order to 'start from the South'. Research and the work of practitioners are integrated here, as they will need to feed into each other to advance the fundamental transformations called for in this book.

Notes

1 https://startnetwork.org/locally-led-action.
2 https://www.partos.nl/werkgroep/shift-the-power-lab-2-0.
3 https://www.near.ngo.
4 https://startnetwork.org/start-fund. For an overview, see Baguios et al. (2021).
5 https://globalfundcommunityfoundations.org. With increased popularity, the meaning of #shiftthepower has broadedened, with participants in the debate using it with reference to a wide range of changes and transformations.
6 https://Grantcraft.org. See also https://www.near.ngo.
7 https://www.trustbasedphilanthropy.org.

References

Aagaard, P., & Trykker, S. E. (2020). The road to partnerships in practice: Practical wisdom as an alternative to managerialism in NGO partnerships. *Development Policy Review, 38*(2), 266–282. https://doi.org/10.1111/dpr.12427.

Allen, V. L., & van de Vliert, E. (1984). *Role transitions. Explorations and explanations*. Boston, MA: Springer.

AWID & Mama Cash. (2020). *Moving more money to the drivers of change. How multilateral and bilateral funders can resource feminist movements*. Retrieved from: https://www.mamacash.org/media/publications/movingmoremoney_mama_cash_awid_cmi.pdf.

Baguios, A. (2022). *Anti-racist and decolonial framework*. Start Network. Retrieved from: https://start-network.app.box.com/s/vxtyzboew8we5d7gcp87nkbx2vv2bzjp.

Baguios, A., King, M., Martins, A., & Pinnington, R. (2021). *Are we there yet? Localisation as the journey towards locally led practice: Models, approaches and challenges*. ODI. Retrieved from: https://cdn.odi.org/media/documents/ODI-SH-Localisation-Report-Oct21-Proof06.pdf.

Banks, N., Hulme, D., & Edwards, M. (2015). NGOs, states, and donors revisited: Still too close for comfort? *World Development, 66*, 707–718. https://doi.org/10.1016/j.worlddev.2014.09.028.

Barbelet, V., Davies, G., Flint, J., & Davey, E. (2021). *Interrogating the evidence base on humanitarian localisation. A literature study*. HPG/ODI/HAG. Retrieved from: https://humanitarianadvisorygroup.org/wp-content/uploads/2021/07/Localisation_lit_review_WEB-1.pdf.

Bheeroo, L., Mafethe, P., & Billing, L. (2021). *Racism, power and truth. Experiences of people of colour in development*. London: Bond. Retrieved from: https://www.bond.org.uk/wp-content/uploads/2022/03/bond_racism_power_and_truth.pdf.

Bond. (2021a). *Catalysing locally-led development in the UK aid system*. London: Bond. Retrieved from: https://www.bond.org.uk/resources/catalysing-locally-led-development-in-the-uk-aid-system.

Bond. (2021b). *Taking British politics and colonialism out of our language. Bond's language guide*. London: Bond. Retrieved from: https://www.bond.org.uk/resources/taking-british-politics-and-colonialism-out-of-our-language.

Bruschini-Chaumet, C., Shama, H., Othman, N., & van Hilten, M. (2019). *The localization of aid in Jordan and Lebanon: Barriers and opportunities for women-led organizations*. Action Aid. Retrieved from: https://arab-region.actionaid.org/sites/arab-region/files/publications/The%20Localization%20of%20Aid%20to%20Jordan%20and%20Lebanon.pdf

Choudry, A., & Kapoor, D. (2013). *NGOization: Complicity, contradictions and prospects*. London: Zed Books Ltd.

Dalberg. (2020). Shifting practices, sharing power? How the US philanthropic sector is responding to the 2020 crises. Retrieved from: https://dalberg.com/wp-content/uploads/2020/09/Shifting-practices-sharing-power_How-the-US-philanthropic-sector-is-responding-to-the-2020-crises_Sep-2020-public.pdf.

De Almagro, M. M. (2018). Lost boomerangs, the rebound effect and transnational advocacy networks: A discursive approach to norm diffusion. *Review of International Studies, 44*(4), 672–693. https://doi.org/10.1017/S0260210518000086.

Development Initiatives. (2020). *Global humanitarian assistance report 2020*. Retrieved from: https://devinit.org/documents/776/Global-Humanitarian-Assistance-Report-2020.pdf.

Fowler, A. (2016). Non-governmental development organisations' sustainability, partnership, and resourcing: Futuristic reflections on a problematic trialogue. *Development in Practice, 26*(5), 569–579. https://doi.org/10.1080/09614524.2016.1188883.

Hayman, R., King, S., Kontinen, T., & Narayanaswamy, L. (2016). *Negotiating knowledge: Evidence and experience in development NGOs*. Bourton on Dunsmore: Practical Action Publishing.

Hodgson, J., Knight, B., & Wilkinson-Maposa, S. (2017). *New horizons for community-led development. Recommendations for funders*. Retrieved from: https://globalfundcommunityfoundations.org/wp-content/uploads/2019/04/NewHorizonsForCommunityLedDevelopment.pdf.

House of Commons International Development Committee. (2022). *Racism in the aid sector*. London: House of Commons. Retrieved from: https://committees.parliament.uk/publications/22698/documents/166821/default/.

Humentum. (2022). *Breaking the starvation cycle. How international funders can stop trapping their grantees in the starvation cycle and start building their resilience*. Retrieved from: https://humentum.org/wp-content/uploads/2022/03/Humentum-ACR-Research-Report-FINAL.pdf.

Ismail, Z. (2019). *Advantages and value of funding NGOs in the global South*. Retrieved from: https://opendocs.ids.ac.uk/opendocs/bitstream/handle/20.500.12413/14392/539_Direct_Funding_for_NGOs_in_the_South.pdf?sequence=1&isAllowed=y.

Jalali, R. (2013). Financing empowerment? How foreign aid to Southern NGOs and social movements undermines grass-roots mobilization. *Sociology Compass*, 7(1), 55–73. https://doi.org/10.1111/soc4.12007

Just Future. (2020). *Just future full narrative proposal*. Retrieved from: http://www.africansecuritynetwork.org/assn/wp-content/uploads/2021/03/Just-Future-Full-Narrative-ENG.pdf.

Khan, A. K., & Kontinen, T. (2022). Impediments to localization agenda: humanitarian space in the Rohingya response in Bangladesh. *Journal of International Humanitarian Action*, 7(1), 1–15. https://doi.org/10.1186/s41018-022-00122-1.

Kluczewska, K. (2019). Questioning local ownership: Insights from donor-funded NGOs in Tajikistan. *Journal of Civil Society*, *15*(4), 353–372. https://doi.org/10.1080/17448689.2019.1668629.

Lijfering, S., Rajeshwari, B., & van Wessel, M. (2022). *Advancing research in CSO partnerships. Localization as a way forward*. Retrieved from: https://wncb.org/report-advancing-research-in-development-partnerships/.

Metcalfe-Hough, V., Fenton, W., Willitts-King, B., & Spencer, A. (2021). *The Grand Bargain at five years: An independent review*. Retrieved from: https://www.econstor.eu/bitstream/10419/251128/1/1778377769.pdf.

Mitchell, G. E., Schmitz, H. P., & Bruno-van Vijfeijken, T. (2020). *Between power and irrelevance: The future of transnational NGOs*. New York: Oxford University Press.

Moyo, B., & Imafidon, K. (2021). *Barriers to African civil society: Building the sector's capacity and potential to scale up*. Retrieved from: https://www.raceandphilanthropy.com/research.

Netherlands Ministry of Foreign Affairs. (2019). *Policy framework strengthening civil society*. The Hague: Netherlands Ministry of Foreign Affairs. Retrieved from: https://www.government.nl/documents/policy-notes/2019/11/28/policy-framework-strengthening-civil-society.

OECD. (2020). *The development dimension. Development Assistance Committee members and civil society*. Retrieved from: https://www.oecd-ilibrary.org/docserver/51eb6df1-en.pdf?expires=1656486351&id=id&accname=guest&checksum=6BFE6DCFC62D2321E0BA350E572823A9.

Oxfam GB. (2020). *For a radically better world*. Retrieved from: https://www.oxfam.org.uk/documents/241/Oxfam_GB_Strategy_Document__FINAL.pdf.

Partos. (2022). Dream paper: Shift the power. Retrieved from: https://www.partos.nl/wp-content/uploads/2022/01/Partos-Dreampaper-Shift-the-Power-v7.pdf.

Patel, S., & van Brabant, K. (2017). *The Start Fund, Start Network and localisation: Current situation and future directions*. Retrieved from: https://reliefweb.int/sites/reliefweb.int/files/resources/The%20Start%20Fund%2C%20Start%20Network%20and%20Localisation%20full%20report%20-%20WEB.pdf.

Peace Direct. (2020). *What transformation takes: Evidence of responsible INGO transitions to locally led development around the world.* Retrieved from: https://www.peacedirect.org/wp-content/uploads/2020/12/What-Transformation-Takes-book-December-2020.pdf.

Paige, S., with Kotsiras, D., & Peace Direct. (2021). *Time to decolonize aid. Insights and lessons from a global consultation.* Retrieved from: https://www.peacedirect.org/publications/timetodecoloniseaid/.

Pritchard, Y. V. (2021). *3 ways NGOs and donors are shifting power through governance.* Retrieved from: https://www.bond.org.uk/news/2021/02/3-ways-ngos-and-donors-are-shifting-power-through-governance.

RINGO. (2021a). *Fostering equitable North-South civil society partnership. Voices from the South.* RightsColab/WACSI. Retrieved from: https://rightscolab.org/wp-content/uploads/2021/03/RINGO-RESEARCH-REPORT-FINAL-V-compressed.pdf.

RINGO. (2021b). Prototype portfolio workshop: Moving from ideas to action. Retrieved from: https://rightscolab.org/wp-content/uploads/2021/12/RINGO-Portfolio-Workshop-Report-Dec21-PUBLIC.pdf.

Roesdahl, M., Peet-Martel, J., & Velpillay, S. (2021). *A global system in flux. Pursuing systems change for locally-led peacebuilding.* Conducive Space for Peace. Retrieved from: https://www.conducivespace.org/wp-content/uploads/2021/12/CSP-A-Global-System-in-Flux-final.pdf.

Schmalenbach, C., Christian Aid, CARE, Tearfund, ActionAid, CAFOD, & Oxfam. (2019). *Pathways to localisation: A framework towards locally-led humanitarian response in partnership-based action.* Retrieved from: https://reliefweb.int/sites/reliefweb.int/files/resources/Pathways%20to%20Localisation_report_oct2019_0.pdf.

Seay, L. (2015). Conflict minerals in Congo: The consequences of oversimplification. In A. De Waal (Ed.), *Advocacy in conflict: Critical perspectives on transnational activism* (pp. 115–137). London: Zed books.

Sriskandarajah, D. (2015). Five reasons donors give for not funding local NGOs directly. *The Guardian*, November 9. Retrieved from: https://www.theguardian.com/global-development-professionals-network/2015/nov/09/five-reasons-donors-give-for-not-funding-local-ngos-directly.

Stephen, M., & Martini, A. (2019). *Turning the tables. Insights from locally-led humanitarian partnerships in conflict-affected situations.* Save the Children/Saferworld. Retrieved from: https://www.saferworld.org.uk/resources/publications/1253-turning-the-tables-insights-from-locally-led-humanitarian-partnerships-in-conflict-situations.

Stopping as Success. (2022). *Responsible INGO transitions and locally led development. Findings from an online consultation.* Retrieved from: https://www.stoppingassuccess.org/resources/responsible-ingo-transitions-and-locally-led-development/.

Stroup, S. S., & Wong, W. H. (2017). *The Authority trap: Strategic choices of international NGOs.* Ithaca, NY: Cornell University Press.

van Brabant, K., & Patel, S. (2018). *Localisation in practice: Emerging indicators and practical recommendations.* Disasters and emergencies preparedness programme. Retrieved from: https://reliefweb.int/sites/reliefweb.int/files/resources/Localisation-In-Practice-Full-Report-v4.pdf.

van Wessel, M. (2021). *Linking and localizing in multilevel advocacy. Lessons from the Capacitating Change programme.* Retrieved from: https://www.civil-society-research-collective.org/repository/blogs/linking-and-localizing-in-multi-level-advocacy.

van Wessel, M. G. J., Deo, N., Sahoo, S., Balasubramanian, R., Katyaini, S., Syal, R., ... & Manchanda, R. (2019). *Starting from the South: Advancing Southern leadership in civil society advocacy collaborations*. Wageningen University & Research. Retrieved from: https://www.civil-society-research-collective.org/images/repository/PB_1_STARTING_FROM_THE_SOUTH_DEF.pdf.

van Zyl, H., & Claeyé, F. (2019). Up and down, and inside out: Where do we stand on NGO accountability? *The European Journal of Development Research*, *31*(3), 604619.

WACSI. (2021). *Localisation agenda, Shift the power and African Philanthropic models in Burkina Faso, Ghana, Nigeria and Senegal*. Accra: WACSI. Retrieved from: https://wacsi.org/localisation-agenda-shift-the-power-and-african-philanthropic-models-in-burkina-faso-ghana-nigeria-and-senegal/.

Willitts-King, B., & Metcalfe-Hough, V. (2021). *Improving quality humanitarian funding through the Grand Bargain 2.0*. Retrieved from: https://odi.org/en/insights/improving-quality-humanitarian-funding-through-the-grand-bargain-20/.

Worden, R., & Saez, P. (2021). *Shifting power in humanitarian nonprofits. A review of 15 NGO governing boards*. Retrieved from: https://www.cgdev.org/publication/Shifting-Power-in-HumanitarianNonprofits-A-Review-of-15-NGO-Governing-Boards.

2

CONCEPTUAL FOUNDATIONS

Reimagining roles, relations, and processes

Margit van Wessel and Tiina Kontinen

Introduction

In this chapter, we establish a conceptual foundation, turning to the academic research literature to investigate the discussions concerning roles, relations, and processes in collaborations among civil society organizations (CSOs) in development. The chapter discusses two main questions. First, we explore the kinds of challenges related to power and privilege that have been identified in the research literature concerning civil society collaborations, explaining how these challenges call for new foundations such as equality and mutuality. Second, we investigate new ideas and practices that have been identified as practical translations of the new foundations for collaboration. The discussion presented in this chapter forms not only an overall conceptual context for the chapters that follow, all of which speak from, but also to this literature and offer new directions for reimagining the investigated CSO roles, relations, and processes.

The chapter proceeds as follows. First, we introduce the concept of imagination as a foundation for social change in general and in the context of civil society collaborations in particular. Second, we scrutinize the challenges and reimaginings concerning CSO roles and relations. Third, we discuss challenges and new imaginings for CSO collaboration processes. In the concluding section of the chapter, we argue that, despite many initiatives and normative prescriptions, there is a great deal of room for reimagining the roles, relations, and processes in CSO collaborations in ways that go beyond the solutions being suggested from within the current aid system.

Imagination

In many contexts and moments in time, the imagination has been a catalyst for social change. Following the French philosopher Ricoeur, imagination, rather

DOI: 10.4324/9781003241003-2

than being only a fantasy to escape reality, can be productive of new realities, as it can help the envisaging of a new reality upon which to act (Geniusas, 2015; Taylor, 2006). From anti-colonial movements to 'future workshops' (Jungk & Mullert, 1987) to questioning 'whose knowledge counts' (Chambers, 1991) to the #Shiftthepower movement, imagination has been called upon to catalyze actors to work towards change by helping them see a way forward. Imagination can bring into view what need not be, what truth and value may lie beyond actors' everyday realities, and what could be instead. As Kelley (2002, p. 5), expressing what has been called a radical black imagination, writes, 'any serious motion towards freedom must begin in the mind', identifying his mother's belief that the map to a new world is in the imagination as the catalyst for his political engagement.

In the context of social change, imagination thus starts with denaturalizing rather than simply escaping reality. It is born of a sense that reality can be questioned, in starting and continuing to question it, and in finding and growing the grounds for that questioning. From this foundation, one can envisage alternatives – or find them outside one's initial reality. Seeing such alternatives facilitates action to realize change.

In development, a major current form of imagining is the call to decolonize collaboration, as one theme within a much larger and long-running debate on decolonizing development (see e.g. Apffel-Marglin & Marglin, 1996; Gudynas, 2011; Plaatjie, 2013). Published work has questioned the realities of collaboration as experienced by many actors in the Global South, envisioning ways to think about and do collaboration differently. Much of the imagining discussed in this previous work revolves around principles of relations among actors in development. CSOs in the Global North commonly conceive collaborations in terms of partnering with CSOs in the Global South to develop and implement development work on the basis of shared agendas and in accountable and efficient ways. However, the literature calls these parameters into question, centring on identifying and denaturalizing power, privilege, and prejudice as foundations for collaboration and pointing out practices of dominance, managerialism, and upward accountability that reveal and reproduce inequality. Alternative approaches imagined to replace these foundations stress the principles of equality and mutuality and emphasize facilitating recognition of diverse capacities, identities, knowledges, rights, and perspectives.

As shown in the introduction to this book, these foundations for collaboration are gaining ground – they are increasingly seen as legitimate, progressively rising from the status of 'alternative' counter-views to be understood as self-evidently true, at least in theory. In this chapter, we review the existing research literature offering new imaginings of civil society collaborations in development that are rooted in these new foundations of equality and mutuality. As this book seeks to facilitate the translation of these foundations into practices of collaboration, we focus on three dimensions of civil society collaborations: roles, relations, and processes. 'Roles' refers to behaviours built on normative expectations associated with a position in the collaboration (drawing on Allen & van de Vliert, 1984). 'Relations' are ties or sets of ties among actors through which roles in the collaboration are defined and reinforced. We use 'processes' to mean a continuous operation or series of operations through which the nature of a collaboration is defined and enacted. We explore the extent and nature of reimaginings of each of these dimensions of collaboration, thus charting the present state of affairs regarding the conceptual foundations, their translation into possible practices, and realized enactment. In this pursuit, we focus on research literature explicitly addressing inequalities among collaborating organizations and on how these inequalities are expressed in the collaborations. Generally, this scholarship has centred on North–South collaborations in the aid system. The imaginings expressed in this literature address various aspects of roles, relations, and processes – denaturalizing and questioning these dimensions of collaboration, as well as advancing alternatives. However, we see little of the decentring of the Global North and recentring of the Global South that can be found in the broader literature on decolonizing development (see e.g. Fiddian-Qasmiyeh, 2020). This broader literature foregrounds, for example, alternative conceptualizations of knowledge and knowledge production that relativize Northern-based forms of expertise and learning (Choudry & Kapoor, 2010) and Southern-centred conceptualizations of 'the good life' like *ubuntu* (Moyo, 2021) and *buen vivir* (Gudynas, 2011), which can guide what development should mean in different contexts.

Also, few examples in the research literature show how to move into new ways of relating by illustrating what changes might look like in practice and how new practices could take the place of old ones. This is in line with the experience in practice of change lagging behind principles and promises, as the widespread disappointment on progress on the Grand Bargain illustrates prominently (see e.g. Martin et al., 2021). One reason may be that there are simply few shining examples for researchers to draw on. However, various organizations are experimenting with new ways of collaborating on more equal ground, as discussed in this book's introduction, and pressure on actors to act to address inequality in civil society collaborations in development has increased in recent years. Signs of stasis and slow progress thus far may not be predictive of the future.

As later chapters will show, reimagining turns out to be happening in many places outside of linear North–South relations and moving beyond power relations as their main focus. Such examples show ongoing efforts to imagine collaboration differently in ways that identify diverse actors as important, relativize the role of Northern CSOs, highlight diverse types of ties among actors, and seek ways of thinking about processes that problematize the focus on management that has thus far dominated concern with processes in CSO relations. With their recentring of imagination, starting from various forms of civil society in the Global South, such reimagining efforts are opening new ground and relativizing the North–South dyad in which the existing imaginings in literature have largely been encapsulated.

Roles and relations

In this section, we discuss CSO collaboration from the point of view of roles and relations, which should be seen as interdependent because role expectations are often relationally constructed. We review how the extant literature discusses the questions of who does what and who matters to whom in a variety of relations. We begin with a brief recap of the critical research literature concerning the manifestations of power. Then, we present four main elements of the reimagining discussion: These reimaginings (1) are based on changes in the mindset of Northern CSOs including notions of reflexivity, mutual learning, and moving from control to trust; (2) draw on the drives to shift the focus away from Northern CSOs' agendas and towards contextualization and localization; (3) are initiated by Southern actors' resistance and alternative ways of operating; and, finally, (4) emphasize fundamental transformations in North–South relations and the idea of development.

Problematizing roles and relations

Power imbalances related to donor–recipient relations in North–South CSO collaborations have been discussed extensively for decades (Banks & Bukenya, 2022; Elbers & Schulpen, 2013). In such a relation, international non-governmental organizations (INGOs) and Northern CSOs assume the role of donors who provide funding, determine the content of the collaboration, control the use of resources, and check for Southern actors' adherence to plans. The role of Southern CSOs is thus to be the recipients of funding, reporting its use in detail according to provided templates, accompanied by thorough narrative reports on the implemented activities and achieved outcomes. An alternative relation – partnership – was adopted to conceptualize needed change and move closer to an ideal form of relation. Research has continuously discussed the possibility of authentic (Fowler, 1998) or equal (Lister, 2000) partnership, reflecting the dissonance between the rhetoric of equal partnership and the unequal practices observed in North–South CSO collaborations (Fowler, 2000; Sander, 2021; Schöneberg, 2017).

The conceptualization of power in these discussions has multiple theoretical underpinnings. For instance, Mueller-Hirt (2012) conceptualized monitoring and evaluation practices in North–South relations as manifestations of governmentality as theorized by Michel Foucault, and Girei (2016, 2022) used the lenses of hegemony and resistance as defined by Antonio Gramsci. Moreover, institutional approaches to power as a tendency to modify Southern CSOs to increasingly resemble their Northern counterparts through organizational capacity building have been used (Kühl, 2009). In drafting their strategies for social change, CSOs themselves often draw on the 'power cube' analysis (Gaventa, 2021) to identify the multi-layered power relations towards which they could gear their transformative efforts. Overall, the CSO partnership literature generally discusses power only in terms of asymmetries and hierarchies related to managerialist practices (Dar & Cooke, 2008; Contu & Girei, 2014).

Therefore, accountability is one of the most discussed relations. In current funding arrangements, financial accountability from South to North is significant, not least because many Northern CSOs act as intermediaries, channelling public aid funding to their Southern partners in an 'aid chain' (Wallace et al., 2006). In financial accountability, the actors' roles are clear – the Northern CSO reports to its back donor, such as a ministry, on the basis of financial reports it receives from its Southern partners. Here, expertise in conducting accounting according to international standards is required. However, relations are not limited to financial accountability, but also include accountability regarding activities, results, and outcomes, which are usually verified through extensive monitoring and evaluation systems (Mueller-Hirth, 2012), as well as accountability to the organizational goals and mission over the long term (Ebrahim, 2005). Here, questions of balance between upwards accountability towards Northern partners and downwards accountability towards constituencies and beneficiaries have been among the main discussions (AbouAssi & Trent, 2016; Ebrahim, 2003; van Zyl & Claeyé, 2019). As INGOs and Northern CSOs have moved from a projects approach to a programme approach, the role of Southern CSOs – whether they are local INGO chapters, leading national organizations, or more local CSOs – has often become that of an 'implementing partner' who reports according to decontextualized outcome indicators explicated in the Northern CSO's programme documents. This role exemplifies and fosters the power relations where the North sets the agenda to be realized by Southern CSOs. At the same time, in recent years conceptualizations of accountability have widened to include a wider array of relations and forms, introducing e.g. inter-agency accountability, accountability to country-level state agencies, informal accountability (Hilhorst et al., 2021), and a more internally oriented horizontal accountability (van Zyl & Claeyé, 2019). Downward accountability is emphasized as important for local ownership, trust, and effectiveness. But there has been little research into accountability strategies implemented by local CSOs (van Zyl & Claeyé, 2019).

Relatedly, questions of legitimacy in diverse relations have been widely discussed. One topic here is the question of the representative role that INGOs arguably take, speaking on behalf of people in the Global South internationally and, in many cases, having a much more prominent presence than Southern CSOs, while also playing a key role in deciding which Southern CSOs get to speak in international fora and shaping their voices to fit internationally defined understandings and agendas (see e.g. Gibbings, 2011; Holzscheiter, 2016). Relatedly, how collaboration with INGOs and Northern CSOs affects the legitimacy of Southern CSOs in their own contexts is a recurrent topic. Adaptation of Northern agendas, understandings of issues (Bownas, 2017), and ways of working to meet the legitimacy demands of INGOs and

Northern CSOs (such as financial management, proficiency in the English language, proposal development, and reporting requirements) can lead towards NGOization, involving mission drift and professionalization, and away from representation of constituencies and organizations' own agendas, developed from their own understandings (Bownas, 2017; Chahim & Prakash, 2014; Choudry & Kapoor, 2013; Jalali, 2013). Southern CSOs thus face contradictory demands regarding legitimacy, leading them to perform complicated balancing acts (Elbers et al., 2022; Matelski et al., 2021). In addition, it has been suggested that the tendency of INGOs and Northern CSOs to fund consensus-oriented voices and ways of working can lead to the strengthening of those voices and the relative weakening of others with more conflict-oriented stances involving constituency mobilization (Banks et al., 2015; Jalali, 2013), resulting in CSO collaboration potentially skewing the representative roles of Southern CSOs within their own societies.

Going beyond these themes, the postcolonial and decolonial literature locates CSO collaborations within a wider set of asymmetries constituting a continuation of colonialism. The CSO relation has been identified as paternalistic (Eriksson Baaz, 2005) and characterized by 'othering' through a discursive practice by which Northern CSOs are constructed as capable and trustworthy, in contrast to their unreliable and incompetent Southern partners. Relations can also be discriminatory, with differing value attached to the professional authority of posted and local staff (Sundberg, 2019). An emerging theme inspired by the literature on decolonization is epistemological injustice (Malavisi, 2018), which refers to the practice of valuing international knowledge over local and indigenous knowledges, despite frequent claims to appreciate the latter (Fernando, 2003). This literature is critical of relations where Northern actors play the role of knowledgeable experts, while Southern actors are portrayed as in need of capacity building, for instance through training in certain kinds of professional expertise where Northern terminologies, approaches, and ideas are prioritized in a taken-for-granted way. The differentiated valuing of work also comes in here – for example, through critiques in the literature of how the complex 'implementing' roles of in-country development workers are misrecognized, remain invisible, or are discounted (Peters, 2020). These critiques are related to the question of whose knowledge and capacities are appreciated in collaborations and whose expertise is perceived as sufficient – especially when it comes to the division of labour between expatriates and local staff, as well as the degree to which different forms of expertise are valued and remunerated (Sundberg, 2019). Other literature critical of the continuity of colonial relations sees Southern development CSOs' partnerships with Northern CSOs as vehicles of imperialism and global neoliberalism (Choudry & Kapoor, 2013; Sakue-Collins, 2021) and argues that CSO collaborations function merely as a channel to strengthen the economic and ideological power of the Global North in the Global South.

Reimagining roles and relations

Challenges related to power and privilege in roles and relations in CSO collaborations have been discussed for at least three decades. The literature has also suggested some ways in which these persistent power relations may be counteracted. In the following paragraphs, we discuss four strands of these discussions.

First, there is literature that emphasizes changes in the mindsets and practices of Northern actors that could lead to changes in relations in CSO collaborations. The literature on reflexivity suggests acknowledging the complex power relations prevalent in collaborations (Eyben, 2004; Groves & Hinton, 2004) and building alternatives on the basis of this acknowledgement. One approach contrasts managerial and transformative approaches to collaborations in aid chains (Kamstra, 2020) while identifying the challenges achieving intended transformation with much of existing managerialist logics and practices remaining in place (Kamstra, 2020; Kumi & Saharan, 2022; van Wessel et al., 2020). Others have suggested that collaborations should be characterized by mutual learning rather than mainly knowledge transfer and capacity building from North to South (Eade, 2007), and a shift from a control-based to a trust-based relation has also been discussed (Mawdsley et al., 2005). These ways of reimagining relations in CSO collaborations share an emphasis on how transformations in these relations will be a consequence of changes in the mindsets of Northern CSOs and their individual staff members, followed by their intentional engagement in mutual learning and trustful relations. Moreover, the importance of individuals' willingness to learn and build close and trustful personal relations has been brought up. Thus, this literature suggests novel relations where both Northern and Southern actors learn from each other instead of assuming the roles of the knowledgeable North educating the needy South. Additionally, the idea of trust rather than control as the basis for the relation challenges the role commonly attributed to Northern CSOs as trustworthy managers who need to observe their 'backward and unreliable partners' (Eriksson Baaz, 2005). However, as Kontinen (2018, p. 33) has argued, learning as reformation or transformation of power relations in development CSOs requires a combination of individual, organizational, and institutional aspects, where learning manifests in actual practices of 'doing differently' and in changes in institutional settings rather than in individual attitudes or mindsets. Kontinen (2018, pp. 100–103) has also pointed out the challenging requirement of unlearning and forgetting long-standing practices as part of learning new ones; the dynamics of this process should receive more attention in discussions of the actual translation of new foundations of collaboration in practice.

A second line of discussion emphasizes the significance of context. In this literature, the general argument is that paying attention to different contexts and so-called 'local actors' offers a major means of changing the dynamics of collaborations. A central concept here is localization, an idea that originated in debates on humanitarian action (Roepstorff, 2020) but that has been taken up increasingly widely. In other domains, the concept of local ownership covers similar topics and is similarly embraced, as reported in the existing literature. Localization and local ownership both primarily involve contextualizing through shifting control and initiative to local actors, giving them more control over funding and decision making. With localization, we also see the moving of headquarters to Southern contexts, the hiring of more local staff for leadership positions, more visibility of Southern CSOs, and higher appreciation of local development expertise (Byskov, 2017). However, questions are frequently raised regarding what 'the local' actually means and how diverging understandings of this problematize the envisioning, justification, and enactment of localization (Melis & Apthorpe, 2020; Roepstorff, 2020). Localization has also been assessed as rooted in Northern dominance and reproducing inequalities in its own right, calling for 'critical localism' (Mac Ginty, 2015).

With the increasingly extensive emphasis on context, there is an emerging literature that reimagines civil society collaborations while moving away from questions centred on North–South CSO collaboration. Some of this literature addresses South–South networking and partnering, also introducing the role of diasporas and relativizing the North–South dyad (Appe, 2022; Garbe, 2022). A similarly nascent literature addresses the need to study CSO roles and collaborations more from within domestic settings, relativizing the transnational processes dominating the literature on CSO collaborations in development thus far (van Wessel et al., 2021). More bottom-up processes of collaboration, starting from adequate understandings of local settings, as held by local actors (Seay, 2015), are emphasized in this literature. Deveaux (2021, p. 113), for example, stresses the key role of place-based movements in generating authentic development alternatives. Occasionally, publications question Northern involvement with Southern CSOs' work (Pallas & Nguyen, 2018).

A third debate revolves around Southern CSOs' resistance and autonomy claims. For instance, Claeyé (2014; in the context of South Africa), Girei (2016, 2022; drawing examples from Uganda and East Africa in general), Sander (2021; discussing women's organizations in Jordan), and Dar (2015; investigating alternative accountabilities in Indian CSOs) have shown how Southern CSOs exercise everyday resistance towards required reporting practices stemming from managerialism. Southern CSOs have been observed to emphasize maintaining local relations over reporting to Northern partners, prioritize oral narratives over quantitative measurement, and refuse to provide required information or to collaborate in alignment with the agendas of Northern partners when these are considered irrelevant for their own actions. The capability to resist and to refuse entering into certain partnerships is related to the balance between Southern CSOs' autonomy and their dependency on Northern partners (Banks et al., 2015; Brehm et al., 2004). The overall idea is that, when the relation is one between two or more autonomous actors that share the same interests and agendas, the roles are those of equal collaborators, and the Southern actors can have an equal voice concerning, for instance, how outcome reporting should be conducted.

A fourth debate has considered more fundamental transformations in the relations in CSO collaborations, drawing on wider ideas on development and postcolonialism (McEvan, 2009), decolonialism (Ndlovu-Gatsheni, 2013), and post-development (Ziai, 2007). Drawing on this literature, instead of partnership, which has become one of the 'buzzwords' circulating within the development system (Cornwall, 2007), relations taking forms different from those common in current CSO collaborations in development should be identified and prioritized. Relations based on solidarity have been proposed as an alternative to donor–recipient relations between CSOs (Kajese, 1987) and to managerialism (Dar & Cooke, 2008, p. 3). Solidarity, traditionally, is used in the context of social movements, where it forms a basis for collective action to address common grievances. In the context of CSO collaborations and the inequalities involved in these, authors have used the concept of solidarity in reference to the centrality of Southern CSOs' agency, understandings, and agendas as starting points for collaboration (Deveaux, 2021; Garbe, 2022). Outsiders like INGOs can then take supportive and complementary roles (Deveaux, 2021; Hellmüller & Santschi, 2014; van Wessel et al., 2021). Solidarity can, for example, mean exerting pressure for a Southern-led campaign internationally, or supporting Southern social movements' self-identified goals and helping to facilitate their actions (Deveaux, 2019; Garbe, 2022). However, solidarity is a complex notion in some of this literature, which acknowledges, for example, how solidarity can be rooted in and reproduce inequality, pointing to the need for deep reflection among the privileged and raising questions around particularity and universality (Garbe, 2022; Wilson, 2017). Drawing on research into transnational advocacy of and with the Mapuche, Garbe (2022) conceptualizes the praxis of solidarity from a critical consciousness, as involving social praxis of presence and participation bringing people together, renouncement of privilege and making them useful for a cause, and sharing between those involved.

In most reimaginings of CSO collaboration, however, the reality of aid-chain relations centred on funding provided through INGOs or Northern CSOs is not tackled. Northern funding is accepted as a vital lifeline for Southern CSOs. Fundamental transformation of donor–recipient relations is thus far even hardly explored in the research literature on CSO development collaboration. It appears that global inequalities related to financial resources continue to be accepted as a given. Direct funding has found limited uptake, and there is little research available on it (see Lewis & Sobhan, 1999). The recently expanding #Shiftthepower movement propagates the common practice of community philanthropy as a route towards locally rooted, autonomous development and emancipation. To date, however, there are only a few research publications framing community philanthropy in these terms (Hodgson, 2020; Kilmurray, 2015). Similarly, there are forms of direct funding from donor states in the Global North to CSOs in the Global South, such as the Dutch 'Strengthening Civil Society' policy programme, but these forms have not yet been addressed in research publications. More research is available on other funding alternatives, including work on civil society initiatives in the Global South funded by members of the diaspora (Appe & Oreg, 2020), by private foundations and businesses (Vestergaard et al, 2021), by individuals through small-scale initiatives (Kinsbergen et al., 2017), or through Internet-based donation platforms (Schwittay, 2019). None of these previous publications has presented these forms of funding as a way of addressing or circumventing inequalities in CSO collaborations, but they do call attention to other forms of relations and roles in development collaborations.

Processes: how to work together

In this section, we build on the discussion above, focusing on processes of collaboration. We start by discussing how collaboration processes have thus far been problematized, before discussing three ways in which collaborations have been reimagined: (1) adaptive management to fit changing conditions for better results, (2) building and sustaining relations of mutuality, and (3) facilitation as central to collaboration.

Problematizing processes

Critiques of the current processes shaping civil society collaborations in development centre on how collaboration has become increasingly defined by managerialist approaches. These developments have been partly discussed above; here, we focus on their impact on processes in CSO collaborations. Managerialism, rooted primarily in instrumental rationality and concerns with control and effectiveness, has brought about an emphasis on strategic planning, efficiency, and outcomes (Eagleton-Pierce, 2020). In practice, this has led to the creation of collaboration processes centred on procedures defining and monitoring programmes and their results in predefined and (often) quantified terms. These stress financial management as an important concern shaping collaboration, seeking to guarantee value for money and adherence to 'due diligence'. Practices for risk management may also place conditions on release of funds in ways that may impact receiving CSOs' space to develop and act (see e.g. Kumi & Elbers, 2022). Procedures such as the reporting requirements discussed above require a great deal of attention. Increasingly, work published in recent years has rejected these approaches, especially those limiting flexibility and ownership. Scholars have criticized the tendency of such approaches to invoke a compliance orientation and to overburden and 'NGOize' civil society in the Global South, taking focus away from the actual work and representation of constituencies (Banks et al., 2015; Crewe, 2014; Jaoul, 2018).

Some of the existing literature problematizing managerialist processes points to how CSOs in the Global South resist the imposed conditions by navigating them. Studies have shown, for example, how Southern CSOs engage in practices of perception management and resistance, escaping or shifting the conditions of collaboration with which they are faced (Crewe, 2014; Elbers et al., 2021; Sander, 2021). Most of the literature, however, addresses the problems of collaboration by changing relations and ways of working. The linearity and control sought and suggested by managerial approaches and practices are typically presented as inadequate for addressing complex changes, noting local actors should have a leading role in many of the alternative imaginings that have emerged, understanding and responding to conditions and opportunities flexibly. Four ways of reimagining processes of CSO collaboration that have been proposed are discussed in the following paragraphs. These are generally rooted in a reconsideration of North–South relations.

Reimagining processes

One major alternative is that of adaptive management. This idea has been defined in various ways, but always in terms that centre on decision making as an iterative process, facing dynamics of uncertain environments to fit changing conditions for better results. Theory of Change is one prominent approach that can be categorized as adaptive management. This approach has replaced log frames as the leading 'tool' for planning, monitoring, and evaluation in many corners of the aid system (see e.g. van Wessel et al., 2020). With Theory of Change, the focus has not been, however, on shifting relations in the development sector towards more local ownership, but rather on reflection, learning, and adaptation. Furthermore, the record on that front has shown that achieving flexibility can be difficult given how the aid system is otherwise structured (e.g. van Es & Guijt, 2015). Another prominent incarnation of the adaptive management idea that more radically addresses collaboration between organizations is the Doing development differently (DDD) manifesto (Doing development differently community, 2014), which has inspired many actors in the years since it first appeared. This manifesto emphasizes achieving contextualization through process qualities. For example, the DDD manifesto presents development as a locally owned process, working through local convenors mobilizing all those with a stake in progress; blending design and implementation through rapid cycles of planning, action, reflection, and revision; and drawing on local knowledge, feedback, and energy. Currently, a limited amount of research is available on the adoption of adaptive management, but the idea has been widely embraced, at least in theory (Honig & Gulrajani, 2018) if not as much in practice (Gutheil, 2021). Gutheil (2021, p. 63) has also questioned the transformative potential of adaptive management, as it is driven by Northern actors. At the same time and in line with the manifesto, imagined alternatives relating to the principles of adaptive management often aim for processes that are flexibly geared towards local contexts and their dynamics and actors and that are thus intrinsically tied to questions of ownership. Control as a value should be questioned in terms of whether it facilitates achieving the desired results (Honig, 2018), and it should be rejected to enable more openly understood results. Expressions of adaptive management approaches working from such notions are, for example, set out in research stressing the need to build programming on an understanding of context. Previously published work has discussed various entry points for this. One is the creation of space for creative and flexible processes for imagining the future (Crewe, 2014). Another is enabling organizations to start from their own strengths (Kacou et al., 2022). Attention has also been dedicated to space for emergence, created by allowing local actors to manoeuvre through their contexts on the basis of their own interpretations (Arensman et al., 2018; Ho et al., 2020). This approach can help build effectiveness on alternative fundamental building blocks such as motivation and autonomy (Honig & Gulrajani, 2018).

A second form of imagining centres on building and sustaining relations of mutuality among CSOs. For some, this imagining centres on mutual coordination and communication as crucial for effective and just collaboration processes, building inclusivity and mutuality through adherence to principles (e.g. of information sharing) in daily practices of collaboration. Relations have also been addressed in fundamental terms. Processes seen as needed here are those that reflect partnership, defined in terms of joint commitment, shared responsibility, reciprocity, and mutual accountability (Jordan & van Tuijl, 2000; Olawoore & Kamruzzaman, 2019). Notably, while some concepts like co-creation, co-production abound as buzzwords in the aid world and have been taken up widely in research on development, to date, they have received little attention in research on civil society collaboration.

Relatedly, a review of research analysing adaptive management involving CSOs conducted by Gutheil (2021) showed that the CSOs saw investment in relationship building and collaborations as the most important aspect of adaptive management, emphasizing trust building as particularly fundamental. Trust, in these CSOs' view, leads to 'more communication, better capacity to respond to changing circumstances because of close relationships, enhanced local ownership and leadership because team members feel that they are taken seriously and can make a difference' (Gutheil, 2021, p. 68) – thus closely connecting the capacity to adapt to the local context with the capacity to relate at a personal level. Similarly, a recent analysis of localization in humanitarian response (Roepstorff, 2021) emphasized a failure of localization because of a lack of trust among the actors involved. In the studied case, the actors held divergent understandings of localization and the best way to implement it, which created conflict and hampered joint efforts of international and local humanitarian actors. Roepstorff (2021, p. 3) found that below the surface lay a deep-seated mistrust among the different actors, and he concluded that

> to fill localization with meaning and implement it in humanitarian practice, the humanitarian sector needs to turn its attention to trust-building between the different actors and invest in the fostering of positive relations between them. This requires also addressing underlying structural and systemic issues of (neo)colonialism, racism and classism.

These imaginations are in line with older and influential work by Lister (2000), who emphasized the role of personal relations in partnerships, calling for more actor-oriented approaches, rather than organizational processes such as capacity strengthening, which are still much more stressed in development practice.

While such imaginings foresee better collaboration by building closer relations and also transforming these fundamentally through personal investment and readiness to give up privilege and abandon prejudice, a third type of imagining seeks to achieve the same goal by establishing distance. Taking facilitation, rather than closeness and mutuality, as central to collaboration processes puts INGOs at the service of their partners. Facilitation works to make Southern leadership possible by centring collaboration on the self-defined needs of Southern CSOs. Such 'hands-off' approaches can reinvigorate Southern CSOs in their ambitions to build and act on their own agendas and political roles in their societies by creating an enabling environment by stepping back (Banks et al., 2015), supporting the strengthening of capacities from self-defined needs (Matturi, 2016), and employing the capacities of Northern-based experts to accompany, connect, and coach Southern-based CSO staff in their work (van Wessel, 2021).

Conclusion

We began this chapter with an idea of imagination as a catalyst for social change, referring to a process that starts with denaturalizing taken-for-granted assumptions and practices. We further proposed imagination as a lens through which to review the research literature on CSO collaborations to examine, first, how this literature problematizes some prevalent practices embedded in unequal power relations, and second, what kinds of ideas for reimagining these relations it provides. We showed how the taken-for-granted power asymmetries and the need to transform them in North–South relations in CSO collaborations have been critically discussed for decades, especially from the point of view of management, accountability, and legitimacy.

The main alternatives that have been explored, adaptive management, building close relations of mutuality, and the establishment of distance, can be characterized as reimaginings within the current aid system. They tend to respond to the challenges of management with ideas for modified management, rather than transforming or reimagining the entire institutional set-up of collaborations. Additionally, many of the suggestions emphasize individual conduct and learning as well as the importance of relations among individuals, rather than addressing the underlying mechanisms that make individuals behave in certain ways when they enter the field of CSO collaboration.

Some approaches, such as those centring on solidarity, international support to Southern CSOs with a more 'hands-off' approach, and community philanthropy are more transformative in nature. Academic research on these appears to be relatively limited though and does not feed much into other lines of research that are more embedded in the existing aid system.

Many proposals for alternative roles, relations, and processes are prescriptive. They articulate, for instance, the necessity of trust and mutuality or further fundamental changes in power relations for the South to take the lead. However, descriptions and analyses of actual processes of 'doing differently' in certain contexts are rare. Here, we sense the risk of continuously re-inventing and re-experiencing challenges on the ground, as the prescriptive ideals turn into nice buzzwords with little relevance for practice. In this sense, CSOs can live in 'perpetual presence' (Lewis, 2009), where few lessons are learned from the past, despite good intentions.

Finally, although debates on decolonization are prominent among practitioners, not much literature has reimagined CSO collaborations from this perspective. Collaborations led by Southern agendas or ideas of 'the good life' and characterized by the decentring of the Northern expertise and epistemologies they build on have not been extensively identified or analysed. Relatedly, there has also been little academic research into the issue of racism in CSO collaborations (but see Garbe, 2022), while there is some research on racism in development more broadly (Pailey, 2020), which could be drawn on.

In light of the existing research and its limitations, we suggest a reimagining of CSO collaborations that offers alternative visions that can promote practices and analysis transcending the ongoing critique of power that suggests 'partnership' as a solution, and provides a critique of managerialism suggesting alternative forms of management as a remedy. Although these ideas have served as fertile ground for reflection and for uncovering the challenges related to power and privilege, more is needed. We need research on novel roles, relations, and processes that moves beyond questions of management and provides alternatives from other foundations than existing systems. We also need more empirically informed work that can put ideas to the test and provide exemplars that can guide and inspire.

References

AbouAssi, K., & Trent, D. L. (2016). NGO accountability from an NGO perspective: Perceptions, strategies, and practices. *Public Administration and Development, 36*(4), 283–296. https://doi.org/10.1002/pad.1764

Allen, V. L., & van de Vliert, E. (1984). *Role transitions. Explorations and explanations*. Boston, MA: Springer.

Apffel-Marglin, F., & Marglin, S. A. (Eds.). (1996). *Decolonizing knowledge: From development to dialogue*. Oxford: Clarendon Press.

Appe, S. (2022). South-South networks among NGOs. In C. L. Pallas & E. Bloodgood (Eds.) *Beyond the boomerang. From transnational advocacy networks to transcalar advocacy in international politics* (pp. 49–61). Tuscaloosa: University of Alabama Press.

Appe, S., & Oreg, A. (2020). Philanthropic entrepreneurs who give overseas: An exploratory study of international giving through grassroots organizations. *Nonprofit and Voluntary Sector Quarterly, 49*(3), 502–522. https://doi.org/10.1177/0899764019878785.

Arensman, B., van Waegeningh, C., & van Wessel, M. (2018). Twinning 'practices of change' with 'theory of change'. Room for emergence in advocacy evaluation. *American Journal of Evaluation, 39*(2), 221–236. https://doi.org/10.1177/1098214017727364.

Banks, N., & Bukenya, B. (2022). Northern and Southern NGOs. In K. Sims, N. Banks, S. Engel, P. Hodge, J. Makuwira, N. Nakamura, J. Rigg, A. Salamanca, and P. Yeophantong (Eds.), *Routledge handbook of global development*, (pp. 106–118). London: Routledge. https://doi-org.ezproxy.jyu.fi/10.4324/9781003017653.

Banks, N., Hulme, D., & Edwards, M. (2015). NGOs, states, and donors revisited: Still too close for comfort? *World Development, 66*, 707–718. https://doi.org/10.1016/j.worlddev.2014.09.028.

Bownas, R. (2017). The upside-down roots of a transnational advocacy network: Applying an 'organizational ecology' approach to the anti-GMO network. *Global Networks, 17*(2), 195–211. https://doi.org/10.1111/glob.12148.

Brehm, V. M., with Harris-Curtis, E., Padraom, L. & Tanner, M. (2004). *Autonomy or dependence? Case studies of North–South NGO partnerships.* Oxford: INTRAC.

Byskov, M. F. (2017). Third wave development expertise. *Oxford Development Studies, 45*(3), 352–365. https://doi.org/10.1080/13600818.2016.1276547.

Chahim, D., & Prakash, A. (2014). NGOization, foreign funding, and the Nicaraguan civil society. *VOLUNTAS: International Journal of Voluntary and Nonprofit Organizations, 25*(2), 487–513. https://doi.org/10.1007/s11266-012-9348-z.

Chambers, R. (1991). Scientist or resource-poor farmer: Whose knowledge counts? Brighton: IDS. Retrieved from: https://opendocs.ids.ac.uk/opendocs/bitstream/handle/20.500.12413/254/rc418.pdf?sequence=2.

Choudry, A., & Kapoor, D, (Eds.). (2013). *NGOization: Complicity, contradictions and prospects.* London: Zed Books.

Choudry, A., & Kapoor, D. (Eds.) (2010). *Learning from the ground up. Global perspectives on social movements and knowledge production.* Houndmills: Palgrave Macmillan.

Claeyé, F. (2014). *Managing nongovernmental organizations: Culture, power, and resistance.* New York, NY: Routledge.

Contu, A., & Girei, E. (2014). NGOs management and the value of 'partnerships' for equality in international development: What's in a name? *Human Relations, 67*(2), 205–232. https://doi.org/10.1177/0018726713489999.

Cornwall, A. (2007). Buzzwords and fuzzwords: Deconstructing development discourse. *Development in Practice, 17*(4/5), 471–484. https://doi.org/10.1080/09614520701469302.

Crewe, E. (2014). Doing development differently: Rituals of hope and despair in an INGO. *Development in Practice, 24*(1), 91–104. https://doi.org/10.1080/09614524.2014.867308.

Dar, S. (2015). Hybrid accountabilities: When western and non-western accountabilities collide. *Human Relations, 67*(2), 131–151. https://doi.org/10.1177/0018726713479620.

Dar, S., & Cooke, B. (2008). *The new development management. Critiquing the dual modernization.* London: Zed Books.

Deveaux, M. (2021). *Poverty, solidarity, and poor-led social movements.* Oxford: Oxford University Press.

Doing development differently community. (2014). *The doing development differently manifesto on doing development differently.* Retrieved from: https://cdn.odi.org/media/documents/5149.pdf.

Ebrahim, A. (2003). Accountability in practice: Mechanisms for NGOs. *World Development, 31*(5), 813–829. https://doi.org/10.1016/S0305-750X(03)00014-7.

Eade, D. (2007). Capacity building: Who builds whose capacity? *Development in Practice, 17*(4–5), 630–639. https://doi.org/10.1080/09614520701469807.

Eagleton-Pierce, M. (2020). The rise of managerialism in international NGOs. *Review of International Political Economy, 27*(4), 970–994. https://doi.org/10.1080/09692290.2019.1657478.

Ebrahim, A. (2005). Accountability myopia: Losing sight of organizational learning. *Nonprofit and Voluntary Sector Quarterly, 34*(1), 56–87. https://doi.org/10.1177/0899764004269430.

Elbers, W., Schulpen, L., & Frobisher, E. (2022). Stuck in a "Catch-22": Why donors fail to include grassroots perspectives on CSO legitimacy. *The European Journal of Development Research, 34*(2), 921–939. https://doi.org/10.1057/s41287-021-00406-z

Elbers, W., & Schulpen, L. (2013). Corridors of power: The institutional design of north–south NGO partnerships. *VOLUNTAS: International Journal of Voluntary and Nonprofit Organizations, 24*(1), 48–67. https://doi.org/10.1007/s11266-012-9332-7.

Elbers, W., Schulpen, L., & Frobisher, E. (2021). Stuck in a 'catch-22': Why donors fail to include grassroots perspectives on CSO legitimacy. *European Journal of Development Research*. https://doi.org/10.1057/s41287-021-00406-z.

Eriksson Baaz, M. (2005). *The paternalism of partnership. A postcolonial reading of identity in development aid*. London: Zed Books.

Eyben, R. (2004). *International aid and the making of a better world: Reflexive practice*. London: Routledge.

Fernando, J. L. (2003). NGOs and production of indigenous knowledge under the condition of postmodernity. *The ANNALS of the American Academy of Political and Social Science, 590*, 54–72. https://doi.org/10.1177/0002716203258374.

Fiddian-Qasmiyeh, E. (2020). Introduction: Recentering the South in studies of migration. *Migration and Society, 3*(1), 1–18. https://doi.org/10.3167/arms.2020.030102.

Fowler, A. (1998). Authentic NGDO partnerships in the new policy agenda for international aid: Dead end or light ahead? *Development and Change, 29*(1), 137–159. https://doi.org/10.1111/1467-7660.00073.

Fowler, A. (2000). *The virtuous spiral. A guide to sustainability for NGOs in international development*. London: Earthscan.

Garbe, S. (2022). *Weaving solidarity: Decolonial perspectives on transnational advocacy of and with the Mapuche*. Bielefeld: transcript Verlag.

Gaventa, J. (2021). Linking the prepositions: Using power analysis to inform strategies for social action. *Journal of Political Power, 14*(1), 109–130. https://doi.org/10.1080/2158379X.2021.1878409.

Geniusas, S. (2015). Between phenomenology and hermeneutics: Paul Ricoeur's philosophy of imagination. *Human Studies, 38*(2), 223–241. https://doi.org/10.1007/s10746-014-9339-8.

Gibbings, S. L. (2011). No angry women at the United Nations: Political dreams and the cultural politics of United Nations Security Council Resolution 1325. *International Feminist Journal of Politics, 13*(4), 522–538. https://doi.org/10.1080/14616742.2011.611660.

Girei, E. (2016). NGOs, management and development: Harnessing counter-hegemonic possibilities. *Organization Studies, 37*(2), 193–212. https://doi.org/10.1177/0170840615604504.

Girei, E. (2022). Managerialisation, accountability and everyday resistance in the NGO sector: Whose interests matter? *Critical Perspectives on Accounting*, published online before print. https://doi.org/10.1016/j.cpa.2022.102418.

Groves, L., & Hinton, R. (Eds.) (2004). *Inclusive aid: Changing power and relationships in international development*. London: Earthscan.

Gudynas, E. (2011). Buen Vivir: Today's tomorrow. *Development, 54*(4), 441–447. https://doi.org/10.1057/dev.2011.86.

Gutheil, L. (2021). Adaptive project management for the civil society sector: Towards an academic research agenda. *International Development Planning Review, 43*(3), 393–418. https://doi.org/10.3828/idpr.2020.17.

Hellmüller, S., & Santschi, M. (Eds.). (2014). *Is local beautiful?: Peacebuilding between international interventions and locally led initiatives.* Cham: Springer Science & Business Media.

Hilhorst, D., Melis, S., Mena, R., & van Voorst, R. (2021). Accountability in humanitarian action. *Refugee Survey Quarterly, 40*(4), 363–389. https://doi.org/10.1093/rsq/hdab015.

Ho, W., van Wessel, M., & Tamas, P. A. (2020). *The hidden life of theories of change.* The Hague/Wageningen: Hivos/Wageningen University & Research. Retrieved from: https://library.wur.nl/WebQuery/wurpubs/fulltext/533885

Hodgson, J. (2020). Disrupting and democratizing development: Community philanthropy as theory and practice. *Gender & Development, 28*(1), 99–116. https://doi.org/10.1080/13552074.2020.1717214.

Holzscheiter, A. (2016). Representation as power and performative practice: Global civil society advocacy for working children. *Review of International Studies, 42*(2), 205–226. https://doi.org/10.1017/S0260210515000145.

Honig, D. (2018). *Navigation by judgment: Why and when top-down management of foreign aid doesn't work.* Oxford: Oxford University Press.

Honig, D., & Gulrajani, N. (2018). Making good on donors' desire to do development differently. *Third World Quarterly, 39*(1), 68–84. https://doi.org/10.1080/01436597.2017.1369030.

Jalali, R. (2013). Financing empowerment? How foreign aid to Southern NGOs and social movements undermines grass-roots mobilization. *Sociology Compass,* 7(1), 55–73. https://doi.org/10.1111/soc4.12007.

Jaoul, N. (2018). Politics against the grain: The Dalit movement of Uttar Pradesh in the throes of NGOization. *Critical Sociology, 44*(4–5), 611–627. https://doi.org/10.1177/0896920516688756.

Jordan, L., & van Tuijl, P. (2000). Political responsibility in transnational NGO advocacy. *World Development, 28*(12), 2051–2065. https://doi.org/10.1016/S0305-750X(00)00078-4.

Jungk, R., & Müllert, N. (1987). *Future workshops: How to create desirable futures.* London: Institute for Social Inventions.

Kacou, K. P., Ika, L. A., & Munro, L. T. (2022). Fifty years of capacity building: Taking stock and moving research forward. *Public Administration and Development.* https://doi.org/10.1002/pad.1993

Kajese, K. (1987). An agenda of future tasks for international and indigenous NGOs: Views from the south. *World Development,* 15(Supplement 1), 79–85. https://doi.org/10.1016/0305-750X(87)90145-8.

Kamstra, J. (2020). Civil society aid as balancing act–navigating between managerial and social transformative principles. *Development in Practice, 30*(6), 763–773. https://doi.org/10.1080/09614524.2020.1801590.

Kelley, R. D. (2002). *Freedom dreams: The black radical imagination.* Boston, MA: Beacon Press.

Kilmurray, A. (2015). Participatory decision-making in contested societies: Examples from the field of community philanthropy. *The Foundation Review,* 7(3), 84–97. https://doi.org/10.9707/1944-5660.1256.

Kinsbergen, S., Schulpen, L., & Ruben, R. (2017). Understanding the sustainability of private development initiatives: What kind of difference do they make? *Forum for Development Studies, 44*(2), 223–248. https://doi.org/10.1080/08039410.2017.1307270.

Kontinen, T. (2018). *Learning and forgetting in development NGOs. Insights from organizational theory*. London: Routledge.

Kühl, S. (2009). Capacity development as the model for development. Aid organizations. *Development and Change*, *40*(3), 551–577. https://doi.org/10.1111/j.1467-7660.2009.01538.x.

Kumi, E., & Elbers, W. (2022). How internationally funded NGOs promote gender equality in horticulture value chains in Kenya. *Third World Quarterly*, 1–17. https://doi.org/10.1080/01436597.2022.2081543.

Kumi, E., & Saharan, T. (2022). Hybridisation of institutional logics and civil society organisations' advocacy in Kenya. *Public Administration and Development*. https://doi.org/10.1002/pad.1989.

Lewis, D. (2009). International development and the 'perpetual present': Anthropological approaches to the re-historicization of policy. *European Journal of Development Research*, *21*, 32–46. https://doi.org/10.1057/ejdr.2008.7.

Lewis, D., & Sobhan, B. (1999). Routes of funding, roots of trust? Northern NGOs, Southern NGOs, donors, and the rise of direct funding. *Development in Practice*, *9*(1–2), 117–129.

Lister, S. (2000). Power in partnership? An analysis of an NGO's relationships with its partners. *Journal of International Development*, *12*(2), 227–239. https://doi.org/10.1002/(SICI)1099-1328(200003)12:2<227::AID-JID637>3.0.CO;2-U.

Mac Ginty, R. (2015). Where is the local? Critical localism and peacebuilding. *Third World Quarterly*, *36*(5), 840–856. https://doi.org/10.1080/01436597.2015.1045482.

Malavisi, A. (2018). Epistemology. Epistemic injustice and distortion in development theory and practice. In J. Drydyk & L. Kelehe (Eds.), *Routledge handbook of development ethics* (pp. 41–51). London: Routledge.

Martin, D., Singer, S., & Mathias, B. (2021). Humanitarian accountability in displacement contexts: Five years on from the Grand Bargain. *Refugee Survey Quarterly*. hdab016. https://doi.org/10.1093/rsq/hdab016.

Matelski, M., Zijlstra, S., & van Kempen, L. (2021). Civil society legitimacy as a balancing act: Competing priorities for land rights advocacy organisations working with local communities in Kenya. *Canadian Journal of Development Studies/Revue Canadienne d'études du développement*, 1–19. https://doi.org/10.1080/02255189.2021.1987202.

Matturi, K. (2016). Progress towards effective knowledge sharing in an NGO. *Negotiating knowledge: Evidence and experience in development NGOs*. In R. Hayman, S. King, T. Kontinen, & L. Narayanaswamy (Eds.), *Negotiating knowledge: Evidence and experience in development NGOs* (pp. 93–111). Rugby: Practical Action Publishing.

Mawdsley, E., Townsend, J. G., & Porter, G. (2005). Trust, accountability, and face-to-face interaction in North–South NGO relations. *Development in Practice*, *15*(1), 77–82. https://doi.org/10.1080/0961452052000321613.

McEvan, C. (2009). *Postcolonialism and development*. London: Routledge.

Melis, S., & Apthorpe, R. (2020). The politics of the multi-local in disaster governance. *Politics and Governance*, *8*(4), 366–374.

Moyo, O. N. (2021). *Africanity and Ubuntu as decolonizing discourse*. Cham: Palgrave Macmillan.

Mueller-Hirth, N. (2012). If you don't count, you don't count: Monitoring and evaluation in South African NGOs. *Development and Change*, *43*(3), 649–670. https://doi.org/10.1111/j.1467–7660.2012.01776.x.

Ndlovu-Gatsheni, S. J. (2013). Perhaps decoloniality is the answer? Critical reflections on development from a decolonial epistemic perspective: Editorial. *Africanus: Journal of Development Studies*, *43*(2), 1–11. https://journals.co.za/doi/10.10520/EJC142701.

O'Brien, N. F., & Evans, S. K. (2016). Civil society partnerships: Power imbalance and mutual dependence in NGO partnerships. *VOLUNTAS: International Journal of Voluntary and Nonprofit Organizations*, *28*, 1399–1421. https://doi.org/10.1007/s11266-016-9721-4.
Olawoore, B., & Kamruzzaman, P. (2019). NGOs, partnership and accountability. A case study of ActionAid and its local NGO partners in Nigeria. *Forum for Development Studies*, *46*(3), 451–471. https://doi.org/10.1080/08039410.2018.1562964.
Pailey, R. N. (2020). De-centring the 'white gaze' of development. *Development and Change*, *51*(3), 729–745. https://doi.org/10.1111/dech.12550.
Pallas, C. L., & Nguyen, L. (2018). Transnational advocacy without northern NGO partners: Vietnamese NGOs in the HIV/AIDS sector. *Nonprofit and Voluntary Sector Quarterly*, *47*(4_suppl), 159S–176S. https://doi.org/10.1177/0899764018758462.
Peters, R. W. (2020). *Implementing inequality: The invisible labor of international development*. New Brunswick: Rutgers University Press.
Plaatjie, S. R. (2013). Beyond Western-centric and Eurocentric development: A case for decolonizing development. *Africanus: Journal of Development Studies*, *43*(2), 118–130. https://doi.org/10.2515/0304-615X/2306.
Roepstorff, K. (2020). A call for critical reflection on the localisation agenda in humanitarian action. *Third World Quarterly*, *41*(2), 284–301. https://doi.org/10.1080/01436597.2019.1644160.
Roepstorff, K. (2021). Localisation requires trust: An interface perspective on the Rohingya response in Bangladesh. *Disasters*. https://doi.org/10.1111/disa.12483.
Sakue-Collins, Y. (2021). (Un)doing development: A postcolonial enquiry of the agenda and agency of NGOs in Africa. *Third World Quarterly*, *42*(5), 976–995. https://doi.org/10.1080/01436597.2020.1791698.
Sander, A. (2021). Reclaiming partnership–'rightful resistance' in a Norths/Souths cooperation. *Third World Quarterly*, 1–14. https://doi.org/10.1080/01436597.2021.1957672.
Schöneberg, J. M. (2017). NGO partnerships in Haiti: Clashes of discourse and reality. *Third World Quarterly*, *38*(3), 604–620. https://doi.org/10.1080/01436597.2016.1199946.
Schwittay, A. (2019). Digital mediations of everyday humanitarianism: The case of Kiva.org. *Third World Quarterly*, *40*(10), 1921–1938. https://doi.org/10.1080/01436597.2019.1625267.
Seay, L. (2015). Conflict minerals in Congo: The consequences of oversimplification. In A. De Waal (Ed.), *Advocacy in conflict: Critical perspectives on transnational activism* (pp. 115–137). London: Zed books.
Sundberg, M. (2019). National staff in public foreign aid: aid localization in practice. *Human Organization*, *78*(3), 253–263. https://doi.org/10.17730/0018-7259.78.3.253.
Taylor, G. (2006). Ricoeur's philosophy of imagination. *Journal of French Philosophy*, *16*, 93–104.
van Es, M., & Guijt, I. (2015). Theory of change as best practice or next trick to perform? Hivos' journey with strategic reflection. In R. Eyben, I. Guijt, C. Roche, & C. Shutt (Eds.), *The politics of evidence and results in international development* (pp. 95-114). Rugby: Practical Action Publishing.
van Wessel, M. (2021). Linking and localizing in multi-level advocacy. Lessons from the Capacitating Change programme. Wageningen/The Hague: Wageningen University & Research/Cordaid. Retrieved from: https://www.civil-society-research-collective.org/images/resources/Linking_and_localizing_in_multilevel_advocacy_Van_Wessel_2021.pdf
van Wessel, M., Hilhorst, D., Schulpen, L., & Biekart, K. (2020). Government and civil society organizations: Close but comfortable? Lessons from creating the Dutch

'Strategic Partnerships for Lobby and Advocacy.' *Development Policy Review*, *38*(6), 728–746. https://doi.org/10.1111/dpr.12453.

van Wessel, M., Naz, F., & Sahoo, S. (2021). Complementarities in CSO collaborations: How working with diversity produces advantages. *VOLUNTAS: International Journal of Voluntary and Nonprofit Organizations*, *32*(4), 717–730. https://doi.org/10.1007/s11266-020-00227-4.

van Zyl, H., & Claeyé, F. (2019). Up and down, and inside out: Where do we stand on NGO accountability? *The European Journal of Development Research*, *31*(3), 604–619.

Vestergaard, A., Langevang, T., Morsing, M., & Murphy, L. (2021). Partnerships for development. Assessing the impact potential of cross-sector partnerships. *World Development*, 143. https://doi.org/10.1016/j.worlddev.2021.105447.

Wallace, T., with Bornstein, L., & Chapman, J. (2006). *The Aid Chain. Coercion and Commitment in Development NGOs*. Warwickshire: Intermediate Technology Publications.

Wilson, K. (2017). Words beyond the political? Post-development approaches in practices of transnational solidarity activism. *Third World Quarterly*, *38*(12), 2684–2702. https://doi.org/10.1080/01436597.2017.1354694.

Ziai, A. (Ed., 2007). *Exploring post-development: Theory and practice, problems and perspectives*. London: Routledge.

PART 1

Reclaiming the lead

3

REFLECTIONS ON USING A COMMUNITY-LED RESEARCH AND ACTION (CLRA) METHODOLOGY TO EXPLORE ALTERNATIVES IN INTERNATIONAL DEVELOPMENT

Lise Woensdregt, Kibui Edwin Rwigi and Naomi van Stapele

Introduction

The official development aid (ODA) system increasingly includes community-based organizations (CBOs) in development arrangements. CBOs are community-led organizations founded and led by people who identify with a specific community.[1] Development discourse justifies the inclusion of CBOs by referring to their local embeddedness, connectedness, and legitimacy, all of which are widely considered critical for sustainable and successful development interventions (Skovdal et al., 2017). The relationships between Northern development actors and Southern CBOs and the meaningful inclusion of communities have become much-debated issues among critical academic researchers and development policymakers and practitioners (e.g. van Stapele et al., 2018). Moreover, despite attempts to include community voices, in practice, Northern actors continue to be in the lead, and CBOs remain at the bottom end of the hierarchy. This shows the urgent need for changing the roles of Northern actors vis-à-vis Southern communities and has led to increased recognition of the importance of using community-centred and decolonizing development approaches and research methodologies (e.g. Zavala, 2013). This chapter seeks to contribute to this emerging field of work by situating its findings within larger discussions of collaborative knowledge production and social justice research.

The chapter introduces community-led research and action (CLRA) as a practical alternative for researchers that supports communities to reclaim the lead in international development. CLRA is a dialogic method used in collaborative and community-driven research. Building on participatory action research (PAR) principles, CLRA has the potential to contribute to a reimagining of the role communities can play in the ODA system. The CLRA work that inspired this chapter was part of a larger research project that interrogated how power is

DOI: 10.4324/9781003241003-4

distributed within aid chains in the ODA system. Our focus was on CBOs, and we were keen to understand the everyday dynamics and practices of CBOs and the 'communities' in which they are embedded. More specifically, our analysis draws on a one-year CLRA project carried out in collaboration with two CBOs in Nairobi – a CBO led by male sex workers (MSWs) and a social justice CBO that focuses predominantly on police violence and economic justice in a 'ghetto' (their term).

Below, we first position CLRA within decolonial and participatory traditions in development planning and discourses. Then, while reflecting on our case studies in Nairobi, we discuss the CLRA approach in more detail, including the possibilities and constraints of this method in terms of contributing to durable change in everyday lived realities on the ground, as well as in the ODA system more generally. Our main question is as follows: what are the opportunities and challenges for a CLRA design in planned development? By answering this question, we contribute to the understanding of the complexities of meaningfully and ethically including the voices of 'communities' in development arrangements and to grasping what is needed for CLRA to support communities to reclaim the lead.

Decolonizing planned development through CLRA

CLRA promotes a horizontal and dialogic approach in community-driven collaborative learning processes and draws on the strengths of ethnographic approaches to expand the understanding of dynamics between individual and collective practices to broader social arrangements. The CLRA methodology can contribute to the decolonization of research and practice in planned development. The contemporary ODA system, (re)produced through both subtle and overt self-perpetuating colonial arrangements (see e.g. Kothari, 2019; Pailey, 2019), strongly affects the inclusion and position of CBOs in development partnerships and other North–South configurations. As described in the introduction to this chapter, CBOs in development partnerships continue to be at the bottom of the hierarchy of partners, conceptualized as 'local collaborators' or on-the-ground community mobilizers. The CBOs in our research referred to the treatment of communities by international and national non-governmental organizations (NGOs) as 'neo-colonialism' (*ukoloni mamboleo* in Swahili). A staff member of a CBO participating in our project described the dynamics of CBO–NGO interactions as follows:

> The problem is they [NGOs] have big salaries and take up all the budget, but they can't do the work on the ground. So, we are partners on paper, but we are also sub-grantees. We don't have the power to change that. That is why we say we are their donkeys. That is why we say they colonize us. We know and they know we would never even have gotten the proposal by the EU if their name was not on it, even if it was our idea and it concerns our

> lives. We are dying and we need change, and we can only work on this by being abused by them [partner NGOs]. That is the real problem. We can't get big proposals as CBOs. We try a lot, but it is really difficult.
>
> *[Youth CBO staff member, February 2020]*

This quote illustrates how CBOs struggle to be included meaningfully and ethically in North–South partnerships. CBO representatives expressed the need to liberate research, activism, and development from neo-colonial bondage.

CLRA is used with the aim of changing neo-colonial relationships between 'Norths' and 'Souths', between development practitioners and communities, and among researchers. It draws inspiration from approaches used in PAR. PAR, which can be traced to anti-colonial movements in Africa, Latin America, and elsewhere (Kapoor, 2009; Mbembe, 2001; Ndlovu-Gatsheni, 2015), is designed to amplify demands and critiques from the 'margins' (hooks, 2000) and the 'bottom' (Matsuda, 1987) and to elaborate alternative possibilities for justice (Zavala, 2013). In the context of planned development, PAR aims to honour the perspectives, voices, and interests of the communities being studied to improve (access to) sustainable and inclusive development (Borda, 2006). In theory, PAR aims to be transformative and encourages ownership of the research and action process. However, despite the promises of community ownership in PAR rhetoric, other authors have pointed to the risks of tokenism and of PAR programmes ending up being perfunctory (e.g. Gardner & Lewis, 2015). Hence, in an attempt to further disrupt neo-colonial structures and prevent the co-optation and tokenism of communities, CLRA builds on PAR, taking it a step further by being fully community led. While PAR often responds to a particular problem or need, the CLRA process is open-ended and iterative, changing with community discussions. This means that, in CLRA, research questions and subjects arise from communities examining their shared realities and co-creating meaning in the context of everyday lived realities. CLRA's community-led nature thus provides a means to re-evaluate power differences among relevant (development) actors and offers an alternative to traditional methods of knowledge production (Mignolo, 2003) and concomitant action. This concerns not only action as part of the research but also as emerging as part of the research process – CLRA can generate long-lasting influence among involved communities after the research activity ends. Finally, CLRA does not move from a university or an NGO to a community and back, as is the case with many PAR projects. Instead, CLRA moves within and through the community, with the university or NGO functioning as a mere facilitator. This facilitating role is delineated by the terms of the community and may only be practised to build an infrastructure that can facilitate freeing up the exchange of ideas, resources, and tools for the greater democratization of knowledge (James & Gordon, 2008).

Below, we describe how we implemented CLRA in the context of two CBOs in Nairobi. While we envision CLRA as a legitimate effort in decolonizing the ODA system, reconfiguring power, and doing things differently, the resources for this project flowed through a Dutch university, and we were held accountable by a Dutch funding agency. Consequently, even though the research proposal was written collaboratively by the academics and the CBOs, the main applicant was still a university based in the North, with the CBOs as co-applicants. Nonetheless, the CBOs did receive and manage their portion of the funding, with an almost equal amount given to the main applicant and the co-applicants, and we all established a structure of mutual accountability, both in the research process and outputs and in financial records. Alongside our somewhat inadequate attempts to be fully equal partners, obstructed by funding structures and ensuing demands, this chapter was developed solely by the academic researchers involved. The CBOs took the lead on certain reports and other project outputs they found more directly relevant to their work and chose not to work on academic articles. Although many reasons informed this decision, which can be partly attributed to differences in academic and community priorities, it does illustrate an interesting boundary we encountered to CLRA being fully community-led.

CLRA in practice: how we did it – an inclusive consortium, research teams, and methodology

In 2018, we implemented a CLRA project with two CBOs in Nairobi, Kenya. Before implementation, to promote co-ownership, we built an inclusive research consortium consisting of academic researchers and the CBOs. The consortium was a site of multiple intersectional points around notions of race, gender and sexuality, social and economic class, and culture. The project's reflexively constituted consortium members were keen to foreground the narratives of marginalized communities represented in the consortium. To further promote CBO leadership, the CBOs independently managed funds in line with assigned consortium roles and tasks. This facilitated the CBOs to monitor and manage the boundaries of the academic researchers' work as facilitators in the CLRA project. The resulting praxis increasingly shaped our collective critical inquiry that made use of all our individual and combined expertise on equal terms, while the ultimate power remained located with the two CBOs.

Regarding the makeup of the two research teams, each of the two CBOs selected and employed ten community researchers (CRs) to participate in the CLRA process. The CRs were selected on the basis of community membership and CBO affiliation. None of the CRs in either team had any formal research training when they came into the project. Hence, in facilitating the project, we assisted 'from behind' by supporting the CRs to create, synthesize, and mobilize knowledge. This also included supporting the CRs with writing and research and co-moderating weekly analysis discussion sessions. In terms of the actual implementation, we conducted the CLRA research process for a period of eight months (April to December 2018). Every Thursday (sex workers) and Friday (youth), one of the teams met at the office of the CBO with which they were affiliated. In these meetings, we started with four weeks of building research skills and trust and getting to know each other. Thereafter, the research process consisted of two parts: (1) data collection and (2) data analysis and dissemination. The first of these parts lasted five months, during which each team of CRs met and collected a wealth of data describing different aspects of community life through the eyes of fellow community members. The CRs kept personal journals in which they recorded their reflections on their everyday activities and experiences. They collected ethnographic data by recording observations in their communities, and they each conducted at least two interviews with fellow MSWs or youths living in the ghettos. Each week, the CRs' data collection revolved around previously designed research questions they developed during the weekly collaborative analysis sessions as they delved deeper and deeper into the issues affecting their life-worlds. While discussing the CRs' weekly journals and interview outcomes, the facilitators recorded emerging themes. Towards the end of each session, the CRs would pick one theme or topic they desired to explore further in the coming week. They would then collaboratively formulate new research questions each week. The MSW team discussed topics including public stigma and discrimination, government-led key population policies, community activism and advocacy, mental health among MSWs, and economic empowerment. The youths team covered topics such as police brutality and extrajudicial killings, youth (un)employment, access to basic services, engaging 'hard-to-reach' youths, peace building, and political violence.

The second part of the research process, which lasted three months, focused on a secondary cycle of data analyses through writing and storytelling. Each CR interacted intimately with their personally collected data and, with the guidance of the facilitators, learned how to code their data. From these codes, the CRs formulated *fununu*[2] statements or research propositions. These propositions were written down on sticky notes, posted on a wall, and rearranged to create a 'mind map'. Then, working in pairs, the CRs were assigned new emergent themes and tasked with writing about them. For the story-writing phase, each CR worked with datasets consisting of the collective data from the whole group of CRs, which provided another collaborative dimension to the writing process. During this phase, the CRs also read their written stories to each other in an exercise we called 'community peer review'. During this exercise, the CRs engaged in critical and constructive feedback in a process that both validated their findings and built on their writing. At the end of this second research phase, the two teams produced 17 community research chapters (see Ghetto Foundation, 2019; Healthy Options for Young Men on AIDS/STI [HOYMAS], 2019). Moreover, the CRs presented the results of their research to the board members of their respective CBOs, to their communities, and during a formal book presentation. This book presentation was conducted at the British Institute of Eastern Africa in Nairobi, and all sorts of relevant stakeholders related to the CBOs were invited, including partner CBOs, NGOs, government officials, and academics. In the remainder of the chapter, we reflect on several of the CLRA project outcomes and, on the basis of our experiences, describe how CLRA may function as a catalyst for durable change.

CLRA project outcomes

Co-creation of knowledge and centring community-identified priorities

The outcomes of the CLRA process generated rich and detailed data of the kind that are often left unregistered with other research methods and that generally remain invisible in the academic literature on (male) sex workers and youth living in the ghettos. For instance, despite being involved in international development partnerships since its founding in 2009, the MSW CBO had largely participated only in quantitative research projects and interventions focusing on the management of HIV and sexually transmitted infections, with community members serving as the key subjects of interest – the 'key populations' (see Woensdregt & Nencel, 2022a). The CRs found out from the CLRA process that, while they (and their communities at large) appreciated the health-oriented programmes CBOs provided, these programmes did not always meet their most immediate or pressing desires and needs. The more hidden aspects of their everyday lived realities, including gender-based violence and economic insecurities, remained largely unaddressed. Through the research, the CRs were able to identify these gaps in current programmes for MSWs, and they unearthed mental health as a root cause of many physical health problems among sex workers. They felt that, if mental health issues are left unaddressed, it will render futile other initiatives focusing on sexually transmitted infections and HIV prevention.

CLRA provides opportunities for long-term action

We learned that CLRA could also be a tool for critical reflection for assessing the sustainability and scalability of development interventions. Our CLRA outcomes illustrate that sustainability in the context of CLRA is a process that leads to a number of actions generating several new events and processes that all have specific potentially transformative effects that, in turn, also result in subsequent steps, and so on. For instance, one of the CRs from the ghetto, inspired by his research work, started a radio programme with his CLRA colleagues. This led to the founding of a new youth group that grew into a formal organization that now collaborates with influential Northern actors in the ODA system. Other CRs from the ghetto used the skills they had learned through this project to start an informal mentor programme engaging younger members of their community in research and action. They now form a wide pool of active researchers supporting CBOs in the ghetto with research and research outputs. When we were writing the research proposal for this work, we could never have predicted such outcomes, which illustrates how CLRA requires flexibility and open-endedness in terms of (sustainable) outcomes. Rethinking programme sustainability indicates the need to focus on the research process more than a rigid continuation of specific pre-set project activities. Sustainability, then, becomes a lens to look at how CLRA leads, in this case, to a specific form of agency which may contribute to increased critical consciousness and engender particular community initiatives far into the future. As these emerging forms of sustainability cannot be observed right away, in terms of either the change or the content, this requires a broader frame of project activities and their specific goals. Ultimately, allowing a broader frame of this kind opens a window of opportunity for people-centred/driven and contextualized transformative activities that follow the rhythm of community members' everyday lives and for leaving space for surprises in terms of both knowledge creation and long-term outcomes.

Capacities of participating CBOs

Compared with other development programmes, the CLRA process builds community capacities in different, and potentially more useful, ways. The CLRA research outcomes, combined with the outcomes of participant observations in the two CBOs and interviews with staff members, suggest that development programmes often use CBO members as mere 'bodies' requested to participate in meetings and trainings to fulfil programmatic indicators. Members of the two CBOs explained that NGOs and research institutions often invite them to capacity-building workshops. These workshops tend to focus on health education, safe sex practices and sex worker rights – in the case of MSWs, and data collection and documentation of police killings and sexual violence – in the case of ghetto youths. Community members explained that these training modules do not always meet community members' needs and aspirations. Moreover, we observed that such trainings generally fail to build skills community members can use outside the planned development context.

We observed that CLRA builds grassroots research experience beyond programmatic needs. Through the CLRA process, the CRs were trained in interviewing, writing, and presentation skills. Although it remains unclear whether training on these skills is more useful than other capacity building in the context of planned development, as noted above, this did provide CRs with the necessary skills to participate in other research projects in the CBO/NGO sector. Moreover, we observed that the CRs gained critical consciousness through the CLRA process in terms of their lives (e.g. realizing that they are more than sex workers or 'thugs') and their capabilities beyond planned development programmes. They became aware that their experiences and stories matter and that they are capable of action. During their collaborative sessions, the CRs often contrasted CLRA with what they termed 'NGO-driven research' and described the CLRA process to each other as an empowering experience, as illustrated by the following comment:

> The [CLRA] research, it taught us what we know, and how much we know, and it also showed us what we can do. We can do research, we can write reports, and we can make decisions. We have voices that we can share and make heard. We can initiate our development projects for change and teach NGOs on what we really need and how we want to work together – or not work together at all. This is what we do, also in our justice work, we suffer from police violence, so it's our story to tell. But we can only tell it in our way, our language. They need to learn to listen.
>
> *[Youth CBO CR, November 2018]*

Speaking to each other, many CRs described the CLRA process as providing them with critical awareness overall and specifically about their societal position and opportunities and about more powerful actors in the ODA system. The CBO leaders wrote down these reflections during the process but only shared them with us after the project had ended when they asked us to evaluate the project with them. Moreover, the research process provided the CRs with access to otherwise inaccessible (intellectual) spaces. For example, the formal book presentation introduced above took place in the garden of a research institute in Nairobi. For most of the CRs, this was their first time to present their work. Many of them came to the venue dressed up and visibly enjoyed the presentations and informal festive gathering afterwards.

Challenges and weaknesses

Although the CLRA showed potential in terms of doing things differently and communities reclaiming the lead, the method did not come without challenges and weaknesses. The CLRA process is intense and time consuming and demands commitments from all parties. Throughout the process, the MSW CBO, which is firmly embedded in the ODA system, was at times preoccupied with the managerial demands of their other projects. The CBO management teams fully supported the CLRA project, but the demands of the ODA system affected management's possibilities for involvement. Moreover, the CRs employed by this CBO were frequently required to do CBO duties (e.g. hosting visitors or attending NGO meetings), which understandably hampered their ability to complete their CLRA research. Using CLRA requires researchers, CBOs, and other people involved to reflect and critically consider the time available and necessitates that CBOs provide the necessary space and time for CRs to do their work.

The power differences between us as academic researchers and the CBO staff, as well as between the CBO staff and members at times kept the CLRA process from being fully community-led. Although the CBOs never made explicit the power differences bestowed on us through the structures in which we operate, we noticed that, ultimately, the decision-making power continued to be with us. Relatedly, existing CBO structures and decision-making power also influenced the topics the CRs could and could not discuss. As described above, the CLRA process encourages CRs to interrogate the nature of their reality collaboratively and critically; in the context of our project, this included reflections on the impact of various programmes the CBOs run. In our experience, however, hegemonic power relations within CBOs impacted the extent to which the CRs could engage in such reflection. For instance, during one of the weekly CLRA sessions, the CRs considered how to improve the CBO's interactions with police officers and other law enforcement workers. Through their activities, both CBOs in this study are keen to cultivate a trusting and cordial working relationship with law enforcement and public administration officers. During the CLRA session, the CRs reflected on a sensitization[3] outreach activity that had been conducted on the previous Saturday at a notoriously corrupt police precinct in the northeast of the city. Although the CRs considered the outreach strategy to be in line with the overall CBO programmatic objectives and to serve as a critical entry point for community–police relations, they felt that CBO activities should aim to engage law enforcement more deeply, going beyond routine outreach exercises. We invited the team to describe and interrogate the activity in light of our past discussions. We agreed that the CRs would design their own police sensitization strategies to feed into the CBO's ongoing re-strategizing processes. However, this exercise was interpreted as an unwelcome critique of the CBO in question. Things took a sharp turn in the days following this CLRA session and resulted in a clash among the CRs and between the CRs and the CBO management. In hindsight, we realize that, as facilitators, we failed to intervene when the CRs said they would 'interrogate' or 'investigate' (fairly innocuous research lingo) the CBO's activities with the police. To the CBO staff and members, the use of these words made it seem as if the CRs, as part of the CLRA process, were intent on digging up dirt on the CBO in the way investigative journalists seek to uncover scandals. This was understandably interpreted as a critique of the CBO and its activities and required us to convince the involved CRs and CBO staff members that the process had a different intention. We talked at length with everyone involved, first separately and then collectively, using locally relevant principles of conflict resolution that we were familiar with from having worked with the CBO for years. It took time to listen to everyone and build a collective understanding of the underlying problem of mistrust, and we also facilitated the discussion on how to rebuild trust. While everyone involved acknowledged that rebuilding trust takes time, they also decided unanimously to commit to the process and continue with the research in this spirit. We also learned to tread even more carefully and to be even more attuned to the perceptions of the CRs and to the internal dynamics of the partnering CBOs.

Another challenge arose when deciding on the layout of the book developed by the CRs. Despite adhering as academic researchers to the ideals of engaged scholarship, accompanying research, and co-creation, for the layout of the popular book that was designed as an outcome of the CLRA process and that was supposed to function as a community tool for dissemination, we failed to leave the final decision making to the CBOs. We considered it a nice idea to create a double-sided book, including the content of the gay sex worker-led CBO on one side and that of the youth CBO on the other. Although we were aware of potential tensions between the CRs from the MSW CBO and those from the youth CBO, we failed to account for youths in the ghettos not wanting to be associated with homosexuality. Because their book included content on gay men and homosexuality, the youth CBO was initially hesitant to disseminate this valuable end product.

The open-ended approach that our CLRA project adopted proved to be a very useful explorative and interpretive process that built rich collective profiles of the MSWs and ghetto youth and their lived experiences. This open-ended approach did a great deal to promote participatory and community-driven knowledge production. We also observed individual action (e.g. starting small businesses, pursuing new community-oriented research opportunities, founding new CBOs, and taking up community leadership roles) and collective action (e.g. the adoption of new advocacy strategies concerning LGBTQ rights, police brutality and extrajudicial killings of ghetto youths, CBO-initiated savings and investment support groups, and collaborations with other like-minded CBOs and individuals across the city) emerging from the two teams of CRs and our partner CBOs. This offers an opportunity and basis for subsequent research and intervention projects with the express purpose of showing the extent to which sustainable action and long-term impact can be attributed to CLRA in various contexts.

Conclusion: the potential of CLRA as a method for communities to reclaim the lead

In this chapter, we introduced CLRA as an experimental methodological approach that can be used to support communities to 'reclaim the lead' in the ODA system. We hope we have shown that CLRA can contribute to making international development efforts more inclusive, effective, and relevant by providing an understanding of the everyday lived realities of community members and generating action long after the project period ends.

In describing CLRA as a form of community ethnography, we have shown how CLRA builds on PAR, taking the approach one step further, as communities are in the lead. We have demonstrated the feasibility of the method, showing that it is capable of generating knowledge about the lived experiences of community members, building research and other practical skills, and generating action beyond mere programmatic goals. We have shown CLRA to be a democratic tool, able to generate a shift in focus from planned development goals towards the goals of the people whose lived realities are at stake.

However, as explained above, CLRA does not come without challenges and weaknesses. In reflecting on our experiences with CLRA, we described the power differences among us as academic researchers, CBOs, and communities and discussed how these kept the CLRA process from being community-led throughout. Nonetheless, although the shift in ownership that CLRA promotes does not eliminate hegemonic power, it flattens traditional hierarchies between academic and community researchers. Supporting CRs to take control of the research and action agenda and facilitating their active involvement and leadership in the research design, implementation, and dissemination reinforces the idea of inclusive and community-centred research. We have shown that this process can be empowering and emancipatory for marginalized groups, who often remain unheard. The CLRA approach is relatively unexplored in previous work; to further develop this approach, our reflections emphasize the importance of flexibility, open-endedness, and continued reflections from researchers, academics, and other actors involved at different levels of the ODA system.

In sum, we argue that CLRA offers a practical alternative by 'doing differently' in international development. CLRA has the potential to reverse certain power dynamics, especially around knowledge production and learning, within the field of development cooperation, as well as in academia. Future work should continue to explore the implementation of CLRA in development practice. Our experiences with CLRA in the context of planned development are among the first to be documented. Future work can explore how CLRA works in different contexts and among different communities to interrogate whether the approaches and outcomes seen in other groups and communities as part of this process are similar or unique. The process we have described here was implemented in a context in which sufficient time and resources were available. Future work could seek to understand how CLRA works in contexts where such resources are in shorter supply. Moreover, future work could seek to understand how CLRA works in the context of planned development approaches – for instance, in the design and implementation of a development partnership. To ensure community ownership and leadership, it is crucial that, when CLRA is used in development arrangements, communities – rather than NGOs – have ownership of the allocated (financial) resources. In thinking about future CLRA implementation, we would like to emphasize that, instead of requiring CLRA to adapt to existing (development) systems and approaches, development practitioners will need to adapt to CLRA.

Notes

1 Being aware of multiple conceptual flaws and conflations in understanding 'communities' (see e.g. Cornwall & Eade, 2010; Gardner & Lewis, 2015), when considering CBOs as well as community-led research and action, we understand 'communities' to mean a group of people with specific interests, often in a shared spatial or identity context. We apply 'community' as an everyday concept (Vijayakumar, 2017) and recognize that it emerges in distinct ways.

2 *Fununu* is a Swahili word that loosely translates to 'the word on the street' or 'alleged account'. We used this concept to help CRs formulate research propositions.
3 See Woensdregt & Nencel (2022b) for more information on the police sensitization method used by this CBO.

References

Borda, O. F. (2006). The North-South convergence: A 30-year first-person assessment of PAR. *Action Research, 4*(3), 351–358. https://doi.org/10.1177/1476750306066806.

Cornwall, A., & Eade, D. (2010). Deconstructing development discourse. Buzzwords and fuzzwords. In A. Cornwall & D. Eade (Eds.), *Deconstructing development discourse* (pp. 1–18). Practical Action Publishing in association with Oxfam GB. https://doi.org/10.3362/9781780440095.

Gardner, K., & Lewis, D. (2015). *Anthropology and development: Challenges for the twenty-first century*. London: Pluto Press.

Ghetto Foundation. (2019). *Narratives that matter: Community Led Research, Activist CBOs & Development Aid in Nairobi – life as a youth in Mathare* (E. K. Rwigi (Ed.)). Retrieved from: https://includeplatform.net/wp-content/uploads/2019/11/Volume-B-Narratives-that-Matter-Mathare-Youths-Community-Led-Research.pdf.

hooks, B. (2000). *Feminist theory: From margin to center.* London: Pluto Press.

HOYMAS. (2019). *Narratives that matter: Community led research, activist development aid in Nairobi. Life as a male sex worker* (E. Kibui Rwigi (Ed.)). Retrieved from: https://includeplatform.net/wp-content/uploads/2019/11/Volume-A-Narratives-that-Matter-MSWs-Community-Led-Research.pdf.

James, J., & Gordon, E. T. (2008). Afterword: Activist scholars or radical subjects? In C. R. Hale (Ed.), *Engaging contradictions: Theory, politics, and methods of activist scholarship*, (pp. 367–373). Berkeley: GAIA Books, Global, Area, and International Archive, University of California Press.

Kapoor, D. (2009). Globalization, dispossession, and subaltern social movement (SSM) learning in the South. In A. A. Abdi & D. Kapoor (Eds.), *Global perspectives on adult education* (pp. 71–92). New York: Palgrave Macmillan.

Kothari, U. (Ed.) (2019). *A radical history of development studies. Individuals, Institutions and Ideologies*. London: Zed Books.

Matsuda, M. (1987). Looking to the bottom: Critical legal studies and reparations. *Harvard Civil Rights - Civil Liberties Law Review, 22*, 323–400.

Mbembe, A. (2001). *On the postcolony*. Berkely: University of California Press.

Mignolo, W. D. (2003). *The darker side of the Renaissance: Literacy, territoriality, and colonization*. Michigan: University of Michigan Press.

Ndlovu-Gatsheni, S. J. (2015). Decoloniality in Africa: A continuing search for a new world order. *The Australasian Review of African Studies, 36*(2), 22–50.

Pailey, R. N. (2019). De-centring the 'White Gaze' of development. *Development and Change, 0*(0), 1–17. https://doi.org/10.1111/dech.12550.

Skovdal, M., Magutshwa-Zitha, S., Campbell, C., Nyamukapa, C., & Gregson, S. (2017). Getting off on the wrong foot? How community groups in Zimbabwe position themselves for partnerships with external agencies in the HIV response. *Globalization and Health, 13*(29). https://doi.org/10.1186/s12992-017-0253-5.

van Stapele, N., Nencel, L., & Sabelis, I. (2018). On tensions and opportunities: Building partnerships between government and sex worker-led organizations in Kenya in the fight against HIV/AIDS. *Sexuality Research and Social Policy, 16*(2), 190–200. https://doi.org/10.1007/s13178-018-0337-x.

Vijayakumar, G. (2017). Collective demands and secret codes: The multiple uses of "community" in "community mobilization." *World Development, 104*, 173–182. https://doi.org/10.1016/j.worlddev.2017.11.009.

Woensdregt, L., & Nencel, L. (2022a). Male sex workers' (in)visible risky bodies in international health development: now you see them, now you don't. Culture, Health & Sexuality, 24(3), 344–357, DOI: 10.1080/13691058.2020.1842499

Woensdregt, L., & Nencel, L. (2022b) Taking small steps: Sensitising the police through male sex workers' community-led advocacy in Nairobi, Kenya. Global Public Health, 17(10), 2316-2328.

Zavala, M. (2013). What do we mean by decolonizing research strategies? Lessons from decolonizing indigenous research projects in New Zealand and Latin America. *Decolonization: Indigeneity, Education & Society, 2*(1), 55–71.

4

REIMAGINING DEVELOPMENT FROM LOCAL VOICES AND POSITIONS – SOUTHERN FEMINIST MOVEMENTS IN THE LEAD

Njeri Kimotho, Catherine Odenyo-Ndekera and Janna Visser

Introduction

In this chapter, we suggest a new vision for the development landscape – a vision where Southern feminist movements are in the lead and are recognized as such. We are writing this chapter from our own position as feminist activists and advocates from the South; our vision is based on our own experiences, as well as examples drawn from literature on Southern feminism. In this chapter, we offer a vision for organizing international development – particularly development in the South – differently, such that Southern feminist movements are stewards of transformative and inclusive development. Ensuring that Southern feminist movements lead development agendas, which are currently driven by Western feminism, will address existing inequalities in power relations between the North and the South and within the South. This approach has been proposed in multiple spheres, including in the decolonizing agenda (Byrne & Imma, 2019). Implementing this vision will build more transformative societies that are based on the actual needs of the people in the South, as shown by the examples that we reflect on in this chapter.

As feminist activists and advocates from the South, we provide an argument for a vision that is rooted in existing structures in the Global South: Southern feminist movements have been built and strengthened over the years, and Southern feminists are thus well-positioned to take the lead in development programming. In this chapter, we suggest four intersecting elements that inform this vision. First, we consider the particular relationship between Southern feminism and patriarchy. Second, we take into account the situated, indigenous knowledge found in Southern feminism. Third, we reflect on how the legacy of colonialism can be seen in feminists' struggles and in the successful approaches used to resist and overcome these struggles. Fourth, we describe the promise of building on

DOI: 10.4324/9781003241003-5

diverse paths to emancipation that continue to progress. These four intersecting elements are interlinked. They have bolstered each other over time, and they form the foundational elements of current Southern feminist approaches.

Below, we start with an argument for the need for change in development agendas and for putting Southern feminism in the lead. Then, we elaborate on each element of the vision and provide examples from diverse Southern feminist movements. Finally, we conclude with more concrete suggestions for how to put Southern feminist movements in the lead in the international development agenda.

The need for a new paradigm: Southern feminism in the lead

In this section, we articulate the current situation in the development landscape, which is in need of a paradigm shift led by Southern feminism, and we provide examples of what we mean when we refer to this shift. The dominant development paradigm has a long history of being centred on Northern thinking and practices, despite the rising call to decolonize development over the past several years (Plaatjie, 2013). Countless present-day practices and attitudes in the development sector stem from the colonial era, although many development practitioners in the Global North are still reluctant to acknowledge this influence. International development that applies modern-day practices and norms reinforces colonial dynamics and beliefs such as the 'white saviour' ideology, which internalizes a narrative assuming that white people, white institutions, and white agendas are more advanced and superior compared with those in the Global South. This assumption is manifested in the communication materials of international development organizations and is salient in their organizational structures and working modalities. The pervasiveness of these ideas has perpetuated the colonial mentality of power relations, which has rarely allowed for contributions from the people from the Global South or for the use of local knowledge in the Global South (Paige & Kotsiras, 2021). In essence, this is also the case in the feminist agenda in international development.

The current development agenda has been informed mainly by the gender connotations in Northern feminist thinking, with minimal input from Southern feminists. This means that development may take a shape that is not beneficial to building more transformative societies among the people of the South, creating a failure in the development paradigm and a waste of resources that do not create the intended impact. This chapter draws on the interplay of intersecting variables that have bolstered feminist movements in the South, enriching their perspectives and enabling their growth, replication, and success over time. These aspects have been ignored in much of the development agenda, which uses Northern thinking to inform development in the South. Additionally, the sharing of the success stories of indigenous feminists from the South has been rendered invisible in academic production and in knowledge sharing more broadly because of a system of knowledge circulation that often favours Northern authors, who do not share lived experiences of the South.

Southern feminist movements

Accordingly, it is time to recentre development efforts on the practices and knowledge of Southern feminists. First, however, it is necessary to define what we mean by 'Southern feminism'. To many people, feminism continues to be a controversial concept with multiple ambiguities. Many contemporary feminist scholars and advocates argue that a singular feminism does not exist (Walby, 2011). In this chapter, we draw on the concept of feminism in reference to the broad notion of advocacy on women's rights. To unpack what is meant by Southern feminism more specifically, we must first define what we mean by the South by building on the work of Byrne and Imma (2019, p. 2): 'The "South" of this designation, therefore, refers to countries that in the late twentieth and early twenty-first centuries, have been marked by middle-to-low income economies, not those situated in any particular geographical location'. Most of these countries are located in Africa, Asia, and South America. The feminist movements within these spaces are what we refer to as 'Southern feminist movements'. We argue that it is time to change the development agenda in the South so that it is led by feminists from the South. This change is envisaged to bring about development that will not only be acceptable to the people in the South but that will also be based on these people's ideologies, needs, indigenous knowledge, cultural acceptance, and social systems.

One can easily be trapped into thinking that feminism is a movement seated in the West or the Global North. However, feminist individuals, movements, and organizations have been well established over time in Asia, Africa, and South America. However, feminists in the South are often invisible in discussions about international development and women's rights. The crucial role of Southern feminists is lost in the rush to show how international donations and policy decisions affect beneficiaries, and these feminists may not be recognized as partners because their organizational structures do not fit within the stringent rules of Northern donors. Although it is right that the focus should be on the women most in need of support to transform their lives, the women who are driving social change are too often overlooked (Chis, 2015).

Highlighting how women's rights activists in the South have fought for and won real change for themselves demonstrates that these achievements have not been handed to them by Northern feminists. Indeed, much has been won by women's organizations and movements outside the North. For example, in Nepal, Women for Human Rights secured significant changes to dangerous and discriminatory laws against widows and single women, and the Women's Coalition of Zimbabwe successfully lobbied for national domestic violence legislation. In one region of Ethiopia, Kembatta Women Standing Together, an indigenous non-governmental organization dedicated to protecting and fostering women's rights, helped reduce the prevalence of female genital mutilation from 97% to 4%, and, in Ghana, the Gender Centre is persuading entire districts to abandon the harmful traditional practice of widow inheritance (Jackson, 2011).

There are many other examples of Southern women driving social change, such as the feminist Sandinistas playing a strong role in attempting to bring gender equality issues to the centre of political struggles in Nicaragua. South African feminists played a similar role in the anti-apartheid movement and now continue to play this role in the movements around HIV and AIDS (Batliwala, 2011). Another successful example is the National Federation of Dalit Women, which was launched by Dalit women themselves and committed itself to carrying out several tasks to bring about positive changes in their lives, such as taking legal action against caste-based atrocities, facilitating political empowerment, supporting economic empowerment against growing pauperization, building self-confidence, and providing leadership. Dalit women have been active throughout history. They were actively involved in the anti-caste and anti-untouchability movements in the 1920s, for example. Today, they are the stalwarts of Dalit movements in thousands of Indian villages. Dalit women continue to play a critical role in movements for land rights and are making their mark as independent thinkers and writers in the literary world and as visionary leaders in the Panchayati Raj institutions, a system of rural local self-government in India (Manorama, 2016).

Elements informing our vision: patriarchy, indigenous knowledge, colonialism, and emancipation

In this section, we articulate four central elements that inform the new vision for development led by Southern feminism that we propose in this chapter. Even though these elements may look detached from a distance, together, they have positioned feminist movements in the South and contributed to their current strength and resistance. The first element demonstrates the continuing resistance and challenging of patriarchal systems embedded in the Global South led by women's movements that were later described as feminists. The second element concerns indigenous knowledge, which is inherently connected to Southern feminism as a powerful resource that offers local perspectives and approaches for engagement, negotiation, and inclusive development. Third, we zoom in on the positionality of Southern feminism through the colonial era, cognizant of the power dynamics and influence of Northern forces that not only created resistance but also further equipped the feminist drivers of this resistance in the South to challenge Northern ideological approaches to development. The fourth element is emancipation, which showcases how the evolution of Southern feminist movements and their communities over time has prospered and strengthened Southern feminists' potential to create the much-needed change in the development paradigm.

Southern feminist movements challenging patriarchal systems

Many societies in the Global South are characterized by patriarchal systems, where male social power is reinforced by the cultural institutions, language, religion, media and popular culture, education, and household dynamics. The ideology of patriarchy seems to have emanated from the idea of the leadership of the fathers being elevated to a position of paramount importance in society (Biesta, 2010). This ideology has been entrenched in the South, embedded within hereditarian systems that are highly protected by Southern cultural institutions. For instance, a study on patriarchy and gender inequalities in the central region of Ghana revealed how a range of social, cultural, and religious factors stemming from patriarchy combine to inform the construction of traditional masculinity. This customarily accepted masculinity is supported by factors such as men's right to make decisions in the home, the existence of distinct and inflexible gender roles, and the ownership of female partners, including the power to engage in sexual intercourse, which is extended to legitimize wife beating as a disciplinary action (Sikweyiya et al., 2020).

In many regions in the South, patriarchy is grounded in cultural institutions, which makes the communities in these localities view the institution of patriarchy as a norm created by previous generations that informs relations and cultural realities. This makes it an uphill task to end practices with patriarchal connotations in many communities in the Global South without damaging their cultural and societal structures. However, there are examples of cases where women have challenged patriarchal norms and demanded their rights and equality in multiple ways. Over time, these actions have strengthened and enriched feminist ideologies in the South. Even in situations where patriarchal norms emphasize that women must not speak up or engage in 'unbecoming' societal behaviour leading to discrimination, harassment, and continuing inequalities, we see examples of women who have challenged the status quo.

For example, women of African descent have used multiple expressions and forms of collective and individual resistance that are often institutionalized in traditional African cultural systems. Invoking the memory of these women, whose names are hardly ever recorded in history books, we provide some examples that denote distinctive female modes of resistance using cultural practices, some with clear patriarchal overtones. Long ago, women first came together to vocalize their feelings about situations that affected them. These meetings built support networks that women could depend on to punish offending men. Collectively, the women would request that the objectionable behaviour stop. If it did not, the women's groups would serve as 'pressure groups', imposing punishment on the guilty party or parties. More specifically, West African women's group tactics included strikes, boycotts, force, nudity as protest, and 'making war' or 'sitting on a man'. 'Making war' or 'sitting on a man' (publicly shaming a man by convening upon his hut or workplace, potentially involving dancing, singing, and detailing grievances about his behaviour) was the toughest measure employed by

West African women for punishing wrongdoers and enforcing compliance with their rules and regulations (Kuumba, 2006). Other examples of women taking collective action include ceremonies and work songs relayed in places such as kitchens and water collection sites, as well as at kinship gatherings and other places where women gathered.

Other evidence shows how feminist movements in the South pushed through patriarchal culturally locked spaces, allowing women to access education and participate in political arenas – domains that were historically only for men. We see similarities across women leaders in societies where women gained positions of authority. An example of this derives from the Queen Mothers of Asanteland in Ghana, who closely influenced the government and political space of Asanteland. The Queen Mothers were women who co-ruled together with the chiefs and kings of Asanteland prior to the colonial era (Aidoo, 1977). Their power stemmed from the matrilineal nature of social organization in the Asante Kingdom. The Asante have a saying that 'it is a woman who gave birth to a man; it is a woman who gave birth to a chief'. The Queen Mother is a member of the governing council or the assembly of state, and her presence is required whenever important matters of state are to be decided. Such women, who had inherent power in social systems in patriarchal settings, encouraged other women to enter spaces considered men's domain.

Successes like those highlighted in this section should be used to inform the development agenda in the South instead of allowing this agenda to merely replay Northern ideas without incorporating knowledge about how Southern cultural frameworks protect patriarchal systems through hereditary lineage. The complex and disruptive phenomenon of patriarchy can only be uprooted by illuminating indigenous systems, structures, and processes, whose dynamics are best understood by indigenous feminists with lived experience in the Global South.

The situatedness of indigenous knowledge within Southern feminist movements

The second element we put forward for our vision is indigenous knowledge – knowledge that evolves from the local environment, built up and adapted by a group of people in a particular society over several generations (World Bank, 1998). Such knowledge is an important resource for Southern feminist movements. Indigenous knowledge has been, and continues to be, an important driver of Southern feminist movements' agendas of resistance, stimulating support and negotiations among these feminists themselves, but also within local communities. With their specific knowledge, skills, social relations, and networks, indigenous Southern feminists have been able to pass along messages, mobilize others to resist, and challenge patriarchy within existing frameworks (Aluko, 2018).

Although indigenous knowledge has played a critical role not only in advancing the work of feminist movements and systems but also in informing common practices such as traditional healing, agriculture, and values for governance in local communities, such knowledge is not always used to inform international development initiatives that impact the livelihoods of hundreds of millions of people in the Global South (Aluko, 2018). Despite growing recognition of the importance of indigenous knowledge, Southern feminist movements, which are shaped and driven by this knowledge, continue to be left out in the current development paradigm. Indigenous knowledge is crucial to a community's sustainability and development. Indigenous women, informed by their lived experiences in particular indigenous contexts, can – and should – contribute to the design and implementation of sustainable development initiatives. Indigenous knowledge from the South is an important part of communities' social capital – 'the institutions, relationships, attitudes, and norms that govern interactions among individuals in a society and contribute to socio-economic development' (Tirmizi, 2005, p. 2). Ignoring this knowledge undermines acceptance by the communities whose values, systems, and structures were shaped by it.

Approaches that have ignored local and indigenous knowledge in the South have faced a myriad of challenges. In a study on non-heterosexual sexualities in Africa and indigenous knowledge, Mkasi (2016) acknowledges that understanding non-heterosexual sexualities in African communities requires a highly complex narrative that incorporates indigenous knowledge and culture. Although there might be a need to interrogate the issue of freedom from Northern theoretical impositions, agendas related to sex and sexualities need to be contextualized and analysed through the eyes of indigenous societies. In the domain of sexual and reproductive health rights, initiatives related to genital mutilation and lesbian, gay, bisexual, transgender, and queer (LGBTQ) rights are two of the many examples. The LGBTQ agenda advocated for in many international development initiatives has underestimated indigenous knowledge and values, increasing resistance to its implementation. For instance, on 3 May 2021, the Uganda Parliament passed the Sexual Offenses Bill, which contains a clause criminalizing same-sex relationships. During the debate on the bill, there was mention of how the LGBTQ agenda should have been positioned differently, in a way that respected the indigenous knowledge and practices. It was made clear that, although this might not have been a new subject, it appeared that way because those pushing this agenda did not consult the indigenous feminists who were already aware that non-heterosexual practices existed silently within the communities (Nakkazi, 2021). We believe that precarious agendas such as this, especially, need to include indigenous feminist knowledge to negotiate, bargain, and facilitate change.

Borrowing from the work of Escobar (1997, p. 98), 'The remaking of development must thus start by examining local constructions, to the extent that they are the life and history of a people, that is, the conditions of and for change'. With their specific knowledge, skills, social relations, and networks, indigenous Southern feminists should play a central role in designing and implementing Southern development solutions.

Between colonialism and development

As a third element, we focus on the positionality of Southern feminist movements throughout the colonial era, cognizant of the power dynamics and the influence of Northern forces, which not only created resistance but also further equipped the feminist drivers in the South to challenge Northern ideological approaches to development. Although this has occurred in different ways in different places, the South has certainly been influenced by the colonial era, which shaped resistant forces to oust negative influences while activists in the South also agitated for access to development priorities such as education and political space. The colonization process reinforced existing power relations inherent in patriarchal cultural structures in the Global South, but this did not stop the previously established feminist forces. Using examples from Africa, Latin America, and Asia, below, we show the interplay between colonization and the resistance and struggles of Southern women's movements.

Europeans began arriving in Africa in the 15th century, most frequently settling in coastal enclaves and pursuing trade in goods such as ivory and gold, as well as in slaves. These Europeans tended to use the power imbalances between men and women to their advantage, stepping into the existing power dynamics between men and women and using these to their advantage, perpetuating the exploitation of women. The years that followed were marked by intense colonialism, with increased warfare that was magnified when the Europeans attempted – and in most areas succeeded – to enforce their political control over African communities. Africans resisted these incursions from the beginning, and the first nationalist movements arose in the early 20th century, culminating in successful transfers to independent status for most African nations in the 1950s and early 1960s (Sheldon, 2018). This did not occur without the involvement of women's movements. Women's involvement and responses to colonial 'power over' was seen in a variety of ways, and they used both formal and informal pre-existing organizations for their activism against patriarchal systems.

Ngwatiko work groups among the Kikuyu people in Kenya are a strong example of such resistance. The Kikuyu, the largest ethnic group in Kenya, occupied the largest proportion of land in the country. They were forced out by white settlers and driven into infertile and inhospitable lands. The Kikuyu women suffered a particularly heavy workload on coffee plantations newly owned by white settlers, and they experienced all forms of gender-based violence and the withholding of their wages. These women relied on a traditional support system, the *gwatiko*. *Gwatiko* was a true identity of collaboration and interaction among Kikuyu women facing the common predicament of oppression and forced into a subordinate relationship with the white settlers. In March 1922, at a mixed-gender mass gathering, women led a public protest using *ngemi* [ululation] to raise crowds to action on women's right to participate in political spaces. Many public protests led by women followed. The success of these public protests established a precedent for women's leadership in public roles while simultaneously winning gains in labour arrangements (Kombo, 2012).

As colonization took shape, Southern feminist movements found that their space grew with development, and they also gained space to resist inequalities that were historically embedded, as well as those that were created as a result of the power relations with the colonialists. Many of the success stories of indigenous women were never shared because a system of circulation of knowledge that favoured Northern authors, who were predominantly white men, meant these women's voices were absent from academic production (Harding, 1991). Nevertheless, there are many successful examples of indigenous women who challenged colonial frameworks to push their agendas. Although these examples are often seen as isolated actions by indigenous peoples, we can highlight successes accomplished through struggle and resistance by the collective voices of social actors and local movements. This is seen, for instance, in the successful struggles for water, dignity, sovereignty, and life and in the defence of Mother Earth and ancestral territories in Latin America and the Caribbean. These regions have changed dramatically to adopt more inclusive perspectives that incorporate the traditions, struggles, and resistance of women and peasant communities (Schutte, 2011).

As touched upon earlier in this chapter, present-day development approaches also carry colonial overtones. Even current feminist development approaches have been criticized by women in the Global South for including colonial practices and solely representing the desires of white, middle-class Western women (Mohanty et al., 1991). Modern-day Western feminism 'isolate "gender" from class, colonialism, and white patriarchy, maintaining racist structures and ignoring the fact that the perception of gendered bodies is socially inscribed, contingent and historically constituted' (Harcourt, 2009, as cited in Chis, 2015, p. 2). An example of this is the problematic use of the term 'third world women' by Western feminists. Mohanty and colleagues (1991) show that women in the so-called 'Third World' are often represented as having needs and problems, with hardly any freedom to act. This not only echoes the structures of colonial development by reinforcing the power dynamics that were brought about by colonialism, but also denies Southern feminist movements a space to influence current development agendas from their own positionality. However, as will be shown in the next section, Southern feminist movements have played a crucial role in emancipating themselves and their communities, which contributes to the argument that it is time to move away from colonial overtones both in general development approaches and in Western feminist approaches to development.

The emancipation process

As a fourth main point, building on diverse paths to emancipation that have been seen and continue to progress, we showcase the evolution over time of Southern feminist movements and the communities of which they are a part, showing how they have prospered and strengthened their potential to create much-needed changes in the development paradigm. The idea of emancipation originally comes from Roman law, where it meant that a son or wife withdrew from the legal authority of the male head of household (i.e. the father or husband). According to Biesta (2010, p. 41), emancipation implies that '...the person to be emancipated, becomes independent and free as a result of the act of emancipation'. We use this positioning with the understanding that emancipation is a process by which people – in this case, women – have been striving to liberate themselves from the authority and control of men and traditional power structures, as well as to secure equal rights.

Over the years, women in different contexts in the South have prided themselves in emancipation processes that have enriched them despite patriarchal structures. For example, in India, using the traditional gender role of a dutiful wife and supporter, women managed to mobilize support for changing the status quo from husbands, other women, and their communities in general. In other instances, while carrying out family traditions within existing structures, women carved out opportunities to engage in politics and leadership. Socially constructed gender roles such as mothering have been applied by older women to influence their relations with power holders in the family and the community by passing on wisdom, thereby influencing the traditional power ranking order. In essence, these women transformed the patriarchal frame from within their assigned gender roles, disguising their actions as 'quietly serving the men' (Rao, 2012, as cited in Patel et al., 2021, p. 16); as a result, women's individual position was improved, and social norms were manipulated for the larger community (Patel et al., 2021).

Other emancipation processes also took shape during the colonial era. For example, in African contexts, the colonial era forced traditional support systems, such as the previously mentioned *ngwatiko* among the Kikuyu in Kenya or the *ebere* among the Ibibio in Nigeria, both of which were set up to resist the patriarchal oppression of women and subordinate relationships with white settlers, to advance from serving as women's movements merely supporting members in their work on white settlers' plantations to public structures for activism and protest (Kombo, 2012). The contributions and significance of these women's movements in terms of the emancipation of women at both the individual level and the political level played a critical role in building the steps towards initiating women's own economic activities and shifting their participation from the household to the market space. Through these organized collectives, diverse skills such as knitting, sewing, cooking, and selling were passed on among indigenous women. These skills contributed to women venturing into generating more income by selling their goods (Afshar, 1998). These types of skills had previously been used mainly in the household, but women began to take their abilities outside the home and put them to use at the marketplace for their own economic advancement. Both gaining these skills and engaging in income-generating activities can be viewed as steps towards the emancipation of women, giving them greater economic freedom.

The 19th–21st centuries have been marked by women progressing in their emancipation trajectories in diverse ways. Women in the South have been emancipated through paths involving, among other things, education, employment, entrepreneurship, and political representation, enabling them to improve their lives and the lives of other members of their communities. The maximization and advancement of individual emancipation can benefit from shared solidarity (Schwabenland et al., 2016). A strong example that emerges from this standpoint is the green scarf movement in Argentina, which gained worldwide recognition and support. In 2018, thousands of women put on a green scarf and hit the Argentinian streets with a clear message: they wanted abortion legalized. This is just one of many examples that show how well Southern feminist movements are positioned to challenge previously locked patriarchal spaces (TeleSUR, 2019).

Starting from the South can enhance the emancipation process; thus, the South should be the main driver in evolving their own emancipation process and demands. They should use their existing indigenous knowledge to transform the social and political structures that control their realities. This will better equip them to enrich the existing systems, instead of 'imposing' strategies designed for them by the North. In essence, Southern feminists can foster emancipation by becoming part of Southern development solutions. This means that emancipation is informed by the inherent indigenous knowledge that has emerged from Southern feminists themselves. This chapter therefore recognizes that, although emancipation is a process, Southern feminists are equipped and well placed to lead their own development agendas, even when their emancipation processes are still ongoing.

The way forward

This chapter has brought forward a vision informed by four intersecting elements: the relationship between Southern feminism and patriarchy, the situatedness of indigenous knowledge within Southern communities and in advancing Southern feminism, the legacy of colonialism in feminists' struggles, and the successful approaches used to resist and overcome these, and the diverse paths to emancipation that have been seen and that continue to strengthen Southern feminism. As feminist activists and advocates from the South, we argue that these elements have created an opportunity to reimagine development from local voices and positions grounded within Southern feminist movements in repositioning development for the South. In this concluding section, we put forward three concrete suggestions for how to ensure Southern feminist movements can take the lead in the future development paradigm.

First, structures and knowledge brought forward by Southern feminist movements that have worked in the past should be valued and given a central position in future Southern development agendas. International development has not been adequately informed by Southern feminist thinking and practices, which has led to a continuous disengagement from Southern feminists' knowledge and practices in the development paradigm (Narayanaswamy, 2014). Undoubtedly, indigenous and Southern feminist knowledge and practices need to be positioned on the agenda for Southern development, and who better to lead this than the feminists in the South who have relevant lived experiences?

The second suggestion is to allow for strategic partnerships between Southern feminist movements and other development actors. Reimagining development from the South as observed by the authors of this chapter ultimately refers to reorganizing and localizing development. Various aspects of knowledge, practices, and resources can be used as complements to local resources and catalysts for advancing the development agenda in the South. Southern feminist movements should not operate in isolation; rather, they should use their local potential to enhance development in the Global South and link these efforts to international systems with optimal terms of development cooperation. Northern feminists can play a critical role in putting in place mechanisms for cross-learning, the exchange of practices, and dialogues aiming to find the most desired development paths in local contexts while building on the accumulated experiences and indigenous knowledge of Southern feminists.

Third, considering the inherent economic challenges Southern feminists face, it is fundamental to continue to support them in their efforts to achieve their mandate in the development agenda. This support should be in the form of financial resources to build their innovative trajectories and accelerate these within the communities. An exchange of best development practices that have worked elsewhere could strengthen and enrich the development paradigm driven by Southern feminists. We would therefore like to emphasize that, although there is still room for synergy and space for external support, having Southern feminist movements in the lead of Southern development offers space for organizing development differently and reimagining emancipation from local voices and positions.

References

Afshar, H. (1998). *Women and empowerment: Illustrations from the third world*. Houndmills: MacMillan Press ltd.

Aidoo, A. A. (1977). Asante queen mothers in government and politics in the nineteenth century. *Journal of the Historical Society of Nigeria*, *9*(1), 1–13.

Aluko, Y. A. (2018). Women's use of indigenous knowledge for environmental security and sustainable development in Southwest Nigeria. *International Indigenous Policy Journal*, *9*(3). https://doi.org/10.18584/iipj.2018.9.3.2.

Batliwala, S. (2011). *Feminist leadership for social transformation: Clearing the conceptual cloud*. Retrieved from: https://creaworld.org/wp-content/uploads/2020/11/feminist-leadership-clearing-conceptual-cloud-srilatha-batliwala.pdf?msclkid=7c5df03fc64911ecb7149086181fa62e.

Biesta, G. (2010). A new logic of emancipation: The methodology of Jacques Rancière. *Educational theory*, *60*(1), 39–59. https://doi.org/10.1111/j.1741–5446.2009.00345.x.

Byrne, D. C., & Imma, Z. é. (2019). Why 'Southern feminisms'? *Agenda*, *33*(3), 2–7. https://doi.org/10.1080/10130950.2019.1697043.

Chis, I. C. (2015). *United by strength or oppression? A critique of the Western model of feminism*. Retrieved from: https://www.e-ir.info/2015/09/29/united-by-strength-or-oppression-a-critique-of-the-western-model-of-feminism/.

Escobar, A. (1997). The making and unmaking of the third world through development. In M. Rahnema & V. Bawtree (Eds.), *The post-development reader* (pp. 85–93). New York: Bloomsbury Publishing.

Harcourt, W. (2009). *Body politics in development: Critical debates in gender and development*. London: Zed Books.

Harding, S. (1991). *Whose knowledge? Whose science? Thinking from women's lives*. Ithaca, NY: Cornell University Press.

Jackson, S. (2011). Feminism in the global south hasn't come from the north. *The Guardian*, October 20. Retrieved from: https://www.theguardian.com/global-development/poverty-matters/2011/oct/20/feminism-south-women-development-response.

Kombo, E. E. (2012). *Women in national liberation wars in the settler colonies of Kenya and Zimbabwe: pathways to political empowerment*. York: University of York.

Kuumba, M. B. (2006). African women, resistance cultures and cultural resistances. *Agenda, 20*(68), 112–121.

Manorama, R. (2016). *Background information on Dalit women in India*. Retrieved from: http://www.wunrn.org/news/2006/12_11_06/121806_india_dalit.htm.

Mkasi, L. P. (2016). African same-sexualities and indigenous knowledge: Creating a space for dialogue within patriarchy. *Verbum et Ecclesia, 37*(2), 1–6. https://doi.org/10.4102/ve.v37i2.1576.

Mohanty, C. T., Russo, A., & Torres, L. (1991). *Third world women and the politics of feminism*. Bloomington: Indiana University Press.

Nakkazi, E. (2021). Uganda's sexual offences bill—A step backwards. *The Lancet Infectious Diseases, 21*(7), 920. https://doi.org/10.1016/S1473-3099(21)00342-X.

Narayanaswamy, L. (2014). NGOs and feminisms in development: Interrogating the 'Southern women's NGO'. *Geography Compass, 8*(8), 576–589. https://doi.org/10.1111/gec3.12150.

Paige, S., & Kotsiras, D. (2021). *Time to decolonise aid: Insights and lessons from a global consultation*. Retrieved from: https://www.peacedirect.org/wp-content/uploads/2021/05/PD-Decolonising-Aid_Second-Edition.pdf.

Patel, T., Romani, L., Oberoi, P., & Ramasamy, C. (2021). Gender role encapsulation as resistance to patriarchy: Women politicians' work and gender equality in India. *Organization*. https://doi.org/1350508421995764.

Plaatjie, S. R. (2013). Beyond Western-centric and Eurocentric development: A case for decolonizing development. *Africanus, 43*(2), 118–130. https://doi.org/10.25159/0304-615X/2306.

Rao, N. (2012). Male 'providers' and female 'housewives': A gendered co-performance in rural North India. *Development and Change, 43*(5), 1025–1048. https://doi.org/10.1111/j.1467-7660.2012.01789.x.

Schutte, O. (2011). Engaging Latin American feminisms today: Methods, theory, practice. *Hypatia, 26*(4), 783–803. https://doi.org/10.1111/j.1527-2001.2011.01200.x.

Schwabenland, C., Lange, C., Onyx, J., & Nakagawa, S. (2016). *Women's emancipation and civil society organisations: Challenging or maintaining the status quo?* Bristol: Policy Press.

Sheldon, K. (2018). *Women and colonialism*. Oxford biographies. Retrieved from: https://www.oxfordbibliographies.com/view/document/obo-9780199846733/obo-9780199846733-0067.xml.

Sikweyiya, Y., Addo-Lartey, A. A., Alangea, D. O., Dako-Gyeke, P., Chirwa, E. D., Coker-Appiah, D., Adanu, R. M. K., & Jewkes, R. (2020). Patriarchy and gender-inequitable attitudes as drivers of intimate partner violence against women in the central region of Ghana. *BMC Public Health*, *20*, 1–11. https://doi.org/10.1186/s12889-020-08825-z.

TeleSUR. (2019). *5 Significant women-led social movements in Latin America in 2018*. TeleSUR. Retrieved from: https://www.telesurenglish.net/news/5-Significant-Women-Social-Movements-in-Latin-America--in-2018-20190308-0020.html.

Tirmizi, S. N. A. (2005). *The contribution of levels of social capital to community development*. Ames: Iowa State University.

Walby, S. (2011). *The future of feminism*. Cambridge: Polity Press.

World Bank. (1998). *Indigenous knowledge definitions, concepts and applications*. The World Bank. Retrieved from: https://chm.cbd.int/api/v2013/documents/4A27922D-31BC-EEFF-7940-DB40D6DB706B/attachments/209070/Hoda%20Yacoub%20-%20IK%20Report%20(1).pdf.

5

BUILDING RESILIENT COMMUNITIES BY GROWING COMMUNITY ASSETS, CAPACITIES, AND TRUST

Stella Wanjiru Chege

Introduction

In this chapter, I explore how communities are 'reclaiming the lead' in development by challenging traditional notions of funding and decision making through home-grown, horizontal systems by which they organize and raise resources locally, strengthening their agency and voice. I have been a development practitioner in Kenya for over ten years, working in human rights, gender, and education spaces. Based on my experience, I argue that grantees' relationships with donors (funding agencies or intermediaries) are mostly hierarchical, with strictly upward accountability and power that flows downward from the funder. In many cases, the funder–grantee relationship follows a prescribed formula: respond to calls for funding with an innovative solution that matches the donor's thematic area of focus and interests; receive funds and implement a programme according to an agreed workplan, logical framework, or, more recently, Theory of Change; and report strictly on the donor's timeline. Failure to adhere to the donor's requirements signals a capacity gap. Though these relationships are referred to as 'partnerships', it is clear that 'he who pays the piper calls the tune', with large international non-governmental organizations (INGOs) often stepping into the role of intermediary between Northern and Southern partners. Although everyone knows their position in the hierarchy, power in these relationships has often remained either unexamined or unacknowledged. However, the recent COVID-19 pandemic has more extensively revealed issues related to power and forced a reckoning among international development stakeholders regarding the capability of Southern organizations to spearhead the response to large crises without the physical presence, leadership, or, in some cases, resources of Northern organizations.

Against this backdrop, I am strongly motivated to explore a radically different model, where power and decision making are shared with communities, which

DOI: 10.4324/9781003241003-6

are enabled to take charge of their development. In this model, communities identify the problem and its solution and raise the resources required to solve the problem. The donor's role – if any – is to serve as a partner in the initiative and actively work to shift power to the community. This approach is based on a notion of *community philanthropy* (Hodgson & Pond, 2018) – a distinct, value-driven form of development practice focused on building community assets, capacity, and trust to drive development, hinging on the premise that communities' own assets – not limited to finances – that can be deployed and that, when pooled, these resources build community power and voice (Hodgson & Pond, 2018). This leads to more community involvement because of a sense of ownership and to the need for horizontal accountability because the donor is the community itself. The mobilization of resources also encourages wider involvement in decision making, which facilitates sustainability because community members consider themselves not only the custodians but also the drivers of their development.

Community philanthropy challenges the notion of international development being donor-centred and pays attention to community foundations, and community-driven initiatives require fewer resources, make use of local expertise, and are sustainable and based on community engagement. *Community foundations* are defined as 'non-profit organizations that pool resources of a community [and] engage business, government and public organizations to contribute into community development and social initiatives' (Knight & Avrorina, 2021, p. 6). These organizations introduce new models of engagement in international development that challenge conventional models based on the top-down dynamics of power and money, promoting community control over resources, as well as a community voice, agency, and power. This shift introduces new ways of working, centred on mutuality and horizontal accountability. Such initiatives work on a small scale but are highly replicable across different communities and situations because the 'formula' is simple and easily adaptable.

We are left with the major question of why this model of development is not being adopted by more donors. In this chapter, my purpose is to invite donors, development practitioners, and researchers to recognize and acknowledge community contributions, which are downplayed in the conventional measurement of development outcomes, and to consider how such principles can be adopted in mainstream development work. Here, I explore the emergent Assets–Capacities–Trust (ACT) framework, which focuses on building community assets, capacities, and trust, which underpin the work of community organizations. Community organizations include both community-led organizations and community foundations, which are sometimes described as community philanthropy organizations or community development foundations.

I begin by describing the context of international development, focusing on power dynamics. Then, I discuss the concept of community philanthropy, before proceeding to introduce the ACT framework and examine its use in community philanthropy. To conclude, I provide practical suggestions on how international development actors can adopt the model of community philanthropy to strengthen resilience and build long-term sustainability, both of which are key to breaking the cycle of community dependence on aid that has long been endemic in development.

Power in international development

In this section, I begin with a snapshot of the impact of COVID-19 on civil society organizations (CSOs) and then provide a brief review of the literature on power in international development, which resonates with my own experience as a development practitioner. This provides a background for the suggestion of a new, alternative model that challenges prevailing power relations.

COVID-19 has exposed weaknesses in current international development models, which are overly reliant on Northern organizations, with an underinvestment in the capacity of Southern NGOs (Centre for Strategic Philanthropy, 2021). Despite lessons learned after Ebola as to the importance of local civil society in such crises and the commitments made under the Grand Bargain to increase flows of international funding to the local level, Southern CSOs are finding themselves on the front lines of the COVID-19 response without the resources necessary to respond.

As the world went into lockdown in early 2020 and many INGOs repatriated staff members to their home countries, local organizations stepped up to fill the gaps left by international actors, including delivering humanitarian aid, mobilizing local resources and mutual aid networks, and forging new coalitions seeking to hold governments accountable. This called into question the widely held notion that Southern organizations do not have the technical capacity to spearhead aid or development efforts and that they rely on INGOs and their expatriate staff for technical expertise (Peace Direct, 2021).

The pandemic also exposed deep-rooted vulnerabilities of Southern civil society resulting from the systematic under-resourcing of institutions and tight restrictions on how the funding that is available is used. In a survey of 125 CSOs from 14 low- and middle-income countries across four global regions published in April 2020, 65% of the respondents reported that they were providing services – including information services, food distribution, and psychosocial support – to respond directly to the COVID-19 pandemic. Of these respondents, one-third had previously provided services, whereas two-thirds had added new services (LINC, 2020). The same survey also revealed that CSOs found themselves facing uncertain futures. Every CSO surveyed had been negatively impacted by COVID-19, with two-thirds reporting that they had to implement cost-cutting measures and 13% anticipating having to close within the next month. Describing the impact of COVID-19 on CSOs in West Africa, Afadzinu (2020) noted, 'To use the language of the times, the morbidity rate is very high especially because of underlying conditions that organizations suffer, due to years of neglect and the lack of support in building strong and resilient institutions'.

Inequality and injustice in international development are expressions of power and symptoms of power structures (Batliwala, n.d.). Before the COVID-19 pandemic, the rise of the 'me too', '#shift the power', 'black lives matter', and 'aid too' movements had begun to catalyse conversations around inequality, exploitation, and racism in international development, raising questions about development funding (Peace Direct, 2021). All these movements call out structural inequalities, challenge power, and demand accountability. Power and decision making in international development rest largely with donor agencies and large international development organizations. Inequality in international development is 'an issue of enduring systematic asymmetries of power and agency' (Hayes et al., 2017, p. 4). Power imbalances are embedded in the practice of focusing on upward accountability and meeting donors' needs, rather than on resolving community needs (Doan & Knight, 2020). Organizations with the structure, capacity, and resources to deliver results in the most efficient ways are considered desirable aid partners (Raeburn-Bruce, 2019), but communities located in the Global South – the recipients of most international aid interventions – feel left out of the decision making (Anderson et al., 2012). Southern organizations often find themselves implementing initiatives that were identified, developed, and funded by actors in the Global North, regardless of whether the initiatives address the most urgent needs or provide the most efficient solutions to the problem.

Despite being a critical part of the relationships between Northern and Southern CSOs, power dynamics in international development are rarely acknowledged or addressed. Power imbalance manifests in different ways, including resource dependency, top-down decision making, and vertical accountability. Because a huge part of international development funding comes from Northern philanthropic organizations, these organizations wield great influence on the practices and institutional frameworks for deploying the philanthropic aid, even though they are not based in the Global South, where the funds are deployed (Centre for Strategic Philanthropy, 2021). Local knowledge and input are rarely considered. This shortcoming could be addressed with the principles of community philanthropy, where accountability and decision making are shared across all stakeholders, including aid recipients.

Community philanthropy as a concept

In many parts of the world, community philanthropy has existed for thousands of years: for centuries, communities pooled their resources after identifying priority issues. In East Africa, specifically in Kenya, community philanthropy takes the form of *harambee*, which means 'pulling together', with people pooling resources and expertise to solve community problems – whether this refers to building a house for a family, raising resources to send a child to school, paying medical bills, or fundraising for a wedding, these actions bond communities together.

Another manifestation of community philanthropy is the Filipino principle of Bayaniham – an altruistic system of mutual help and concern – 'a practical response to both individual and community needs which, under certain circumstances would be difficult to achieve if people with meager means did not organize themselves and pool together their resources' (Ang, 1979, p. 91).

In southern Africa, the concept of community philanthropy is more radical, drawn from the African humanist philosophy espoused by Desmond Tutu (as cited in Jolley, 2011) that a person is a person because of other people – the idea that personhood is intertwined with the collective. This is referred to as *ubuntu*, from the Zulu '*umuntu ngumuntu ngabantu*', meaning 'I am because we are', or the Xhosa translation of '*umntu ngumntu ngabantu*', which expresses the belief in a universal bond of sharing that connects all humanity.

For each of these forms of community philanthropy, mutuality, cooperation, and communalism lie at the heart of the principle. The idea is that pooling resources results in something far greater than its individual parts because the collective gain is a multiplicative (rather than additive) function of individual contributions. Faciolince (2021) proposes shaking up our working cultures to dismantle existing hierarchical structures and replace them with collective power.

Community foundations in the modern sense have existed in North America for over 100 years (Sachs, 2014). However, as a global phenomenon, the community foundations movement has gained momentum over the last two decades. The emergence of this movement is driven by, among other factors, limitations in traditional funding, clashes over priorities, power dynamics, and community disenfranchisement (Hodgson, 2020). A very basic definition of community foundations is the act of individuals giving back to their communities; this can follow an immediate and informal set-up to address a specific need or the more structured and formally organized provision of longer-term support to meet community needs (Sachs, 2014).

Community foundations are often perceived simply as intermediaries – channelling funds from large donors to community initiatives (Kingman, 2003), providing in-country technical assistance, awarding modest grants, and helping to select grantees on behalf of large donors, especially bilateral donors funding initiatives in multiple countries or regions. However, the work of community foundations is not just about more control of resources from Northern donors being given to local/Southern organizations; rather, this concept is also about recognizing that local communities can and do identify priorities and raise resources to solve them. Community philanthropy departs from community development in the role assigned to beneficiaries. Community philanthropy promotes placing target communities at the centre of the decision making through active participation to promote empowerment and social justice. In other words, in community development, target communities are participants, whereas they are the drivers of change in community philanthropy.

The Assets–Capacities–Trust framework of community philanthropy

In this section, I first briefly define the concept of community as it is applied in this chapter. I then describe the ACT framework of community philanthropy. This approach has been articulated by the Global Fund for Community

Foundations (Knight & Avrorina, 2021), and it has been used in a number of development initiatives around the world (Hodgson, 2020).

The concept of 'community' has various meanings, with varying degrees of divergence from each other. Community is usually defined by shared geography, identity, interests, commonality, or connection (Littlejohn & Foss, 2009). In this chapter, drawing on Hodgson and Pond (2018, p. 10), I define community as 'networks of connections between people and a shift from the individual to the collective'. Community has the dual function of being the 'glue' that binds individuals together through 'a shared sense of belonging' and at the same time the 'engine' that drives their collective 'voice and action in relation to others' (Hodgson et al., 2017, p. 17). Communities in the diaspora are a good example. They may not reside on the same continent, but they are united by their sense of kinship or a link to a specific place (for example, a community or school), time, or identity, and they are driven to develop their home communities. Such communities are a powerful tool for development because they can harness their networks and other resources to contribute to their local communities 'back home'. This can be in the form of, for example, providing scholarships or developing their local school or health centre.

Over the last decade or so, a growing number of community foundations have lent their voices to conversations around how to 'do development differently', defining and amplifying an emergent framework focused on the principles of building the community assets, capacities, and trust that underpin the work of community philanthropy (Hodgson, 2020) The ACT framework, building on the principle of mutuality, postulates that fostering agency enables the community to be the architects of their own development and results in sustainability and broad-based accountability.

Assets are resources held by a community that ensure the long-term independence of the community foundation and its work (Knight & Avrorina, 2021). These can take various forms, which includes – but is not limited to – money. In community philanthropy, the value of money as an asset is not considered only in monetary terms but also as a signifier of trust: people give to causes or organizations they trust. Assets can also be in the form of knowledge, skills, and expertise. Different forms of social capital are an important part of community philanthropy; bonding (within a group), bridging (between groups), and linking (an extension of bridging, where power dynamics are of significance) social capital help communities navigate internal relationships within the community, as well as external relationships with others outside of their community.

Proponents of community-based asset development argue that using external experts to solve community problems creates dependency, as it assumes communities need rescuing because they cannot solve their problems – that they need a professional to solve their problems (McNight, 1995, as cited in Green, 2010). This professionalization of community problem-solving creates 'clients who are in need [of] continued care' (Green, 2010, p. 3) and heightens dependence on external parties to solve issues. Additionally, as external experts may not fully understand the local context, they may offer generic solutions to the problem that may not fully address the needs or be the most efficient or effective way of solving the problem.

To understand the value of local knowledge, one should look at the distinction between the community foundations' definition of local knowledge and international development notions of local vs. world class. In international development, local is the polar opposite of 'world class' or 'global'. Nowhere is this distinction more clearly expressed than in the remuneration of 'local staff' vs. expats; locally hired staff members are often viewed as 'would-be beneficiaries' of the programmes being implemented (Peace Direct, 2021, p. 25). In contrast, community foundations, searching for solutions within their environment, tend to view people with local knowledge as the experts, as they are more intimately acquainted with the problem and have a good understanding of the local context. Many times, the target communities are also the local experts on the problem. There is a recognition that the people in need of the help know exactly what solution is required; what they may be lacking is not knowledge but the resources and/or capacity necessary to resolve the problem. By pooling their knowledge, skills, funds, and networks, they are able to work out a solution to the problem, often at a lower cost than when external support is sought. This is because local experts volunteer their knowledge and skills to the initiative. In the case of *Bayanihan* in the Philippines, people with few resources pool them together to resolve problems facing part of their community. In defining 'local' as *internal*, Hodgson and Pond (2018) describe the existence of a latent power that may not be visible externally but that, when circumstances and conditions are right, can be harnessed or deployed and becomes transformational. These are the 'superpowers' of community philanthropy – the ability to deploy relatively low levels of resources in a short time to resolve emerging community needs with a high level of flexibility and adaptability, which is not possible with other international development actors, who are encumbered by layers of accountability and bureaucracy.

Faciolince (2021) describes growing forests of knowledge, which begins with confronting the 'white gaze of development' through questioning whose knowledge counts, making space for diverse forms of knowledge, elevating other forms of expertise, and broadening the definition of what it means to 'live well', challenging the continued underappreciation (e.g. in research) of collective well-being and indigenous worldviews, cultures, and practices.

Capacity is sometimes referred to as agency, which is simply defined as the ability to act. Agency connotes free will and choice (Littlejohn & Foss, 2009). Local people's capacity is therefore their ability to do things they see as important within their communities. After the assets that exist within a community have been recognized and acknowledged, they can be activated by mobilizing people and money in service of the society local people want. Two factors are key to building capacity – the participation of local people (bonding capital) and partnership with other organizations (bridging or linking capital; Knight & Avrorina, 2021).

A good sign of trust within a community is when community members contribute money towards a project because, as mentioned above, people tend to give money to those they know and trust. The value of the money becomes greater than its fiscal worth, as it underpins the relationships in a community, contributing to peace, harmony, and prosperity. It is the social glue that welds local people together to achieve what they want in their communities, a measure of social significance, and a reflection of the community's attitude towards community foundations (Knight & Avrorina, 2021). In a Maasai pastoralist community adjacent to the Maasai Mara Game Reserve in Kenya, many children were unable to attend school because there was only one school in the community (Kenya Community Development Foundation [KCDF], 2014) Some children had to walk as far as eight kilometres to reach the school, facing danger from wild animals in the area. They also had to cross a seasonal river that flooded every year during the rainy season. Therefore, parents were reluctant to send their children to school, especially when the children were young. The Nkoilale Community Development Organisation was established in 2009, in partnership with a Dutch organization (the Osotua Foundation) to address the challenges to education faced by the community in Nkoilale. With the support of their partners, the Nkoilale Community Development Organisation mobilizes resources from the local community to build extra classrooms and dormitories for the primary school, as well as additional 'satellite' schools located closer to the community to reduce the distance children must cover to get to school. The community comes together periodically, raising resources for one classroom or dormitory at a time. As this is a pastoralist community, residents donate livestock (goats or cows) that are then auctioned, and the money raised is used to build the classrooms (KCDF, 2014). In this way, the community has managed to build two additional schools to meet the growing need for education among children in the community.

There is fluidity/interconnectedness between building assets, agency, and trust. In community philanthropy, trust is considered a valuable currency: funds raised by communities have greater value than their monetary amount because of what they can unlock. The money raised has a multiplier effect in terms of building trust and increasing the community's confidence in their ability to 'do for themselves' and solve their problems without looking outside for resources or expertise. It also helps them to leverage external capital and other resources required. Communities do not operate in isolation; rather, they work with different actors to achieve their goals. The difference is that, with community philanthropy, they drive the process – there is recognition that they are not just passive beneficiaries.

Community ownership increases meaningful participation: when people contribute their time and resources, they feel a deeper sense of ownership and belonging because they have invested something of value. It also infuses communities with a sense of dignity when they feel empowered to act to resolve the problems they face. The act of giving becomes a catalyst for sustainable impact because, when communities have a vested interest in something, they work towards improving it, and, the next time they are faced with a problem, they apply the same tools, methods, skills, and resources to resolve it. Tewa is a Nepalese feminist fund working to develop community philanthropy both to minimize the 'social costs incurred in rapid transition for self reliant development and for the empowerment of emerging groups in Nepal' (TEWA, n.d., Introduction). Tewa raises funds locally in Nepal to increase the local ownership and sustainability of their work and to reduce dependency on external donors. For Tewa, the act of giving is 'both an assertion of humanity and an expression of power' (Global Fund for Community Foundations, 2021). Tewa works with other organizations adopting their model of local fundraising as a pathway to philanthropic giving for self-reliance. They hope to build a critical mass of women and men who believe in self-reliant development for equitable justice (TEWA, n.d.). They also build the capacity of local Nepalese organizations in resource mobilization and grant making. The Kenya Community Development Foundation (KCDF) is a community foundation that employs a matching grant model, where communities raise at least 50% of the required resources, and this is then matched by a grant from the foundation. What makes the model distinctive is that KCDF recognizes and quantifies non-cash contributions as part of the community contribution. These come in the form of manpower, skills, and non-monetary donations provided by the community; these contributions are either used directly in a project or exchanged for money (KCDF, 2016).

Community foundations face challenges around resilience and sustainability. They struggle to survive, raise resources, and build a local support base, and they are dependent on local support for survival, raising some, if not most, of their resources from their local community. It takes time to build local support and shift the mindset from being recipients to being donors, especially in communities that have been recipients of aid in the past or that are accustomed to giving to causes rather than to institutions. Building trust is a second challenge related to building local support, especially in places where NGOs may be viewed as corrupt or as working for external interests. If a community foundation is established by an 'outsider', it may take additional time to build trust. A third challenge for community foundations is the struggle to enlist institutional support to strengthen their internal capacity, which is critical for their survival. This challenge is not unique to community foundations, as many CSOs struggle to raise money to cover operational costs. As a fourth challenge, community foundations often find it difficult to strike a balance between immediate needs and the necessity of raising long-term resources for the sustainability of the organization. It is easier to address emerging issues, problems, and needs than it is to build assets; thus, when communities prioritize what to do with the few resources available, long-term problems tend to take a back seat to immediate and emerging issues (McNight, 1995, as cited in Green, 2010). This begs the question of whether a community that is struggling to meet day-to-day needs can afford to build long-term assets. Organizations like KCDF have demonstrated that it is possible to address emerging needs while simultaneously building long-term assets through multi-pronged approaches such as raising resources both locally and internationally, building an endowment, providing matching grants to community organizations, and building the capacity of community organizations in local resource mobilization and advocacy.

Lessons from community philanthropy for international development actors

Community foundations have demonstrated that the needs and interests of donors and those of Southern organizations do not have to be mutually exclusive. Communities pool their resources to resolve a felt need. In this process, they are not only identifying the problem and designing the solution but also mobilizing the resources required to implement this solution. They are not passive recipients but rather architects of their development. This is a powerful departure from the notion in international development that communities are synonymous with beneficiaries, with the accompanying connotation of helplessness. It is possible to build partnerships between Northern and Southern organizations even when most of the funds are flowing from the North. The role of the donor is to facilitate the process by recognizing and addressing power dynamics in the relationship and to foster the development of a partnership of equals. Of course, there is irony in the donor being the one raising the conversation on power, but, because of the nature of the relationship, Southern organizations may not feel entitled to demand an equal partnership with their donors unless that option is presented to them.

To successfully adopt the principles of community philanthropy, international development actors can adopt ten lessons. First, they must *recognize that communities are resource rich*. This also means recognizing that money is not the only asset to consider and that communities can leverage other resources to address their needs. These can be in the form of natural resources, knowledge, skills, social capital, networks, or other assets that the community may possess.

Second, partnering with community foundations requires *flexibility and adaptability* in funding to meet not just the immediate needs, but also the longer-term, changing needs of communities. During the pandemic, funders have shown a high level of flexibility, allowing the repurposing of grants to respond to immediate needs. In many instances, they have allowed grantees to make the decisions that they felt would respond to the largest need or consulted grantees in making decisions about repurposing grants. This is a good test of the local stewardship of international development funds and could either cement the notion that locals cannot be trusted or demonstrate that they have the capacity to handle large grants and deliver results. Donors should endeavour to fund ideas and be responsive as opposed to prescriptive. Flexibility also brings more partners to the table

– especially social movements, youth networks, and local collectives, which tend to be particularly fluid and unstructured.

Third, for these relationships to work, there must be *mutual transparency* and the avoidance of multiple layers of secrecy around funding. Community foundations are well placed to provide a bridge between informal community structures and donors. Aid transparency is crucial for increasing aid effectiveness and accountability to achieve better development outcomes, as it enables communities to see exactly what has been allocated for development, which, in turn, helps with decision making and strengthens trust and accountability. As mentioned above, with community philanthropy, communities give to organizations they trust.

Fourth, the COVID-19 pandemic has exposed the need for more non-financial input from donors to build resilience (Centre for Strategic Philanthropy, 2021) – the need for input into *building the institutional capacity* of local organizations for sustainability and to enable them to manage large grants independently. This means investing in the operations and technical capacity of the organizations, including governance, finance, reporting, and implementation capabilities, to enable them to implement projects effectively, thereby addressing the shortcomings of local organizations perceived by international organizations and donors while also safeguarding partner organizations' sustainability.

Fifth, Northern INGOs need to discard the funder mentality and create space for change to happen to catalyze processes that will allow for equal engagement. This will require *ceding some control*, which should be taken up by Southern organizations; however, this takes time, as each party involved needs to be confident that they can trust the other. Language is very important in communicating power. Words like 'partnership' sometimes lose their meaning in international development because, although organizations form 'partnerships', the relationships are anything but equal, and the grantees are still at the bottom of the decision-making hierarchy. It is therefore the role of funders and international organizations to begin conversations on addressing power in their partnerships. They must also be ready to deal with uncomfortable truths about how power is vested and who holds power. They should be prepared to cede or share power with others in their partnerships.

Sixth, international development actors should *explore different funding models* that give more decision-making power to the recipient organizations or target communities and act as catalysts to spur local resource mobilization (i.e. through matching grants). Another example of this is FRIDA, a feminist fund partnering with young feminist-led organizations to dismantle patriarchy, address human rights violations, overturn inequalities, and co-create new feminist realities (FRIDA, 2015). They address the issues of power, decision making, and transparency in philanthropy through their participatory grant-making process, which puts young feminists at the centre of the decision-making process. Organizations that apply for funding are invited to vote on which of the applicants should receive funding. They also give core funding that is flexible and allows grantees to listen to their communities and be highly responsive in a rapidly changing world, as they can make decisions about what is needed and where to direct their funds.

Seventh, all parties in the partnership must be prepared to be *invested for the long term* because building relationships and gaining trust take time.

Eighth, *timing* is key – community organizations should have decision-making/governance processes in place, be clear about their mission and vision, and have a solid strategy or strategic direction. Organizations that are still defining their identity or work may not be the best fit for this kind of partnership because they may not be ready for the kind of effort required to manage successful partnership relationships. However, this is likely to be a short-term position. A funder or larger organization can still work with these organizations, investing in their growth for future partnerships.

Ninth, international development actors should plan for leadership transitions and safeguard against political interference, especially in organizations established and rooted in the community. The process of partnership should include *due diligence* to ascertain that the organization is a good fit and has compatible values.

Finally, donors need to think about how to reduce local organizations' dependence on short-term grant funding and adopt more sustainable models. *Local resource mobilization* could fund part of the work, but there are other forms of sustainability that can be explored, including growing the assets of local organizations and the communities they serve to strengthen their sustainability and self-reliance.

The current climate in the international development sector, where organizations are challenging the status quo, coupled with the changes in funding for development work and the COVID-19 pandemic, has demonstrated that the current situation is unsustainable. The community philanthropy model provides a viable and scalable solution for international development. The future of development is community-driven, and community foundations are well placed to spearhead the emergence of a strong, bottom-up international development paradigm.

References

Afadzinu, N. A. (2020). *The third sector in West Africa - Maimed by COVID-19*. Accra: WACSI. Retrieved from: https://wacsi.org/the-third-sector-in-west-africa-maimed-by-covid-19/.

Anderson, M. B., Brown, D., & Jean, I. (2012). *Time to listen: Hearing people on the receiving end of international aid*. Cambridge, MA: CDA collaborative Learning Projects. Retrieved from: https://www.cdacollaborative.org/wp-content/uploads/2016/01/Time-to-Listen-Hearing-People-on-the-Receiving-End-of-International-Aid.pdf.

Ang, G. (1979). The bayanihan spirit: Dead or alive? *Philippine Quarterly of Culture and Society*, 7(1/2), 91–93.

Batliwala, S. (n.d.). *All about power: Understanding social power and power structures*. CREA. Retrieved from: https://reconference.creaworld.org/wp-content/uploads/2019/05/All-About-Power-Srilatha-Batliwala.pdf.

Centre for Strategic Philanthropy. (2021). *Philanthropy and COVID-19: Is the North–South power balance finally shifting?* Retrieved from: https://www.jbs.cam.ac.uk/wp-content/uploads/2021/03/2020-csp-report-covid.pdf.

Doan, D., & Knight, B. (2020). *Measuring what matters.* Candid & Global Fund for Community Foundations. Retrieved from: https://globalfundcommunityfoundations.org/wp-content/uploads/2020/10/MeasuringWhatMatters.pdf.

Faciolince, M. (2021). *Creating new horizons: Paths to shift power and imagination in development- from poverty to power.* Retrieved from: https://bit.ly/3tKMOCB.

FRIDA. (2015). *Letting the movement decide: FRIDA grantmaking report.* Lafayette Practice & FRIDA Young Feminist Fund. Retrieved from: https://youngfeministfund.org/wp-content/uploads/2017/05/FRIDA-Grantmaking-Report.pdf.

Global Fund for Community Foundations. (2021). *Tewa celebrates 25 years of advancing women's rights and building local philanthropy in Nepal.* Retrieved from: https://globalfundcommunityfoundations.org/news/tewa-celebrates-25-years-of-advancing-womens-rights-and-building-local-philanthropy-in-nepal/.

Green, P. G. (2010). Community assets: Building the capacity for development. In P. G. Green & A. Goetting (Eds.), *Mobilizing communities: Asset building as a community development strategy* (pp. 1–13). Philadelphia, PA: Temple University Press.

Hayes, N., Introna, L. D., & Kelly, P. (2017). Institutionalizing inequality: Calculative practices and regimes of inequality in international development, *Organization Studies, 39*(9), 1203–1226. https://doi.org/10.1177/0170840617694067.

Hodgson, J. (2020). Disrupting and democratizing development: Community philanthropy as theory and practice. *Gender & Development, 28*(1), 99–116. https://doi.org/10.1080/13552074.2020.1717214.

Hodgson, J., Knight, B., & Wilkinson-Maposa, S. (2017). *New horizons for community development: Recommendations for funders.* Retrieved from: https://assets.ctfassets.net/zsfivwzfgl3t/XYMRGEFupoyCThDoUaIEr/6ddb46b9c723a158496576c9319e6b8e/new-horizons-for-community-development.pdf.

Hodgson, J., & Pond, A. (2018). *How community philanthropy shifts power: What donors can do to make that happen.* Retrieved from: https://learningforfunders.candid.org/content/guides/how-community-philanthropy-shifts-power/.

Jolley, D. R. (2011). *A person is a person through other persons.* Master's thesis Southern Utah University. Retrieved from: https://www.suu.edu/hss/comm/masters/capstone/thesis/jolley-d.pdf.

Kenya Community Development Foundation. (2014). *Entrenching local resource mobilisation: Nkoilale classroom project* [video file]. Retrieved from: https://www.youtube.com/watch?v=xJ46aHMVIk0.

Kenya Community Development Foundation. (2016). *Community philanthropy: The journey of KCDF's Pamoja for Change project.* Retrieved from: https://www.kcdf.or.ke/Community-philanthropy.pdf.

Kingman, A. (2003). What role for intermediaries? *Alliance Magazine*, June. Retrieved from: https://www.alliancemagazine.org/feature/what-role-for-intermediaries/.

Knight, B., & Avrorina, L. (2021). Assets, capacity, trust: Role of community foundations in development of local philanthropy. Charities Aid Foundation Russia, Global Fund for community Foundations & Philanthropy for Social Justice and Peace. Retrieved from: https://globalfundcommunityfoundations.org/wp-content/uploads/2021/03/AssetsCapacitiesTrust_Feb2021.pdf.

LINC. (2020). *How civil societies in the global south are impacted by COVID-19.* Retrieved from: COVID-19-Impact-on-CSOs_LINC-report.pdf (linclocal.org).

Littlejohn, S., & Foss, K. (Eds.). (2009). *Encyclopaedia of communication theory.* Thousand Oaks, CA: SAGE.

Paige, S., Kotsiras, D., & Peace Direct. (2021). Time to decolonise aid: Insights and lessons from a global consultation. Peace Direct, Adeso, the Alliance for Peacebuilding, and Women of Color Advancing Peace and Security. Retrieved from: https://www.peacedirect.org/wp-content/uploads/2021/05/PD-Decolonising-Aid-Report.pdf.

Raeburn-Bruce, A. (2019). *Opinion: International development has a race problem.* DEVEX. Retrieved from: Opinion: International development has a race problem | Devex.

Sachs, E. (2014). *Community Foundations around the world: An examination of the Community Foundation Movement.* Council of Foundations. Retrieved from: https://core.ac.uk/download/pdf/71359692.pdf.

TEWA. (n.d.). *Introduction.* Retrieved from: https://www.tewa.org.np/introduction.php.

TEWA. (n.d.). *Model adaptation initiative.* Retrieved from: https://www.tewa.org.np/tmai.php.

6

CONTESTING PRACTICES OF AID LOCALIZATION IN JORDAN AND LEBANON

Civil society organizations' mobilization of local knowledge[1]

Elena Aoun, Lyla André and Alena Sander

Introduction

This chapter explores the unfulfilled promises of the Northern-led 'aid localization' that has been initiated in the fields of humanitarian aid and development, as well as the opportunities this shift has nonetheless created for local actors from the South[2] to reclaim the lead in decision making in cooperation with donors.[3] The idea of localizing aid dates back to the 1980s (Ettlinger, 1994), and practices and discourses around this idea have evolved and developed in varied ways ever since. In the last couple of decades, these practices and discourses have merged with wider frames of development aid and humanitarian assistance. Analysis of this evolution has concluded that it is constitutive of a new paradigm of 'self-reliance' (Joseph, 2013, 2014; Juncos, 2017). Seen as the ability of individuals and communities to meet their own needs, self-reliance is meant to empower local actors so they can shape their own fortunes through 'aid localization', 'a collective process by [which] the different stakeholders' of the humanitarian and development systems aim to put local actors at the centre and give them a greater role (de Geoffroy & Grunewald, 2017, p. 1).

Aid localization approaches based on self-reliance are also meant to transfer power and to level the asymmetry between Northern donors and Southern recipient states and communities. However, the literature points to the persistence of unequal power relations (Eriksson Baaz, 2007; Sander, 2021; Schöneberg, 2017). While agreeing that the alleged transfer of power mostly equates to a re-adjustment of Norths–Souths power relations in subtler forms of governmentality, this chapter explores how local actors, especially civil society organizations (CSOs), find leverage and resources in the discourse that precisely frames localization and power transfer for the purpose of reclaiming, if not leadership, at least an enhanced agency. The chapter argues that, using, notably, the resource of

DOI: 10.4324/9781003241003-7

contextual knowledge, local actors try to assert themselves as necessary and full-fledged partners rather than passive implementers. In doing so, they project significant agency and provide genuine 'starting from the South' approaches as they strategically navigate the web of power relations pervading the world of international development and humanitarian aid, as well as local political settings.

The argument builds on two case studies, both based on extensive fieldwork. Grounded in the development field, the first case study explores the cooperation between Jordanian women's non-governmental organizations (NGOs) and their Northern-based donors around women's rights in Jordan. Located at the core of the 'humanitarian–development nexus', the second case study examines the relationship between local actors involved in Syrian refugee education in Lebanon and their European donors. The field research in Jordan took place in 2017 (one month) and 2018 (three months) through semi-directed face-to-face interviews and online in 2021 with representatives of Jordanian women's organizations and donor agencies. In addition to 63 interviews, three months of participant observation with one organization was conducted. The field research in Lebanon took place in 2019 (one month) and 2021 (two months). A total of 56 semi-structured interviews (face-to-face or online depending on COVID-related restrictions) were conducted with representatives of local organizations, Lebanese officials, and donor representatives working in the field of Syrian refugee education. All participants provided informed consent for the use of their anonymized data.

These two cases seem to share very little. Yet, their very differences provide much ground to examine how local actors try to seize the opportunities provided by aid localization to gain more say in spite of the power relations in which they are entangled.

Unfolding its argument in three sections, the chapter starts by retracing the shifts in the wider paradigms in which the discourse and practice of localization are embedded. Building on critical approaches to Western-led development and humanitarian aid, this first section below not only highlights the ongoing limitations to localization and the persistence of power relations throughout the shifts but also the new opportunities created for Southern-led agency with these changes. Following Batliwala (2019), we focus on how knowledge, as a significant tool for Southern actors, along with intangible resources, is used to reclaim a greater role. After presenting a brief overview of donors' localization discourses in both settings, the second section explores the power relations within which CSOs in Jordan and Lebanon are entangled – whether these are with their donors or with the state. The third section focuses on how Jordanian and Lebanese CSOs push for more symmetrical relationships to alter persisting power relations through the day-to-day assertion of their contextual knowledge, contestation of their side-lining, and claims for a more genuine localization. The conclusion offers some recommendations on the basis of Southern CSOs' perceptions of what is lacking that would be required for a real localization of development and crisis responses to make good on pledges to start from the South.

Paradigmatic shifts around localization

Development and humanitarian assistance have traditionally been interwoven with power relations. Both fields still are, though they have absorbed the discourse on localization and despite paradigmatic shifts in international approaches spurred by a mix of regular critiques and political, social, and economic developments.

Meant to include local communities in the processes aimed at bolstering their development and/or assisting them in facing humanitarian challenges, 'localization' can be understood as a dominant discourse that has evolved in development and humanitarian action over the past several decades. Today, 'localization' is found within the paradigm of self-reliance, which is itself embedded in transnational neo-liberal discourses of colonial continuities (i.e. the dynamics of colonial power that are based on racism and culturalism and that continue to shape present-day ideas and practices in development and humanitarian action (Ziai et al., 2020).

As argued by Escobar (1995/2012) and Kothari (2005), since the beginning of the so-called development era, Western development and humanitarian efforts have been accompanied by the conviction that 'expert knowledge' is possessed only by a privileged group – the former colonizers – and is necessary to achieve development for the formerly colonized. This discursively constructed superiority of Western knowledge became one of the main arguments for top-down development programmes and humanitarian action financed and led by the West – and so it remains, particularly because local actors have had hardly any say in the emergence of the wider paradigm within which donors approach them today. Therefore, localization remains structurally embedded in a paradigm that somehow negates it; consequently, power relations persist when the discourse translates into practice.

Discourse about localization is not new. It emerged from the early critiques of Western-led development interventions. Often influenced by feminist, postcolonial, and post-development thought, these critiques highlighted the failure of Western interventions to value and include Southern knowledges and experiences, calling for a 'local turn' (Mac Ginty & Williams, 2009). By the late 1980s, this turn had been achieved, mostly bearing the hallmark of the social, economic, and political developments of the decade. Indeed, neo-liberal capitalism, belief in the power of the free market, and the failure of liberal state building through the instruments of the Washington Consensus led to a general 'state fatigue'. This new idea, also referred to as 'state phobia' (Villadsen & Dean, 2012), was also based on the assumption that Southern states were not stable or efficient enough to effectively respond to development and humanitarian challenges like poverty, hunger, and conflict. In this context, 'localization' mostly meant that some money trickled down to local NGOs so they could implement in the Souths what was often conceived in the Norths.

Paradigmatic developments took place in the mid-1990s, with the shift from 'state security' to 'human security' (UNDP, 1994). This more liberal conception of security put the individual at the centre of international security policy discourses (Chandler, 2012, p. 214). By discursively relocating the roots of crises in socioeconomic disparities, this discourse directly linked security to both humanitarian and development issues. In addition to establishing a triple nexus among all three terms, this paradigm added a new dimension to localization, as ordinary people in poverty- and disaster-prone societies were increasingly seen as the targets of international efforts aimed at 'empowering' them so they could become 'resilient' (Hilhorst, 2018).

Faced with persistent critiques and significant developments at the international level nurturing fears of state failure and showing the limitations of humanitarian and development interventions, the paradigm shifted again. The initially 'broad' and 'emancipatory' vision of 'human security' was progressively replaced by a 'narrow' and institutional conception promoting 'the creation of liberal institutions to protect security', thus bringing back the Southern state (Richmond, 2007, p. 460). Moreover, the paradigm discursively moved away from the assumption that Western intervention is needed to secure the Souths, shifting 'towards a concern with facilitating or developing' self-reliance of all local actors, including the state, civil society, local communities, and the individual (Chandler, 2012, p. 213).

At first glance, through this multidimensional recentring on Southern actors, the self-reliance approach enhances localization, providing a fair way of including local needs, experiences, and knowledge at various levels, flattening out persisting power imbalances between aid-givers and aid-receivers. However, research into recent international responses to humanitarian/development challenges suggests that this neo-liberal approach consists only of a transfer of 'responsibility' at the level of implementation 'onto local actors' (Joseph, 2014, p. 290). The approach thereby invites target populations in the Souths 'to take responsibility for their welfare and economic and social well-being', without giving them power (Joseph, 2013, p. 44). Indeed, as Northern donors turned from 'builders' into 'facilitators' (Haldrup & Rosén, 2013, p. 131), they kept the power to influence 'who gets what, who does what, who decides what, and who sets the agenda' (Batliwala, 2019, p. 13), maintaining control over most resources in Batliwala's extended notion of social power.

Nevertheless, development and humanitarian action today are much more than a Western-dominated knowledge regime. Instead, these fields are a battlefield that has been turned upside down, especially by the discourse of localization, which puts greater emphasis not only on local responsibility but also on local knowledge. This creates new opportunities for Southern actors to reclaim the importance of local social power (Batliwala, 2019) and to incrementally contribute to a redefinition of Norths–Souths relationships (Mosse, 2014). As resources of power are not only economic and material but also include 'the various human and social resources which serve to enhance' social power, defined as 'the ability to exercise choice' (Kabeer, 1999, p. 437), knowledge, along with other intangible resources, has become a resource for Southern actors (Kabeer & Sulaiman, 2015). Resources of this type include 'relational' and 'invisible' resources of power such as 'who you know, social support networks, membership of social movements or unions' (Batliwala, 2019, p. 39).

CSOs' power entanglements in Lebanon and Jordan

Both in the field of women's rights in Jordan and in that of Syrian refugee education in Lebanon, Northern-based donors' discourse largely echoes localization objectives. In Jordan, donors who work with Jordanian women's organizations may be diverse in their approaches and intervene in different areas of women's rights. However, they all put a particular focus on the promotion of women's political and economic participation and leadership, aiming at empowering women to become self-reliant. Illustratively, USAID claims that it 'aims in all its programming in Jordan to reduce gender disparities and empower women and girls to realize their rights, determine their own life goals, and help Jordan build an economically stable, self-reliant future' (USAID, 2020, p. 1).

Additionally, donors claim to perceive – and treat – Jordanian CSOs as their partners. Partnership, according to several donor representatives, is based on mutual respect and trust. Even if it mostly plays out as a discourse and less as actual practice, partnership further associates local actors with the overall development objectives pursued by donors through support for women's rights projects, as it purports to aim for equal responsibility sharing between donors and the women's NGOs.

In Lebanon, the international discourse is even more explicit on both self-reliance and localization. Building 'resilience for all' is showcased as the paramount objective of the United Nations (UN)-led Regional Refugee Resilience Plan addressing the Syrian refugee crisis. The major instrument of the European Union (EU) in the country, the MADAD Fund, echoes this objective, aiming at addressing 'early recovery, as well as resilience and self-reliance needs of refugees and IDPs [internally displaced persons] [...] in a manner that also benefits local communities' (European Commission, 2021). Beyond this focus on the individuals and communities at the receiving end of international and EU efforts, local civil society actors are regarded as key partners. For instance, the UN's 2021–2022 regional strategic overview for the Regional Refugee Resilience Plan (UNHCR, 2020, p. 13) states the aim of fostering 'local service delivery through greater partnership with local actors, including NGOs' while 'enhancing local and national capacities'. Likewise, the EU insists on the need to '[step] up cooperation with local partners', considering that local and national NGOs are 'often the first to respond when a disaster strikes, [...] a part of the local communities, and [...] more perceptive of the local cultural and political dynamics in which they operate' (European Commission, 2021).

Despite the efforts described above, the experiences of local actors in the two settings examined here do not indicate a search for genuine partnerships. Rather, CSOs that implement donor-funded projects in Lebanon and Jordan remain deeply entangled in several layers of power relations. These are similar in both settings, with CSOs depending completely on donors and being heavily influenced by the context where they operate, which is framed by the state. These similarities notwithstanding, the shape power relations assume differs slightly between Lebanon and Jordan. These differences have an impact on how localization plays out in each context and on how organizations mobilize local knowledge to reclaim localization.

Interviewees in both settings confirmed that their relationships with donors were far from equal and that aid localization, which is meant to acknowledge and enhance their agency, has been realized to a very limited extent. Several reasons for this were emphasized: donors refuse to hand over financial responsibility to local CSOs, retain agenda-setting and decision-making power, and, finally, often decide unilaterally which projects by which CSOs will be funded, frequently in ways that remain opaque for the CSOs themselves. Moreover, the respondents asserted that donors continue to exercise power in terms of capacity building, although such activities are at the core of the objectives of resilience and self-reliance for local individuals and communities.

Thus, viewing aid localization more as rhetoric than actual practice, representatives of CSOs in both settings expressed disappointment. In Lebanon, one respondent spoke about a 'missed opportunity' for effectively localizing funding to local civil society:

> After almost ten years now, [...] this should have shifted; international donors, the EU, and other donors could have directly donated to the local organizations, and a lot of money could have been saved and spent on the refugees or the local community [...]. But this didn't happen.
>
> *[Lebanese CSO representative, 4 February 2021]*

In Jordan, a CSO director echoed this perception, stating, 'Donors are not implementing localization; it's just semantic and lip service and how they are playing along, against the values they claim. They are not truly investing in [us]. It's just an industry' [Jordanian CSO representative, 5 May 2021]. For CSOs, this often meant that they were expected to 'abide [by] donors' expectations' [Lebanese CSO representative, 29 January 2021]; consequently, they perceived their relationships with donors as 'patriarchal' [Lebanese CSO representative, 10 November 2021] or 'colonial' [Jordanian CSO representative, 23 April 2021].

As both cases examined here show, the reality of humanitarian and development aid has little to do with partnership, as CSOs rarely feel respected or trusted. CSO representatives claimed that donors often unilaterally decide what 'respect' and 'trust' mean – and expect their local partners to earn these Northern-defined forms of respect and trust. In addition, the CSO representatives believed that donors do not fully trust local organizations. Among other reasons for thinking this, respondents mentioned that donors usually maintain financial control over project budgets and monitor CSOs' work closely through extensive reporting, evaluation, and audit procedures. While donors expect CSOs to fully open their books and justify every dinar or lira spent, the donors themselves usually remain completely opaque in how they disburse project funding. In Jordan, donors often approach women's organizations with pre-designed projects, pushing the CSOs into the role of service providers or project implementers. This practice sharply contrasts with donors' discourse on partnership and with the objective of self-reliance they pursue through projects meant to empower women to become leaders. In Lebanon, although local actors seem to enjoy more negotiation space on project design and implementation, they take issue with donors' 'paperwork' expectations and pressure relating to CSOs' 'accountability' [Lebanese CSO representative, 29 January 2021].

While CSO representatives in both settings perceived their relationships with donors as unequal, there nevertheless seems to be a difference: whereas the women's organizations in Jordan resisted all active interventions from donors in the field of women's rights, the CSOs in Lebanon seemed to accept a certain involvement of donors in the field of emergency education. This can be understood in relation to the differing characteristics of these issues. Women's rights in Jordan are perceived as a local matter in which the active involvement of the West might harm the cause of women's organizations because women's rights are often dismissed as a Western import in Jordanian public discourse. Jordanian women's organizations therefore try to keep donors out of their decision making as much as possible and are primarily interested in accessing their funding; hence, these CSOs make an absolute claim to aid localization. Emergency education in Lebanon, however, is not perceived as just a local matter. On the contrary, responsibility for Syrian refugees is considered something that must be shared by the international community, where the North plays a leading role. This does not mean that Lebanese organizations are unaware of power relations; rather, it indicates that they may strategically call for significant donor involvement in decision making because they are aware of the stakes of burden sharing in the international refugee regime.

Regarding their relationships with the state, the representatives of CSOs in both settings agreed that the state also engulfs them in a web of power relations and is the primary factor influencing the context in which they operate, as well as how localization takes place. In Jordan, the state's role was mostly perceived as restricting, and the state was often viewed as an opponent invested in 'shrinking civic spaces', co-opting civil society, and promoting patriarchal values in society. Although Jordanian organizations must obtain approval from national ministries before they start implementing projects and prior to being allowed to access foreign funding, the women's organizations in Jordan, like other CSOs in the country, are free to engage in direct cooperation with foreign funders. The situation is completely different in Lebanon, where the Lebanese Ministry of

Education functions as an intermediary between donors and CSOs in the field of emergency education and has been leading the response since 2014. This led to the consolidation of political authorities' control over the implementation of the response to the domestic refugee crisis, at the expense of Lebanese CSOs, despite the fact that CSOs provided a significant part of refugee education on the ground and continue to supply valuable information to both the state and donors. In practice, the localization process contributed to enhancing the 'resilience' of national institutions rather than CSOs' capacities. Because the Lebanese state plays such a vital role in the diffusion and management of aid in the field of emergency education, it also heavily influences and restricts the potential of aid localization at the level of civil society. In contrast, in Jordan, the potential to localize aid at the CSO level is relatively high, which is one of the reasons why Jordanian women's organizations are able to claim full localization.

Mobilizing local knowledge

Jordanian and Lebanese CSOs use different strategies to assert themselves in the face of power relations and to reclaim a more genuine localization. Knowledge resources related to project management and implementation, along with more intangible resources such as contextual knowledge, local coalition building, networking, and information sharing, are tools commonly used by local actors in both settings.

One way of using local knowledge is to challenge donors' expertise on local matters. By doing this, local actors reassert an expertise that their partners from the North cannot have. In Jordan, for example, research participants especially questioned donors' knowledge of women's situation in Jordan, which many donors use as a basis for pre-conceiving projects. Western-based 'Google experts', as one interviewee called them, who sit in their offices somewhere in the Norths, draw their expertise from the Internet [Jordanian CSO representative, 27 April 2021]. However, she continued, these 'experts' completely ignore the everyday challenges of women living in Jordan. Therefore, she asserted, many development projects fail to yield positive change for women in Jordan. Staff members of women's organizations in Jordan linked this failure first to the fact that projects are based on inaccurate knowledge regarding the context, as Western knowledge about Jordan is often prioritized over local knowledge. Second, they linked the failure to the fact that Jordanian women's organizations are not sufficiently included in decision making about programming and strategizing. The research participants also explained how they sometimes confront donors directly or correct them in meetings when they speak about women in Jordan, or about Jordan in general. By doing this, local actors mobilize their insider knowledge about broader topics of interest for donors, such as democratization and shrinking civic spaces in the country. Some research participants even described themselves as teachers who educate the donors, whereas others spoke about themselves as the ones who bring the 'truth' to the donors. Using donors' rhetoric about partnership and localization, local actors, as described by the research participants, obviously argue for a shift of power based on the claim that local knowledge about 'the field' trumps Western knowledge. According to the research participants, they deserve a place at the table as full-fledged partners because they 'know the field' [Jordanian CSO representative, 23 April 2021], 'have eyes and ears on the ground' [Jordanian CSO representative, 5 October 2017], are 'trusted by the people' [Jordanian CSO representative, 5 May 2021], and 'know what [they]'re doing' [Jordanian CSO representative, 15 November 2021].

For CSOs involved in providing education to Syrian refugees in Lebanon, the recognition of and reliance on local expertise by Northern donors seem to flow more naturally. As one interviewee noted, donors often strictly fund programmes and

> don't tell us what to do [...]; they fund it – this is how it goes, and in return we offer them papers, documents, how much money was spent. But as regards to the activities, it is up to us to say what we want to really do.
>
> *[Lebanese CSO representative, 21 January 2021]*

In this case, the very nature of the task supports local actors' claim to do the job without having donors telling them what to do. Indeed, refugee education is part of public policy, requiring local knowledge – notably, regarding the linguistic ability to teach Syrian children and/or the accreditation to provide the Lebanese curriculum. Moreover, local CSOs were the first to meet the educational needs of Syrian refugee children, making use of their contextual knowledge by leading the response through direct relationships with Syrian children well before donors or the state began to react to the crisis.

However, local actors in Lebanon also take issue with the fact that they are routinely excluded from Northern-led coordination and deprived of the possibility of having a wider view on the overall efforts in the field of refugee education. Our interviews revealed that, consequently, local actors rely on coordination and coalition building to enhance their position with donors and to avoid being side-lined and missing key information. One interesting example is an alliance of some well-established national CSOs, not only to claim ownership of knowledge as a resource but also to strategically build this knowledge to strive for more localization. In 2014, this initiative gave rise to the Lebanese Humanitarian and Development NGOs Forum, which has steadily grown, reaching up to 100 members. The goal of this forum '[...] is that everyone [among Lebanese NGOs] has access to the information and spread the information' but also to 'bridge the gap between the coordination [in] the field and the very formal coordination handled by the UN' [Lebanese forum representative, 21 January 2021]. The forum also issues a yearly briefing note in the framework of the Brussels Conference[4] and is particularly active in terms of advocacy.

Contextual knowledge, local coalition building, networking, and information sharing are not the only resources local actors mobilize to assert themselves as key players. Knowledge resources related to project management and implementation, including budgeting and monitoring, are often emphasized. Especially in Jordan, research participants mobilized two interrelated strains of argumentation to claim strong project management skills. The first is related to the long experience that most of the organizations have in the field of project implementation. Indeed, some of the CSOs date back to well before the 2000s and have been implementing development projects for decades. This has given them and their staff members opportunities to acquire considerable experience. The second argument is related to the many trainings and workshops the CSO staff members have attended in the context of donor-funded capacity building on topics such as project management, finances, and budgeting. At least for the older Jordanian women's organizations, this has led to knowledge transfer in the field of project management to the extent that the CSOs have perfected the skill and are able to meet donors' standards and, accordingly, demand more horizontal relationships based on genuine partnership.

In Lebanon, local actors involved in the field of refugee education are relatively diverse: some already have a long history and strong experience in Northern-funded project implementation and voice claims regarding genuine partnerships with donors that are very similar to those observed among the Jordanian CSOs. Interestingly, on the other side of the spectrum, local actors with less exposure to cooperation with international donors and those that newly materialized in the wake of the Syrian refugee crisis highlight the lack of capacity building provided by the international community. Representatives of such CSOs see this lack as a clear disregard of localization objectives and proof that discourses about self-reliance are mostly void of real meaning. Against this backdrop, one respondent from a national NGO concluded that 'It is a shame to have an instrument such as [the] EU MADAD Fund that is used to enhance aid localization' when, in the end, only 'some local organizations indirectly benefit from it' [Lebanese CSO representative, 21 January 2021]. Other respondents from smaller CSOs further acknowledged that 'unfortunately, [...] donors prefer to have international NGOs to be the umbrella [above] local NGOs to conduct auditing, all documentation' [Lebanese CSO representative, 27 January 2021], wondering 'why the aim is not to build local CSOs' capacities and why would we always need a "foreigner"?' [Lebanese CSO representative, 20 August 2020]. Consequently, local actors try to push for access to capacity building by bridging gaps among researchers, experts, practitioners, and activists through CSOs such as The Centre for Social Sciences Research and Action (Abi Yaghi & Troit, 2020).

Finally, local actors also use the power to decide whether they want to cooperate with international actors and take their money. Staff members of the Jordanian women's CSOs explained that, even though they depend on foreign funding, they do not necessarily accept any conditions that donors try to put on them, and, at times, they reject funding or even blacklist donors. One respondent claimed that 'donors have their conditions, and so do we. We often say "no" if we don't agree with their terms. We have our own rules' [Jordanian CSO representative, 29 September 2017]. The founder of a small Lebanese educational CSO remembered rejecting requests from donors such as providing data on the identity of refugee recipients as a funding condition [Lebanese CSO representative, 20 August 2020]. Similarly, the artistic director of a CSO running a music school also mentioned strongly rejecting a German cultural institution's demand for quantitative indicators, considering that the musical progress of refugee children, who are often traumatized, could not be evaluated via any quantitative measurement tool. This refusal had consequences because the funding was not reallocated to the NGO [Lebanese CSO representative, 10 September 2020].

Such incidents reveal the extent to which local actors are aware of the discrepancy between donors' talk about localization and the reality of their practices, as well as their intentions to use diverse strategies to make their voices more audible. The CSO representatives often stressed the interdependency of their local knowledge and the donors' funding, and they emphasized that one cannot go without the other if development and humanitarian objectives are to be achieved. Accordingly, local organizations present themselves as indispensable sources of real expert knowledge for donors and as actors that need to be fully associated with plans aimed at achieving shared objectives, whether it is for advancing women's rights in Jordan or for providing refugee education in Lebanon.

Local actors' demands for a shift of power, notably through focusing on the importance of local knowledge – a resource they argue that they have more of, compared with donors – have been made possible through the dominant discourses. For many research participants, reclaiming the power of local knowledge is a way of holding donors accountable for their promises of localization, empowerment, and self-reliance. Thus, local actors do not just challenge those in power; they also redefine the contours and contents of Norths–Souths partnerships, which, according to the interviewees, has been dominated by donors' rules for too long.

Conclusion

Very active in the fields of development and humanitarian aid, local CSOs in the Souths are keen supporters of localization, which is purportedly meant to enable them to engage in horizontal partnerships with Northern-based donors and to provide them with the financial means and capacities to conceive and conduct the projects they deem useful and relevant, considering their intimate contextual knowledge of the target populations and the stakes involved. However, individuals working in the fields of refugee education in Lebanon and women's rights in Jordan expressed disappointment in how localization has played out, perceiving their cooperation with their Northern 'partners' as unequal. Many research participants felt that they are required to primarily be compliant service providers and implementers located at the far end of a process in which their input is nowhere near the central position that would be implied by real localization. However, CSOs are confident in the worth of their actions regarding not only the target populations but also the donors' objectives. Their local knowledge and experience empower them to challenge the content and method of Northern donors' approaches, even if this is often done discreetly and 'behind the scenes'. In addition to the mobilization of contextual knowledge to assert themselves, CSOs are keen to build their capacities, make up for their marginalization by creating platforms to collectively build knowledge and know-how, share information, and come together to strengthen their voices and increase their weight when facing donors.

This everyday struggle demonstrates that localization is far from being a lived reality in the Souths and that actors from the Souths are currently striving to translate the localization discourse into practice in the field. Starting from our interactions with Southern CSOs, we offer a few recommendations.

Our first recommendation involves the need for context-specific definitions of localization through the inclusion of local civil society actors. This need is important because local settings may differ widely, notably in terms of power relations between national authorities and local civil society actors. To be effective, localization must not over-strengthen authoritarian and/or corrupt states at the expense of civil society.

Very pragmatically, Northern-based donors could also take the following steps:

- Adapt their funding requirements and expectations to facilitate diverse local CSOs to ask for funds.
- Move away from the idea of the superiority of quantitative tools for monitoring and evaluation over qualitative and intangible knowledge owned by local actors.
- Engage with local CSOs through strategic and coordination meetings where they have more than an observer status, and ensure that the same level of information is maintained and that CSOs' locally grounded ideas are taken on board through horizontal discussions.
- Increase the budgetary and strategic decision-making power of local actors while maintaining transparency standards.

These recommendations seem relatively easy to implement, as they are in line with the wider paradigm in which development aid and humanitarian assistance are embedded today. However, if localization someday comes to mean a shift in both responsibility and power, the broader neo-liberal paradigm, embedded in colonial continuities, may need to be questioned.

Notes

1 This chapter derives from a research programme funded by the UCLouvain, entitled 'ARC-SERTIS: resistance to international prescriptions and injunctions in Africa and the Middle East today'.

2 The terms 'Souths' and 'Norths' are used in their plural forms to reflect the heterogeneity and diversity of countries, cultures, and identities in both the Souths and the Norths.
3 The definition of 'donors' used here follows Southern CSOs' use of the term to describe the ensemble of Northern-based organizations that fund Southern-based organizations directly or channel funding to them. This ensemble includes bilateral and multilateral donors, private foundations, and international non-governmental organizations.
4 The Brussels Conference has taken place yearly since 2017. Its objectives are to continue supporting the Syrian people, to mobilize the international community to achieve a comprehensive and credible political solution to the Syrian conflict, and to provide a platform for dialogue with civil society organizations from Syria and the broader region.

References

Abi Yaghi, M.-N., & Troit, V. (Eds.). (2020). *Transition humanitaire au Liban: Humanitarian Transition in Lebanon*. Paris: Karthala.

Batliwala, S. (2019). *All about power: Understanding social power and power structures*. CREA. Retrieved from: https://namati.org/resources/all-about-power-understanding-social-power-power-structures/.

Chandler, D. (2012). Resilience and human security: The post-interventionist paradigm. *Security Dialogue*, *43*(3), 213–229. https://doi.org/10.1177%2F0967010612444151.

de Geoffroy, V., & Grunewald, F. (July 2017). *More than the money: Localisation in practice*. Trocaire - Working for a Just World. Retrieved from: https://www.trocaire.org/documents/more-than-the-money-localisation-in-practice-2/.

Eriksson Baaz, M. (2007). Paternalism: The 'outside' or 'rejected Inside' of partnership? *New Glocal Times* (7). Retrieved from: https://ojs.mau.se/index.php/glocaltimes/article/view/148.

Escobar, A. (2012 [1995]). *Encountering Development: The making and unmaking of the Third World*. Princeton, New Jersey: Princeton University Press.

Ettlinger, N. (1994). The Localization of development in comparative perspective. *Economic Geography*, *70*(2), 144–166. https://doi.org/10.2307/143652.

European Commission. (2021). *European civil protection and humanitarian aid operation. Grand Bargain. Factsheet*. Retrieved from: https://ec.europa.eu/echo/what/humanitarian-aid/grand-bargain_en.

Haldrup, S. V., & Rosén, F. (2013). Developing resilience: A retreat from grand planning. *Resilience*, *1*(2), 130–145. http://dx.doi.org/10.1080/21693293.2013.804659.

Hilhorst, D. (2018). Classical humanitarianism and resilience humanitarianism: Making sense of two brands of humanitarian action. *Journal of International Humanitarian Action*, *3*(1), 1–12. https://doi.org/10.1186/s41018-018-0043-6.

Joseph, J. (2013). Resilience as embedded neoliberalism: A governmentality approach. *Resilience*, *1*(1), 38–52. https://doi.org/10.1080/21693293.2013.765741.

Joseph, J. (2014). The EU in the Horn of Africa: Building resilience as a distant form of governance. *Journal of Common Market Studies*, *52*(2), 285–301. https://doi.org/10.1111/jcms.12085.

Juncos, A. E. (2017). Resilience as the new EU foreign policy paradigm: A pragmatist turn? *European Security*, *26*(1), 1–18. https://doi.org/10.1080/09662839.2016.1247809.

Kabeer, N. (1999). Resources, agency, achievements: Reflections on the measurement of women's empowerment. *Development and Change, 30*(3), 435–464. https://doi.org/10.1111/1467-7660.00125.

Kabeer, N., & Sulaiman, M. (2015). Assessing the impact of social mobilization: Nijera Kori and the construction of collective capabilities in rural Bangladesh. *Journal of Human Development and Capabilities, 16*(1), 47–68. https://doi.org/10.1080/19452829.2014.956707.

Kothari, U. (2005). Authority and expertise: The professionalisation of international development and the ordering of dissent. *Antipode, 37*(3), 425–446. https://doi.org/10.1111/j.0066-4812.2005.00505.x.

Mac Ginty, R., & Williams, A. J. (2009). *Conflict and development*. London: Routledge.

Mosse, D. (2014). Knowledge as relational: Reflections on knowledge in international development. *Forum for Development Studies, 41*(3), 513–523. https://doi.org/10.1080/08039410.2014.959379.

Richmond, O. P. (2007). Emancipatory forms of human security and liberal peacebuilding. *Canada's Journal of Global Policy Analysis, 62*(3), 459–478. http://dx.doi.org/10.1177/002070200706200302.

Sander, A. (2021). Reclaiming partnership: 'Rightful resistance' in a Norths/Souths cooperation. *Third World Quarterly, 39*(2), 1–14. https://doi.org/10.1080/01436597.2021.1957672.

Schöneberg, J. M. (2017). NGO partnerships in Haiti: Clashes of discourse and reality. *Third World Quarterly, 38*(3), 604–620. https://doi.org/10.1080/01436597.2016.1199946.

UNDP. (1994). *Human development report: New dimensions of human security*. Retrieved from: http://hdr.undp.org/en/content/human-development-report-1994.

UNHCR. (2020). *Syria 3RP Regional Strategic Overview 2021–2022*. Retrieved from: https://data2.unhcr.org/en/documents/details/84022.

USAID. (2020). *Promoting gender equality and women's empowerment. Jordan*. Retrieved from: https://www.usaid.gov/sites/default/files/documents/1883/Enhancing_Gender_Equality_and_Female_Empowerment_.pdf.

Villadsen, K., & Dean, M. (2012). State-phobia, civil society, and a certain vitalism. *Constellations, 19*(3), 401–420. http://dx.doi.org/10.1111/cons.12006.

Ziai, A., Bendix, D., & Müller, F. (2020). Introduction. In A. Ziai, D. Bendix, & F. Müller (Eds.), *Beyond the master's tools? Decolonizing knowledge orders, research methods and teaching* (pp. 1–16). Lanham: Rowman & Littlefield.

PART 2

Displacing the North–South dyad

7

SOUTHERN CIVIL SOCIETY ORGANIZATIONS AS PRACTICAL HYBRIDS

Dealing with legitimacy in a Ugandan gender advocacy organization

Tiina Kontinen and Alice N. Ndidde

Introduction

Analysis of civil society collaborations often focuses on how Northern civil society organizations (CSOs), including international non-governmental organizations, conduct their programming in cooperation with their Southern partners, frequently featuring critical discussion of the asymmetries in such North–South collaborations. Focusing on the North–South dyad easily excludes the examination of the web of influential relationships in which Southern CSOs are embedded. In this chapter, we scrutinize how CSOs navigate between diverse audiences and logics in negotiating their organizational legitimacy while trying to maintain their aspirations for social change and transformation. Previous research on the legitimacy of development CSOs has focused on, for instance, the challenge for international non-governmental organizations to be simultaneously seen as legitimate by their audiences in the Global North and their partners and beneficiaries in the Global South (Dodworth, 2014; Lister, 2003; Mitchell et al., 2020; Ossewaarde et al., 2008; Walton et al., 2016). Some studies have examined Southern CSOs' efforts to gain legitimacy vis-á-vis the field of international development through certain management practices and 'development speak' (Claeyé & Jackson, 2012), whereas others have investigated the divergence among accountability mechanisms perceived to be legitimate by international donors, governments, and local communities (Buchard, 2013; Claeyé, 2014; Dar, 2014); scrutinized different interpretations of sources of CSO legitimacy held by donors and grassroots organizations (Elbers et al., 2021); and investigated sources of legitimacy of local advocacy CSOs in their relationships with communities (Matelski et al., 2021). Scholars have also discussed the ability of CSOs to act as legitimate representatives of those they claim to speak for, and the extent to which CSOs legitimately follow their own explicit values in terms of societal goals (Atack, 1999; Dodworth, 2014; Mitchell et al., 2020, p. 100).

DOI: 10.4324/9781003241003-9

To contribute to debates on CSO legitimacy, in this chapter, drawing on two distinct bodies of literature, we discuss diverse legitimacy audiences and logics in relation to which legitimacy is assessed and negotiated. First, we join the debate on 'going with the grain' (Booth, 2011; Crook & Booth, 2011; Kelsall, 2008, 2012) in development studies. This literature leads us to view CSOs as 'practical hybrids' (Booth & Cammack, 2013, p. 99; Rusca & Schwartz, 2014) that must balance between being embedded in existing institutionalized practices and promoting the transformation of these practices. Second, we draw on organization studies literature on hybrid organizations – organizations combining diverse institutional logics to perform legitimacy in the eyes of different audiences in varying fields (Battilana & Dorado, 2010; Battilana et al., 2017; Deephouse et al., 2017; Pache & Santos, 2013).

We explore CSO legitimacy through the case of Action for Development (ACFODE), a Ugandan gender advocacy organization that negotiates its legitimacy in alignment with diverse audiences and logics while striving to maintain its core concern – gender equality. We ask, first, what the main legitimacy audiences for ACFODE are, and second, according to which different logics its legitimacy is assessed. We reflect on the ways in which the organization negotiates across differing legitimacy expectations. In the following sections, we first briefly discuss the notions of practical hybrids, hybrid organizations, and legitimacy. Then, we introduce the case of ACFODE and present our findings concerning legitimacy audiences and logics. We conclude with some ideas concerning the implications of our findings for North–South CSO collaborations.

Practical hybrids: balancing between diverse perceptions of legitimacy

In this section, we introduce our understanding of CSOs as practical hybrids, building on the bodies of literature concerning 'going with the grain' and organizational legitimacy. In both the Global South and the Global North, CSOs are often preoccupied with transforming existing ideas, practices, and institutions. However, these organizations typically need to anchor their approaches within the very institutions they seek to eventually change. CSOs in this position are conceptualized as 'practical hybrids' (Booth & Cammack, 2013, p. 99) in the literature on 'going with the grain', a notion that originated in research on African power and politics as an alternative to the 'good governance agenda' that mostly promoted Western-type CSOs in Africa and that faced many implementation and sustainability challenges (Booth, 2011; Booth & Golooba-Mutebi, 2012; Kelsall, 2008, 2012). The idea of 'going with the grain' emphasizes working with the existing social fabric, such as extended family, religion, women's organizations, and clientelism, instead of importing a new kind of 'civil society' (Kelsall, 2008, pp. 637–640). Practical hybrids consider existing institutions' potential resources rather than old-fashioned hindrances to be 'swept aside' and emphasize anchoring development interventions in local cultural repertoires to ensure their sustainability (Booth & Cammack, 2013, p. 101), thus seeking to promote something new in culturally legitimate ways (Rusca & Schwartz, 2014).

However, the legitimacy of CSOs can also be defined more broadly than the cultural legitimacy of their interventions. In organization studies, legitimacy is understood as 'a generalized perception or assumption that the actions of an entity are desirable, proper, or appropriate within some socially constructed systems of norms, values, beliefs, and definitions' (Suchman, 1995, p. 574) and therefore also as a kind of 'perceived appropriateness' of an organization (Deephouse et al., 2017, p. 32). Moreover, this appropriateness is assessed by multiple audiences (Deephouse & Suchman, 2008, p. 62) in a continuous process (Suddaby et al., 2017, p. 462) and embedded in social relationships (Meyer et al., 2013). Further, as suggested by the literature on hybrid organizations (Battilana & Dorado, 2010; Battilana et al., 2017; Fisher et al., 2017; Pache & Santos, 2013), legitimacy can be evaluated vis-á-vis different institutional logics. Here, 'logics' refers to the 'socially constructed, historical pattern of material practices, assumptions, values, beliefs, and rules by which individuals produce and reproduce their material subsistence, organize time and space, and provide meaning to their social reality' (Thornton & Ocasio, 1999, p. 804), further discussed in reference to organizations rather than individuals (Thornton et al., 2012). Logics do not refer to characteristics of certain actors but rather to institutionalized rationalities available in society, such as the market or religion (Friedland & Alford, 1991), that hold up different models, goals, and practices as appropriate – and thus legitimate (Thornton et al., 2012, p. 108).

Using these two bodies of literature in combination, we define Southern CSOs as practical hybrids, as well as hybrid organizations that negotiate their legitimacy vis-á-vis varied institutional logics and in the eyes of diverse audiences. Such legitimacy is needed so that CSOs can both anchor their work in existing practices and promote the transformation of these practices.

Introduction to the case and methods

ACFODE is a Ugandan gender advocacy organization that was established in 1986 to catalyze action on issues related to women. The organization was initiated by a few concerned activists, including many academics, in the aftermath of the United Nation's Third World Conference on Women in Nairobi in 1985. The organization played an important role in flourishing the women's movement in Uganda, which contributed to several legislative advancements in the early years of the regime of National Resistance Movement (NRM) and President Yoweri Museveni, starting in 1986 (Tripp, 2001; Tushabe, 2008).

One research participant narrated how ACFODE was born as a 'handbag organization' hosted in a founding member's office at Makerere University in the capital city of Kampala, at a time when all the organization's documents and assets could be placed in the handbag of one of the founding members. It has since evolved into a professional organization that owns an office building and has a fully functioning secretariat (Kontinen & Ndidde, 2020). From the beginning, knowledge production and dissemination, research publications, and media presence have been central to ACFODE. For example, the organization has published the biannual *Arise Magazine*, which covers a range of gender-related issues, since 1991. The organization depends on donor funding, which accounts for almost 90% of its current budget. Consequently, ACFODE is familiar with balancing its core concerns related to gender equality with diverse donor agendas, including the good governance agenda. Long-term and constant support from some of its development partners, especially the Konrad Adenauer Foundation, has played an important role in ACFODE's stability.

ACFODE's 2019–2023 Strategic Plan describes how the organization 'engages in evidence-based advocacy working with the central and local government, development partners and other civil society actors to influence gender policy development and implementation'. The Strategic Plan goes on to state that it targets 'non-traditional gender advocates like cultural, religious leaders and other informal authorities and undertakes women's economic empowerment and community development programmes covering all the regions of the country'. Clearly, ACFODE must negotiate its legitimacy with a number of audiences and within varied logics. We explore these negotiations based on qualitative research material, including documents, interviews with 12 organization members and staff, and discussions held at two workshops on ACFODE's history and interactions with stakeholders. Additionally, selected parts of interviews with 60 project participants in rural communities in Namutumba and Kiboga Districts are used. We analysed the material in two rounds. First, we identified diverse legitimacy audiences, their expectations, and their organizations' responses, as perceived by ACFODE. Second, after analysing the different expectations of legitimacy defined as appropriateness in the eyes of diverse audiences, we interpreted these through the analytical lens of logics.

Findings: legitimacy audiences and logics

In this section, we present our findings concerning the main legitimacy audiences and logics revealed by our analysis. We first briefly discuss the audiences by whom ACFODE seeks to be perceived as appropriate, before proceeding to the identified logics in relation to which the organization's legitimacy is negotiated.

Legitimacy audiences

Five main, internally heterogenous audiences appeared to be the most significant for ACFODE's legitimacy. First, the central government (i.e. the President, Cabinet Ministers, Members of Parliament, and other policymakers) is a significant legitimacy audience in two primary ways: First, the central government is one of the targets of ACFODE's lobbying on the formulation and implementation of policies and legislation that promote gender equality, and second, overall legitimacy in the eyes of the central government is also needed for any CSO to be able to function in Uganda. ACFODE, like many other gender advocacy organizations, balances between being perceived as a legitimate participant in policy-making processes, being co-opted, being subject to control to be seen as posing no threat to the government's gender agenda, and being delegitimized (Nabacwa, 2021, p. 316). In the 1980s, ACFODE's relationship with the National Resistance Movement and President Museveni was mainly one of cooperation, as the regime perceived women's empowerment a shared agenda item. The overall stance towards ACFODE and non-governmental organizations (NGOs) and CSOs in general changed with the shift to a multi-party system after the Referendum in 2005, and a move on the part of CSOs to adopt the good governance and human rights agenda. The increasingly suspicious and restrictive climate was exemplified by the 2016 NGO Act, which introduced new government control measures for organizations. The government considers ACFODE appropriate and legitimate as long as the organization focuses on women's empowerment programmes and supports government gender policies. However, ACFODE's activities concerning good governance or democracy are sometimes regarded as inappropriate, 'partisan' action, or 'elitist', and as not having the legitimacy to represent women in general. With recent restrictions on civil society, such as abruptly suspending the work of some CSOs in August 2021, ACFODE is in constant fear of encountering issues such as de-registration or the freezing of their bank accounts.

Second, the legitimacy audience of local government includes the Resident District Commissioners, councillors, and technical officers at different levels – groups to which ACFODE needs to demonstrate appropriateness to be able to work on its projects in communities across the country. In ACFODE's early years, the organization went directly to communities to implement their women's empowerment agenda. However, since the organization began to take up themes such as good governance and training local women councillors, the organization's legitimacy has been questioned at times by local government, leading to, for example, harassment and the interruption of events. To regain its legitimacy, ACFODE adopted the practice of 'signing a memorandum of understanding with the district leadership', inviting local leaders to raise any issues 'they may not be comfortable with' at review meetings, and asking local authorities to facilitate trainings so that 'they know what we are doing and will not consider it a sabotage'.

A third important audience consists of diverse project participants in the communities. ACFODE has faced several legitimacy negotiations related to its role and activities. In the beginning, the organization focused on training women only, which created suspicion and resistance among men. To increase their overall legitimacy in the eyes of communities, ACFODE started to train women and men together, which led to increased perceptions of appropriateness, as one participant stated: 'now [that] they taught the entire community, the message was more acceptable'. Additional legitimacy negotiations revolved around the question of whether to focus on gender awareness training or livelihood improvements. In response to the expectations of the most impoverished communities, ACFODE began to include livelihood components such as farming and adding value to agricultural products in its activities. For example, in Namutumba District, the women interviewed considered ACFODE a fully appropriate organization because it has supported the improvement of farming methods and adding value to agricultural products, responding to the most pressing local needs.

Fourth, an extremely important audience is the organizations ACFODE calls 'development partners'. Over the years these have included the Ford Foundation, Hivos, the Konrad Adenauer Foundation, EIRENE, Diakonia, We Effect, the European Union, and the British Council. Obviously, these partners do not constitute a coherent audience, and each assesses ACFODE's appropriateness on the basis of their own goals, programmes, and partnership criteria. Some have engaged in long-term partnerships, whereas others have worked with ACFODE to implement individual projects. Generally, all these organizations base their perception of appropriateness on assessments of ACFODE's expertise in gender issues, fluency with changing development discourses, and ability to implement activities and manage funding according to the partner's particular requirements.

Fifth, other Ugandan gender CSOs are an important audience that may be collaborators or competitors, depending on the situation. Women's organizations have proliferated at both national and local levels since the mid-1980s. Currently, according to the National Association of Women Organisations in Uganda, over 120 women's organizations are officially registered with the National NGO Bureau. Although many of them have specialized mandates in certain sectors or issues, they often expect ACFODE to provide leadership in advocacy on national gender issues and concerns. ACFODE has participated in many networks and coalitions, where it has been considered appropriate because of its ability to represent and work with women from diverse societal positions and because of its advocacy's strong evidence base.

Logics of patrimonialism: ACFODE as a nod to patronage networks

In this section, we discuss the logics in relation to which ACFODE's legitimacy is assessed, often simultaneously. According to the logics of patrimonialism, a legitimate organization is one that affirms reciprocal patronage networks characterized by power and support, both upwards towards the national power holders and downwards towards communities. 'Going with the grain' literature identifies patrimonialism as an institution that must be worked with (Kelsall, 2008). Patrimonialism and neo-patrimonialism, sometimes referred as 'big men politics', characterize governance in Africa in general (Hydén, 2013) and in Uganda in particular (Therkildsen, 2014). In the patrimonial system, political power is established through reciprocal relationships between patrons and clients, where the latter provide the former (e.g. a parliamentary candidate) with support, such as votes, in exchange for financial assistance, protection, and jobs (Cheeseman, 2018). Patrimonial logics influence social relationships far beyond state politics

(Hydén, 2013). Going beyond power, patronage networks involve moral virtues related to giving assistance (Cheeseman, 2018, p. 47).

In Uganda, President Museveni's regime has built extensive patronage networks through which the regime's supporters are rewarded, whereas opponents and competitors are suppressed or harmed, often violently (Loozekoot, 2021). In this situation, CSOs are pushed towards co-optation by the regime, seeking to be included in the networks rather than treated as enemies (Nabacwa, 2021; Tripp, 2001, 2010; Tushabe, 2008). Following patrimonial logics, in the eyes of the regime, an 'appropriate' ACFODE occupies the position of a client to the government, providing expert support for government policies to ensure its freedom to act. ACFODE has long noted that the 'President refers to himself as the driver of the vehicle of [the] women's movement'. Within these logics, ACFODE is invited to comment on policies and access power holders for lobbying purposes. Sometimes, government officials perform patronage by appearing at ACFODE's events as guests of honour. Moreover, as an illustration of a typical co-optation strategy (Nabacwa, 2021), some ACFODE members have been offered leadership positions in government administrative bodies.

While patrimonial logics based on social networks rather than institutions are often perceived as corrupt and nondemocratic, such logics are nevertheless an influential part of the social fabric and norms determining what is morally appropriate (De Herdt & Olivier de Sardan, 2015; Olivier de Sardan, 2008) and thus commonly expected to be followed. In this vein, ACFODE occasionally aligns with these logics; for instance, by inviting top political figures to their events or building their own social network of 'friends' within the regime, ACFODE has been able to further push its core agenda and maintain the potential to act.

Patrimonialism manifests in everyday social life in communities as the moral obligation of those who are well off to assist others (Kelsall, 2008). Likewise, CSOs are often expected to function as patrons – sources of continuous assistance (Swidler, 2009). In Ugandan context, Scherz (2014) shows how community members can stop participating in CSO programmes if they consider the organization as a bad patron not willing to assist them in their needs. In our case, community members said that an appropriate organization provides long-term support, noting that ACFODE 'abandoned us at [the] breast-feeding stage', making them feel 'like someone is pulling your hand trying to save you from drowning; then, when you reach the middle of the waters, they let your hand go and they disappear from you'. There were expectations that the organization would have a continuous community presence and respond frequently to immediate problems by 'giving money for the school fees' or 'helping me to build a house'. Similarly, there was much discussion on the allowances paid for participation in ACFODE's activities. Training workshops, in general, create an arena for patrimonialism (Smith, 2003), as they offer access to financial resources and networks in exchange for participation, which is essential for the CSOs' reported success. Allowances paid to women participants sometimes made ACFODE legitimate in the eyes of their husbands, who would not let their wives to participate without such payments.

Thus, the organization must continuously balance between participants' expectations for the provision of continuing assistance and ACFODE's core concern of empowerment. ACFODE's response has not been to assume the role of a patron, delivering assistance to meet needs in exchange for loyalty from community members; rather, the organization has used alternative strategies described by a staff member as follows: 'Often, our beneficiaries keep asking for money, so we have adjusted our training packages to include things like proposal writing or general resource mobilization strategies because you cannot sustain by giving groups money all the time'.

Logics of professionalism: ACFODE as a modern advocacy organization

Following the logics of professionalism, an appropriate organization possesses specific substantive and management expertise. Professional logics have been described as meaning using paid staff instead of volunteers, engaging in strategic planning, and conducting systematic programme evaluation (Hwang & Powell, 2009). The skills required thus include professional management practices, which are often related to the global trend of managerialism in CSO development cooperation (Claeyé, 2014; Girei, 2014).

Professionalism and pursuing the model of a modern, rational organization (Meyer & Bromley, 2013) were at the core of the organizational capacity-building programmes that gained momentum in the late 1990s. Encouraged by its development partners, ACFODE went through an organizational restructuring process in 2000 (Kontinen & Ndidde, 2020), transitioning from a purely voluntary organization to a professional organization, and started to conduct regular strategic planning and recruit staff based on competence. During the process, the organization's legitimacy was challenged on the grounds that it had lost aspects such as its members belonging to a community and doing things together, notwithstanding their formal competencies. Nevertheless, alignment with professional logics plays an important role in gaining legitimacy in the eyes of development partners, who appreciate ACFODE's competence with multiple planning and reporting frameworks, as 'all donors have their way of doing things, their reporting formats, their concept notes, the requirements they have for us'. Additionally, it is essential for ACFODE to be able to adapt to constantly changing development terminology. ACFODE has shifted from talking about 'women's empowerment' to discussing 'gender equality'. Additionally, aligned with the 'good governance agenda', ACFODE has adopted vocabularies such as 'public expenditure tracking' and 'civic engagement', and they have long used models such as the human-rights-based approach, as one senior staff member narrated:

> For instance, we began to use the word 'right-holders' from one of our development partners. In a number of trainings, they introduced the whole

> concept of [the] rights-based approach. I think we were already doing some rights-based approach, but it was not deliberate or clear-cut.

Many issues aligned with professional logics initially emerged in response to demands from ACFODE's development partners. These logics then gradually grew into everyday practices. Although staff members considered frequently changing approaches and numerous different reporting demands time consuming, they also perceived such changes as opportunities to learn something new.

Logics of community: ACFODE as a locally embedded organization

In community logics, an appropriate organization is part of everyday life in the community. Thornton et al. (2012, p. 73) argue that legitimacy in community logics is based on 'unity of will' and belief in trust and reciprocity and builds on common boundaries and group membership. Accordingly, an appropriate CSO would be located in the community and build trust on a daily basis. Such legitimacy would be difficult to achieve for an organization located in the capital city and implementing programmes nationwide. Initially, ACFODE was a group of educated urban women who went to communities to 'teach and preach gender equality', as a long-term member described it. The community response was hesitant and even hostile, as ACFODE was seen as promoting changes in cultural practices that were unwanted and lacking legitimacy.

ACFODE continues to be judged as an elite organization that did not emerge from underprivileged communities – the kind of organization that is often criticized as being distant from community needs (Banks et al., 2015; Elbers et al., 2021). However, ACFODE has undertaken a variety of strategies to align with community logics. The organization has moved its training events from towns to communities, employed local trainers, engaged community volunteers, and worked with traditional and religious leaders and existing community groups. Thus, ACFODE has gradually shifted towards being a practical hybrid, using the existing social fabric to advance its core concerns regarding gendered power relations. ACFODE has made efforts to contextualize its training material and translate it into local languages, as a staff member noted: 'We use local languages, local terminologies for rights [and] freedoms; the terms are there, so that is what we use, and we contextualize'.

Logics of activism: ACFODE as part of the Uganda women's movement

The legitimacy of an organization in terms of the logics of activism, typical of social movements, is related to its ability to promote change and transformation through mobilizing for collective action (Schneiberg & Lounsbury, 2017). Logics of activism are related to the possibilities to contest existing arrangements and propose alternatives (Thornton et al., 2012, p. 97). Therefore, from this perspective, an appropriate gender organization introduces equal gender relations that differ from the existing unequal relations and succeeds in mobilizing people to act together to change their views and practices towards these alternatives.

In alignment with the logics of activism, as an integral part of the African women's movement, which is concerned with women's economic status, representation in politics, cultural positions, and legal rights (Ahikire & Mwine Ashaba, 2015, p. 6; Tripp et al., 2008, p. 14), ACFODE has always promoted change in unequal power relationships. In Uganda, the women's movement was robust from the 1940s until 1970, when it was suppressed by the dictatorial regimes of Presidents Milton Obote and Idi Amin. At the time of ACFODE's inception in 1985, the women's movement was reigniting simultaneously with the beginning of President Museveni's regime in 1986 (Ahikire & Mwine Ashaba, 2015; Tamale, 2020; Tripp, 2001; Tripp & Kwesiga 2002; Tushabe, 2008). Since then, ACFODE has been a legitimate part of the movement, showing success in lobbying for women's representation in policy processes and policy formulation commissions such as the Constituent Assembly. However, the legitimacy of some ideas, especially related to the Domestic Relations Bill, which was tabled in 2003, was not seen as appropriate by the government, whose representatives accused ACFODE of being 'funded by the enemies of state', 'elitists' and 'anti-African'. The response was the founding of the Uganda Women Network, a platform for the Coalition of 24, which pushed for the revised Domestic Violence Bill in 2018.

Therefore, ACFODE is a legitimate organization from the perspective of the logics of activism in terms of mobilizing for changes in policies, legislation, and women's participation in national politics. However, as Tripp (2021, p. 23) argues, without concrete changes in 'the daily practice of communities, the impact of changes at the national level are necessarily limited'. Aligning with activist logics means introducing changes in communities, where gender relations are ingrained in societal customs and culture. As described above, ACFODE has employed multiple strategies to align with community logics, but, as a practical hybrid, the organization couples these with activist logics in an attempt to promote transformation. Additionally, ACFODE often combines livelihood and gender issues as a strategy to introduce alternatives. Project participants talked enthusiastically about their improved farming practices and increased appreciation for their children's education in parallel with changing attitudes regarding gender violence and women's political participation.

In interviews, the project participants described how their practices had changed as a result of the human rights education they received through ACFODE: 'We studied about human rights; they told us that all of us have rights, including women. We did not know that even women have a right, children have a right, and men also have rights'. In addition, starting from the grassroots, ACFODE has encouraged community members to identify their own advocacy issues related to domestic violence and girl-child education and devise strategies for addressing them. Consequently, some communities in Namutumba and

Kiboga Districts came up with by-laws against these issues. These examples illustrate how working with activist logics led to ACFODE's legitimacy in the eyes of communities, who appreciated the changes, although the main reason for adopting an activist stance was ACFODE's own core concern and the agendas of the organization's development partners.

CSOs as practical hybrids: lessons learned for starting from the South

This chapter has shown how Southern CSOs balance between different legitimacy audiences and logics. For ACFODE, negotiating the logics of patrimonialism, professionalism, community, and activism is central. In advocacy relations with the government, ACFODE balances between the logics of patrimonialism, professionalism, and activism; in community projects, the main negotiations are between the logics of patrimonialism, community, and activism, and the emphasis with development partners is on balancing between professional, community, and activist logics. We thus see Southern CSOs as hybrid organizations (Battilana et al., 2017) seeking to perform legitimacy through combining diverse logics, as well as practical hybrids (Booth & Cammack, 2013) balancing between being embedded in and transforming institutionalized practices. In ACFODE's case, this means contributing to transforming gender inequality in legislation, policy, the societal division of labour, and community-level practices by 'going with the grain' – for instance, utilizing patronage networks to gain entry points for lobbying decision makers or working with existing community groups and traditional leaders to promote gradual change in gender roles in the community.

Understanding Southern CSOs' need to continuously negotiate their legitimacy in relation to diverse audiences and logics challenges the perception of them as merely 'partner organizations' whose main source of legitimacy is the successful implementation of Northern programmes. Often, different audiences simultaneously judge Southern CSOs as being too donor-driven to be indigenous activist organizations, too activist to be legitimate government collaborators, too unprofessional to master international partners' reporting frameworks, and too elitist to be community organizations. Faced with such challenges to their legitimacy, CSOs can successfully combine diverse logics and balance between working within and transforming existing institutions. Being a practical hybrid can enable organizations to preserve their own core concern in determining how they respond to diverse legitimacy demands, avoiding simply adopting a single set of logics imposed by one external legitimacy audience. Accordingly, when entering into collaborations, Northern CSOs could start with identifying the role they, as a significant legitimacy audience, could play in advancing their partners' core concerns, rather than primarily searching for somebody to implement their programmes.

Acknowledgements

We would like to acknowledge funding received from the Academy of Finland for writing this chapter under the project 'Hybridity in African civil society organizations: examples from Tanzania and Uganda' (decision number: 327210) and for enabling the data collection under the project 'Growth into citizenship in civil society encounters' (decision number: 285815).

References

Ahikire, J., & Mwiine Ashaba, A. (2015). *The politics of promoting gender equity in contemporary Uganda: Cases of the domestic violence law and the policy on universal primary education* (ESID Working Paper No. 55). Manchester, UK: University of Manchester. http://dx.doi.org/10.2139/ssrn.2695727.

Atack, I. (1999). Four criteria of development NGO legitimacy. *World Development, 27*(5), 855–864. https://doi.org/10.1016/S0305-750X(99)00033-9.

Banks, N., Hulme, D., & Edwards, M. (2015). NGOs, states, and donors revisited: Still too close for comfort? *World Development, 66*, 707–718. https://doi.org/10.1016/j.worlddev.2014.09.028.

Battilana, J., Besharov, M., & Mitzinneck, B. (2017). On hybrids and hybrid organizing: A review and roadmap for future research. In R. Greenwood, C. Oliver, T. B. Lawrence, & R. E. Meyer (Eds.), *The SAGE handbook of organizational institutionalism* (2nd ed., pp. 128–162). Los Angeles, CA: Sage Publications. https://dx.doi.org/10.4135/9781446280669.n6.

Battilana, J., & Dorado, S. (2010). Building sustainable hybrid organizations: The case of commercial microfinance organizations. *The Academy of Management Journal, 53*(6), 1419–1440. https://doi.org/10.5465/amj.2010.57318391.

Booth, D. (2011). *Working with the grain and swimming against the tide: Barriers to uptake of research findings on governance and public services in low-income Africa* (APPP Working Paper No. 18). London, UK: ODI. Retrieved from: https://cdn.odi.org/media/documents/appp-wp18-working-with-the-grain-and-swimming-against-the-tide-david-booth-april-2011.pdf.

Booth, D., & Cammack, D. (2013). *Governance for development in Africa: Solving collective action problems*. London, UK: Zed Books.

Booth, D., & Golooba-Mutebi, F. (2012). Developmental patrimonialism? The case of Rwanda. *African Affairs, 111*(444), 379–403. https://doi.org/10.1093/afraf/ads026.

Buchard, M. (2013). Faith-based humanitarianism: Organizational change and everyday meanings in South Africa. *Sociology of Religion, 74*(1), 30–55. https://doi.org/10.1093/socrel/srs068.

Cheeseman, N. (Ed.). (2018). *Institutions and democracy in Africa: How the rules of the game shape political development*. Cambridge, UK: Cambridge University Press. https://doi.org/10.1017/9781316562888.

Claeyé, F. (2014). *Managing nongovernmental organizations: Culture, power, and resistance* (1st ed.). New York, NY: Routledge. https://doi.org/10.4324/9781315850856.

Claeyé, F., & Jackson, T. (2012). The iron cage re-revisited: Institutional isomorphism in non-profit organizations in South Africa. *Journal of International Development, 24*(5), 602–622. https://doi.org/10.1002/jid.2852.

Crook, R. C., & Booth, D. (2011). Conclusion: Rethinking African governance and development. *IDS Bulletin, 42*(2), 97–101. https://doi.org/10.1111/j.1759-5436.2011.00215.x.

Dar, S. (2014). Hybrid accountabilities: When western and non-western accountabilities collide. *Human Relations, 67*(2), 131–151. https://doi.org/10.1177/0018726713479620.

Deephouse, D. L., Bundy, J., Tost, L. P., & Suchman, M. C. (2017). Organizational legitimacy: Six key questions. In R. Greenwood, C. Oliver, T. B. Lawrence, & R. E. Meyer (Eds.), *The SAGE handbook of organizational institutionalism* (2nd ed., pp. 27–54). Los Angeles, CA: Sage Publications. https://dx.doi.org/10.4135/9781446280669.n2.

Deephouse, D. L., & Suchman, M. (2008). Legitimacy and Organizational Institutionalism. In R. Greenwood, C. Oliver, K. Sahlin, & R. Suddaby (Eds.), *The SAGE handbook of organizational institutionalism* (1st ed., pp. 49–77). Los Angeles, CA: Sage Publications. https://dx.doi.org/10.4135/9781849200387.n2.

de Herdt, T., & Olivier de Sardan, J.-P. (Eds.). (2015). *Real governance and practical norms in Sub-Saharan Africa: The game of the rules* (1st ed.). London, UK: Routledge. https://doi.org/10.4324/9781315723365.

Dodworth, K. (2014). NGO legitimation as practice: Working state capital in Tanzania. *Critical African Studies, 6*(1), 22–29. https://doi.org/10.1080/21681392.2014.889522.

Elbers, W., Schulpen, L., & Frobisher, E. (2021). "Stuck in a "Catch-22": Why Donors Fail to Include Grassroots Perspectives on CSO Legitimacy." *European Journal of Development Research, 34,* 921–939. https://doi.org/10.1057/s41287-021-00406-z.

Stuck in a "Catch-22": Why donors fail to include grassroots perspectives on CSO legitimacy. *European Journal of Development Research, 34*(2), 921–939. https://doi.org/10.1057/s41287-021-00406-z.

Fisher, G., Kuratko, D. F., Bloodgood, J. M., & Hornsby, J. S. (2017). Legitimate to whom? The challenges of audience diversity and new venture legitimacy. *Journal of Business Venturing, 32*(1), 52–71. https://doi.org/10.1016/j.jbusvent.2016.10.005.

Friedland, R., & Alford, R. R. (1991). Bringing society back in: Symbols, practices, and institutional contradictions. In W. W. Powell & P. J. DiMaggio (Eds.) *The new institutionalism in organizational analysis* (pp. 232–266). Chicago, IL: Chicago University Press.

Girei, E. (2014). NGOs, Management and Development: Harnessing Counter-Hegemonic Possibilities. *Organization Studies, 37*(2), 193–212. https://doi.org/10.1177/0170840615604504.

Hwang, H., & Powell, W. W. (2009). The rationalization of charity: The influences of professionalism in the nonprofit sector. *Administrative Science Quarterly, 54*(2), 268–298. https://doi.org/10.2189/asqu.2009.54.2.268.

Hydén, G. (2013). *African Politics in Comparative Perspective* (2nd ed.). New York, NY: Cambridge University Press. doi:10.1017/CBO9781139343756.

Kelsall, T. (2008). Going with the grain in African development? *Development Policy Review, 26*(6), 627–655. https://doi.org/10.1111/j.1467-7679.2008.00427.x.

Kelsall, T. (2012). Neo-patrimonialism, rent-seeking and development: Going with the grain? *New Political Economy, 17*(5), 677–682. https://doi.org/10.1080/13563467.2012.732275.

Kontinen, T., & Ndidde, A. (2020). Learning in a Ugandan gender advocacy NGO: Organizational growth and institutional wrestling. In K. Holma & T. Kontinen (Eds.), *Practices of citizenship in East Africa: Perspectives from philosophical pragmatism* (pp. 176–193). London, UK: Routledge. https://doi.org/10.4324/9780429279171-12.

Lister, S. (2003). NGO legitimacy: Technical issue or social construct? *Critique of Anthropology, 23*(2), 175–192. https://doi.org/10.1177/0308275X03023002004.

Loozekoot, A. (2021). We are not the president's 'yes' men and women: How legislative budget scrutiny improved in Uganda. *The Journal of Legislative Studies, 27*(2), 246–265. https://doi.org/10.1080/13572334.2021.1909955.

Matelski, M., Zijlstra, S., & van Kempen, L. (2021). Civil society legitimacy as a balancing act: Competing priorities for land rights advocacy organisations working with local communities in Kenya. *Canadian Journal of Development Studies/Revue canadienne d'études du développement*, November, 1–19. https://doi.org/10.1080/02255189.2021.1987202.

Meyer, J. W., & Bromley, P. (2013). The worldwide expansion of "organization." *Sociological Theory, 31*(4), 366–389. https://doi.org/10.1177/0735275113513264.

Meyer, M., Buber, R., & Aghamanoukjan, A. (2013). In search of legitimacy: Managerialism and legitimation in civil society organizations. *Voluntas: International Journal of Voluntary and Nonprofit Organizations, 24*(1), 167–193. https://doi.org/10.1007/s11266-012-9306-9.

Mitchell, G. E., Schmitz, H. P., & Bruno-van Vijfeiken, T. (2020). *Between power and irrelevance: The future of transnational NGOs*. New York, NY: Oxford University Press. https://doi.org/10.1093/oso/9780190084714.001.0001.

Nabacwa, M. S. (2021). Relations between gender-focused NGOs, advocacy work, and government: A Ugandan case study. In J. De Coninck & A. Larok (Eds.), *Uganda's civil society: History, challenges, prospects* (pp. 312–324). Kampala, Uganda: Fountain Publishers.

Olivier de Sardan, J.-P. (2008). *Researching the practical norms of real governance in Africa* (APPP Discussion Paper No. 5). London, UK: ODI. Retrieved from: https://assets.publishing.service.gov.uk/media/57a08bbe40f0b652dd000e6a/APPP-Discpaper5.pdf.

Ossewaarde, R., Nijhof, A., & Heyse, L. (2008). Dynamics of NGO legitimacy: How organizing betrays core missions of INGOs. *Public Administration and Development, 28*, 42–53. https://doi.org/10.1002/pad.472.

Pache, A.-C., & Santos, F. (2013). Inside the hybrid organization: Selective coupling as a response to competing institutional logics. *Academy of Management Journal, 56*, 972–1001.

Rusca, M., & Schwartz, K. (2014). 'Going with the grain': Accommodating local institutions in water governance. *Current Opinion in Environmental Sustainability, 11*, 34–38. https://doi.org/10.1016/j.cosust.2014.09.010.

Scherz, C. (2014). *Having people, having heart. Charity, sustainable development, and problems of dependence in Central Uganda*. Chicago, IL: The University of Chicago Press.

Schneiberg, M., & Lounsbury, M. (2017). Social movements and dynamics of institutions and organizations. In R. Greenwood, C. Oliver, T. B. Lawrence, & R. E. Meyer (Eds.), *The sage handbook of organizational institutionalism* (2nd ed., pp. 281–310). Los Angeles, CA: Sage Publications. https://dx.doi.org/10.4135/9781446280669.n12.

Smith, D. (2003). Patronage, per diems, and the workshop mentality: The practice of family planning programs in Southeastern Nigeria. *World Development, 31*(4), 703–715. https://doi.org/10.1016/S0305–750X(03)00006–8.

Suchman, M. C. (1995). Managing legitimacy: Strategic and institutional approaches. *Academy of Management Review, 20*(3), 571–610. https://doi.org/10.5465/amr.1995.9508080331.

Suddaby, R., Bitektine, A., & Haack, P. (2017). Legitimacy. *Academy of Management Annals, 11*(1), 451–478. https://doi.org/10.5465/annals.2015.0101.

Swidler, A. (2009). Dialectics of Patronage. Logics of accountability at the African AIDS-NGO Interface. In Hammack, D.C., and Heydemans, S. (Eds.) *Globalization, Philanthropy, and Civil Society. Projecting Institutional Logics Abroad* (pp.192-220). Bloomington and Indianapolis: Indiana University Press.

Swidler, A. (1986). Culture in action: Symbols and strategies. *American Sociological Review, 51*(2), 273–286. https://doi.org/10.2307/2095521.

Tamale, S. (2004). Gender trauma in Africa: Enhancing women's links to resources. *Journal of African Law, 48*(1), 50–61. https://doi.org/10.1017/S0021855304481030.

Tamale, S. (2020). *Decolonization and afro-feminism*. Ottawa, ON, Canada: Daraja Press.

Therkildsen, O. (2014). Working in neopatrimonial settings: Public sector staff perceptions in Tanzania and Uganda. In T. Bierschenk & J.-P. Olivier de Sardan (Eds.), *States at work: Dynamics of African bureaucracies* (pp. 113–144). Leiden, The Netherlands: Brill.

Thornton, P. H., & Ocasio, W. (1999). Institutional logics and the historical contingency of power in organizations: Executive succession in the higher education publishing industry, 1958–1990. *American Journal of Sociology, 105*(3), 801–843. https://doi.org/10.1086/210361.

Thornton, P. H., Ocasio, W., & Lounsbury, M. (2012). *The institutional logics perspective: A new approach to culture, structure and process*. Oxford, UK: Oxford University Press. https://doi.org/10.1093/acprof:oso/9780199601936.001.0001.

Tripp, A. M. (2001). The politics of autonomy and co-optation in Africa: The case of the Ugandan Women's Movement. *The Journal of Modern African Studies, 39*(1), 101–128. https://doi.org/10.1017/S0022278X01003548.

Tripp, A. M. (2010). *Museveni's Uganda: Paradoxes of power in a hybrid regime*. Boulder, CO: Lynne Rienner Publishers.

Tripp, A. M. (2021). Expanding 'civil society": Women and political space in contemporary Uganda. In J. De Coninck & A. Larok (Eds.), *Uganda's civil society: History, challenges, prospects* (pp. 13–33). Kampala, Uganda: Fountain Publishers.

Tripp, A. M., Casimiro, I., Kwesiga, J., & Mungwa, A. (2008). *African women's movements: Transforming political landscapes*. Cambridge, UK: Cambridge University Press. https://doi.org/10.1017/CBO9780511800351.

Tripp, A. M., & Kwesiga, J. C. (Eds.) (2002). *The women's movement in Uganda: History, challenges and prospects*. Kampala, Uganda: Fountain Publishers.

Tushabe, C. (2008). The autonomy of Ugandan women's organizations: How it matters in creating and maintaining a dependable democracy. *Wagadu: A Journal of Transnational Women's and Gender Studies, 6*, 45–59.

Walton, O. E., Davies, T., Thrandardottir, E., & Keating, V. C. (2016). Understanding contemporary challenges to INGO legitimacy: Integrating top-down and bottom-up perspectives. *Voluntas: International Journal of Voluntary and Nonprofit Organizations, 27*(6), 2764–2786. https://doi.org/10.1007/s11266-016-9768-2.

8

BEYOND THE NORTH–SOUTH DYAD

Diaspora-led organizations in development collaborations

Susan Appe

Introduction

This chapter addresses a way in which diasporas in the United States are engaging in development collaborations through grassroots international non-governmental organizations (GINGOs). In the United States, GINGOs make up a majority of the over 16,000 non-profit organizations doing development aid.[1] GINGOs are small, volunteer-run aid initiatives that fundraise and manage funds from private individual donors in the United States to send to recipient communities abroad. They raise these funds to deliver services in the Global South. It is estimated that approximately 10% of US-based GINGOs are founded by diaspora members (Appe & Chen, 2021).

GINGOs led by a member of a diaspora are the focus of this chapter. Diasporas are 'ethnic minority groups of migrant origins residing and acting in host countries but maintaining strong sentimental and material links with their countries of origin – their homelands' (Sheffer, 1986, p. 3). Diaspora members have begun to be part of the academic conversation about GINGOs (e.g., Appe & Oreg, 2020, 2021; Schnable, 2021), but there has been little theorization of the extent to which or how organizations led by individuals who identify as part of a diaspora contribute to development collaborations. Indeed, the diasporas themselves 'started' in the South and, over time, have built a transnational identity because of their migration. Because of this background, diaspora members have deep links with networks and communities in their homelands that allow them to assume Southern leadership even though they are based in the North.

Here, I situate GINGOs as an outlet for diaspora philanthropy, which is the transfer of private donations back to the homeland. Diaspora philanthropy also shows up in the literature as 'collective remittances' and 'communal philanthropy among migrant workers' (Babis et al., 2021, p. 373) and has also been called

DOI: 10.4324/9781003241003-10

'homeland philanthropy', 'migrant philanthropy', 'transnational giving', and 'diaspora for development' (Espinosa, 2016). There has been a lot of attention given to the relationship between migration and development, namely framing migrants as 'enablers of development' (Espinosa, 2016) and thus directing specific focus to remittances by diaspora groups (i.e. direct financial transfers usually to family and friends in the homeland), but much less attention has been paid to the forms and mechanisms of diaspora philanthropy (Desai & Kharas, 2018).

The chapter asks how diaspora-led GINGOs challenge the common perceptions of 'Northern-led' and 'Southern-led' development aid. Common perceptions include that Northern-led and Southern-led development aid are distinct phenomena. However, here, I present case studies that espouse 'starting from the South', that is, the shaping of roles and collaborations in development on terms that are defined by Southern actors based in the North. Most of the literature on diaspora philanthropy has centred on diasporas as potentially effective fundraisers for initiatives in their homelands (Desai & Kharas, 2018; Flanigan, 2017), which tends to reinforce the North–South dyad. However, GINGOs led by diaspora members open up possibilities to understand development collaborations differently. Through an interpretive approach, this chapter explores ways in which diasporas contribute to development collaborations through Northern-based GINGOs and Southern networks in their homelands. The chapter contributes to rethinking the North–South dyad in development by capitalizing on what diasporas bring to development collaborations.

The context of development aid for diasporas

The typical chain of development aid includes (institutional and private) donors in the North providing funding, often to international NGOs that then find Southern ('local') organizations as partners and implement development projects and programmes (Smith, 1998). This chain has most often been comprised of traditional aid donors, including multilateral channels through United Nations agencies and international and regional development banks; bilateral channels via governments in the Global North transferring aid to the South; and civilateral channels, which usually consist of funding channelled through Northern NGOs for projects in the Global South (Kinsbergen & Schulpen, 2013).

This chapter narrates important shifts in development aid that have opened spaces for new development collaborations – what Kinsbergen and Schulpen (2013) call 'philanteral aid'. The private actors of philanteral aid, the so-called 'fourth pillar' of development aid, are considered distinct from more traditional aid donors (Develtere, 2012), as the former are characterized by voluntary characteristics and philanthropic behaviours. Philanteral aid includes an expanding array of other private actors, including celebrities, philanthrocapitalists, athletes, tourists, and everyday consumers. It is in this context that I have selected GINGOs started by and/or led by diaspora members based in the United States as the centre of my enquiry.

Grassroots INGOs

In the mix of philanteral aid, GINGOs highlight voluntary and philanthropic attributes in development aid particularly strongly. GINGOs are a type of citizen aid (Fechter & Schwittay, 2019) or humanitarianism 'defined primarily by individuals' (Berman, 2016, p. 227). Scholars have suggested that these initiatives democratize aid and allow for innovations and relationships to occur at both international and local levels (e.g. Haaland & Wallevik, 2017; Kinsbergen, 2019). GINGOs represent the expressive functions of organized civil society (Appe & Oreg, 2020; Schnable, 2021), allowing founders, board members, and other supporters to express their 'motivations, characteristics, and personal commitment', which profoundly structure the organizations and the services they provide (Appe & Oreg, 2020, p. 504). While research on GINGOs is expanding, we still have a limited understanding of GINGOs that are led by diaspora members.

Diaspora in development

As has previously been observed, GINGOs are a venue for diaspora philanthropy, the transfer of private donations back to one's home country (Johnson, 2007; Newland et al., 2010). Immigrants and refugees living in the United States, for example, who engage in diaspora philanthropy, 'can convey information about their home countries to prospective individual funders. Immigrants may also directly mobilize resources by funding home-country recipients through private aid or microlending exchanges outside of remittance flows' (Desai & Kharas, 2018, p. 506).

Diaspora philanthropy comprises more than economic transfers of resources and is greater than a desire to contribute to development. Rather, as explained by Espinosa (2016), it is not '"just remittances" or "just philanthropy". It is imbued with so much hope to bring about development, share wealth and distribute social justice' (p. 363). Diasporas dream about helping their homelands. Given this, I explore diaspora members in development, beyond remittances and their potential as fundraisers only, through their role as leaders of GINGOs. I focus on the relational processes that position diasporas, 'starting from the South', as both Southern leaders and partners (based in the North) in development collaborations.

Research approach: comparative case studies

To answer my research question, I seek to understand how diaspora members are engaging in development collaborations through GINGOs. The chapter presents four case studies of diaspora-led, US-based GINGOs. The four cases were purposively chosen given the involvement of diaspora members in these GINGOs' day-to-day operations; these diaspora members perform the everyday duties of running the organization, such as record keeping and maintaining ties to partners and donors. While all these organizations have diaspora leadership, they vary in terms of where they serve and some of the services they provide (see Table 8.1).

TABLE 8.1 Selected GINGOs with diaspora leadership

Organization name	*Diaspora member*	*Role*	*Founding date*	*Country of origin and service provision*	*Mission*	*US location*
Banda Bola Sports Foundation	Kalekeni 'Coach' Banda	Founder	2009	Malawi	To use soccer to promote education and social change	Guilderland, NY
Building Minds in South Sudan	Sebastian Maroundit	Founder	2010	South Sudan	To provide educational and entrepreneurial opportunities for villagers in the Republic of South Sudan	Pittsford, NY
Victor Foundation	Alice Marcus	Founder	2017	Nigeria	To provide water, education, and homes to orphans, as well as providing other social services	Schenectady, NY
Advance and Embrace Community-USA (AEC-USA)[2]	Monica Bright	Board member	2005	Kenya	To support education, health care, and sanitation, AEC-USA hopes to promote social and economic justice around the world	Clarence, NY

In-depth case studies allow for a better understanding of how these Southern-led, Northern-based organizations are shaping new (or repackaged) development collaborations. The case study data are from ongoing fieldwork that began in 2016 on GINGOs that are based in New York State in the United States and that serve communities abroad.

To date, my research on GINGOs has included in-depth interviews with organizational founders, board members, and other supporters, as well as the analysis of social media and organizational archival documents (e.g. Appe & Oreg, 2020). I use ethnographic interviewing, which entails 'repeated, semi-structured and unstructured interviews with the same participant' (Rhodes, 2019, p. 10). I have had continued contact with many research participants during the research period since 2016, and this contact is ongoing. My analysis uses an interpretive approach, which centres on meaning making and analyses meaning 'through a focus on situated agents' (Rhodes, 2019, p. 22). Transcriptions of interviews, archival documents, and extensive fieldnotes were analysed to illuminate patterns and trends across the data. Memoing was conducted to further develop themes and produce major findings. The case studies are descriptively introduced below, followed by a presentation of the major findings of the research.

Grassroots INGOs: four case studies

The Banda Bola Sports Foundation is a non-profit organization that was informally founded in 2009 and incorporated in 2019. The organization was founded by **Kalekeni 'Coach' Banda** to serve rural Malawi. Coach Banda grew up in Chituka, a farming village in Malawi. As a child, he played sports in the village; when he moved to the United States with his family, he continued playing sports like soccer and running track. Coach Banda created the Chituka Village Project to serve the children of his home village. It uses soccer to promote education and social change in Malawi. The organization is based in Guilderland, NY, in the United States and is entirely volunteer based.

Building Minds in South Sudan (BMISS) is a non-profit organization that was founded by cousins **Sebastian Maroundit** and Mathon Noi in 2010. Sebastian and Mathon grew up in the rural village of Mayen-Abun in Twic State, South Sudan. At the age of ten, they were both separated from their families because of the civil war and forced to migrate to Ethiopia. They then left Ethiopia and walked across the desert to reach a refugee camp in Kenya. In 2001, they were selected to resettle in the United States, and they remained committed to improving opportunities for people in their village, eventually forming BMISS. BMISS builds schools to promote education for girls, improve gender equality, provide teacher training, and allocate microfinance grants to women. The all-volunteer organization is based in Pittsford, NY.

The Victor Foundation was started by Nigerian-born **Alice Marcus** in 2017. In Nigeria, Alice grew up in poverty, as part of a large family, including many siblings. She came to the United States because of an arranged marriage, and after enduring challenges with the marriage, she separated and re-settled in upstate New York with her three-year-old son. She created the Victor Foundation with the hope to 'uplift girls and give hope to the hopeless'. The organization supports women's empowerment projects and helps students by providing them with laptops, books, and menstrual pads. The Victor Foundation also has a child feeding program, through which it provides meals for children to ensure they have a nutritious and balanced diet. Based in Schenectady, NY, the Victor Foundation does not have staff, but many volunteers in Nigeria deliver food and support the organization's projects there.

Monica Bright was born in Kenya. In 2003, she married an American she met in Kenya and moved to the United States shortly thereafter. It was happenstance that she met Eleanor Smith, the founder of **Advance and Embrace Community-USA (AEC-USA)** in Buffalo, NY, at a physical therapy practice. AEC-USA funds projects across Kenya, including building bore wells, sponsoring students to attend school, funding micro-loans for women, providing sanitary pads, and funding agricultural projects. Since meeting Eleanor, Monica has served on AEC-USA's board, where she has played a prominent role. AEC-USA does not have any paid staff and is governed by a board of eight members, all of whom are volunteers.

As their descriptions suggest, these GINGOs are small in scale and rely on volunteers and donations from private individuals. Consistent with other GINGOs in the United States, diaspora-led GINGOs are rooted in personal experiences. I present findings through three main themes outlined below. First, the personalness of these organizations provides further context about their presence in development collaborations. As the second and third themes, I elaborate on these diasporas through the lenses of their roles as (Northern-based) *Southern leaders* and *Southern partners* in development collaborations.

Personal projects by diaspora members

These organizations, as well as their missions and projects, are informed by the diaspora members' lived experiences. Three of the organizations were started after a meaningful trip back to the homeland. For all four organizations, the actions of collecting and sending funds were soon coupled with regular in-person visits to the country of origin. This makes these initiatives even more personal for these Northern-based Southern leaders.

For example, after becoming a US resident, Alice visited her home village in Nigeria and soon began to send back her annual tax refund. This led to the founding of the Victor Foundation and the soliciting of volunteers and donations. Alice seeks to provide new opportunities to Nigerian women and girls. Reflecting on caring about the girls in her village, in particular, she noted that she had 'been there' [A. Marcus, 17 December 2020]. Alice remembers going to bed hungry as a child and described being sent to the city to live with and care for a family at the age of 16. While the Victor Foundation is the youngest and most fledging of the four organizations, Alice identifies it as 'a dream to be able to help' her Nigerian homeland.

Sebastian of BMISS is forthright that 'coming to the United States was not a personal decision' [S. Maroundit, 17 July 2017]. When he was asked as young man if he wanted to go to the United States after years living in refugee camps, he said yes, but only if he would be able to go to school. After resettling in the United States and attending school, in 2007, Sebastian became a US citizen; that same day, he applied for a passport to return to what was then Sudan. In Sudan, he met with his family who had assumed he had died years ago during the war. He took on some responsibility for his younger brother's education, promising to send him to boarding school in Kenya. Soon after, Sebastian spoke to other young boys in his village; he explained, 'They asked me very directly "What about us?" [...] They didn't ask for clothing or shoes. They asked for what? Access to school' [S. Maroundit, 17 July 2017]. It was then that Sebastian started to envisage BMISS.

As is the case for Alice's and Sebastian's GINGOs, the Banda Bola Sports Foundation is personal for Coach Banda. Its mission is soccer based, as Coach Banda's entire life has been focused on playing sports. In addition, he experienced hardship because of the political instability in Malawi during its dictatorship and also as it democratized in the 1990s. When he left Malawi as a young adult because of the political instability, ending up in the United States, he had 'about $40 in [his] pocket'. At that time, he remembers thinking, 'I'm now a refugee [...] My life was changed right in front of me' [K. Banda, 1 May 2020]. Indeed, his sadness about the political situation in Malawi shaped Coach Banda's life and drove his desire to someday be able to give back to his homeland.

Although Monica did not create AEC-USA, she is deeply connected to its mission. As observed above, it was coincidental that she met AEC's founder in Buffalo, NY. When asked to join the board, she jumped at the chance to help children in Kenya. It was personal. She referenced the Kenyan ideal of *harambee*, which partially drives her work with AEC:

> When [Kenya] had our independence, we had to say *harambee*; [it] means that we have to pull together if we want to be able to push out the British. That word *harambee* [...] expanded to communities. With communities, [if] they want to do something like, let's say, [...] if a child is stranded and that child is bright, they'll come together and they will say, 'Let us make *harambee*'. You and I and everybody else will come together; the community, they'll chip in with what they have. They'll collect some money and they'll send this child to school. That's how that word *harambee* came in. It's like, 'Let's come together, and together we can do something'.
>
> *[M. Bright, 6 December 2016]*

Diaspora members as Southern leaders

Going from sending money to family and friends in the homeland in an ad hoc way to funding larger community projects to then incorporating into a formal organization is an act of Southern leadership for all the diaspora members, positioning these individuals as leaders in forming and shaping new futures for their homeland. The projects that these organizations take on are what diasporas describe as 'bold thinking' in their homelands. Coach Banda's vision includes girls and women playing soccer in Malawi, Sebastian and his cousin are committed to girls' education in South Sudan, Alice hopes to help Nigerian girls and women to have financial independence, and Monica is committed to serving children in Kenya – girls and boys – who have been deeply affected and stigmatized by HIV and AIDS.

As an example of this 'bold thinking', Sebastian's vision for BMISS centres on girls' education, which took some convincing of the village elders. He himself observes that he would not have even considered this prior to living in the United States and being educated there. He admits that 'Sebastian of 2001 and Sebastian of today would fight a lot about girls and women's rights' [S. Maroundit, 17 July 2017]. Other board members of BMISS describe the Sebastian of today as 'very much a feminist' [BMISS board member, 17 July 2017]. Sebastian described his commitment to girls' education as intrepid in his village, noting that there was serious doubt that BMISS would come to fruition. Sebastian committed to building two classrooms and continuing his work thereafter – but only if girls were allowed to go to school. Sebastian stated,

> It took them a year to consider it completely, but the village chief said, 'I think we can do it'. It was not official yet, but when he said that, the mothers started dancing. It was so amazing, because all the woman in the village, including my mom, do not know how to read and write.
>
> *[S. Maroundit, 17 July 2017]*

Although Monica did not found AEC-USA, as a board member, she has taken on a leadership role and influences the organization. As an example, she linked AEC-USA to her cousin in Kenya who runs a local community-based organization. In 2014, Monica's cousin, Mary, founded Angels in Kenya to provide accommodation, nutrition, and education to orphans who are living with HIV and AIDS. On the basis of this introduction, AEC-USA opened a second branch in Kenya to more effectively serve the children of Angels in Kenya. In 2019, the organization was officially registered as a community-based organization in Kenya, with the full name of the Advance and Embrace Community-Angels in Kenya.

At times, there are caveats to the leadership roles assumed by diaspora members. In some instances, their leadership can be met with suspicion and hesitation. In the case of Banda Bola Sports Foundation, for example, Coach Banda explained that villagers assumed he had an agenda, such as running to be President of Malawi. These suspicions can sometimes hinder the progress of projects and stymie trust building. Similarly, Sebastian's family questioned his intentions with BMISS. He explained, with a smile,

> My mom says, 'Go back to United States and have a life. You are not a Catholic priest. You are not a government official, to be able to build a school. A school is built by an institution, not a person like you. If you keep telling people this, they will think you're a liar, because you will not do it'. I said, 'Mom, in America you do what you think you can do. I'll do it'. She did not believe me [...]
>
> *[S. Maroundit, 17 July 2017]*

In addition to pushing forward projects that at times made local actors in the villages hesitant, all the diaspora members acknowledged the intimacy created by the focus on their home villages. Many of them also discussed the pressures, needs, and challenges of expanding or scaling up their development collaborations. As Monica explained,

> There's so many poor people in Kenya – not only in one village [...] I just don't really believe in my village alone. If you have to help a community, you have to be national. You have to help whoever is really, really in need. That's my way of thinking [...] Okay you still help your community, but there could be other places which really, really need help.
>
> *[M. Bright, 24 March 2018]*

Likewise, Alice explained that she has started with 'her' village but that she also sees further need in other communities. Other communities hear about the work in her village and are interested in reaching out to her to come to their villages as well. Alice wants to assume this leadership role and expand services, as Nigeria's government does not reach many villages and there are clear service gaps, and even when larger INGOs are more present than the government, services are not consistent, Alice reported. Alice remembers being a child in the village and sometimes receiving immunizations from nurses from an INGO, but she noted that she does not know who they were, that they did not come back, and that this is the perception of INGOs among the villagers. Like the leadership of many GINGOs, she situates the Victor Foundation as different from these INGOs – as an alternative.

Sebastian's leadership is also sometimes challenged because of the village's experience with other INGOs, but he has remained committed to keeping to his promises to his village and leading its development. He explained,

> A senior elder in the community says, 'Too many Western NGOs came over, did a ceremony, promised, and they never delivered. What make you

> think you could be the one to do it?' and I explain, 'Yes, maybe, and those were Westerners; we are your sons'.
>
> *[S. Maroundit, 20 May 2019]*

In this case, Sebastian underlines the intimacy of being from the village, which allows him to assume the leadership role needed for BMISS.

Diaspora members as development partners

As (Northern-based) Southern leaders, diaspora members forge development collaborations. Diasporas facilitate partnerships in the South and in the North, and they bridge the South and the North. Whereas GINGOs have been observed to work in isolation (Appe & Schnable, 2019), based on the cases presented here, organizations with diaspora leaders challenge this. That is, because of their location and agency in both the South and the North, organizations with diaspora leaders are more likely than other GINGOs to build development collaborations across a diverse set of partners.

First, as they are 'starting in the South', diaspora members are able to form links with key figures in their homelands. These links are often based on personal, kin, and familial relations. This can mean a link between a Northern GINGO and community-based organizations on the ground in the homeland, as is the case in Monica's connecting AEC-USA to Angels in Kenya. These connections not only require 'knowing' the homeland, but they are also contingent on familial relations. Coach Banda often mentioned the role of his siblings on the ground in Malawi, who help Banda Bola Sports Foundation in multiple ways – from storing equipment to setting up meetings with the community. Likewise, Sebastian stressed the importance of his uncle, who is a village elder, and Alice relied on family members as key volunteers in Nigeria to distribute the goods and services provided by the Victor Foundation.

The interviewed diaspora members also leverage their connections to US-based partners. Both Banda Bola Sports Foundation and the Victor Foundation, which are located near each other in New York State, partner with The Mooncatcher Project. The Mooncatcher Project is a GINGO that was founded by New York native Ellie von Wellsheim with a mission 'to optimize girls' lives worldwide by removing barriers related to menstruation. The Mooncatcher Project works in over 15 countries around the world and supports eight different sewing guilds in Africa . Banda Bola Sports Foundation and the Victor Foundation have sent kits that include reusable pads, soap, and washcloths to Malawi and Nigeria, respectively, advancing their missions of serving girls as well as the mission of The Mooncatcher Project.

As Banda Bola Sports Foundation and the Victor Foundation are both based in the Capital Region of New York, they have participated in the informal African Support Alliance (ASA), which is 'a loose affiliation of projects and people supporting work in Africa' [ASA, 9 February 2020]. Both Alice and Coach Banda are plugged into this group, which is comprised of religious and secular organizations working in various parts of Africa. ASA's purpose is to network among organizations, share information, and, most importantly, learn from each other and from people outside the group. Before the 2020 global pandemic, they met somewhat regularly and shared challenges and promising practices. Such spaces for peer learning have been recognized in the literature as a potentially effective way to improve GINGOs' organizational performance and development outcomes (Appe & Schnable, 2019). This is a space for learning and building partnerships, and it is also where these organizations first came into contact with The Mooncatcher Project.

These Southern leaders and development partners have positioned themselves as local non-profit leaders in the United States. They speak at different events and give regular community presentations. In the case of Banda Bola Sports Foundation, audiences include local soccer leagues and clubs. Sebastian often speaks at schools, as BMISS engages students in small fundraising events. All the interviewed leaders are regularly invited to speak to churches and Rotary Clubs, as these spaces have helped with fundraising and getting the word out to their local US-based communities.

Reshaping Northern-led and Southern-led?

Diasporas might very well be effective fundraisers for their homelands, as migration and development studies have suggested. However, this literature tends to situate diasporas in development, with a limited focus on remittances (usually to family and friends). The cases presented in this chapter, rather, broaden this idea to theorize more about collective remittances, or diaspora philanthropy, via GINGOs. My findings expand thinking about the North–South dyad in development collaborations. The chapter contributes to our understanding about individuals from diasporas engaging in development by establishing, leading, and/or serving GINGOs based in the United States but serving their homelands.

First, how do diaspora members challenge the common perceptions of 'Northern-led' and 'Southern-led' development aid? In three of the cases described in this chapter, diaspora members created a Northern-based organization to support initiatives in their homeland; in the fourth case, a diaspora member contributed to the governance of a GINGO as a board member and brought new Southern-based initiatives from their homeland to the organization. These instances illuminate expanded modes of collaborations in development aid across the Global North and the Global South while also making fuzzier the binary of 'the North' and 'the South' in development collaborations.

Second, in many ways, these organizations show characteristics of the broader organizational field of GINGOs in the United States. These are personal projects that rely on development in the everyday by everyday people; the projects are volunteer-based, expressive work grounded in relationships (Appe, 2022).

However, my analysis further illuminates the fuzziness of 'Northern' and 'Southern' designations in diaspora-led GINGOs and underlines how GINGOs led by diaspora members as a form of philanteral aid can contribute to and open up new possibilities for development collaborations.

Third, although I cannot generalize to the entire subset of diaspora-led GINGOs, I can emphasize through the cases presented here that diaspora leaders leverage and elevate Southern agency in their homelands. For example, AEC-USA, which has the longest history of the selected cases, broadened its partner network in Kenya several years ago because of Monica's leadership on the board. Angels in Kenya, a Southern-led community-based organization, is now a trusted partner of AEC-USA. Without Monica, this partnership likely would not have come to fruition. Monica's knowledge of the context and her relationship with her cousin facilitated AEC-USA's expansion in Kenya.

The findings outlining the characteristics of diaspora leaders in development, particularly at the grassroots scale, suggest that diaspora philanthropy and diaspora-led GINGOs might also fit into the conversations about localization in humanitarian and development fields (Barakat & Milton, 2020; Global Fund, 2020; Roepstorff, 2020). Localization advocates suggest that donors need to invest in local knowledge and look to the grassroots for innovation – which these Southern leaders offer in development collaborations. In this respect, these diaspora-led GINGOs align with some of the tenets of localization. Motivated by caring relationships, such efforts often spring up when there are 'inadequate or non-existent public services in resource-poor settings' (Lentfer, 2017, p. 19), as Alice noted in her commitment to filling service gaps in Nigeria. Localization initiatives seek processes that aim to create funding mechanisms to 'support (not distort) local civil society' (Nolan, 2017, p. 31). Based on the case studies in this chapter, diaspora-led GINGOs may provide such a mechanism.

In addition, while outside the scope of this research, further study is warranted about GINGOs' relationships with governments, both in the United States and in the homeland. Diaspora-led GINGOs are not discussed in the literature on migration governance (e.g., Espinosa, 2016), and, partially because of the perceived isolation of GINGOs, not much work on these organizations and their relationships with governments has appeared in the development literature. Representation comes up in discussions about development organizations and governments, as 'representation often means performing the role of an intermediary between constituencies and the state' (van Wessel et al., 2019, p. 8). This dimension is not fully articulated by these Southern leaders. Rather, as demonstrated in the examined cases, they tend to focus on first-generation strategies of service provision, usually related to education, health, and sanitation services (Korten, 1987).

Diaspora members' role in development as fundraisers is well documented, including the transfer of resources – often to family and friends through remittances, and this cross-border flow of resources is important. However, this is not the only role in development for diasporas. With GINGOs, diaspora members assume (Northern-based) Southern leadership and can become effective partners in development collaborations. Given their knowledge of both contexts – the North and the South – diaspora members provide the know-how that might produce more effective and sustainable aid delivery. While we need further research about their actual development outcomes, these engaged diaspora members have deep links and commitment to networks and communities in their homelands and in the United States. These relationships shape how these development collaborations begin and likely influence their potential to be effective and sustainable.

Acknowledgements

The author would like to thank Rachel Morris for her research assistance for this project. In addition, the author expresses deep gratitude to the research participants, particularly for their time and for the passion they have for the work they do.

Notes

1 Almost 80% (n = 12,539) register as having a budget of US$250,000 or less. This is the budget threshold that tends to tip non-profit organizations in the United States from volunteer-based to operating with hired staff.

2 The names of this organization and the individuals associated with it are pseudonyms. The other organizations have given permission to use their identifiers, and/or I have previously published on them using their identifiers.

References

Appe, S. (2022). Grassroots international NGOs in Africa: Perspectives on what they are (and are not?). *Nonprofit and Voluntary Sector Quarterly, 51*(2), 125–147. https://doi.org/10.1177/0899764021991672.

Appe, S., & Chen, X. (2021). *Cross-border giving for development: Grassroots INGOs as a channel for diaspora philanthropy*. Working Paper. Available from the author.

Appe, S., & Oreg, A. (2020). Philanthropic entrepreneurs who give overseas: An exploratory study of international giving through grassroots organizations. *Nonprofit and Voluntary Sector Quarterly, 49*(3), 502–522. https://doi.org/10.1177/0899764019878785.

Appe, S., & Oreg, A. (2021). Is effective altruism driving American grassroots philanthropic giving overseas? *Third World Quarterly, 42*(12), 2841–2862. https://doi.org/10.1080/01436597.2021.1969910.

Appe, S., & Schnable, A. (2019). Don't re-invent the wheel: Possibilities and limits to building capacity of grassroots international NGOs. *Third World Quarterly, 40*(10), 1832–1849. https://doi.org/10.1080/01436597.2019.1636226.

Babis, D., Zychlinski, E., & Kagan, M. (2021). Comparing transnational and communal diaspora philanthropies among temporary migrant workers: The case of the Filipino Community in Israel. *Voluntas, 32*(2), 372–382. https://doi.org/10.1007/s11266-020-00304-8.

Barakat, S., & Milton, S. (2020). Localisation across the humanitarian-development-peace nexus. *Journal of Peacebuilding & Development, 15*(2), 147–163. https://doi.org/10.1177/1542316620922805.

Berman, N. (2016). Contemporary German MONGOs in Diani, Kenya: Two approaches to humanitarian aid. In G. R. Witkowski & A. Bauerkamper (Eds.), *German philanthropy in transatlantic perspective* (pp. 227–243). Berlin: Springer Nature.

Desai, R. M., & Kharas, H. (2018). What motivates private foreign aid? Evidence from internet-based microlending. *International Studies Quarterly, 62*(2), 505–519. https://doi.org/10.1093/isq/sqy023.

Develtere, P. (2012) *How do we help: The free market in development aid.* Leuven: Leuven University Press.

Espinosa, S. A. (2016). Diaspora philanthropy: The making of a new development aid? *Migration and Development, 5*(3), 361–377. https://doi.org/10.1080/21632324.2015.1053305.

Fechter, A.-M., & Schwittay, A. (2019). Citizen aid: Grassroots interventions in development and humanitarianism. *Third World Quarterly, 40*(10), 1769–1780. https://doi.org/10.1080/01436597.2019.1656062.

Flanigan, S. T. (2017). Crowdfunding and diaspora philanthropy: An integration of the literature and major concepts. *Voluntas, 28*(2), 492–509.

Global Fund for Community Foundations (GFCF). (2020). *An open letter to International NGOs who are looking to "localise" their operations.* Retrieved from: https://globalfundcommunityfoundations.org/news/an-open-letter-to-international-ngos-who-are-looking-to-localise-their-operations/.

Haaland, H., & Wallevik, H. (2017). Citizens as actors in the development field. *Forum for Development Studies, 44*(2), 203–222. https://doi.org/10.1080/08039410.2017.1305444.

Johnson, P. D. (2007). *Diaspora philanthropy: Influences, initiatives, and issues.* The Philanthropic Initiative, Inc. and The Global Equity Initiative, Harvard University. Retrieved from: https://www.cbd.int/financial/charity/usa-diasporaphilanthropy.pdf.

Kinsbergen, S. (2019). The legitimacy of Dutch do-it-yourself initiatives in Kwale County, Kenya. *Third World Quarterly, 40*(10), 1850–1868. https://doi.org/10.1080/01436597.2019.1644497.

Kinsbergen, S., & Schulpen, L. (2013). From tourist to development worker. Private development initiatives in the Netherlands. *Mondes en Développement, 0*(1), 49–62.

Korten, D. C. (1987). Third generation NGO strategies: A key to people-centred development. *World Development, 15*(supplement 1), 145–159. https://doi.org/10.1016/0305-750X(87)90153-7.

Lentfer, J. (2017). The real experts. In J. Lentfer & T. Cothran (Eds.), *Smart risks: How small grants are helping to solve some of the world's biggest problems* (pp. 37–40). Rugby: Practical Action Publishing.

Newland, K., Terrazas, A., & Munster, R. (2010). *Diaspora philanthropy: Private giving and public policy.* Washington: Migration Policy Institute.

Nolan, R. (2017). Peace begins at home. In J. Lentfer & T. Cothran (Eds.), *Smart risks: How small grants are helping to solve some of the world's biggest problems* (pp. 27–32). Rugby: Practical Action Publishing.

Rhodes, R. (2019). Public administration, the interpretive turn, and storytelling. In A. Massey (Ed.), *A research agenda for public administration* (pp. 12–27). Cheltenham: Elgar Research Agendas.

Roepstorff, K. (2020). A call for critical reflection on the localisation agenda in humanitarian action. *Third World Quarterly, 41*(2), 284–301. https://doi.org/10.1080/01436597.2019.1644160.

Schnable, A. (2021). *Amateurs without Borders*. Berkeley: University of California Press.

Sheffer, G. (Ed.). (1986). *Modern diasporas in international politics*. London: Croom Helm.

Smith, B. H. (1998). Nonprofit organizations in international development. In W. W. Powell & E. S. Clemens (Eds.), *Private action and the public good* (pp. 217–227). New Haven: Yale University Press.

van Wessel, M. G. J., Katyaini, S., Mishra, Y., Naz, F., Balasubramanian, R., Manchanda, R., & Sahoo, S. (2019). *Civil society dynamics: Shaping roles, navigating contexts*. Wageningen: Wageningen University & Research. Retrieved from: https://includeplatform.net/publications/civil-society-dynamics-shaping-roles-navigating-contexts/.

9

EXPLORING MUTUAL DEPENDENCE THROUGH NON-FINANCIAL RESOURCE EXCHANGES

A Tanzanian non-governmental organization network case study

Sandy Zook, Samantha Temple and Emmanuel Malisa

Introduction

International partnerships between Southern and Northern non-governmental organizations (NGOs) are characterized by fiscal and structural power imbalances (Edwards & Hulme, 1996; Elbers & Schulpen, 2013; Fowler, 1991). Historically, research on North–South NGO networks presents a dyadic relationship, with resource dependency theory depicting financially secure Northern partners wielding power over financially dependent Southern partners (AbouAssi, 2012; Elbers & Arts, 2011; Hudock, 1995). This paradigm discounts the complexity of North–South networks – namely, the range of network structures, such as those where financial resources are not the network's primary goal, and efforts to decentralize authority and leadership (van Wessel et al., 2019, 2020). In such networks, one can observe the mutual dependence (i.e. balance of power) arising from the exchange of non-financial resources (i.e. legitimacy, local knowledge,[1] and information; O'Brien & Evans, 2016). Narratives focusing solely on financial resources exchanged limit the ability of NGO partners to reimagine their collaboration structures and leave little room for learning and change.

This chapter addresses the question of how to collaborate differently, posed in the book's introduction. We answer this question in terms of research and practice by examining resource exchanges in a Tanzania-based North–South NGO network that is actively engaged in reimagining collaboration. Here, social exchange theory (SET), which uses a network approach to situate 'dependence' through resource exchanges as a proxy for 'power', is the theoretical framework. SET defines power not as one partner over another (i.e. donor versus recipient), but rather as a structural attribute of a relationship created and altered through (both financial and non-financial) resource exchanges (Barbalet, 2017; Cook et al., 1983; Molm, 2015). Dependency occurs on a continuum between

DOI: 10.4324/9781003241003-11

unbalanced power (one actor's complete dependence on another; i.e. donor–recipient) and power balance (resources mutually provided, received, and equally valued by the actors).

This inquiry uses a case study approach, investigating the resources exchanged within a Tanzania–United States (i.e. North–South) network. We draw on organizational documents, interviews with founders, and a survey to articulate the establishment, structure, and evolution of the network. These methods serve three critical functions: (1) measuring what resources are exchanged within the network, as well as the importance each partner places on these resources; (2) understanding whether resource exchanges result in mutual or skewed dependencies; and (3) understanding key attributes of the network (e.g. communication processes and perceptions of organizational agency).

Our results support growing calls for greater Southern NGO agency (see Banks et al., 2015; Bawole & Langnel, 2016; van Wessel et al., 2019, 2020). While our findings are specific to one North–South NGO network, we provide a replicable survey tool for use in other partnerships and networks. The study confirms that a variety of non-financial resources are exchanged and identifies strategies for Southern and Northern partners to reshape non-financial roles and relationships to advance Southern partners' leadership. We distinguish three primary themes in our findings. First, non-financial resources (sharing information and opportunities) are the primary resources exchanged in this network. Second, resource exchanges are reciprocal and multidirectional, resulting in mutual dependence among partners. Finally, the use of democratic principles within the network allows partners to have individual agency through open communication, which occurs formally and informally between partners.

The chapter begins by examining the establishment and evolution of the Tanzania–United States NGO network. Next, we outline SET as a framework for the survey tool, followed by a discussion of the survey findings. We then conclude with implications for research and practice.

Establishment and evolution of the Tanzanian NGO network

This research was conducted in Tanzania, East Africa, in collaboration with a North–South NGO network consisting of nine NGO partners, including eight 'local' (Southern) NGOs registered in Tanzania – staffed and managed by Tanzanian nationals. The founding partner of the network is a United States-based (Northern) NGO registered in the United States, funded by US donors, and managed by co-founders – a US national located in the United States and a Tanzanian national residing in Tanzania.

Tanzania is categorized as a non-industrialized economy in the Global South (OECD, 2021). The country is home to over 8,000 local and international NGOs and is considered a 'donor darling' for international aid (National Council of NGOs Tanzania, 2017). In 2018, Tanzania was among the top ten recipients of US donor aid (OECD, 2021). Many local Tanzanian NGOs have experience working with or receiving funding from Northern NGOs and therefore understand the dynamics of North–South fiscal partnerships.

In general, the NGOs in the studied network have relatively small budgets, with annual reported revenue of less than US$5,000 for the smallest NGOs and US$85,000 for the largest. Most of the organizations report annual revenue between US$25,000 and US$35,000. As the budgets indicate, these are localized organizations receiving small-scale international funding for local projects (as opposed to large multi-million-dollar grants and contracts). The Tanzanian NGOs are embedded in and provide services directly to specific communities, in contrast to NGOs operating at a broader national or international level.

Over the last three years (2018–2021), the NGO network has undergone a three-phase evolution from a grant-making structure to a collaborative network focusing on capacity building and information sharing. In 2018, the network was initiated by the Northern NGO, whose co-founders had work history and experience in Tanzania's Southern Highlands. Because of this history, the Northern NGO knew that the Southern NGOs in this region struggle with access to international resources and opportunities – particularly non-restrictive funding opportunities outside the traditional aid system.

In the first phase, the founders built the network in accordance with the perceived needs of Tanzanian NGOs to 'create a bridge for resources, from the US to Tanzania' (Northern NGO, personal communication, 2021). Thus, the primary focus was for the US NGO to provide grants and donations, as well as access to an online donation platform to expand the NGOs' reach to new donors. Initially, the network did not provide technical support, trainings, or programmes, instead resembling a series of dyadic fiscal relationships between the US NGO and each Tanzanian partner (as the NGOs were not connected through previous partnerships). After a year, however, it was clear that this model only served a handful of the NGOs – those with capacity and experience soliciting grants and donors. Through internal dialogue over the first year, the Tanzanian NGOs expressed shared interest in a different model, moving into phase two.

In the second phase (roughly 2019–2020), the network evolved from a dyadic fiscal partnership to a trainer–trainee model. The Tanzanian partners requested organizational capacity-building support from the US NGO, including strategic planning, local fundraising, and board-of-directors development. This support was provided through group workshops where all partners were invited to attend in person. It also included individual consulting, with the US NGO's Tanzanian director visiting each partner quarterly for a one-on-one site visit and consultation. Although this phase expanded the emphasis to include fiscal and information exchanges, it continued to centre on the US NGO as the trainer – the holder of the information – and the Southern NGOs as knowledge recipients. In this phase, however, the group workshops had an unanticipated outcome, resulting in networking and cohesion that brought forward opportunities to break away from the dyadic North–South relationship and build South–South relationships by sharing ideas for reimagining the network, leading to the third phase.

Phase three, the current phase of this North–South network (roughly 2020–present), is the transition from dyads to what the partners call a 'network' – some even refer to it as a 'family'. In this phase, partners are encouraged to collaborate, share best practices, advertise projects and funding opportunities, and work together to strengthen the local NGO sector in their communities. This includes formal (i.e. newsletters) and informal (i.e. WhatsApp group text) opportunities for information exchange. Aspects of the previous phases are still in place – mainly that the Northern NGO provides resources for group workshops. However, side projects have begun to materialize outside and without the involvement of the Northern NGO. For example, two partners recently signed a separate partnership agreement whereby one partner provides expertise and experience in water, sanitation, and hygiene (WASH) and the other provides access to and knowledge about a local youth population, with the goal of creating a 'WASH Innovation Academy.' Both partners are in the same community, but they had not previously collaborated. Projects like this show that the network has evolved beyond its original dyadic structure, with collaboration not only flowing North–South but also South–South.

Currently, the focus of the network is on improving power relations between partners, specifically 'to equalize voices, both in reality and in perception' (Northern NGO, personal communication, 2021). The aim is to devolve power from the Northern NGO by shifting leadership to a board operated by elected Southern NGO representatives and to expand the network to include more than the original eight Southern NGOs. For this leadership transition to be successful, the original convener acknowledged that perceptions of power differentials must be addressed and that 'all partners must be able to see the value that they bring to the network and not only think of the network as something they receive benefits from' (Northern NGO, personal communication, 2021).

The three phases described here have evolved quickly and represent a North–South NGO network 'doing differently', because each iteration is driven by the willingness of the partners to solicit communication and feedback, identify needs-based practices, and engage in strategic agility to act on the feedback received. The survey and other methods deployed in this study assist the network in achieving its third-phase goals – to highlight the value provided by each partner through the resources exchanged and the mutual dependencies that result from these exchanges. The following section explores the theoretical background and literature that guided the survey tool creation.

Social exchange theory: dependence as a proxy for power

SET's power-dependence principle defines power (i.e. dependence) within relationships not as one partner positioned over another (i.e. donor versus recipient), but as a structural attribute created and altered through the exchange of economic and social goods (i.e. financial and non-financial resources; Barbalet, 2017; Cook et al., 1983; Molm, 2015). The result is a map of dependencies, where equal dependence between two partners equates to balanced power and unequal dependence equates to an imbalance in power.

Three criteria are critical to SET: Resource value is (1) subjective and (2) temporal, and (3) there is no information asymmetry between exchange partners. For example, if partner A values funding and partner B has funding to provide, partner A might perceive their power in the relationship to be diminished, as they will need to depend on partner B for funding. This equation, however, is missing one important aspect – the resource provided in exchange for funding. Resource exchanges are rarely unidirectional. If partner B values access to a new community as much as partner A values funding, SET says both partners are mutually dependent, and one could characterize the partnership as balanced through mutual dependence.

Unlike the simple dyadic relationship in this example, however, calculations and estimations of dependence become more complex as actors and resources are added to an exchange network, making SET's network approach useful in this case study. Moreover, as the number of actors in a network increases, information asymmetry becomes a central barrier between partners. It affects an actor's valuation of their dependence within a network and ability to gauge the value other actors place on each resource. Thus, information sharing and information transparency among partners is a central strategy to combat information asymmetry in resource exchange. The survey used in this research aimed to uncover these value perceptions and to share the survey results with each NGO participant to reduce information asymmetry through improved accuracy of each partner's estimation of their power and dependence within the network.

Resource exchanges

Our examination of resource valuation within the NGO network consisted of financial and non-financial resources. To define both types of resources for the survey, we consulted the extant NGO literature and found support for three important non-financial resources in North–South NGO partnerships: legitimacy, local knowledge, and information exchange (AbouAssi, 2015; Elbers & Arts, 2011; Fowler, 1991; Mitchell, 2014). To define the role of financial resources, drawing on the context of this Tanzania network, we identified three relevant financial resources: grants, scholarships for trainings, and vehicles/equipment. Table 9.1 provides a summary of each resource and its nested concepts.

Legitimacy

Legitimacy is defined as public trust and support (AbouAssi, 2015). Here, 'public' refers to the community benefiting from a given NGO's mission. In North–South partnerships, it is rare that Northern NGOs engage directly with Southern communities, meaning Southern NGO partners are called on to provide legitimacy in these contexts (Fowler, 1991; O'Brien & Evans, 2016). In South–South

TABLE 9.1 Categories of resource exchanges

Non-financial
Legitimacy
Extending public trust and support to another NGO
Providing avenues for the popularization of another NGO's work
Local knowledge
Access to a new community
Knowledge about needs in a new community
Knowledge about solving needs in a new community
Information exchange
New opportunities
Technical information
Financial
Grants
Scholarships for trainings
Vehicles/equipment

NGO partnerships, each NGO has the potential to provide legitimacy in the communities they uniquely serve and can transfer that legitimacy to other NGOs through partnership.

In the context of the Tanzanian NGO network, partners exchange legitimacy by lending their public trust and support in a particular community to another organization or by raising the visibility of an organization new to their community, thus creating an avenue for the popularization of another organization's work. Thus, the survey uses two measures of legitimacy as an exchange: (1) lending public trust and support to another NGO and (2) popularizing the work of another NGO.

Local knowledge

Northern NGOs working in the Global South are often disconnected from Southern communities and their needs, relying on Southern NGOs to bridge this gap. It is rare for a Northern NGO to have a comprehensive understanding of the needs and the appropriate tools available to address them. Southern NGOs are better positioned to provide this information. Regarding local knowledge as a non-financial resource, Southern NGOs provide information about the needs, proper tools for intervention, and challenges and threats in the delivery of specific services (Fowler, 1991; Mitchell, 2014).

Local knowledge can also be transferred South–South when one Southern NGO, with experience in a local community, extends their knowledge and community access to another Southern NGO new to that community. Therefore, we identified three concepts nested under local knowledge: access to a new community, knowledge about the needs in a new community, and knowledge about meeting the needs in a new community.

Information exchange

Information exchange is the process of producing and sharing information among partners (Elbers & Arts, 2011; O'Brien & Evans, 2016). This can include the sharing of any type of information, such as development data or project opportunities (O'Brien & Evans, 2016). Information is exchanged formally through newsletters or policy memos and informally between partners through personal communication (e.g. SMS messages or WhatsApp).[2] Both types of information exchanges provide opportunities to exercise power and influence among partners.

As highlighted in Table 9.1, information exchange was divided into two categories – opportunities and technical support. Information on new opportunities included trainings, funding, and calls for new projects, whereas technical support included 'how-to' information, such as monitoring and evaluation practices, benchmarking, fundraising, and strategic planning.

Data collection

The survey measured (1) resources provided and received by each partner within the network, (2) each partner's importance and priority placed on the resources, and (3) structural attributes of the network. To measure the resources provided and received, respondents selected 'yes' or 'no' for each resource listed in Table 9.1, selecting all resources that applied to them. A follow-up question asked the respondents to indicate the most and least important resources provided and received. Finally, to triangulate priorities, each partner was also asked to prioritize resources using a five-point Likert scale, responding to the following question stem: 'If your organization is deciding on a new partnership with another NGO, how do you prioritize…' (meaning within a hypothetical future partnership). This technique allowed comparison between financial and non-financial resources. To measure the structure (i.e. rules, norms, and practices) of the network, survey items asked about overall network/partnership satisfaction, network strengths and challenges, communication processes, and perceived individual agency within the network. Pilot surveys ensured the accuracy and cultural appropriateness when translating the survey from English to Swahili and back to English.

Findings

To measure the exchange of resources within the network, survey respondents were asked to identify which resources their organization provided to and received from other network partners, and which resources were the most important and least important. Overall, the results demonstrate strong alignment between the priorities of each partner and the resources exchanged. Our analysis revealed that non-financial resources were both the most prioritized and most important resources exchanged. This aligns with the evolution of the network, as it has intentionally transitioned to increasingly emphasize non-financial resources.

When asked about the most important resource received within the network, as shown in Table 9.2, 78% of the partners selected non-financial resources – specifically, 56% selected information exchange (this category included 'new opportunities' and 'technical information'). Of the two partners selecting financial resources as the most important, both chose 'scholarships for trainings' (22%). Interestingly, although the category of 'new opportunities' was the most important resource received (Table 9.2), as well as the most exchanged resource (Table 9.3), no organization reported 'new opportunities' as the most important resource provided to the network. Rather, two-thirds of the organizations identified some form of local knowledge as the most important resource provided to the network. This demonstrates awareness among partners of their embeddedness in local Tanzanian communities, as well as their willingness to share and extend this embeddedness to other partners in the network.

Overall, Table 9.2 indicates an implicit agreement within the network, where partners exchange local knowledge for information (i.e. trainings, funding, and collaboration projects). Two-thirds identified local knowledge as the most important resource they provided to the network; in exchange, over half identified information exchange as the most important resource received.

Table 9.3 indicates the top four most exchanged resources, all of which are non-financial resources. The data on resources exchanged demonstrate the diversity of needs and exchanges occurring within the network. Local knowledge was the most provided (Table 9.3) and most important (Table 9.2) resource exchanged, whereas the category of 'new opportunities' was the most received resource (Table 9.3) and the most important resource received (Table 9.2).

The distributions of providing and receiving resources, however, demonstrate that a variety of resources are mutually exchanged, with few resources showing a skewed balance in terms of who gives and who receives. The exception is 'scholarships for trainings', which is further discussed in the 'Financial Resources' section below. Only one organization (the Northern NGO) provided scholarships, and all the other organizations reported receiving scholarships from the Northern NGO. After removing the receipt of scholarships, we found strong symmetry among the most provided and most received resources in the network.

Legitimacy

The nested concept of public trust and support in a new target community was the third most exchanged resource, with 56% receiving and 89% providing this resource. Additionally, while the category of avenues for the popularization of another organization's work was not one of the top-ranked resources exchanged, 78% provided this resource and 45% received it. Most partners rated these resources as a high priority when deciding on a new partnership.

TABLE 9.2 Most important resources provided and received

	Most important provided (%)	*Most important received (%)*
Non-financial resources		
Legitimacy		
Public trust and support	0	0
Avenues for the popularization of work	11	0
Local knowledge		
Knowledge about solving needs in a new community	**22**	**11**
Knowledge about needs in a new community	**22**	**11**
Access to a new community	**22**	**0**
Information exchange		
New opportunities	**0**	**56**
Technical information	11	0
Financial resources		
Scholarships for training	**11**	**22**
Vehicles/equipment	0	0
Grants	0	0
Total	**100**	**100**

Note: The most important resources are shown in bold text.

TABLE 9.3 Distribution of resource exchanges

	Provide (%)	*Receive (%)*
Non-financial resources		
Legitimacy		
Public trust and support	**89**	**56**
Avenues for popularization of work	78	45
Local knowledge		
Knowledge about solving needs in a new community	**89**	**67**
Knowledge about needs in a new community	**78**	**56**
Access to a new community	67	45
Information exchange		
New opportunities	**78**	**100**
Technical Information	33	44
Financial resources		
Scholarships for training	11	89
Vehicles/equipment	33	11
Grants	11	11

Note: The most exchanged resources are shown in bold text.

Local knowledge

The 'local knowledge' category included three nested concepts (see Table 9.2). Combining these three concepts, local knowledge was the most important resource across all questions: It was the most prioritized resource when deciding on a new partnership, the most important resource provided in this network, and the most exchanged resource. Most partners reported providing and receiving all three types of local knowledge resources. Indeed, local knowledge was the most reciprocally exchanged resource.

Interestingly, although the extant literature describes local knowledge as a resource provided to Northern or non-indigenous NGOs in exchange for other resources, we found multidirectional relationships in South–South local-knowledge exchanges and dependencies. This is illustrated in the abovementioned description of the history of the Tanzanian network, where two Southern partners in the same region of Tanzania recently entered a formal partnership agreement for a WASH programme. In this example, one partner brings technical expertise, and the other brings access to a specific youth population.

Information exchange

The 'information exchange' category included two nested concepts: (1) information on new opportunities (i.e. information on trainings, funding opportunities, and collaboration opportunities) and (2) technical information. Information on new opportunities was the most exchanged resource in this network. All partners (100%) received some form of information on new opportunities, and 75% reported providing this kind of information. Additionally, information on new opportunities was the most prioritized resource when deciding on a new partnership.

In addition to the Likert-type scale questions, the survey included open-ended items about the mechanisms for information exchange in the network. These open-ended questions uncovered two avenues for information exchange within this partnership: (1) formally through partnership meetings, workshops, and newsletters organized by the Northern NGO and (2) informally through one-on-one and group communication and platforms, such as WhatsApp groups and SMS messaging. Moreover, the formal partnership exchanges appear to facilitate informal exchanges, as one partner highlighted: 'Knowledge and information is shared among partners through workshops and communication between individual organizations [as] a result of networking'.

Information exchange is also an important priority for the continued development of the partnership, as evidenced by this quote from the Northern NGO's US director: 'We are beginning to implement a new process... The goal is to make the information sharing a more 360 experience. Each partner organization just designated a new partnership liaison to help increase information sharing and response time'.

Financial resources

Of all the resources, financial resources were the most centralized and unidirectional. As mentioned above, all the Southern NGOs reported receiving scholarships for trainings (89%), but only the Northern NGO provided these scholarships (11%). Additionally, only the Northern NGO provided small grants, and one partner was the recipient of that grant. As for the third type of financial resource, vehicles, and equipment, three partners provided (33%), and one received (11%) this resource. An example of this exchange occurs when one partner provides an office location for training and the other partner benefits from free or reduced-cost use of that space.

Despite the initial goals in the first phase of the partnership structure, only two partners (22%) ranked financial resources as the most important resource received from the network. There were additional comments suggesting an interest in cultivating more financial resources within the partnership. Thus, the demand for financial resources was not entirely decentred or removed. When asked how the network could be improved, two participants responded as follows:

> [The US NGO] should support partners to meet their running costs in order to avoid collapsing/weakening of organizations. Weakening of an organization may weaken its partnership with other organizations.
>
> Identifying a new partner who will join the partnership as a donor, providing funds for [all] partners to implement projects.

Mutual dependence through resource exchanges

The findings demonstrate that all partners provided and received a variety of financial and non-financial resources, indicating a degree of mutual dependence built into this network. This is apparent among the categories of non-financial resources, with approximately three-fourths of the partners claiming to provide legitimacy, local knowledge, and information exchange. On the receiving end, most partners also received these resources. Notably, all partners (100%) received information on new opportunities, and approximately three-fourths (78%) provided that information within the network.

We found evidence of skewed dependence on the Northern NGO in the financial resources exchanged. This was not unexpected; however, resources also flowed South to North. The Northern NGO depended on Southern NGOs for intermittent in-kind donations, including borrowing a vehicle, equipment, and office space.

Structural attributes of the network: strengths and opportunities

When asked about their level of satisfaction with the network, all the partners reported being 'moderately satisfied' or 'very satisfied' with the partnership, with answers split 50/50 across these two responses. None of the partners reported that they were not satisfied. The respondents identified several strengths of the partnership, including the network's collaborative nature (50%) and the use of workshops to share skills and provide networking opportunities (38%). Three respondents expanded on the importance of collaboration, workshops, and networking:

> Workshops bring us together whereby we know each other better. Workshops should continue, especially on writing project proposals.
>
> Meetings/workshops/training/seminars bring partners together and strengthens togetherness which is important in collaboration.
>
> Knowledge and information shared among partners through workshops and communication between individual organizations is a result of networking.

All the partners agreed that they have agency within the network to communicate feedback, propose new ideas (i.e. for trainings or projects), and implement new projects and trainings. Only one partner reported not feeling they had agency in terms of influencing the network's future agenda. This indicates some success of the network's efforts to establish a democratic governance model, encouraging an open culture for communication such that partners feel free to not only report opportunities and ideas but also implement them within the network. Remembering that the Northern NGO initiated the network and held a more centralized position in the first two phases of the partnership structure's evolution, this finding highlights the fruitful work put into opening communication channels and creating a more collaborative culture of sharing.

Two opportunities for improvement include developing more participatory leadership among all partners and improving the recruitment of new partners. Despite the evolution in the structure, fewer than half of the partners (38%) felt they could invite new members to the network, and half (50%) expressed a desire for more participatory leadership among all partners. The desire for more participatory leadership included efforts to formalize the network's structure, leadership, expectations, and processes. We expand on these next-step efforts in the final section of this chapter.

Conclusion

To date, research and practice do not give equal attention to the exchange of non-financial resources (in comparison to financial resources) within North–South partnerships and networks. We recognize that financial resources are paramount to organizational sustainability and that this NGO network may be somewhat unique in its focus on non-financial resources. Nevertheless, the lessons and strategies from our analysis have the potential to be useful to a broad array of North–South NGO partnerships and networks. First, this is because other examples of non-financial partnerships and networks exist in practice (e.g. communities of practice and learning, NGO membership organizations, and non-financial incubators for new social-purpose organizations and entrepreneurs), where practitioners come together to learn, share ideas, and exchange information. Moreover, even North–South partnerships that focus exclusively on financial resource exchanges could utilize this survey instrument as a low-cost strategy to introduce dialogue around the types of non-financial resource exchanges implicitly occurring within the partnership.

Opening dialogue around non-financial resource exchanges can aid North–South NGO networks. As demonstrated in the analysis, opening channels of communication can foster a culture where partners have increased agency to make decisions and engage in agenda setting. In our case, the act of administering the survey provided a mechanism for information exchange and should be viewed as a strategic tool other North–South NGO networks can use to reduce information asymmetry around resource exchanges. The survey can draw attention to specific resources exchanged, identify partnership opportunities, and aid organizations in identifying individual and collective strengths and challenges for strategic development. Thus, providing the results of this survey to the partners continues the feedback loop. Viewing the survey as an information exchange opportunity allows networks to engage in discussions of the survey findings, the future of resource exchanges within the network, and strategic next steps.

Our analysis demonstrates that this NGO network has developed an impressive recognition of mutual dependence. Our findings indicate that, although there are opportunities for growth and improvement, the network has done well to build a foundation of resource sharing. Moreover, despite the highly centralized mechanisms used in the founding of the network, the partners have adapted quickly by facilitating open communication and supporting partner agency.

The findings on resource exchange, specifically information exchange, support the use of SET as a viable theoretical frame for examining resource exchanges in North–South NGO networks. This NGO network breaks away from the stereotype of North–South dyadic relationships characterized by the flow of financial resources from Northern to Southern actors. Instead, this chapter highlights a multidirectional flow of many financial and non-financial resources exchanged between Northern and Southern partners. The success of this network is attributed, in part, to the framework of the network emphasizing a variety of non-financial resource flows between Southern partners.

Our survey identified information exchange as the most important resource exchanged, in the eyes of the network partner organizations. The survey responses highlighted how the partners used formal networking (i.e. workshops, trainings, and seminars) to facilitate informal and organic opportunities (i.e. WhatsApp groups and one-on-one exchanges). This informal communication builds trust, which then bolsters open communication in the formal mechanisms, creating a feedback loop effect. This process, however, is not without challenges, such as the cultivation and distribution of financial resources continuing to be points of discussion and the building of opportunities for participatory leadership and new partner recruitment.

Next, we found evidence of trust among partners and in the resources exchanged. First, most partners were willing to provide their individually held local knowledge (i.e. knowledge about new communities, solving problems in new communities, and access to new communities) in exchange for information (i.e. new opportunities and technical information). This indicates high levels of trust within the network because partners are willing to exchange their knowledge to receive collective information and further their strategic goals and organizational sustainability. Second, we found strong alignment between the most important resources exchanged in the network and the priorities for evaluating a 'hypothetical' future partnership, indicating strong symmetry between the importance of resources exchanged and the priority each partner places on those resources.

There are several clear limitations affecting the findings and generalizability of this study. Specifically, this is a case study of one small NGO network, with a single Northern NGO partner. Moreover, the network is young, having been in existence for only three years, and in a continual process of evolving its goals and governance structure. We do not measure outcomes of success, nor can we deduce the likelihood of the sustainability of the network. Extending this research by including a comparative case study of other types of NGO networks (e.g. more NGOs in the network, more years of existence, different ratios of Northern to Southern NGOs, or larger national NGOs) or NGO networks that vary in terms of the number and types of resources exchanged, as well as in the structure of the network (i.e. rules, norms, and practices) may lead to different insights and could increase the validity of our findings. However, our case study does provide an opportunity to observe a network as it evolves, builds trust, and grapples with opening communication and resource exchange to build a communal vision of the future of the network.

In summary, our findings depict a North–South NGO network that is truly reimagining collaboration. In this network, partners place importance on the exchange of non-financial resources – even in the prioritization of resources when considering new partnerships. The variety and degree of exchanges result in many layers of multidirectional dependencies (i.e. North–South, South–North, and South–South). This case study network departs from the traditional North–South narrative, instead revealing a nuanced image of collaboration.

Acknowledgements

The authors of the chapter are grateful to the NGOs that participated in this research. Without their valuable time and insight, this research would not have been possible.

Notes

1 In this context, 'local' means the community or geographical area of an NGO's work.
2 SMS stands for Short Message Service. It is a commonly used means of communication in Tanzania. WhatsApp is a messaging application for cell phones that allows users to send text and voice messages, make and receive voice and video calls, and share images, documents, and other content.

References

AbouAssi, K. (2012). Hands in the pockets of mercurial donors: NGO response to shifting funding priorities. *Nonprofit and Voluntary Sector Quarterly*, *42*(3), 584–602. https://doi.org/10.1177/0899764012439629.

AbouAssi, K. (2015). Testing resource dependence as a motivator for NGO self-regulation: Suggestive evidence from the Global South. *Nonprofit and Voluntary Sector Quarterly*, *44*(6), 1255–1273. https://doi.org/10.1177/0899764014556774.

Banks, N., Hulme, D., & Edwards, M. (2015). NGOs, states, and donors revisited: Still too close for comfort? *World Development*, *66*, 707–718. https://doi.org/10.1016/j.worlddev.2014.09.028.

Barbalet, J. (2017). Social exchange theory. In B. Turner, K. Chang, C. Epstein, P. Kivisto, J. Ryan, & W. Outhwaite (Eds.), *The Wiley Blackwell encyclopedia of social theory* (pp. 1–11). Malden, MA: Wiley-Blackwell.

Bawole, J. M., & Langnel, Z. (2016). Downward accountability of NGOs in community project planning in Ghana. *Development in Practice*, *26*(7), 920–932. https://doi.org/10.1080/09614524.2016.1210094.

Cook, K. S., Emerson, R. M., Gillmore, M. R., & Yamagishi, T. (1983). The distribution of power in exchange networks: Theory and experimental results. *American Journal of Sociology*, *89*(2), 275–305. https://doi.org/10.1086/227866.

Edwards, M., & Hulme, D. (1996). Too close for comfort? The impact of official aid on nongovernmental organizations. *World development*, 24(6), 961–973. https://doi.org/10.1016/0305-750X(96)00019-8.

Elbers, W., & Arts, B. (2011). Keeping body and soul together: Southern NGOs' strategic responses to donor constraints. *International Review of Administrative Sciences*, 77(44), 713–732. https://doi.org/10.1177/0020852311419388.

Elbers, W., & Schulpen, L. (2013). Corridors of power: The institutional design of North-South NGO partnerships. *VOLUNTAS: International Journal of Voluntary and Nonprofit Organizations*, *24*(1), 48–67. https://doi.org/10.1007/s11266-012-9332-7.

Fowler, A. (1991). Building partnerships between Northern and Southern developmental NGOs: Issues for the 1990s. *Development in Practice*, *1*(1), 5–18. Retrieved from https://www.jstor.org/stable/4029179.

Hudock, A. C. (1995). Sustaining Southern NGOs in resource-dependent environments. *Journal of International Development*, 7(4), 653–667. https://doi.org/10.1002/jid.3380070407.

Mitchell, G. E. (2014). Strategic responses to resource dependence among transnational NGOs registered in the United States. *VOLUNTAS: International Journal of Voluntary and Nonprofit Organizations*, *25*, 67–91. https://doi.org/10.1007/s11266-012-9329-2.

Molm, L. D. (2015). Power-dependence theory. *The Blackwell Encyclopedia of Sociology*. https://doi.org/10.1002/9781405165518.

National Council of NGOs Tanzania. (2017). *Tanzanian government verifies over 2,000 NGOs*. Retrieved from: https://www.nacongo.or.tz/resources/view/tanzanian-govt-verifies-over-2000-ngos

O'Brien, N. F., & Evans, S. K. (2016). Civil society partnerships: Power imbalance and mutual dependence in NGO partnerships. *VOLUNTAS: International Journal of Voluntary and Nonprofit Organizations*, *28*, 1399–1421. https://doi.org/10.1007/s11266-016-9721-4.

Organization for Economic Co-operation and Development (OECD). (2021). *Aid at a glance*. Retrieved from: https://public.tableau.com/views/AidAtAGlance/DACmembers?:embed=y&:display_count=no?&:showVizHome=no#1.

van Wessel, M., Katyaini, S., Mishra, Y., Naz, F., Rajeshwari, B., Manchanda, R., ... Sahoo, S. (2019). Civil society dynamics: Shaping roles, navigating contexts. *Wageningen University & Research, Indian Institute of Technology Delhi and Lehigh University, Wageningen, the Netherlands*. Retrieved from: https://edepot.wur.nl/511476.

van Wessel, M., Naz, F., & Sahoo, S. (2020). Complementarities in CSO collaborations: How working with diversity produces advantages. *VOLUNTAS: International Journal of Voluntary and Nonprofit Organizations*, *32*(4), 717–730. https://doi.org/10.1007/s11266-020-00227-4.

PART 3

Asking Southern-centred questions

10

ADVOCATING FOR LAND RIGHTS IN KENYA

A community-based organization's attempt to reconcile external funding with local legitimacy

Selma Zijlstra and Marja Spierenburg

Introduction

In response to the critique that Northern non-governmental organizations (NGOs) have weak roots among the local civil society, a growing number of scholars have called for aligning development support with already-existing social movements (Banks et al., 2015). Thus, programme development by Northern NGOs should be 'turned upside down' by starting programmes from organizations that are already active on the ground, enhancing Southern leadership (van Wessel et al., 2019). However, it has also been well documented that donor support professionalizes movements, potentially causing them to lose their grassroots ties (Jalali, 2013). This presents a challenge to local organizations, which are expected not only to be locally embedded but also to become incorporated into the global aid system. How can these seemingly contradictory processes be reconciled?

Remarkably, much of the existing literature paints a rather bleak picture of 'NGOization', yet rarely takes the story beyond the observation that donor support undermines civil society organization (CSO) legitimacy. With some exceptions, which we highlight below, scant effort has been invested in documenting how CSOs try to maintain or regain legitimacy vis-à-vis their constituents.

In this chapter, we address the following research question: What has been the effect of professionalization on CSOs' legitimacy, and how do CSOs address legitimacy challenges? Through the lens of the social construction of legitimacy (Lister, 2003), we show that legitimacy is not a 'fixed' characteristic of an organization; rather, it is a relational process. Here, our account therefore documents interactions among CSO staff members, their international NGO (INGO) partners, and community members. However, we also argue that a CSO's legitimacy is not dependent only on the triad of INGO–CSO–constituent relations; it is also

DOI: 10.4324/9781003241003-13

contingent upon other social interactions. This is especially true in the case of land conflicts, where government and private-sector strategies may divide communities and affect CSOs' capacity to mobilize (Kirsch, 2014).

This chapter is based on nine months of fieldwork in Kenya conducted in 2018 and 2019, during which we studied several cases of land investments where CSOs engaged in land rights advocacy, with two weeks of follow-up data collection in November 2021. This contribution centres primarily on the perspective of a local community-based organization (CBO), Malindi Rights Forum (MRF), which was engaged in a struggle against salt mining on the coast of Kenya.[1] In the following section, we discuss the literature on professionalization and legitimacy. We then present our case study, followed by a conclusion and brief recommendations.

Literature overview

'NGOization' refers to a process through which the formal requirements of funding agents impact the strategies of civil society actors (Jalali, 2013), promoting processes centred on rational and results-driven 'project-logics' (Alvarez, 2009). Scholars have described how this can shift movements' priorities to focus on institutional survival and accountability towards donors instead of mobilizing their constituents (Igoe, 2003; Jalali, 2013). Movements depoliticize as they change focus from political work to service delivery in response to donor demands (McKie, 2019) or shift to more moderate goals and tactics (Corrigall-Brown, 2016). Incorporation into the aid system also leads to professionalism, which refers to aspects such as salaried employment, staff with adequate education and/or expertise, and 'organizational rationalization', including strategic planning, audits, and reporting (Hwang & Powell, 2009). The resulting emphasis on skills and expertise can lead to the devaluation and marginalization of uneducated volunteers (Choudry & Kapoor, 2013).

Scholars have, however, also paid attention to NGOs' agency. NGOs creatively manage to remain political (Jaoul, 2018; Mosse & Nagappan, 2021; Robins, 2008) and maintain their grassroots ties as long as they have strong internal and downward accountability (AbouAssi & Trent, 2016). Some organizations have consciously attempted to 'de-NGOize' by emphasizing spontaneity versus project planning, being selective in accepting donor funding, and promoting equal treatment of staff and volunteers (Shrestha & Adhikari, 2011).

We aim to complement this strand of literature by bringing in the concept of legitimacy, as we hypothesize that NGOization and professionalization impact grassroots legitimacy. According to one of the most cited definitions of organizational legitimacy, the term refers to, 'a generalized perception or assumption that the actions of an entity are desirable, proper or appropriate within some socially constructed system of norms, values, beliefs and definitions' (Suchman, 1995, p. 574). Lister (2003) and Ossewaarde et al. (2008) distinguished pragmatic (enhancing a self-interest goal of constituents), normative (collective goals and mission statements of organizations), cognitive (the acceptance of an NGO as 'one of us'), and regulatory (the conformity with rules, laws, and regulations) legitimacy. Matelski et al. (2021) added political legitimacy, which includes trust in leadership; representation (whether they have the mandate to act as a spokesperson for the community); and representativeness (whether they *resemble* the community). Without the local constituents participating, being consulted, engaging in decision making, and sharing information, representational legitimacy is reduced (Bawole & Langnel, 2016).

In line with the ideas of several scholars, we view legitimacy as a relational construct rather than as a 'fixed' characteristic of a CSO. Lister (2003) described legitimacy as a dynamic process – a product of continuous interaction with various stakeholders, such as local communities. Similarly, international and local actors and underlying power dynamics may affect an organization's legitimacy (Walton et al., 2016). These relational and power dynamics are especially relevant in the context of (large-scale) land acquisition, where business and government investments are at stake, as is seen in Kenya.

Case study

In Kenya, land ownership and governance are hotly contested. When Kenya became independent, the government inherited a land administration system that was highly controlled by the centre, leading to a predatory state using land allocation for political rewards and speculation (Boone et al., 2019). On the country's coast, the indigenous Mijikenda peoples became 'squatters', while land titling schemes benefited mainly those within patronage networks (Kanyinga, 1998). In 2010, Kenya adopted a fairly progressive constitution and subsequent land laws, pushed by a reform movement led by CSOs. However, implementation remains a challenge (Klopp & Lumumba, 2017), and CSO are hindered in their advocacy role as the government attempts to shrink civic space (Wood, 2016). Kenya's civil society has seen vast growth since the 1980s, mostly relying on donor funding (Brass, 2012). As drivers of reform movements, CSOs have also been accused of being elitist (Mati, 2013). However, the legitimacy of rural-based advocacy CBOs that have been incorporated into the aid chain has not yet been adequately captured in the Kenyan context. We now turn to one example of this type of organization.

Along the coastal Lamu-road, ponds stretch over an area of approximately 50 kilometres. When the sun shines long enough, workers with little protective gear face the heat to harvest salt from the ponds. This is to be refined as consumer salt for the Kenyan and regional market. In the small town centre of Marereni, a sandy road leads to the MRF office. The office consists of a room with a big table where you can usually find the MRF staff engaged in conversations with community members, as well as a smaller room that holds archival documents and a desktop computer where staff members take turns writing their reports, hoping that power cuts will not interrupt their work. When they visit the villages by *bodaboda*,[2] most rides are interrupted because they meet other MRF members along the way.

This humble office is the epicentre of the decades-long struggle against the salt companies. MRF originated in local farmer groups resisting eviction by salt mining companies, which started acquiring land in the 1980s. Upon the farmer groups' invitation, the Kenya National Human Rights Commission issued a devastating report about forced evictions and environmental impacts (Kenya National Human Rights Commission, 2006), which drew the attention of national NGOs. The farmer groups were advised to form an umbrella organization, which became MRF in 2006. MRF currently has 3,000 members, who are also members of the local farmer groups. It has two major funding sources: the US-led American Jewish World Service (AJWS), which has a branch in Nairobi, and the INGO ActionAid, with a national head office in Nairobi and branches worldwide. The AJWS has sponsored MRF on a long-term basis since 2009, providing, among other support, funding for salaries and for court cases, in partnership with the Kenyan NGO Kituo cha Sheria, which is based in Mombasa. ActionAid supports advocacy mobilization efforts and dialogue forums. Since 2015, ActionAid's support has also taken on a long-term character, assuring funding for five consecutive years (part of the Dialogue and Dissent policy framework of the Dutch Ministry of Foreign Affairs).[3]

We first assess the impact of donor funding on MRF's practices, as well as MRF's attempts to exert agency by staying in touch with their roots. We then bring in the voice of the communities to analyse their perspectives on the CSO and scrutinize how professionalization is interlinked with processes of legitimacy vis-à-vis communities.

Funding impacts on MRF's practices

Donor funding impacted several of MRF's practices; some of these consequences manifested directly, whereas others crept in indirectly. We highlight a few of these consequences in the realms of staff and leadership, activities and strategies, thematic focus areas, and networks. Equally important, however, is how MRF retained its autonomy – mainly through considering adherence to its main mission and careful donor selection.

MRF ensured that they upheld their constitution, which was adopted at MRF's founding. This constitution established MRF's main mission as advocating for land rights. Because MRF adhered to this constitution, it chose its donors selectively (at least in the years up to 2021, to which we will come back later). MRF was aware that donors came with their own priorities, and the organization refused to cooperate with donors that would use MRF for their own gain. This was a luxury MRF could afford, given the long-term funding they received.

The relations between MRF and its INGO partners were both cordial and instrumental; in the words of the MRF coordinator, 'we are one big family'. In many respects, ActionAid and MRF were a good match. ActionAid drew its legitimacy from working with the grassroots, and ActionAid distinguished itself from other INGOs by emphasizing dissent.[4] ActionAid engaged in creative juggling to match its own priorities to the capricious trends in the donor world. For example, it narrated its land rights programme in such a way that fit Dutch donor priorities on livelihoods and trade, stressing that, without access to land, neither trade nor livelihoods would materialize.

MRF's priority to fight for the land rights of people impacted by the salt companies thus did not change, but certain themes were added, most notably a strong emphasis on women's rights instilled by ActionAid, which struck a chord in communities where gender-based violence cases were rampant. MRF's workload thus grew as the office became an advice centre on gender-based violence, marriage cases, and child rights, and the MRF staff were also expected to join nationwide campaigns on women's land rights.[5] Further, MRF was expected to roll out activities in the broader ActionAid network.

Although the INGO partners did not depoliticize MRF's mission, their involvement did *deradicalize* its strategies. In the past, MRF staff members, working alongside farmers, used disruptive tactics. Confronted with police retaliation and following advice from their partners, MRF replaced these tactics with moderate strategies, such as mobilizing the media, writing petitions and letters, and filing court cases. The MRF coordinator described this change as follows:

> Until [the] NGOs came to us, we were like savages. We burned the pumps. We hit casual laborers. Our approach was – You hit us; we hit you. Through [the] NGOs, we engaged in the proposal writing zone; that's when our strategy started changing.

Abandoning these former tactics was also a deliberate strategy to avoid arrests and protect the organization against a government with authoritarian tendencies and a penchant for delegitimizing CSOs as inciters. In a context of shrinking civic space, CSOs also had to be careful not to jeopardize their registration, which was necessary to get donor funding, as well as to be able to have uninterrupted meetings.

Incorporation into the aid system brought professionalization in leadership and management. After MRF was funded, the staff received (modest) salaries. Several staff members were employed based on their long-term engagement in the struggle, whereas others – including MRF's accountant – were selected based on their experience and education level. The staff members were required to come from the area, although this was broadly interpreted and did not refer to the *directly* impacted communities. Nonetheless, the modest appearance of the MRF staff and office gave off an air of accessibility, and the office door always stood – both literally and figuratively – open. To lead the organization and educate community members on their rights, staff members needed to be conversant with the laws and advocacy strategies, and they thus attended multiple training sessions. Though the earlier volunteerism was replaced with professionalization, MRF ensured that they maintained their links with the farmer groups through their organizational structure and procedures, with a board consisting of the chairs of the farmer groups and a supervisory committee chaired by one of MRF's founders. Professionalization, thus, was combined with rootedness.

However, the reporting requirements necessary to receive the next round of funds meant that, often, staff members struggled to meet report deadlines (that were often not communicated well in advance). Stress was particularly high when power cuts hit the office. This form of 'regulatory legitimacy', which is valued by INGO partners but driven by donors' accountancy departments, unavoidably took away from time that could have been dedicated to the community. Activities were scheduled on a project basis, as funds could not be disbursed without a clear plan. This hampered spontaneity in doing activities. Although the MRF coordinator indicated they negotiated with their partners regularly, which resulted in a fair amount of flexibility for new plans, these had to fit within the overall programme.

Furthermore, ActionAid was bound by managerial rules dictating that new funding could only be disbursed after activities had been completed. For MRF, this meant that new funds were not always disbursed on time, sometimes causing activities to be postponed. Therefore, MRF's activities had to follow the account balance rather than the dynamics on the ground. It also proved difficult to fund lawyers or research. This led to a significant delay in one of MRF's main strategies, a public interest litigation case that required a study on the health effects of the salt companies' operations.

MRF managed to find some creative ways to overcome budget limitations. Through the local CBO network, they pooled their resources. For example, if MRF's budget had been spent while other organizations had activities that needed to be finalized before a deadline, MRF's activities would be integrated into these budgets, and vice versa. Thus, organizations assisted each other through local networks to maintain leniency.

The impact of donor funding on MRF's legitimacy

How did MRF's integration into the aid system impact their legitimacy in the eyes of their constituents? MRF still enjoyed considerable legitimacy, as we noted during community engagements. It was mainly the normative and pragmatic legitimacy that was engrained among MRF members, as people shared their main goal of getting the land back, as well as shorter-term goals such as getting education on land rights or fighting for short-term results such as land titling. The new emphasis on women's rights was embraced and also attracted more women to the movement. MRF also showed representational legitimacy, as they were seen as a genuine spokesperson for the people. People referred to MRF as their 'umbrella', indicating that they perceived MRF as 'one of them' (representativeness).

The legal strategies that had been enhanced by funding were a new source of MRF's legitimacy, as the organization brought expertise. Even though community members sometimes recalled with nostalgia the collective spirit and different tactics they had used in the past, people preferred to use 'the law instead of the *panga*'[6] because of police repression but also because they had come to understand their rights, which enabled them to fight back with something more forceful than before. One of the founders of MRF, who had long presided over one of the farmer groups and was currently one of MRF's most loyal members, noted, 'If you fight with the knowledge that the law is on your side, you fight with much more confidence'.

However, the shift in strategies demanded a different skill set: a good command of English, knowledge of the law, and the ability to use computers to write letters. Hence, most strategic actions were carried out by MRF instead of by the farmer group leaders. Because legal advocacy relies less on active MRF member participation, compared with the earlier, more collective strategies, the loss of collective spirit necessary for the 'embodied' defence of land rights reinforced processes of demobilization.

Furthermore, MRF's cognitive legitimacy (constituents seeing MRF as 'one of us') was impacted, as community members started to look at the office differently when the volunteers from the early days were replaced by professional staff members. The previous MRF leaders were directly affected, as it was their land that was being taken, and it was felt that the younger generation did not always understand the issues. Additionally, even though the staff's salaries were modest, the fact that they received salaries at all created a sense of distance in the eyes of other community members. Several MRF members indicated that the organization's staff were not seen as equal members of the community but as professionals who could leave any time if the funding dried up.

Pragmatic legitimacy is about being able to satisfy the needs of the community. Many community members indicated that MRF had helped with stopping some of the salt companies' expansions. However, the organization's funding also created high expectations. People anticipated they would get their land back quickly; when this proved to be a long and protracted struggle, people started to lose trust in MRF. One senior MRF member indicated that people could not understand why their problems were not solved when the office was receiving millions of Kenyan shillings. The influx of money also created other expectations, such as school bursaries and assistance with hospital visits.

Perhaps the biggest challenge for MRF revolved around their representational legitimacy. Both MRF members and MRF staff recalled how, in the past, community members chipped in with their own resources. The MRF coordinator recounted with nostalgia how people had previously mobilized resources – how they would sell their farm produce and collect money for the cause during burials to finance court cases or other expenses. However, at the time of the interviews, people instead expected the office to have sufficient resources and felt that their former sacrifices were no longer required. Without contributing in this way, though, the MRF staff felt that people had also lost ownership of the struggle.

Another unintentional consequence of funding was the culture of reimbursement, which impacted collective action and inclusion. This practice served to compensate people for their time when they could have been engaged in income-generating activities, considering the high levels of poverty in the area. However, it also created 'monetization of mobilization'; people came to expect allowances in return for their participation in civic education. Although it is fair to say that many people still came to meetings without demanding to receive a payment, the *institutionalized practice* of reimbursements drained the budget, causing MRF to have to drastically scale down its meetings. Big public *barazas*[7] became a thing of the past. Instead, MRF focused on just a few spokespersons to represent the community. Meetings were mainly held in rented meeting halls instead of under trees in the villages, where meetings had traditionally been held. The same people showed up to most of these meetings. Although these were highly committed volunteers who often chipped in with their own money to cover transport, the consequence was that MRF became more of a closed network. Many people were not aware that meetings were held, and some indicated 'it is only for the selected few'.[8] Though the community leaders were expected to pass on information and knowledge, in practice, this rarely happened.[9] Many people did not feel they were included in the decision making and were disappointed that community meetings were no longer held locally. They did not get regular information or updates – about the public interest litigation case for which many people had provided statements, for example. 'This is demoralizing [to] the groups', one farmer asserted. MRF members therefore called for a reintroduction of meetings 'under the tree'. Thus, MRF and community members kept each other somewhat in a stranglehold, as MRF complained that people only wanted to attend when they were given allowances, while community members missed having large regular meetings.

In short, monetization had some sobering consequences. As the MRF coordinator summarized, 'Funding has helped the programme, but it has killed the spirit'. However, as we demonstrate below, funding was not the only (or even the main) cause of the waning spirit of the movement.

Power relations and contested legitimacy

MRF's legitimacy was not affected only by donor funding but also by changes in the practices and strategies of other actors. One of the recurring themes during our fieldwork was that the farmer groups had become 'dormant', in the words of the MRF staff and active farmer group members. Some of the more seasoned farmer group members who had been involved in resistance activities for many years observed that the unity and solidarity that had once existed were gone. The reason most often offered by active farmer group members and MRF staff members was that people had grown tired of the struggle and had lost hope. Even those who participated actively in the struggle sometimes muttered, after we had finalized our focus group discussions, that they would just give up. During one community meeting, a young man joked, 'Land, rest in peace', which provoked an explosion of laughter in the community but indicated the sense of fatigue with a seemingly never-ending struggle. This reveals the relevance of psycho-social factors in community mobilization. Other people indicated they were just too busy with their sheer survival – poverty forced them to prioritize short-term goals.

Community members also recounted how the salt companies had deployed strategies to curb resistance, promising jobs and school bursaries and having those who continued to confront them fired or arrested. The companies convinced some people to sell their land, after which those who continued to resist sometimes found themselves completely encircled by company land. This created internal community divisions that impacted MRF's representational ability, as participation in the struggle had dwindled. The biggest farmer group became fragmented and stopped functioning. Community members felt a sense of hopelessness, lacking trust that justice could be achieved by any government institution – including the courts. It was suspected that high Kenyan government officials had a stake in the land and that any form of justice would therefore be stalled – a belief reinforced by past experiences with judicial processes characterized by irregularities, continuous delays, and lawyers who suddenly disappeared.

How MRF tried to regain its legitimacy

MRF did not stand by passively; rather, they actively tried to mitigate these adverse consequences in their interactions with their INGO partners and communities. When the new MRF coordinator began the job in 2018, reviving the farmer groups was at the top of his priority list. 'It is no use having a CBO that has a gap with the community', he confided. Thus, he called all the leaders of the groups together to learn about the groups' status, activities, and challenges and to design a way forward. After that, meetings meant to revive the groups were planned in each location. For the biggest farmer group, a new leader was elected.

When we revisited Marereni in 2021, the picture we encountered was mixed. We joined a training session on social media for a youth group, who enthusiastically started twittering with the #LandNotSaltKilifi. This was in line with MRF's plan to involve community members more broadly beyond the farmer groups, including the youth. A team of these youths started to make a documentary about the struggle against the salt mines.

When we visited the villages, it was clear that the farmer groups had become more active again. Ironically, their revival was sparked by the same actors who had been responsible for their dormancy: the salt companies. Arguably anticipating the looming public interest litigation, the salt companies had attempted to expand their areas of operation. Faced with a renewed imminent threat, the communities resisted by removing the beacons that the salt companies had recently placed to demarcate their boundaries and engaging in small acts of protest. The farmer groups resumed their meetings and reconnected with MRF for assistance, aided by MRF's leaders, who pushed them to meet frequently.

However, despite the farmer groups having resumed their activities, there was a sense of despair among them. They were hit hard by a severe drought, which came on top of the environmental effects caused by the salt companies. It was ironic to ask a farmer whose goats just had died because of lack of grass, one who could not pay school fees for their children, or one who sat in a meeting without having had breakfast if they could return to mobilizing their own resources. They described having done this in the past, but how could resources be mobilized if there were none? Furthermore, there was still distance between MRF and its members, as the latter still perceived there to be a lack of meetings, despite MRF making several visits. Gossip was not uncommon, especially among community members who had little interaction with MRF; those with long-term and frequent interactions remained loyal to the organization. Some MRF members missed their old leaders, including a few who had passed away. These members felt that the gap they left behind had not been adequately filled by the new leadership.

MRF's staff members themselves were, in the meantime, anticipating the phasing out of the AJWS funding. Even though MRF was psychologically prepared for this, it still hit them hard, especially as the public interest litigation case was finally getting in full swing and because new cases had been started in response to the recent salt mining activities. AJWS's goal was to fund emerging movements for seven years – a time frame they had already extended. They expected that, once organized, these movements would find their own way. However, with this funding stream ending, the MRF coordinator was compelled to do something MRF had skilfully avoided since their foundation – spending time and energy on finding donor funding. The staff volunteered for Nairobi-based organizations that wanted to roll out their daily programmes in the area to receive daily allowances that could keep their work going for a while and support their young families. While working overtime and even chipping in with his own resources, the coordinator was blamed by the community for not doing enough. At the same time, MRF felt pressured by ActionAid to be active in the INGO's networks. For the coordinator, the pressure had become so intense he had even considered quitting, but his loyalty to the community members and their struggle against the salt companies kept him going.

One of the strategies MRF adopted was professionalizing the farmer groups. MRF wanted to make these groups more autonomous, but the communities were not seen as having the capacities necessary to adequately use legal methods of advocacy. This meant they first had to be trained in proposal writing and donor mapping. MRF assisted one of the groups with a funding proposal. Interestingly, further professionalization, reaching to the level of the farmer groups, was thus advanced as a response to the negative impacts of professionalization. One could argue that the logic of professionalization had entered into MRF's 'every-day world' (Hwang & Powell, 2009, p. 256) to such an extent that the only viable way they could see to give autonomy back to the farmer groups was to professionalize them as well. As the coordinator stated, 'We have to win back the community and integrate them in the formal'.

However, some community members proposed simpler solutions. They did not necessarily need to become professionals: They only requested a small amount of funding so they could do step-down trainings[10] on the ground, which are cheaper than meetings in central halls because of lower transport costs. Others proposed using the money to generate small income-generating activities for the farmer groups. They did not want to feel dependent upon MRF to provide them with money to pay for transport each time there was a court case; they could fund themselves with their own resources. Others proposed rolling out educational activities in schools so that youth from the affected areas could engage in capacity building, making them eligible for jobs at MRF. Other farmer group members did not propose anything; they just wanted to be informed about what was happening.

The tragic truth was that nothing much was happening. Even though the public interest litigation case had been filed, the first hearing date was not set for a year. It was difficult for staff members to visit the communities without having any good news to share, as they anticipated not being able to respond to the community's needs because of a lack of funding for the public interest litigation case and for the many other court cases between the salt company and communities. The lack of funding for court cases ultimately obstructed MRF's legitimacy on the ground because they felt they could not adequately respond to what the communities demanded. ActionAid does not fund litigation because of the high costs involved; its focus is on dialogue and campaigns. MRF's partner Kituo cha Sheria is tasked with assisting in court cases, but this organization saw their resources dwindling just as the public interest litigation was about to start. The staff of Kituo cha Sheria had been trying to get funding for litigation from major donors such as the European Union and the Dutch Embassy, but one of these staff members said that they had encountered unwillingness to support court cases. The staff member criticized donors' emphasis on multistakeholder partnerships, wondering how to communicate with a government that 'is not willing to listen' and 'tramples people's rights', expressing his wish that – in the spirit of the strategic partnerships – the Dutch Embassy could use its influence to put pressure on the Kenyan government. As stated by the MRF coordinator,

> If you say you do bottom up, but then in the end you do not follow the priorities of people on the ground, then is it really bottom up? You can create awareness, but if you don't fund the tools for people to seek justice, then what is the awareness for? It cannot stop with just advocacy alone.

Discussion and conclusion

We found evidence similar to some typical accounts of 'NGOization' but also showed that MRF did not depoliticize or shift to service delivery (McKie, 2019), which was also thanks to the INGO partners that supported MRF's political efforts and creatively matched their own priorities to those of donors. Despite reporting and accountability pressures, MRF continued to focus on its grassroots connections, and representational legitimacy thus continued to be built (AbouAssi & Trent, 2016). Although this is by no means an easy task, MRF continuously engaged in critical reflexivity on its roles. However, like Rahman (2006), we warn against a unidimensional focus on the links between Northern donors and Southern CSOs. Counterstrategies of companies and the government broke many people's spirit of resistance, and some never had this spirit in the first place. CSOs rarely represent a 'homogeneous' community (Gilfoy, 2014), and legitimacy is contested in politically volatile spaces such as land investments.

The case study presented here shows an example of how Northern NGOs can support movements that are already active on the ground, but it also demonstrates how professionalization can create both synergies and trade-offs in terms of grassroots legitimacy. Added expertise and results through more sophisticated advocacy strategies can enhance normative legitimacy and potentially also pragmatic legitimacy, but there are trade-offs because professionalization can hamper cognitive legitimacy and may result in diminished representational legitimacy. However, legitimacy is a continuous, interactive, and dynamic process that requires commitments not only from the CSO in question but also from the communities in which they operate, as well as their INGO partners and donors. Legitimacy is furthermore dependent on the responses from the advocacy targets and the prevailing power relations in the contexts where CSOs work. As has been documented by Mosse and Nagappan (2021), the sobering reality is that even the most legitimate organizations have a hard time challenging powerful forces.

To conclude, aligning with already-existing social movements is paramount to make sure local priorities lead. We present some general recommendations to avoid NGOization on the basis of our findings. First, donors should maintain funding for advocacy work, as it avoids depoliticization. Nevertheless, it is also necessary to continue to improve flexibility in planning and reporting. This latter recommendation also applies to INGO partners, for whom it means relinquishing some of their built-in control routines. Loyal partnerships with local CBOs are paramount, as these enhance the local CBOs' credibility in society. Equal partnership should be practically translated to entrusting local CBOs with larger tranches of funding, which would enable them to create 'buffers' for larger expenditures, such as research or lawyers. Funding for legal advocacy should be drastically scaled up. Teaching social movements the legal tools they need to defend their rights is not sufficient: They should also be supported once they use the tools to demand these rights. Deserting movements at a critical stage risks engendering feelings of abandonment towards CSOs in the community. Furthermore, in the spirit of strategic partnerships, donor partners can use their influence to put pressure on the Kenyan government.

For CBOs, in addition to building new capacities among members, we also recommend building on the capacities that people already have, which includes nurturing the surviving spirit, assisting with collective organization, and considering non-violent forms of collective contestation instead of relying exclusively on skills-based advocacy. Specific and targeted service delivery projects could be considered to address people's immediate needs that drive them to depend on the companies. Such efforts can perhaps be outsourced to other CSOs, but donors and INGOs can help with networking – if they start to view transformation as a holistic endeavour.

Finally, we advocate creating more space for reflexivity throughout the aid system. It is the system – not just one partnership – that should be remediated. We do not propose a ready-made solution, but rather a willingness to listen – not only to the evaluative reports of overburdened staff but also to their ideas about how to improve their work; to the accounts of not only the hardships the communities face but also the solutions they offer. Leading from the South requires a multi-layered perspective: Leading from the capital is not enough. Leading from a local CBO is not enough. It is about leading from the communities that stand at the heart of the struggle.

As MRF is still finding its ideal solution to combine external funding with local legitimacy, their strong commitment to start from the concerns of the local communities and their ability to reflect on their role can serve as an example.

Acknowledgements

This study was supported by WOTRO Science for Global Development, Nederlandse Organisatie voor Wetenschappelijk Onderzoek (Netherlands Organisation for Scientific Research; NWO) under Grant W 08.311.108, funded by the Dutch Ministry of Foreign Affairs and the Catharina van Tussenbroek Funds.

Notes

1 The first author conducted participant observation; held formal and informal talks with CBO staff and 10 community members; organized 12 community focus group discussions; conducted a survey among 120 respondents, with the assistance of 4 Kenyan research assistants; and interviewed 2 business representatives and 4 government officials. The second author joined three focus group discussions during a one-week field visit.

2 A local means of transport – young men riding a motorbike.

3 This was extended in 2020 by another five years through the Power of Voices programme.

4 For example, during several talks we had with ActionAid Kenya, they expressed wariness of cooperation with the government, which may lead to co-optation – a fate that, in their perception, had befallen some other NGOs.

5 An example is the Women2Kilimanjaro initiative.

6 Kenyan knife used in agriculture.

7 A *baraza* is a big public meeting held at village level, often called to create awareness of a specific issue, disseminate information, or give community members an opportunity to voice their concerns and share in decision making.

8 This idea was also reflected in our survey, where just 27.5% of the respondents reported having interacted with MRF.

9 Our survey confirmed this; 80% of those who were not in direct contact with MRF also did not get updates from others.
10 A session where representatives who have received training or civic education from MRF teach local community members about what they learned.

References

AbouAssi, K., & Trent, D. L. (2016). NGO accountability from an NGO perspective: Perceptions, strategies, and practices. *Public Administration and Development, 36*(4), 283–296. https://doi.org/10.1002/pad.1764.

Alvarez, S. E. (2009). Beyond NGO-ization?: Reflections from Latin America. *Development, 52*(2), 175-184. https://doi:10.1057/dev.2009.23.

Banks, N., Hulme, D., & Edwards, M. (2015). NGOs, states, and donors revisited: Still too close for comfort? *World Development, 66*, 707–718. https://doi.org/10.1016/j.worlddev.2014.09.028.

Bawole, J. N., & Langnel, Z. (2016). Downward accountability of NGOs in community project planning in Ghana. *Development in Practice, 26*(7), 920–932. https://doi.org/10.1080/09614524.2016.1210094.

Boone, C., Dyzenhaus, A., Manji, A., Gateri, C. W., Ouma, S., Kabugu Owino, J., … Klopp, J. M. (2019). Land law reform in Kenya: Devolution, veto players, and the limits of an institutional fix. *African Affairs, 118*(471), 215–237. https://doi.org/10.1093/afraf/ady053.

Brass, J. N. (2012). Blurring boundaries: The integration of NGOs into governance in Kenya. *Governance: An International Journal of Policy, Administration, and Institutions, 25*(2), 209–235. https://doi.org/10.1111/j.1468-0491.2011.01553.x.

Choudry, A., & Kapoor, D. (Eds.). (2013). *NGOization: Complicity, contradictions and prospects.* London, UK: Zed Books.

Corrigall-Brown, C. (2016). Funding for social movements. *Sociology Compass, 10*(4), 330–339. https://doi.org/10.1111/soc4.12362.

Gilfoy, K. (2014). Land grabbing and NGO advocacy in Liberia: A deconstruction of the 'homogeneous community'. *African Affairs, 114*(455), 185–205. https://doi.org/10.1093/afraf/adu078.

Hwang, H., & Powell, W. W. (2009). The rationalization of charity: The influences of professionalism in the nonprofit sector. *Administrative Science Quarterly, 54*(2), 268–298. https://doi.org/10.2189/asqu.2009.54.2.268.

Igoe, J. (2003). Scaling up civil society: Donor money, NGOs and the pastoralist land rights movement in Tanzania. *Development and Change, 34*(5), 863–885. https://doi.org/10.1111/j.1467-7660.2003.00332.x.

Jalali, R. (2013). Financing empowerment? How foreign aid to Southern NGOs and social movements undermines grass-roots mobilization. *Sociology Compass*, 7(1), 55–73. https://doi.org/10.1111/soc4.12007.

Jaoul, N. (2018). Politics against the grain: The Dalit movement of Uttar Pradesh in the throes of NGOization. *Critical Sociology, 44*(4–5), 611–627. https://doi.org/10.1177/0896920516688756.

Kanyinga, K. (1998). Politics and struggles for access to land: 'Grants from above' and 'squatters' in coastal Kenya. *The European Journal of Development Research, 10*(2), 50–69. https://doi.org/10.1080/09578819808426716.

Kenya National Commission on Human Rights. (2006). *The Malindi inquiry report: Report of a public inquiry into allegations of human rights violations in Magarini, Malindi.* Nairobi, Kenya: Author. Retrieved fromhttps://tinyurl.com/7xj4n8cx.

Kirsch, S. (2014). *Mining capitalism: The relationship between corporations and their critics*. Oakland: University of California Press.

Klopp, J. M., & Lumumba, O. (2017). Reform and counter-reform in Kenya's land governance. *Review of African Political Economy, 44*(154), 577–594. https://doi.org/10.1080/03056244.2017.1367919.

Lister, S. (2003). NGO legitimacy: Technical issue or social construct? *Critique of Anthropology, 23*(2), 175–192. https://doi.org/10.1177/0308275X03023002004.

Matelski, M., Zijlstra, S., & van Kempen, L. (2021). Civil society legitimacy as a balancing act: Competing priorities for land rights advocacy organisations working with local communities in Kenya. *Canadian Journal of Development Studies/Revue canadienne d'études du développement*, November, 1–19. https://doi.org/10.1080/02255189.2021.1987202.

Mati, J. M. (2013). Antinomies in the struggle for the transformation of the Kenyan constitution (1990–2010). *Journal of Contemporary African Studies, 31*(2), 235–254. https://doi.org/10.1080/02589001.2013.785145.

McKie, K. (2019). International donor funding and social movement demobilization: The Barabaig land-rights movement in Tanzania. *Africa Today, 66*(1), 72–95. https://doi.org/10.2979/africatoday.66.1.04.

Mosse, D., & Nagappan, S. B. (2021). NGOs as social movements: Policy narratives, networks and the performance of Dalit rights in South India. *Development and Change, 52*(1), 134–167. https://doi.org/10.1111/dech.12614.

Ossewaarde, R., Nijhof, A., & Heyse, L. (2008). Dynamics of NGO legitimacy: How organising betrays core missions of INGOs. *Public Administration and Development, 28*(1), 42–53. https://doi.org/10.1002/pad.472.

Rahman, S. (2006). Development, democracy and the NGO sector: Theory and evidence from Bangladesh. *Journal of Developing Societies, 22*(4), 451–473. https://doi.org/10.1177/0169796X06072650.

Robins, S. L. (2008). *From revolution to rights in South Africa: Social movements, NGOs & popular politics after apartheid*. Woodbridge, UK: Boydell & Brewer Ltd.

Shrestha, C. H., & Adhikari, R. (2011). NGOization and de-NGOization of public action in Nepal: The role of organizational culture in civil society politicality. *Journal of Civil Society*, 7(1), 41–61. https://doi.org/10.1080/17448689.2011.553420.

Suchman, M. C. (1995). Managing legitimacy: Strategic and institutional approaches. *The Academy of Management Review, 20*(3), 571–610.

van Wessel, M., Deo, N., Manchanda, R., Sahoo, S., Rajeshwari, B., Katyaini, S., … Mishr, Y. (2019). *Starting from the South: Advancing Southern leadership in civil society advocacy collaborations* (Policy Brief No. 1 December). Civil Society Research Collective. Retrieved from: https://includeplatform.net/wp-content/uploads/2019/12/Policy-brief-1-Starting-from-the-South.pdf.

Walton, O. E., Davies, T., Thrandardottir, E., & Keating, V. C. (2016). Understanding contemporary challenges to INGO legitimacy: Integrating top-down and bottom-up perspectives. *Voluntas: International Journal of Voluntary and Nonprofit Organizations*, 27(6), 2764–2786. https://doi.org/10.1007/s11266-016-9768-2.

Wood, J. (2016). Unintended consequences: DAC governments and shrinking civil society space in Kenya. *Development in Practice, 26*(5), 532–543. https://doi.org/10.1080/09614524.2016.1188882.

11

SURREPTITIOUS SYMBIOSIS IN PROMOTING ADVOCACY? COLLABORATION AMONG NON-GOVERNMENTAL ORGANIZATIONS, SOCIAL MOVEMENTS, AND ACTIVISTS IN WEST AFRICA

Emmanuel Kumi and Albert Arhin

Introduction

In recent years, many West African countries have witnessed increases in the active participation of social movements, activists, and non-governmental organizations (NGOs) in civic mobilization (Ajala, 2021; Wienkoop, 2022). Civil society mobilization efforts involving these groups have played a role in resisting and challenging elite-led democratic backsliding and in demanding social justice by drawing attention to inequalities and other social problems (Wienkoop, 2022). Most existing studies on social movements in West Africa have focused on their resource mobilization, framing strategies, and roles in establishing democracy (see Maccatory et al., 2010; Ndiaye, 2021; Wienkoop, 2022), neglecting the investigation of how social movements constantly collaborate with NGOs and activists in their advocacy activities and the value added by such collaborations. Additionally, in the civil society literature in West Africa, the focus has largely been on organized or institutional organizational forms such as NGOs, with limited research on social movements and activists (Noll & Budniok, 2021), which tend to have informal organizational structures and forms, work as loose networks, and sometimes have tempestuous relations with organized civil society (Della Porta & Diani, 2006).

Although some social movements have historically existed across the West African region, their ability to mobilize large numbers of followers has been relatively limited (see e.g. Maccatory et al., 2010; Ndiaye, 2021). However, in recent years, with emerging technologies, the region has seen the materialization of new, organic social movements characterized by flexible memberships and organizational structures, as well as the ability to work on multiple issues (Zihnioglu, 2019). For example, recently created social movements such as Y'en a Marre (Enough-is-Enough), Mouvement du 23 Juin (the June 23 Movement),

DOI: 10.4324/9781003241003-14

Balai Citoyen (the Citizen's Broom), EndSars, Occupy Ghana, Revolution Now, and the Coffin Revolution, among many others, have emerged in countries such as Senegal, Burkina Faso, Nigeria, Ghana, and Cameroon to mobilize citizens through collective action. Because of this shift, social movements and activists have played significant roles in mobilizing collective action for social change. It is particularly important to understand how these groups collaborate with NGOs in promoting their advocacy activities. Social movements and activists align themselves with NGOs to gain political leverage domestically and also as a means of survival during times of repression (Ismail & Kamat, 2018). NGOs provide important organizational resources for social movements and activists (Della Porta, 2020). However, this usually comes with 'strings attached', which puts the social movements and activists in a 'delicate' position as they seek to satisfy external and local demands that arise because of resource dependency (Ndiaye, 2021).

Despite the significance of cross-sector collaborations among social movements, activists, and NGOs (Della Porta, 2020; Glasius & Ishkanian, 2015; Youngs, 2017), the experiences and nature of these collaborations remain poorly understood. Existing studies on social movements and NGOs often focus on single countries rather than taking a cross-border or transnational perspective; hence, comparative analysis is lacking. In addition, thorough empirical analyses of the value added by advocacy collaboration and how donor funding influences social movements and activists in West African countries are limited. This echoes the observation by Della Porta (2020) that there is an urgent need to build bridges between social movement studies and NGO studies given the empirical and theoretical overlaps between the two areas. This chapter contributes to filling these gaps in the literature by addressing the following questions: What is the nature of collaboration among NGOs, social movements, and activists around advocacy in West Africa, and what is the value added by such collaborations? How are these collaborations influenced by donor funding?

To answer these questions, we draw on qualitative research involving semi-structured interviews and focus group discussions (FGDs) with representatives of NGOs and social movements as well as activists across 14 West African countries. This chapter positions itself within the literature on collaborations in civil society and social movement studies and makes two contributions. First, it presents empirical evidence on the added value of advocacy collaborations among NGOs, social movements, and activists in West Africa, expanding and enriching our understanding of alliance building by showing how Southern-based civil society actors work together to promote and achieve their advocacy goals through increasing the voice and impact of advocacy campaigns, knowledge sharing, and enhanced visibility and credibility. Ndiaye (2021) has argued that NGOs are hesitant to collaborate with West African social movements working on contentious actions such as anti-government protests because of potential repercussions for their operations and relationships with the government. However, this chapter shows that both local and international NGOs do collaborate with social movements and activists on advocacy activities through the provision of financial and non-financial resources, which facilitates activists' advocacy work. However, we also show that such collaboration produces unintended effects such as unequal power dynamics in agenda setting and the loss of autonomy for social movements and activists. As the second major contribution of the chapter, we highlight how the dependence of social movements and activists on NGO funding influences their collaborations through movement capture, with NGOs dominating the agenda-setting and decision-making processes. Thus, NGOs' priorities tend to dominate in their engagements with social movements and activists. We also show the risks linked to co-optation of social movements and activists, which can negatively affect these actors' credibility and legitimacy at the grassroots level. This chapter contributes to the objective of the book to reimagine collaborations by providing empirical evidence on the added value collaborations among Southern-based civil society organizations (CSOs) bring to their advocacy work and on the challenges associated with these collaborations. Southern CSOs' perspectives on these issues have received relatively little attention in the existing literature examining collaboration.

The remainder of the chapter is structured as follows. The following section discusses existing research on collaboration between social movements and NGOs. We then summarize the research methods used, before presenting the research findings. The last section of the chapter discusses the findings and offers some concluding remarks.

Collaboration among NGOs, social movements, and activists

Collaboration involves joint efforts by organizations with shared goals and mutual interests. While the literature lacks a common definition, Agranoff and McGuire (2004, p. 4) defined collaboration 'as the process of facilitating and operating in multi-organisational arrangements to solve problems that cannot be solved, or solved easily, by single organisations'.

Globally, collaboration has become increasingly important because of the changing political, economic, and social environments where activists, social movements, and NGOs operate (Maccatory et al., 2010; Ndiaye, 2021). For example, in recent years, many CSOs have experienced the closing of civic space, and transnational collaboration has become a mechanism for addressing the restrictions and repression of CSOs (Fransen et al., 2021). Such collaborations have become possible partly because of the marked increase in the use of mobile phones and the Internet for both online and offline mass mobilization (Sanches, 2022). However, although anecdotal evidence suggests that activists and social movements are collaborating with NGOs, the nature of collaborations between these actors has received little attention (see Glasius & Ishkanian, 2015; Zihnioglu, 2019). Nevertheless, a limited amount of research does shed some light on this phenomenon. For instance, von Bülow (2017) described how the Coalition for Democratic Political Reform and Clean Elections was formed in 2013 as a joint initiative between 114 social movements and traditional CSOs in Brazil, with the aim of advocating for changes in Brazil's electoral systems. In Egypt, Halawa (2017) found that rights-based CSOs and activists worked together to bring communities online to advocate for political freedom.

The rise of activists and social movements has not eclipsed NGOs' activism because the relationships among these groups are not antagonistic (Glasius & Ishkanian, 2015; Zihnioglu, 2019). Studies conducted in Kenya, Tunisia, and Turkey have suggested that NGOs work together with activists and social movements by influencing their advocacy activities and operations (Youngs, 2017). Indeed, some scholars have argued that the activities of NGOs, social movements, and activists complement each other's efforts because of their differing strengths and weaknesses (Glasius & Ishkanian, 2015; Zihnioglu, 2019). In their analysis of collaborations between NGOs and street activists in London, Athens, Cairo, and Yerevan, Glasius and Ishkanian (2015) found that, although NGOs did not initiate protests, they did provide financial and non-financial resources (e.g. technical support, expertise, contacts, meeting space, and legal aid) to support activists' activities. Collaborations among activists, social movements, and NGOs are thus reinforced by mutual resource dependence (Wienkoop, 2022; Zihnioglu, 2019). NGOs depend on activists because of the latter group's ability to mobilize people and draw media attention to issues of critical concern to NGOs. Activists tend to have high visibility for their activities and are independent of donors; these factors provide opportunities for them to speak out on issues that directly affect NGOs. In addition, collaboration between these actors results in successful campaigns, as the size and voice of each organizational participant in the collaboration is increased.

Existing research has thus shown the significance of collaboration among NGOs, social movements, and activists and illustrated the need for further exploration of this phenomenon to advance our knowledge concerning its nature, added value, and challenges in various contexts. The study presented in this chapter contributes to addressing this need by analysing perspectives and experiences of NGOs, social movements, and activists from West Africa. As we discuss below, in these groups' view, collaboration enhances CSOs' advocacy by amplifying their voice and impact, facilitating knowledge sharing, and allowing enhanced visibility and credibility. At the same time, these actors also identify challenges, such as the limited nature of transnational advocacy collaborations, as well as movement capture by NGOs through agenda-setting and decision-making processes. On the basis of these findings, the chapter presents recommendations for enhancing collaborations among these groups. The next section presents the research methods we used.

Research methods

This study used qualitative research methods. The choice of qualitative research methods was driven by the need to obtain a deeper understanding and critical insight into the dynamics of advocacy collaborations. Data for this study were gathered through FGDs and in-depth interviews from September to December 2019. Two FGDs were conducted with 21 representatives of NGOs and social movements and 34 activists in Accra, Ghana, during two separate workshops on collaboration organized by the West Africa Civil Society Institute (WACSI). The participants in the first FGD comprised 21 NGO and social movement representatives from 14 countries (Burkina Faso, Benin, Cameroon, Chad, Cote d'Ivoire, The Gambia, Ghana, Guinea, Mauritania, Niger, Nigeria, Senegal, Sierra Leone, and Togo). The second FGD comprised 34 activists from seven countries (Cameroon, Togo, Ghana, Cote d'Ivoire, The Gambia, Guinea, and Burkina Faso). The discussions in the two FGDs were open-ended and guided by a set of questions relating to participants' perceptions and experiences on the value added and challenges associated with collaborations among NGOs, activists, and social movements.

In addition to these FGDs, semi-structured interviews were also conducted with NGO and social movement representatives and with activists. These participants were purposively selected because of their experience with and knowledge about collaboration. The interviews were conducted with eight NGO staff members, including executive directors and project officers, and ten activists[1] from Nigeria, Cote d'Ivoire, Togo, Burkina Faso, Cameroon, Niger, Mauritania, Senegal, The Gambia, and Ghana.

All interviews were conducted face-to-face in Accra. Some of the activists also self-identified as leaders in social movements, which blurred the distinction between social movement representatives and activists. The FGDs and interviews were recorded with the consent of the participants and were subsequently transcribed. The data were coded using NVivo 12. Thematic analysis and discourse analysis were employed in analysing the data. The thematic analysis was inductive and iterative in nature, which helped in the identification of emergent themes and patterns in the data. Discourse analysis was used to understand how participants made meanings and framed their experiences of collaboration.

Findings

Nature and experiences of collaborations among NGOs, social movements, and activists in West Africa

The empirical evidence from this study indicates that collaboration is becoming an important resource for NGOs, social movements, and activists in West Africa. According to the study participants, a growing number of collaborations are emerging as different types of actors seek to promote social justice and deepen democratization processes in the region. In particular, NGOs, social movements, and activists are collaborating in mobilizing collective action to promote social change and draw attention to social justice issues through campaigns and protests.

Participants from Benin, Cameroon, Sierra Leone, Togo, The Gambia, Ghana, and Nigeria shared their experiences of collaboration among NGOs, social movements, and activists. For example, a participant from Cameroon recounted how the Centre for Human Rights and Democracy in Africa, which is at the forefront of seeking change in the context of the Anglophone crisis,[2] has been collaborating with grassroots social movements like the Coffin Revolution[3] and with activists (e.g. Cameroonian politician and activist Kah Walla) to stand against human rights violations and marginalization by the government. The Centre has also been collaborating with the Open Society Initiative in West Africa – for example, to build their capacity and advance social justice issues [FGD, activists, November 2019].

A participant from Senegal also shared experiences of how the Y'en a Marre Movement, which started with a group of young activists, has collaborated with multiple NGOs, initially to stop former President Abdoulaye Wade from overstaying his term and later to keep the succeeding government on its toes to improve the socioeconomic state of the country. The participant explained that the movement built strong alliances with human rights-based NGOs and other social movements, which resulted in the formation of the Mouvement du 23 Juin, with 25 organizations and movements participating [FGD, social movements, September 2019]. A participant from Sierra Leone explained how an alliance formed with a local NGO, the Sierra Leone chapter of Defence for Children International, has been instrumental in building the technical capacity of grassroots social movements. Similarly, activists from The Gambia said that certain NGOs had coordinated the activities of social movements and activists during the Occupy Westfield movement, which protested against the National Water and Electric Company because of power cuts and water shortages. These NGOs also offered technical support and legal advice for activists and social movements seeking to petition the Gambian parliament and the Office of the Vice President [FGD, activists, November 2019].

Importantly, NGOs play a crucial role in helping social movements and activists to self-organize through collective action. A case in point is the #IamToufah movement (named for Gambian sexual assault survivor Fatou 'Toufah' Jallow), which led to the #MeToo campaign in The Gambia. Speaking about his experience of collaboration among NGOs, social movements, and activists, one participant explained, 'When Fatou Jallow came out to talk about her rape case, we had a lot of activists, NGOs like Think Like a Woman, Girls Agenda, and other social movements, who joined her campaign to achieve a particular cause' [interview, activist, November 2019].

In Ghana, a representative of Activista Ghana (a social movement) shared experiences of successful collaborations with the Media Foundation for West Africa and the Centre for Democratic Governance to resist the introduction of the 'spying' bill (officially, the Interception of Postal Packets and Telecoms Messages Bill, 2016). This collaborative effort between social movements and NGOs led to the withdrawal of the bill from parliament [interview, social movement representative, September 2019]. Likewise, activists from Benin shared experiences of how they came together and worked with NGOs with reputable 'brands' and credibility to communicate their issues on social media platforms, and in Nigeria, the #BringBackOurGirls campaign involved collaborations among women-led NGOs, activists, and online communities of bloggers [FGD, November 2019]. Notably, the reported experiences of collaboration among NGOs, social movements, and activists varied, ranging from one-off collaborations to continuous engagements.

The added value of collaboration in advocacy

The participants identified three main types of value added by advocacy collaboration. These are (1) increased voice and impact resulting from 'strength in numbers', (2) enhanced credibility and visibility, and (3) resource provision and knowledge sharing.

Increased voice and impact resulting from 'strength in numbers'

Our interview data suggest that collaboration among NGOs, activists, and social movements is crucial in amplifying the collaborators' voices. Many activists argued that, by working together with NGOs, they are able to influence and persuade policymakers and political actors to make commitments to protect human rights because of 'strength in numbers', which amplifies their voices. For example, an activist from Guinea argued that collaboration among NGOs, social movements, and activists resulted in the formation of the Voice of the People campaign in the education sector in 2017 and that this campaign subsequently led to the removal of Ibrahima Kourouma, the Minister of Pre-university Education. NGOs, social movements, and activists are thought to have a greater impact when they collaborate with each other. This was aptly captured in the following statement from an activist:

> There is value addition because, at the end of the day, we are supporting each other. So that will be a way to add some weight to the cause we're all fighting to achieve. So, I think it's necessary, and it will have a great impact on whatever work that we will do.
>
> *[interview, activist, November 2019]*

Enhanced visibility, credibility, and legitimacy

Another element of value added by collaboration among these actors mentioned is that such collaboration enhances the visibility of protests and campaigns organized by NGOs to promote their advocacy activities. This was attributed to the activists' ability to leverage their broad social base and grassroots connections. During interviews, some activist bloggers and social movement representatives suggested that their ability to engage with many followers on social media afforded them the opportunity to increase the visibility and credibility of their programmes. Their use of social media contributed to their capacity to attract large numbers of protesters and draw public attention. Many activists and social movement representatives explained that this made working with them very attractive to NGOs, especially on campaign initiatives, where the activists could enhance the visibility of the NGOs' advocacy programmes. In the words of one activist, 'I think because I was known [popular], I started to work with them [NGOs] and becoming involved in projects that were related to my cause [interest] such as transparency in elections' [interview, activist, November 2019]. These findings demonstrate how activists use their visibility and mobilization capacities to promote the work of NGOs. Some NGO representatives also affirmed the added value of working with well-known activists in terms of enhancing the visibility of their campaigns.

We also found that NGOs, because of their organized structure, capacity, and relationship with political actors, sometimes play a crucial role in giving activists the credibility and the sustainability needed for advocacy interventions. Many NGO representatives felt that activists and movements are ill-equipped to bring about policy changes, partly because of their inability to develop strong relationships with policymakers or to sustain their programmes over the long term. In this regard, collaboration with NGOs with knowledge, expertise, and an organized structure allows activists and social movements to sustain their interventions and work with government officials. For example, some activists explained that their collaborations with certain local NGOs gave them recognition and credibility in the eyes of local stakeholders. This largely results from the NGOs supporting the activists and social movements in enhancing their capacity to use facts or evidence in their advocacy work because 'As [a] social activist, you just don't go on social media and make pronouncements about things that are not factual and you cannot verify' [interview, social movement representative, November 2020].

According to some NGO representatives, the perceived inability of some activists to use facts led to the assumption that 'activists are negatively perceived by traditional media' [FGD, NGO representatives, September 2019]. However, working with certain respected NGOs was seen as bringing an 'additional blessing' to activists, helping to reduce the negative labels attached to them, which enhances their credibility in the eyes of various types of stakeholders. Collaboration with NGOs also gives activists exposure and access to wider audiences. One participant succinctly described this as follows: 'The hands they [NGOs] lend us boosts our prowess in gaining audience on local, regional, and global scales' [interview, activist, November 2019]. Thus, developing relationships with NGOs helps activists to bring their advocacy programmes to the attention of global audiences.

Resource provision and knowledge sharing

Activists and social movement representatives mentioned that collaborations with NGOs brought access to financial resources they needed. They emphasized that, on their own, they were unable to secure adequate funding because donors prefer to fund organizations with formalized governance structures. For this reason, NGOs fund social movements and activists by supporting their campaigns, actions, and programmes, acting as their behind-the-scenes donors: 'We collaborate with NGOs since we sometimes face challenges of limited resources. I think such partnerships have immensely contributed to our work because they tend to augment our limited resources' [interview, activist, November 2019].

In addition to having financial benefits, collaboration with NGOs also leads to the provision of capacity-strengthening support to activists and social movements. The study participants explained that advocacy programmes require activists and social movement representatives to have specialized knowledge and technical skills for policy engagement. However, they often lack such skills and therefore depend on NGOs to provide them with the needed knowledge and training. Many activists acknowledged, in the words of one participant, that 'NGOs are more established than us, and they use their resources to help us in order to enhance our work [...] They [NGOs] have the knowledge and skills and show us the way things are done' [FGD, activist, September 2019].

Activists and social movement representatives also shared knowledge and experiences regarding successful practices for engaging stakeholders, as an NGO representative suggested: 'We invite activists to share their experiences with us if their work inspires us' [interview, NGO representative, September 2019].

Challenges and limits of collaboration

Despite the added value of collaboration among NGOs, social movements, and activists, we found that collaboration with NGOs is sometimes detrimental to the legitimacy of activists and social movements at the grassroots level. This is because activists and social movements perceived to be close to NGOs are accused of promoting the NGOs' agendas rather than advocating for grassroots causes and values. One social movement representative lamented this, saying,

> So, there have been issues with some NGOs in Gambia, and that causes credibility issues because a lot of people are saying these NGOs exist to finance homosexual lobbying and all that [....] So, the moment you [a social movement] work with these NGOs, it means you share in their ideals. So that's where the credibility issue comes in.
>
> *[interview, social movement representative, November 2019]*

In contrast, some NGOs also raised concerns that collaborations with 'radical' activists perceived as 'enemies of the government' could often result in the NGO '[...] being targeted by the government' [FGD, NGO representatives, September 2019].

Collaboration with activists, despite its benefits, exposes NGOs to risks, which potentially affects their reputation and relationships with government officials. The NGO representatives argued that this stems in part from incompatible ideologies and approaches:

> Sometimes, the problem is where donors do not allow you to do certain collaborations. There are always some restrictions by donors when you want to work with some groups [activists or social movements] [....] So, donor influence is one of the threats to collaboration.
>
> *[FGD, NGO representative, November 2019]*

This is because of differences in organizational structures, where activists and social movements are quick to react to situations through confrontational approaches like protests and demonstrations because of these groups' flexible organizational structures. However, in the view of some NGOs and their donors, working with 'radical activists' has the potential to negatively affect their credibility by exposing them to government scrutiny.

Another challenge found in this study was that, while in-country collaborations and solidarity messages appear to be growing, there is weak cross-country or transnational collaboration among NGOs, social movements, and activists in West Africa in practice. For instance, the following statement made by a participant in one of the FGDs reflects a general view shared by other FGD participants regarding the lack of transnational advocacy collaboration:

> We have been busy battling issues in our countries, but an area [in which] my organization and those I have heard from have not done well relates to collaborations across countries. It will be great for us to move out and build strong friends across the sub-region. Friends that will be crucial for us to call upon when it gets tougher but also to even shape the decisions [of] our regional policymakers.
>
> *[FDG, NGO representative, September 2019]*

This statement suggests that collaborations among NGOs, social activists, and social movements have often focused on country- or national-level issues. In addition, while some INGOs work at the international level, the concern among many participants was that INGOs often do not support social movements and activists in amplifying their voices at regional and international levels. Thus, our empirical findings suggest that transnational advocacy collaboration is limited among NGOs, social movements, and activists, as these groups tend to focus on issues within their own countries. Moreover, the participants mentioned that there are limited platforms, including coalitions and networks, that bring these actors from different countries together to share their advocacy experiences.

Influence of donor funding on collaboration among NGOs, social movements, and activists in West Africa

The interview data from this study suggest that effective collaboration among NGOs, social movements, and activists is considerably influenced by donor funding. This section discusses the pathways through which donor funding acts as a constraint to advocacy collaboration.

Donor funding, professionalization, and collaborations

Our interview data suggest that activists and social movements are reluctant to collaborate with NGOs because they perceive them as being professionalized and bureaucratic in nature, which negatively affects their autonomy and independence. A participant from Sierra Leone, for example, argued that, given that most activists and social movements are not 'elitists', when working with NGOs, 'they [social movements] are often seen as not doing it the Sierra Leone way [through informal and less structured engagements] but more of [the] European way of doing things [professionalized and bureaucratic in nature]' [interview, activist, September 2019]. This affects social movements' grassroots mobilization because they are perceived as being distant from the constituents as they tend to reorient their activities away from the grassroots.

Many social movement representatives further argued that collaboration with professionalized NGOs has the potential to change their own organizational structures because they would be required to operate, in the words of one social movement representative, in 'certain ways in order to attract funding from donors' [interview, social movement representative, November 2019]. An underlying reason for the professionalization of social movements cited by many participants was that donors are unwilling to provide funding directly to social movements because they do not have a formalized structure. For example, a social movement representative from Benin explained that it was initially difficult to obtain funding from donors because the organization was not formalized. For this reason, donors kept insisting that 'there are rules and procedures to be followed if you want to get their funding' [interview, social movement representative, September 2019]. This assertion was confirmed by many participants, who argued that social movements becoming formalized organizations open up funding opportunities, which helps them to sustain their activities and increase their influence on the ground.

However, the participants also explained that social movements receiving donor funding are often criticized by grassroots actors or accused of being distant, which affects their legitimacy and credibility. The participants further maintained that social movements that are dependent on external donor funding are often perceived as serving the interests of their 'pay masters abroad' [interview, social movement representative, September 2019], as stated by one study participant. In addition, participants from Cote d' Ivoire, Benin, and The Gambia raised concerns that some donors channel their funding through government institutions, and social movements receiving funding from the government are often susceptible as targets for manipulation in the form of co-optation: '[…] People have moved to work for the government […] Those who were once vocal have been bought by the government' [interview, social movement representative, September 2019].

Movement capture and unequal power dynamics due to resource dependency

A key concern raised by the participants involved the issues of movement capture and unequal power relations between NGOs and social movements. It was explained that, although NGOs provide social movements with logistical support such as safe spaces for meetings, as well as programmes creating synergies in their advocacy collaborations, some NGOs ended up dominating the advocacy agenda setting and operations rather than actively engaging the social movements and activists in their day-to-day activities. According to some activists, this occurred because of their resource dependence on NGOs. For this reason, many participants expressed the view that, instead of approaching collaborations with an open mind regarding what social movements and activists need, some NGOs come in with predefined goals. Thus, in terms of agenda setting and decision making, NGOs' priorities prevail because they control the resources – especially financial resources – given that donors are often unwilling to fund social movements and activists directly. This creates unequal relationships, mainly because decision making is largely in the hands of the NGOs. In this way, these collaborations are mainly instrumental, with social movements and activists serving as a means for NGOs to conduct their programmes rather than being recognized as equal partners.

Discussion and Conclusion

The findings in this chapter highlight the added value of collaboration among NGOs, social movements, and activists in West Africa. The chapter suggests that collaboration amplifies the voice and impact of advocacy campaigns because of 'strength in numbers'. In addition, having a large number of actors involved in advocacy enhances the credibility and legitimacy of advocacy campaigns. The findings in this chapter further suggest that resource provision and knowledge sharing are important elements of the added value of collaboration. We show that, by acting as donors, NGOs expand the access of activists and social movements to financial and non-financial resources. This helps social movements to effectively undertake their advocacy activities. Overall, the findings in the chapter therefore broaden our understanding of collaborations by highlighting how social movements and activists perceive their complex and mutually interdependent relationships with NGOs in West Africa. The chapter further indicates that cross-country and transnational collaboration involving NGOs, social movements, and activists in West Africa is weak, as these collaborations often occur at the national rather than the transnational level. A plausible explanation for this is the lack of regional networks creating spaces for and coordinating the activities of civil society actors across the region, which negatively affects these collaborations.

Our findings also highlight the challenges associated with collaborations among NGOs, social movements, and activists. Specifically, we demonstrate that donor funding can produce unintended effects for advocacy through movement capture and unequal power dynamics. Because of their access to donor resources, NGOs tend to dominate the agenda-setting and decision-making processes in their engagements with social movements. Overall, although donor funding has the potential to enhance advocacy collaboration with social movements and activists, it can also hinder advocacy. Building on the findings presented in this chapter, we make the following overarching recommendations for NGOs and social movements and on collaboration in general.

Recommendations for NGOs

First, to maximize the benefits of collaborations, there is a need for NGOs to focus more on their added value by providing some level of flexibility when working collaboratively with social movements and activists. Given that NGOs tend to be more bureaucratic in nature compared with these other groups, it is imperative that they provide this flexibility to social movements and activists and avoid controlling them by setting the advocacy agenda and priorities because of their unequal access to resources. Second, the findings highlight the need for NGOs to be more supportive in terms of sharing financial and non-financial resources, including technical expertise, with social movements and activists to enable them to undertake their advocacy activities more effectively.

Recommendations for social movements and activists

Given that NGOs tend to have technical and policy expertise, it is important for social movements and activists to be open to learning from them to build and improve upon their own capacities. This will also require trust building, as many social movements and activists are unlikely to initiate collaborative relationships with NGOs because of their perceptions of the potential for unintended negative effects on their advocacy campaigns. Social movements need to complement the work of NGOs by showing solidarity and a willingness to share resources, including grassroots mobilization tactics and approaches, with NGOs, enhancing the effectiveness of their advocacy activities.

Recommendations regarding collaboration in general

The findings in this chapter have indicated that transnational advocacy collaboration among NGOs, social movements, and activists in West Africa is very weak. There is therefore a need for these civil society actors to leverage information and communication technology and digital media platforms to enhance information sharing and continuous transnational engagement. Our findings also stress the need to develop stronger Southern-based regional-level CSO networks and coalitions that create spaces for NGOs, social movements, and activists to interact with one another. Creating transnational advocacy networks and coalitions in West Africa has the potential to help CSOs recognize each other's work and also see themselves as important allies who can collaborate to achieve bigger impacts in their advocacy work.

Acknowledgements

This study draws on data from a research study on collaboration among social movements, activists, and NGOs in West Africa commissioned by the West Africa Civil Society Institute (WACSI) and the Fund for Global Human Rights. We are therefore grateful to Nana Afadzinu for granting us permission to use data from the study. We would also like to thank James Savage, John Kabia, Jimm Chick Fomunjong, Christian Elongue, and Charles Vandyck for their comments on earlier drafts of the research report.

Notes

1 In this chapter, 'activist' refers to someone who is personally involved in a cause and is passionate about an issue. The goal of an activist is to bring about change in society through his/her participation and involvement in campaigns and protests. Activists can therefore work independently of social movements, but they can also be part of these movements.
2 For details about the Anglophone crisis in Cameroon, see Pommerolle and Heungoup (2017).
3 The Coffin Revolution was started by Mancho Bibixy, an activist who stood in an open casket in the city of Bemenda in Cameroon to draw attention to the socioeconomic marginalization of English-speaking Cameroonians. For details on this movement, see https://africasacountry.com/2017/05/the-coffin-revolution.

References

Agranoff, R., & McGuire, M. (2004). *Collaborative public management: New strategies for local governments*. Washington, DC: Georgetown University Press.

Ajala, O. (2021). Evolution and decline: Transformation of social movements in Nigeria. *Review of African Political Economy*, November, 1–18. https://doi.org/10.1080/03056244.2021.1996344.

Della Porta, D. (2020). Building bridges: Social movements and civil society in times of crisis. *Voluntas: International Journal of Voluntary & Nonprofit Organizations, 31*(5), 938–948. https://doi.org/10.1007/s11266-020-00199-5.

Della Porta, D., & Diani, M. (2006). *Social movements: An introduction* (2nd ed.). Malden, MA: Blackwell Publishing.

Fransen, L., Dupuy, K., Hinfelaar, M., & Zakaria Mazumder, S. M. (2021). Tempering transnational advocacy? The effect of repression and regulatory restriction on transnational NGO collaborations. *Global Policy, 12*, 11–22. https://doi.org/10.1111/1758-5899.12972.

Glasius, M., & Ishkanian, A. (2015). Surreptitious symbiosis: Engagement between activists and NGOs. *Voluntas: International Journal of Voluntary and Nonprofit Organizations, 26*(6), 2620–2644. https://doi.org/10.1007/s11266-014-9531-5.

Halawa, H. (2017). Egypt and the Middle East: Adapting to tragedy. In R. Youngs, (Ed.), *Global civic activism in flux* (pp. 13–18). Washington, DC: Carnegie Endowment for International Peace. Retrieved from: https://carnegieendowment.org/files/Global_Civic_Activism_INT_Final_Full.pdf

Ismail, F., & Kamat, S. (2018). NGOs, social movements and the neoliberal state: Incorporation, reinvention, critique. *Critical Sociology, 44*(4–5), 569–577. https://doi.org/10.1177/0896920517749804.

Maccatory, B., Oumarou, M. B., & Poncelet, M. (2010). West African social movements 'against the high cost of living': From the economic to the political, from the global to the national. *Review of African Political Economy, 37*(125), 345–359. https://doi.org/10.1080/03056244.2010.510631.

Ndiaye, B. (2021). Social movements and the challenges of resource mobilization in the digital era: A case from Francophone West Africa. *Africa Today, 68*(1), 49–71. https://doi.org/10.2979/africatoday.68.1.03.

Noll, A., & Budniok, J. (2021). Social protest and the middle class in Ghana: A social movement approach of three cases. *Journal of Contemporary African Studies*, August, 1–15. https://doi.org/10.1080/02589001.2021.1931056.

Pommerolle, M. E., & De Marie Heungoup, H. (2017). The "Anglophone crisis": A tale of the Cameroonian postcolony. *African Affairs, 116*(464), 526–538. https://doi.org/10.1093/afraf/adx021.

Sanches, E. R. (2022). *Popular protest, political opportunities, and change in Africa* (1st ed.). Abingdon, UK: Routledge. https://doi.org/10.4324/9781003177371.

von Bülow, M. (2017). Brazil: New activism, changing politics. In R. Youngs (Ed.), *Global civic activism in flux* (pp. 7–12). Washington, DC: Carnegie Endowment for International Peace.

Wienkoop, N.-K. (2022). Cross-movement alliances against authoritarian rule: Insights from term amendment struggles in West Africa. *Social Movement Studies, 21*(1–2), 103–117. https://doi.org/10.1080/14742837.2020.1770068.

Youngs, R. (Ed.). (2017). *Global civic activism in flux*. Washington, DC: Carnegie Endowment for International Peace.

Zihnioglu, Ö. (2019). The prospects of civic alliance: New civic activists acting together with civil society organizations. *Voluntas: International Journal of Voluntary and Nonprofit Organizations, 30*(2), 289–299. https://doi.org/10.1007/s11266-018-0032-9.

12

MOVING BEYOND (EN)FORCED NORTH–SOUTH COLLABORATION FOR DEVELOPMENT

Possibilities from Pakistan

Themrise Khan

Introduction

Discussion of Northern donors' and international NGOs' (INGOs) relationship with and role in the development of civil society organizations (CSOs) in the Global South has been particularly prominent in recent years. Calls for 'decolonization' and 'localization' of the international aid system are becoming more common, shifting the power of decision making, funding, and implementation from North to South. However, these terms ('decolonization' and 'localization'), which have largely been introduced by the Global North, are not very clearly defined in the context of development. The concepts also do not specify whether such processes would entail a reduction or the complete removal of Northern institutions from the North–South development equation. The underlying assumption is that major decisions would remain in the hands of the Global North, with their counterpart organizations in the South remaining at the receiving end of funding, policy choices, and programming approaches.

As a result, the pursuit of development in the South appears to necessitate an '(en)forced' collaboration between the North and the South, with the latter being forced to contend with power filtering down from the North because of the North's control over a high volume of funding. This relationship is enforced using Northern policy and practice, rather than Southern knowledge and capabilities. Hence, the title of this chapter is not just a play on words; there is an actual enforcement of conditions on the South by the North that is almost forcibly placed on institutions that receive Northern funding for development.

This chapter asks whether it is possible for the South to move away from such (en)forced collaboration with the North and instead devise a locally led form of development that is less dependent on Northern funding and its conditions. Here, collaboration is defined as including both technical and financial collaboration,

DOI: 10.4324/9781003241003-15

with the balance heavily skewed in favour of the North in both cases. Likewise, 'development' refers to 'soft' aid (i.e. bilateral and multilateral aid through grants for social-sector development and infrastructure in sectors such as education, health, empowerment, and humanitarian aid). This chapter does not cover 'hard' aid, as defined by the International Monetary Fund/structural adjustment loans.

To answer this question, the chapter will draw on the case of CSOs in Pakistan working in development. Among other types, CSOs in Pakistan include INGOs, non-profit NGOs, philanthropic and charitable trusts, corporate foundations, research-based think tanks, and grassroots social movements (Ahmad, 2021). Some of these follow the Northern playbook on development (and some were even created specifically to make use of incoming Northern funding), but many also rely heavily on non-Northern avenues of funding with little to no dependence on the North. The latter type of CSOs provides similar levels of – if not more – life-saving development services to the general population. The fact that such organizations have existed for decades challenges the assumption that development in the South is not possible without North–South collaboration, including receiving Northern funding and/or incorporating Northern approaches to development.

Using the Pakistan case and defining locally led development in this context, this chapter identifies how development in the Global South, rather than being carried out only in collaboration with organizations from the Global North, has already been taking place through various locally led organizations. In this chapter, I use examples of locally led development to attempt to create an alternative narrative, suggesting how CSOs in the Global South could function independently of Northern influence, thus moving beyond the current North–South (en)forced collaboration for development. I begin by defining and contextualizing decolonization and localization, the two main buzzwords surrounding North–South collaboration. I then present an overview of Northern development funding to Pakistan, followed by examples of locally led development in four thematic social sectors. Finally, I use these examples to critically analyse the limitations of North–South collaboration and present the potential implications of these limitations for purely Southern-led efforts for development as a future movement.

Unpacking the buzz in North–South collaboration

Several buzzwords have been circulating in recent discussions on how international development aid from the North to the South can be redesigned to address imbalances of power. The most prominent of these buzzwords are 'decolonization' and 'localization'. These terms are seen as differing from collaboration in that they allude to some level of independence and detachment of aid receivers from aid providers.

The term 'decolonization' can be traced back to mid-20th-century Europe and is associated with anti-colonial voices exemplified by scholars such as Frantz

Fanon in his seminal work, *The Wretched of the Earth*, and later Edward Said in his scholarly work on the Palestinian occupation. The term was later used in discussions of the independence movements seen in many former colonial states that achieved sovereignty over their colonizers (Peace Direct et al., 2021). In the context of aid, which emerged at the end of colonization after World War 2, decolonization is seen as the removal of the colonial roots of aid and the creation of an equilibrium between the former colonizers and the formerly colonized.

As the term is used in this chapter, localization differs from local ownership, one of the pillars of the 2005 Paris Declaration on Aid Effectiveness. The former term refers to a process where organizations in the Global North hand over decision-making and financial power structures to those in the Global South, whereas the latter term refers to countries being able to acknowledge their role in their own development that has occurred through foreign aid interventions. Localization was introduced in its current usage in 2016 in the context of humanitarian assistance and peacebuilding, as part of the Grand Bargain agreement that was signed by 52 national and international humanitarian and development organizations. The purpose of this agreement was to ensure that a minimum of 25% of funds allocated in the humanitarian sector go directly to local organizations in country, as opposed to being fully controlled by institutions in the Global North (Barakat & Milton, 2020). A common theme in academic and practitioner definitions of localization is 'the need to recognize, respect, strengthen, rebalance, recalibrate, reinforce or return some type of ownership or place to local and national actors' (Barbelet, 2018, p. 5).

I argue that both terms, used in the context of redefining the relationship between the North and the South in development, are in many ways disconnected from reality. First, neither term includes the idea that development in the Global South could be possible without the involvement of the Global North. This indicates the intention of the North to continue to hold on to the power, as opposed to divesting itself of it. Second, when it comes to civil society, the discussion mostly emphasizes the role of Northern INGOs as intermediaries in the development process rather than stressing the independent role of Southern organizations. In fact, critics of localization claim that the term is both narrow and unclear in its conceptualization of 'local' and that the localization 'agenda' of many Northern donors and INGOs risks reproducing a colonial approach to the discourse between international and local (Roepstorff, 2020). Third, these discussions are commonly led by and centred on Northern stakeholders in development. Southern government leaders, civil society, and development actors are rarely given the opportunity to interpret these concepts from their point of view.

As a result, development collaboration is (en)forced on the Global South by the Global North, leading to a misguided understanding of the practice of development collaboration. The case of Pakistan illustrates how such buzzwords and discussions ignore existing practices in development in the South. These practices bring a much-needed Southern perspective to such discussions and, in essence, completely change the meaning and nature of North–South collaboration for development.

Northern-led development in Pakistan

There is no formal definition of Northern-led development in the development literature. However, references to Northern-led development focus on the practices of multilateral and bilateral donor institutions in the Global North, primarily from Organisation for Economic Co-operation and Development (OECD) countries, who invest in economic and social development in the Global South. For the present analysis, Northern-led development is defined as approaches and practices initiated by institutions of the Global North with objectives of achieving economic and social development in countries in the Global South. This currently includes the modalities of funding, project design and management, implementation, evaluation, and in-country staffing, all of which tend to be controlled by actors in the Global North.

Pakistan has been a recipient of Northern bilateral and multilateral funding since the early 1950s, soon after it gained independence. Since the beginning, foreign aid to Pakistan has been dominated by aid from the United States (Anwar & Michaelova, 2004; Zaidi, 2019). The United Kingdom also became a significant donor in later years, and the World Bank, United Nations, European Commission, and Asian Development Bank are major multilateral donors to Pakistan and part of the country's long-term development landscape.

It is difficult to find exact figures for international aid to Pakistan broken down by category of recipient (e.g. the government or an NGO). However, as a broad example, the latest figures for fiscal year 2019–2020 show that the Pakistan government signed new aid agreements worth US$10,447 million with various multilateral and bilateral development partners and foreign commercial banks (Government of Pakistan, 2020). Only 1% of this total amount was allocated as official development assistance. The remainder of these aid agreements took the form of loans from international finance institutions for items including budgetary support and debt restructuring. The last five years have shown a similar breakdown in official development assistance to Pakistan (Economic Affairs Division, 2020).

Pakistan's key CSOs, such as the All Pakistan Women's Association, were established in the early 1950s, soon after the partition of India and Pakistan (Ahmad, 2021). Others, such as the Aga Khan Rural Support Programme and the Orangi Pilot Project, emerged in the 1980s, when Northern donor funding increased in Pakistan, prompted by the Afghan refugee crisis (Pasha & Iqbal, 2002). In the 1980s, a vibrant women's movement emerged, with the creation of the Women's Action Forum and the introduction of INGOs such as Oxfam and Save the Children in Pakistan. The 1990s saw a further proliferation of large national organizations such as the Pakistan Poverty Alleviation Fund and the National Rural Support Programme, which were established with the help of large-scale investment by multilateral and bilateral donors (Pasha & Iqbal, 2002). After 9/11, there were massive increases in social sector funding for development purposes (relative to previous years) by the United States (Zaidi, 2011). This increased the pool of foreign funding available to civil society for a host of sectors, including girls' education, women's empowerment, rural development, and democratic strengthening (Democracy Reporting International [DRI], 2019).

This post-9/11 scenario and Pakistan's involvement in the subsequent 'war on terror' eventually led to a destabilization and shrinking of civic space in Pakistan. The subsequent killing of Osama bin Laden in Pakistan by US forces in 2012 heralded the end of the presence of many long-standing INGOs in Pakistan, such as Save the Children, Plan International, and Action Aid, some of which were accused of perpetuating 'an anti-state agenda' through their development programming (Sayeed, 2017). As militant and jihadi activity increased in the region, INGOs and foreign-funded CSOs – particularly those working for advocacy, women's rights, and human rights – became targets of the Pakistani state. In 2015, Pakistan's government imposed further restrictions on national NGOs, requiring them to re-register with added documentation if they received any funding from international sources (Mohmand, 2019). There were also concerns regarding financing terrorism raised by international regulatory bodies such as the Financial Action Task Force, resulting in the Pakistani government putting in place an even more rigorous framework to monitor and regulate incoming funding in the aid sector (DRI, 2019). As a result, although Northern donors still provide most of the funding received by development NGOs in Pakistan, the work of these NGOs is increasingly scrutinized, which has created the need to find alternative forms of both funding and development approaches.

Locally led development in Pakistan

In the grey literature, locally led development is defined as development that is locally owned, negotiated, and delivered by those who receive the aid, rather than by those who provide the aid. Locally led development focuses on locally salient issues, employs local capacity to implement solutions, and has 'the power to support, influence or block change' (Booth & Unsworth, 2014, p. 3). Simply put, locally led development refers to initiatives and approaches that 'prioritize the participation of people and their communities in their own development decisions' (Bond, 2021, p. 8).

This understanding of locally led development, again, concerns the approach of Northern development organizations vis-à-vis their Southern counterparts. It ignores the possibility that these 'local' organizations could be the result of Northern funding opportunities, rather than of development outside the international aid system. For instance, many INGOs would claim that the work they support is clearly 'locally led' by virtue of having country offices based in the South. However, these definitions do not acknowledge that 'locally led' does not refer only to local ownership and management, but also to local creation and funding. Thus, the defining feature of locally led initiatives is that they are completely uninfluenced by Northern-centric views of development.

This kind of locally led development has taken a range of forms in Pakistan, including philanthropic and welfare organizations and private institutions catering to a wide population with various levels of service provision. Unlike organizations funded by Northern donors, these organizations are financially supported by philanthropic and charitable giving by individuals and/or private-sector organizations. The scope and objectives of these organizations range from providing no-cost services to hybrid models, including charging those who can afford to pay. The services provided by these organizations, many of which are also provided by Northern-led development organizations through project funding, range from providing free meals and shelter to the poor to offering primary education, quality health care, micro-credit, and technical and vocational training.

To demonstrate how locally led development in Pakistan can transcend the conventional development approaches of Northern-led development, I present the following examples in four sectors: education, public health, micro-credit, and humanitarian assistance. On the basis of these examples, I attempt to develop an alternative narrative featuring the independence of Global South civil society from Northern influence.

Education

The Citizens Foundation (TCF) was established in 1995 as a network of over 1,200 schools across Pakistan by a group of Pakistani businessmen; to date, these schools have graduated almost 300,000 students (www.tcf.org.pk). TCF pursues a completely locally designed and created model, as seen in the custom design and construction of its schools, curriculum, recruitment of teachers (who mostly belong to the communities where the schools are located), and teacher training. TCF has offices across Europe and North America with the sole purpose of fundraising among the Pakistani diaspora overseas. According to its 2020 annual report, 75% of TCF's income in that year was in the form of support donations, with the rest coming from investments, government support, fees, and assets (The Citizens Foundation, 2021). The organization has also branched out into community-driven initiatives such as adult literacy, safe drinking water, and vocational training for women.

Public health

The Indus Hospital and Health Network (IHHN), set up in 2007, follows a relatively new model of free/hybrid health care provision, with care ranging from clinical and blood donation services to rehabilitation and public health initiatives across a range of campuses throughout Pakistan (www.indushospital.org.pk). Established by former public service medical practitioners and initially supported by Pakistani businesses and philanthropists, the IHHN is currently supported by donations and grants from a variety of local and international sources, which, similar to TCF, include funds from a range of international affiliates or 'Friends of the Indus Hospital'. Most of IHHN's funding comes from *zakat* (alms) donations, which have benefited over 70% of the hospital's patients. Several of the IHHN's campuses follow the public–private partnership model, managing and operating government hospitals. In 2017, the organization also established the Indus University of Health Sciences.

Micro-credit

The Akhuwat Foundation was established in 2001 and is now the largest interest-free microfinance loan institution in the country, supported by donations and public grants – especially *zakat* donations (www.akhuwat.org.pk). To date, the Akhuwat Foundation has provided over 2 million loans of an average of US$200, with over 800 branches across 400 cities and towns. Given its emphasis on Islamic financing and the Islamic principle of solidarity, Akhuwat has purposely stayed away from the Northern-supported approaches to micro-credit and lending that charge interest to their beneficiaries. This has not only earned the organization the goodwill of its borrowers, but also a massive financial and charitable support base. The organization's work recently won the prestigious Ramon Magsaysay Award, also known as the 'Asian Nobel Prize', in 2021 (Express Tribune, 2021).

Humanitarian assistance

Founded in 1951, the Edhi Foundation is Pakistan's oldest and most well-known humanitarian assistance organization. With a network of humanitarian support that is global rather than only national, this organization manages orphanages, women's shelters, and food banks, as well as providing burial services and disaster assistance, to name just a few of its activities. The Edhi Foundation is run entirely by donations and volunteers across the country. The organization has always been family-run – first by its late founder and his wife, and now by his widow and son. Such a model, because of its relative informality, may contrast with the conventional illustration of a 'development model', but there is no denying that the Edhi Foundation is through-and-through locally led.

Although these four organizations may solicit minor levels of programme funding from Northern donors, these are limited to a small component of the larger whole. Such funding is usually in the form of grants and is not included as part of the organizations' core programming. These organizations see such funding as one part of a much larger fundraising strategy, as opposed to being completely dependent on it. All four examples define and implement their programmatic approaches without Northern-led collaboration.

An interesting observation across these organizations is that they have all been instrumental in providing immediate financial assistance and support to their communities during the COVID-19 pandemic. Their non-reliance on Northern funding has allowed them to promptly address the impact of the pandemic through the provision of social protection mechanisms, including public health facilities. This contrasts with INGOs and other non-local organizations, who have either had to wait for new funding to be approved by their Northern headquarters or divert existing programme funds to the crisis.

It is important to note that these examples are not (and should not be) a replacement for state provision of basic services to citizens, particularly because exactly the same argument is often made about Northern development programming through organizations in the Global South. However, while organizations like these four examples cannot compensate for state provision of services, they are completely capable of playing a large part of the role currently filled by North–South collaboration for development. The success of these locally led ventures is demonstrated by these organizations' vision, which is embedded purely in the Pakistani context, as opposed to catering to a 'donor-funded agenda' that forces organizations to adapt their priorities depending on the funding pools available. These organizations have proven that they can achieve not just long-term sustainability, but also a national expansion – something Northern-led development has still not been able to successfully manage. Consequently, these types of locally led organizations are well able to challenge the idea that North–South collaboration is necessary for development in the South.

A critical view of the limits of (en)forced collaboration

The purpose of this chapter is to show that there is a world beyond North–South collaboration, where development efforts already exist and sometimes even predate the arrival of donor-funded models in many countries in the South. Moreover, these efforts are sustainable, scalable, and replicable, thus achieving the three outcomes continually emphasized in the Northern-led development approach. The examples described above illustrate the ability to achieve these three outcomes in a purely Pakistani context, which demonstrates that CSOs in the South are completely capable of functioning independently of the North – both financially and conceptually – in some of the key sectors of social service delivery.

I now turn to look at each of the three outcomes more closely, beginning with sustainable funding. All four example organizations are financially supported through charitable and philanthropic donations both from within Pakistan and from the Pakistani diaspora overseas. The diaspora largely comprises either individuals living overseas who donate to charity at a personal level or groups of individuals in other countries who have come together specifically to help raise money for organizations such as TCF or the IHHN. These are not external diaspora organizations that 'fund' such initiatives; therefore, they do not have the kind of influence or structures that foreign donors or INGOs may have. These are also not all ad hoc measures – they are systematically established mechanisms. For instance, TCF and the IHHN receive funds through their international 'chapters' that continually fundraise among the Pakistani diaspora. While charity and philanthropy can never (and should never) be the only way to contribute to a country's development, this type of giving remains an indelible part of Pakistan's culture because of its Islamic underpinnings. This makes it not only a legitimate form of financing but also a sustainable one.

The second outcome is the national scalability seen in all four examples. Northern-led models of development are rarely able to achieve national scalability or target the numbers reached by these organizations. An exception to this statement is the integrated development Rural Support Programme model, which can be argued to have reached the national scale, with thousands of beneficiaries. This model has been heavily influenced and funded by Northern donors. The organizations discussed here were also not established based on a set project-based time frame, which is common among Northern-led models. For instance, Akhuwat's reliance on local donors meant that, unlike Northern donor-dependent microfinance institutions, it was not under any pressure to scale up quickly and did so over the span of almost a decade (Ranjha, 2019).

The third outcome is replicability. Because of their focus on giving and charity, these locally led models can easily be replicated by others, as the concept of charitable giving is very much ingrained among Pakistanis. Moreover, the space for these kinds of locally led organizations is also unlimited because of major gaps in the state provision of basic services. Unlike Northern-led programming, which works in tandem with either governments or individual partner organizations, the four examples described in this chapter are independent of both. Although these locally led organizations do engage in public–private partnership arrangements when necessary, they only do this when these arrangements support their vision and approach – not because of an external funding requirement.

In contrast to locally led models, the traditional development program/project model relies almost completely on Northern donors for survival. Organizations in the development sector are often forced to obtain funds from Northern donors in the absence of adequate public funding, or they may be attracted by the more substantial funds available to them from the Global North. However, this funding comes with the added burden of models and approaches such as logical frameworks, results-based management, and Theories of Change – models that are imported and imposed by Northern donors. Recipient organizations' compliance includes answering to headquarters in the Global North, as opposed to their own government and beneficiaries. Under the traditional development model, monitoring and evaluation mechanisms are also led by Northern donors instead of by the recipient countries themselves.

It must be said, however, particularly in the case of financial sustainability, that depending on the Islamic concept of *zakat* and charity has certain pitfalls and is in no way perfect. For instance, this approach gives religion a large role in development, which is *a* model but not *the only* model. Although all four examples do rely largely on the Islamic practice of charity, they are not religiously motivated or faith-based organizations. This is a crucial distinction to highlight:

the motivation behind faith-based organizations is to use Islamic principles to address a particular issue, whereas these organizations are motivated to address a particular issue and use Islamic principles as one way to elicit funding.

Another limitation of personal philanthropy-based models is that, although they are effective in meeting tangible needs like health, education, and financial independence, they may not be so effective at social and political advocacy – for example, championing women's rights and freedoms, minority rights, or even child rights – because advocacy seeks to contribute to a long-term change in mindset and requires more intensive efforts, such as lobbying for legislative reform. Philanthropy and a local funding base would be hard to find for organizations involved purely in advocacy efforts.

Implications for North–South collaboration

So what does this mean for (en)forced North–South collaboration for development? The current narrative on Northern-led development revolves around external power and resources, where the terms of collaboration are defined by the party with the most bargaining power. This takes us back to the 'buzzwords' describing attempts to dismantle such power: decolonization and localization. These concepts are not applicable to locally led development because they do not imply a complete replacement or even end of North–South collaboration. In fact, these terms suggest a continuation of power relationships that still put Northern donors in the driving seat (Khan, 2022). The examples discussed in this chapter, in contrast, consciously disassociate themselves from the colonial history of aid, with both their origin and their survival independent of traditional Northern-led aid models. These were fully 'decolonized' and 'localized', to use those terms, long before the terms were popularized in the aid discourse.

Considering these examples reveals an important implication for the future of North–South collaboration if there is one. This involves the lack of alignment between foreign aid and local philanthropic initiatives. Organizations like those presented here are still viewed by the aid industry as charitable endeavours rather than structured, professionally led organizations. Despite the popularity and success of such organizations in Pakistan, the Northern aid community does not view these as models in best practices in health, education, micro-credit, and humanitarian assistance. This illustrates the one-dimensional way development in the South is perceived by the North (i.e. in terms of how Northern aid institutions define successful models of development). However, it might be a blessing for such organizations to remain independent of the Northern-centric 'projectized' approach that has the potential to constrain local innovation and resource mobilization. Indeed, the Edhi Foundation has pioneered a novel form of voluntary philanthropy, which North–South collaboration models would never have been able to envision because of the Northern emphasis on bureaucratic procedures.

Relatedly, many governments in the Global South do not see philanthropy as an intrinsic part of national economic and social development because its benefits are not seen in the contexts of economic growth and social service provision, which are often only connected to aid and public spending. The issue here is to change the narrative to view charitable and philanthropic initiatives not as alms, but rather as a legitimate form of development funding that can be harnessed to improve the social sector, in combination with public spending. The 'innovation' aspect, if there must be one, would be the formalization of this model as an institutional form of locally led development. Already registered in Pakistan as charities and non-profits, organizations such as TCF and the IHHN can provide blueprints for this, with their formal operational structures, including fundraising and accountability mechanisms. Many studies have shown the existence of alternative funding mechanisms for development that can reduce the need for dependence on Northern donor funding, further supporting the case for local philanthropic fundraising. These mechanisms include more efficient use of taxation, diaspora contributions, and *zakat* (Akram & Afzal, 2014).

Conclusion

The examples in this chapter reinforce the idea of the leading role that a civil society organized in line with local priorities, resources, and methods can play in the South. The success of such organizations shows that locally led organizations are perfectly capable of taking over the role often played by Northern development actors, including donors and INGO intermediaries. These examples can change the existing narrative of development into a purely locally led one, where validation is not sought from the North; on the contrary, in this alternative narrative, it is the North that can turn to such development models as the impetus to guide its priorities. Northern priorities should not aim to create new models in the South but to allow the existing models to dictate what support, if any, Southern organizations need from the North.

Despite the limitations of locally led models, these models remain far more realistic and attainable in a variety of contexts, compared with Northern-led collaboration, because of the three key outcomes of sustainable funding, scalability, and replicability. These benefits are not seen just because local organizations' vision is rooted in founders who belong to and have always lived in the country they have chosen to support; the benefits are also the result of the human and financial resources and capital investments made being entirely home-grown. Most importantly, the approach is fully sensitive to the country context, a point on which North–South collaboration constantly flounders when trying to create hybrid development models.

The example cases presented in this chapter cater to the South, from the South, and in the South. This rootedness also gives such organizations greater leverage to negotiate with Northern partners if the need arises. This is perhaps their biggest success – that they do not need to pander to external donors because they have already garnered sufficient support elsewhere. It is possible for such approaches to take hold in other countries of the South as well. Each context may be different – for example, some countries may not have very active diasporas overseas, and others may not subscribe to religious charity as a funding option – but the crux of the situation remains the same: as long as organizations continue to develop independently in their own contexts, they will always find a way to survive independently of conventional North–South collaborative models.

References

Ahmad, S. M. (2021). Clearing misconceptions about civil society in Pakistan. In P. B. Andersen, M. Rubya, & P. Amit (Eds.), *Re-interrogating civil society in South Asia: Critical perspectives from India, Pakistan and Bangladesh* (pp. 56–71). Abingdon: Routledge.

Akram, M. M., & Afzal, M. (2014). *Dynamic role of Zakat in alleviating poverty: A case study of Pakistan*. Retrieved from: https://mpra.ub.uni-muenchen.de/56211/.

Anwar, M., & Michaelova, K. (2004). *The political economy of US Aid to Pakistan*. Hamburg Institute of International Economics. Retrieved from: https://papers.ssrn.com/sol3/papers.cfm?abstract_id=625944.

Barakat, S., & Milton, S. (2020). Localization across the humanitarian-development-peace nexus. *Journal of Peacebuilding & Development, 15*(2), 147–163. https://journals.sagepub.com/doi/pdf/10.1177/1542316620922805.

Barbelet, V. (2018). *As local as possible, as international as necessary. Understanding capacity and complementarity in humanitarian action*. London: Overseas Development Institute. Retrieved from: https://cdn.odi.org/media/documents/As_local_as_possible_as_international_as_necessary_understanding_capacity_and_comp.pdf.

Booth, D., & Unsworth, S. (2014). *Politically smart, locally led development*. London: Overseas Development Institute. Retrieved from: https://cdn.odi.org/media/documents/9204.pdf.

Bond. (2021). *Catalysing locally-led development in the UK aid system*. Retrieved from: https://www.bond.org.uk/wp-content/uploads/2022/03/catalysing_locally-led_development_in_the_uk_aid_system.pdf.

Democracy Reporting International. (2019). *Civil society and social development in Pakistan: How the state can support its development through effective regulation*. Retrieved from: https://democracyreporting.s3.eu-central-1.amazonaws.com/images/2341BP-101-Final_Pakistan_English.pdf.Economic Affairs Division. (2020). *Sectoral analysis of foreign economic assistance. Policy report* 1/2020. Policy Analysis and Development Wing. Economic Affairs Division. Government of Pakistan. Retrieved from: http://ead.gov.pk/SiteImage/Misc/files/EAD_Secotralanalysis1%2C2020.pdf.

Express Tribune. (2021). *Pakistani microfinance pioneer wins Asia's 'Nobel Prize'*. Sept. 1. Retrieved from: https://tribune.com.pk/story/2317947/pakistani-philanthropist-wins-asias-highest-honour.

Government of Pakistan. (2020). *Annual report on foreign economic assistance (FY 2019–2020)*. Ministry of Economic Affairs. Government of Pakistan. Retrieved from: http://www.ead.gov.pk/SiteImage/Misc/files/Final%20Debt%20Bulletin%20 11_12_2020_New.pdf.

Khan, T. (2022). *The narrative of decolonization of development aid. Are non-Western alternatives the real issue?* Department of External Development, Government of

Catalonia. Retrieved from: https://revistaidees.cat/en/the-narrative-of-decolonization-of-development-aid/.

Mohmand, S. K. (2019). *The implications of closing civic space for sustainable development in Pakistan*. Sussex: Institute of Development Studies. Retrieved from: https://www.ids.ac.uk/publications/the-implications-of-closing-civic-space-for-sustainable-development-in-pakistan/.

Pasha, A. G., & Iqbal, M. A. (2002). Non-profit sector in Pakistan: Government policy and future issues. *The Pakistan Development Review, 41*(4), 879–908. Retrieved from: https://www.pide.org.pk/pdf/PDR/2002/Volume4/879-908.pdf.

Peace Direct, Adeso, Alliance for Peacebuilding & Women of Colour Advancing Peace and Security. (2021). *Time to decolonize aid. Insights and lessons from a global consultation*. Retrieved from: https://www.peacedirect.org/wp-content/uploads/2021/05/PD-Decolonising-Aid-Report.pdf.

Ranjha, M. S. A. (2019). Akhuwat. New microcredit stories. In J. B. Shahid, A. C. Iftekhar, & E. B. Asad (Eds.), *Pakistan at seventy: A handbook on developments in economics, politics and society* (pp. 241–248). London: Routledge.

Roepstorff, K. (2020). A call for critical reflection on the localization agenda in humanitarian action. *Third World Quarterly, 41*(2), 284–301. https://doi.org/10.1080/01436597.2019.1644160.

Sayeed, S. (2017). *Pakistan Closes 27 NGOs in what activists see as widening crackdown*. Reuters, 22 December. Retrieved from: https://www.reuters.com/article/us-pakistan-rights-idUSKBN1EG0SJ.

The Citizens Foundation. (2021). *Keeping dreams alive. Annual report 2020*. Retrieved from: https://view.publitas.com/the-citizens-foundation/tcf-annual-report20/page/1.

Zaidi, A. S. (2011). Who benefits from US Aid to Pakistan? *Economic & Political Weekly, 46*(32), 103–109.

Zaidi, A. S. (2019). The death wish in Pakistan's aid dependence. *Current History, 118*(807), 154–156. https://doi.org/10.1525/curh.2019.118.807.154.

13

SHIFTING THE NARRATIVE

Localization and 'shift the power' in the African context

Emmanuel Kumi, Thomas Yeboah, Nancy Kankam Kusi, Jimm Chick Fomunjong and Charles Kojo Vandyck

Introduction

In recent years, there has been a growing emphasis on the need to reform the aid system's structure, culture, and practices, particularly in terms of challenging and changing existing power dynamics (Bond, 2021; Hodgson, 2020; Knight, 2019). This has resulted in critical voices demanding that development be done differently (Honig & Gulrajani, 2018). The growing emphasis on the need to do development differently is informed by the fact that many development interventions have had limited impact because of the lack of involvement of local communities and organizations in the development process. In fact, as Knight (2019, p. 5) contends, 'well-meaning external interventions into communities frequently produce results that local people do not want'.

As a result, there is an increasing emphasis on the need to reform the structure, culture, and practices of aid, particularly regarding challenging and changing existing power dynamics. This has led to multiple conversations and narratives regarding topics such as localization, Reimagining International Non-governmental Organizations (RINGO), Charter4Change, power shift, and the #ShiftThePower campaign (Bond, 2021, p. 4; Charter 4 Change, 2015; Emmens & Clayton, 2017; Hodgson, 2018; RINGO, 2020). In addition, at the 2016 World Humanitarian Summit, global humanitarian actors signed the Grand Bargain, committing to change their working practices to improve the efficiency and effectiveness of the humanitarian aid system (Austin et al., 2019; Roepstorff, 2020).

With growing debate and contestation with regard to the current humanitarian aid system and its underpinnings (Pincock et al., 2021; Roepstorff, 2020), actors in the development ecosystem are becoming increasingly interested in understanding the opportunities and best practices for local civil society organizations

DOI: 10.4324/9781003241003-16

(CSOs) – especially those from the Global North – to shift power to the Global South. The goal is to put 'local actors' at the centre of development work (Al-Abdeh & Patel, 2019; Hodgson, 2020). For this reason, localization and 'shift the power' narratives have received much attention in the literature (Barbelet et al., 2021; Hodgson, 2020; Pincock et al., 2021; Roepstorff, 2020). However, conversations and engagement around efforts to localize and 'shift the power' are increasingly dominated by Northern-based donors and organizations (Barbelet et al., 2021). Additionally, recent work by Barbelet et al. (2021) has acknowledged the need to contextualize the interpretation of localizations.

However, few systematic research efforts have examined how CSOs in the Global South understand localization and 'shift the power' narratives, the role of these CSOs in realizing these goals, and the challenges and opportunities associated with achieving localization and shifting the power. This represents a knowledge gap that this chapter seeks to contribute to filling by answering the following research questions: How are localization and 'shift the power' understood by African CSOs? What role do African CSOs play in promoting the localization and 'shift the power' agendas? What are the underlying constraints and opportunities for African CSOs to implement the localization and 'shift the power' agendas? By answering these questions, we aim to contribute to the emerging literature by shifting the focus of debate and dominant narratives from the perspectives of actors in the Global North to those of actors in the Global South.

The findings presented in this chapter are based on a study commissioned by the West Africa Civil Society Institute (WACSI). The study was funded by the Global Fund for Community Foundations and overseen by the NEAR Network and Save the Children Denmark as part of the 'Innovation for Localisation' project, which was funded by the Danish International Development Agency. The outcome of the study was published in a report entitled 'Localisation agenda, shift the power, and African philanthropic models in Burkina Faso, Ghana, Nigeria, and Senegal' (see WACSI, 2021).

The remainder of the chapter is structured as follows. The next section presents the research approach and methods. We then summarize and discuss our research findings. Finally, in the last section, we provide some concluding remarks.

Approach and methods

This study employed a qualitative research design involving semi-structured interviews with 18 local CSO professionals and experts from eight African countries (Burkina Faso, Cameroon, Ghana, Nigeria, Kenya, Togo, Sierra Leone, and South Africa). Qualitative research approaches are deemed useful when one wants to explore and gain an in-depth picture of the meanings and subjective views that individuals or groups ascribe to a social phenomenon. It is worth mentioning that, although this study sought to explore how the interviewees framed and understood the localization agenda and 'shift the power' narratives, the definition of these terms was left open so that interviewees could interpret them on the basis of their own perspectives rather than following a predetermined definition. This was also a useful mechanism for assessing participants' knowledge and awareness of localization and 'shift the power'.

Purposive sampling was used to select 18 CSO representatives, who served as key informants. These individuals were selected because they were deemed information-rich and because they had been involved in discussions about the localization agenda and 'shift the power' narratives at local, national, regional, and global levels. The participants were selected from CSOs, including philanthropic organizations, non-governmental organizations (NGOs), and humanitarian organizations. In addition to the semi-structured interviews, this chapter also draws on insights from a webinar on 'The localisation agenda: questioning the intermediary donor system', which was hosted by WACSI and the Global Fund for Community Foundations on 29 April 2021. The webinar aimed to critically discuss and explore how the intermediary structure within the philanthropy/donor funding system is changing the localization agenda.

Data collection for this study took place over five months, from March to July 2021. All interviews were conducted using a virtual means (i.e. the Zoom platform) because of the ongoing COVID-19 pandemic and its associated social-distancing protocols. With the participants' informed consent, all interviews were recorded, and they were later transcribed. A coding frame containing themes and sub-themes was developed from the transcripts. Reflective thematic analysis was employed in analysing the interview data. The validity and credibility of the findings were established using multiple sources of evidence from the interview data, peer debriefing, and the researchers' reflexivity.

Findings and discussion

This section presents and discusses the research findings on how African CSOs frame their understanding and their roles, as well as the challenges and opportunities related to the localization agenda and the 'shift the power' movement. The data discussions in this section are based on empirical evidence gathered from interviews. Direct quotes from the interviewees are provided to support specific themes.

Understanding of localization among African CSOs

In the literature, localization is considered to be reaction to the long exclusion of local people from decision making and to funding models favouring large INGOs, which has left local organizations under-resourced (Centre for Humanitarian Leadership and RINGO, 2022). However, the interview data in this study suggest that the driving factors behind the high awareness of localization in the Global South revolve around the increasing outcry against racial injustice and the need to decolonize development. According to the interviewees, the discussion of localization is situated in contexts where humanitarian actors in the Global South, particularly CSOs, reflect on how best to remain relevant in the context of ongoing political, economic, social, and cultural changes in their field of operation. Different interpretations emerged in terms of how the interviewees understood localization and what it meant for them and their organizations. These differing understandings of localization among the interviewees are in line with Barbelet et al.'s (2021) observation that there is a no single definition of localization. In this study, two key themes around localization emerged from the interviews: empowerment of local organizations and localization as local ownership and mutual partnership.

Empowerment of local organizations

One key understanding of localization emerging from the interviews is closely linked to the concept of empowerment. Key informants framed the localization agenda as a means to deepen and strengthen African organizations' agency, power, and capacity. They further emphasized the need for CSOs to come together as one unit to speak with a common voice against longstanding practices of, for example, the dominance of international NGOs (INGOs) and the lack of recognition of local actors' role in the humanitarian aid system. The interviewees maintained that localization entails a shift or transfer of power away from international organizations based in the Global North to local organizations in the Global South. This process allows local organizations to lead the development and delivery of interventions. To many interviewees, localization meant shifting the balance of power and reversing the current paradigm, where international actors dominate the aid architecture. As one interviewee explained,

> [The localization agenda] is about deepening and strengthening the agency, power, and capacity of organizations rooted in the Global South. It's about transferring power away from the Global North to embed that power in local organizations to take the lead in [the] development process.

Interviewees further reported that empowering local actors and organizations requires the provision of holistic capacity-strengthening initiatives rather than donors' tokenistic, one-off capacity-building efforts, which are mostly tied to specific short-term projects. Many interviewees further argued that donors should implement the Grand Bargain commitments by providing resources to strengthen African CSOs' capacity. According to these interviewees, this would help address the perceived lack of capacity of some African CSOs to manage funds, which is used to justify donors' preference for INGOs. In the view of some interviewees, this justification is rooted in colonial ideologies and mindsets:

> Donors and INGOs have to change their colonial mindset that CSOs in the Global South do not have the absorptive capacity or the required

> capacity to manage their grants and its related projects [...]. We have seen a lot of disrespect by INGOs towards local CSOs, and that in itself is creating some tension.

Localization as local ownership and mutual partnership

Another important understanding of localization revolves around using local knowledge and ensuring local ownership of development programmes and interventions. Many interviewees vehemently argued that localization is all about how support can be garnered locally from individuals, organizations, and local communities to strengthen the ability of CSOs to achieve the desired impact:

> My understanding of localization is about how we, the locals, support the works that local CSOs including NGOs do instead of depending solely on international organizations [...] I believe it is about time we look at this and find ways of supporting CSOs operating within the country.

Other interviewees framed their understanding of localization in terms of genuine and equitable partnership. In their view, localization revolves around how humanitarian organizations at global, national, and local levels increasingly need to be treated as equal partners in initiating development interventions. However, in the view of these participants, the role of local organizations within this partnership, in terms of leading, coordinating, and bringing their local knowledge and expertise to the execution of projects, is crucial. One interviewee explained this as follows:

> The localization agenda is a call from local actors that the humanitarian system treats them more as equals, in line with the outcome of the World Humanitarian Summit, which recognizes the role of the locals as crucial stakeholders in humanitarian action. It's this notion of shifting the balance, where donors and INGOs recognize that they are not the ones coming in to dominate the humanitarian aid system in the Global South. Rather, they should be working to complement and strengthen the long-term growth of the local actors.

Localization is generally understood to mean strengthening the leading and coordinating role of local actors and organizations in the Global South (Brabant & Patel, 2018). However, the interviewees suggested that, in reality, localization has been reduced to foreign organizations, particularly INGOs, 'localizing' their operations without local actors' active participation or involvement. One interviewee noted that localization, as it is currently being practised, focuses mostly on 'how institutions in the Global North are taking over development in countries in the Global South, often through the mobilization of local resources'.

African CSOs' understanding of 'shift the power'

The interview data suggest that, as is the case for the localization agenda, African CSOs have a general awareness but different interpretations of 'shift the power'. Interviewees repeatedly mentioned being aware of the increasing emphasis on 'shift the power', especially in development and humanitarian aid discourses, in recent years. They attributed their increasing level of awareness of 'shift the power' to global discourses on, for example, the decolonization of humanitarian action, racial injustice, and the acknowledgement of power imbalances in the aid sector (see e.g. Centre for Humanitarian Leadership & RINGO, 2022; Fellow et al., 2020). Speaking about the underlying factors driving 'shift the power' narratives, an interviewee mentioned that

> I think 'shift the power' is receiving attention because there is an outcry at different levels. I mean, in the West, we are having uprisings or movements like the Black Lives Matter [movement] and there is a lot of discussion on racial injustice. There is a whole movement around decolonization of development, and this is affecting the 'shift the power' discourse at different levels [...]. It is also affecting the discourse among INGOs, who are themselves looking at their own roles within the development system and looking at how they can decolonize themselves and their work.

The literature describes 'shift the power' as seeking to challenge and reform development aid practices and institutional philanthropy by advocating for a 'more equitable people-based development' (Bond, 2021; Hodgson, 2020; Knight, 2019, p. 5). The interviewees described their understanding of 'shift the power' in three ways, which are discussed below.

'Shift the power' as changing power dynamics

The consensus among the interviewees was that 'shift the power' is the effort to change existing power asymmetries in agenda setting and decision making in relationships between actors in the Global North and those in the Global South. The interviewees further explained that 'shift the power' focuses on changing the dominant narrative by giving local actors and organizations in the Global South a voice and full participation in deciding on how development interventions should be planned and implemented, arguing that the movement was born mainly because of 'epistemic injustices' such as discrimination based on characteristics like gender, social background, ethnicity, or race in the aid sector. For instance, an interviewee shared his perspective, noting that 'Shift the power is about the localization of decision-making processes [...] We should fight against injustices in the humanitarian aid system because our voices must be heard'. Another interviewee stated that 'shift the power' entails 'changing the dominant, top-down decision-making and agenda-setting process from the Global North to be more inclusive of voices of different stakeholders and allowing them to contribute to decision making on development priorities'.

Promoting local participation, ownership, and trust building with community members

In addition to the involvement of Southern-based organizations in decision-making processes, the consensus among interviewees was that 'shift the power' is about efforts aimed at promoting the ownership and local participation of the intended beneficiaries or community members in the development process. For example, one interviewee argued that 'shift the power' concerns making local people feel that they have ownership of what they are doing and ensuring that development targets those who are poor and unemployed. Another interviewee shared the following perspective:

> We need 'shift the power' because, over the years, we have seen that there is 'business as usual'. Humanitarian aid is not helping us move forward, and there is a need for a kind of modification in the whole process so that humanitarian aid can be able to make sense because as of now it is nonsense.

Interviewees further emphasized that 'shift the power' is about the need to build trust with community members; this trust, in turn, leads to increased community participation in CSOs' activities, which helps them to become sustainable organizations. An interviewee addressed this directly in saying that 'shift the power' 'has a lot to do with creating and enabling trust [...]. So, for us, it is about centring trust with community members in everything we do'.

Thus, 'shift the power' is about the direct involvement of community members in CSOs' operations and activities, which facilitates giving more power to the grassroots to make decisions regarding their development needs and priorities. Building trust with grassroots actors helps to enhance CSOs' organizational legitimacy and credibility. Thus, 'closeness to the grassroots', as phrased by an interviewee, is crucial in creating a perceived sense of acceptance and legitimacy. However, many interviewees added that building trust requires time and deliberate effort from development stakeholders, including governments and CSOs. The following interviewee statement sums up the connection among the trust building, legitimacy, and credibility arising from 'shift the power':

> 'Shift the power' is a question of trust building, which also increases our credibility and legitimacy as an organization in the areas in which we are working and also increases a sense of loyalty within the groups or communities you are serving.

Equal partnership between Southern-based organizations

Although 'shift the power' is usually framed around shifting the power dynamics between the Global North and South, the interviews strongly demonstrated that this also entails efforts by Southern-based CSOs operating at the national level not to reinforce existing power dynamics with their local counterparts, such as community-based organizations. Thus, according to the interviewees, 'shift the power' is not limited to only the relationships of donors and INGOs with their partners in the Global South – it also strongly emphasizes mutual relationships among Southern-based organizations. One interviewee explained that '"shift the power" is not only for Global North organizations, but even in the Global South, there are power imbalances in the way organizations at the national and local levels engage'. The interviewees also understood this notion as being about efforts to bridge the unequal power relationships between governments and CSOs in the Global South. According to some interviewees, many governments in the Global South wield enormous power in these relationships, mainly because of their ability to regulate CSOs' activities. Many governments use their regulatory powers against CSOs they perceive as 'threats', especially by restricting the civic space or limiting the environments where these CSOs can operate.

The role of African CSOs in promoting 'shift the power' and the localization agenda

Many interviewees mentioned that African CSOs, in their own capacities, have played active roles in promoting localization and 'shift the power' in the Global South. The analysis of the interview data suggests that the roles of African CSOs could be categorized into two categories: (1) engaging in advocacy and discussions and (2) carrying out implementation through projects and programmes.

Engaging in advocacy and discussions on 'shift the power'

The interview data suggest that African-based CSOs, including philanthropic organizations in Ghana, Nigeria, and Sierra Leone, have played active roles by engaging in advocacy and discussions on 'shift the power'. The interviewees mentioned that organizations such as WACSI have been at the forefront of discussions about the 'shift the power' movement or campaign in the West African region. For instance, speaking about their involvement in 'shift the power' discussions at the global and national levels, an interviewee stated, 'I was actually part of the forum that came up with the #ShiftThePower'. Southern-based organizations have been involved in promoting discussions about 'shift the power' through their work with global networks and projects that seek to change the power dynamics between the Global North and South, as illustrated in the following interview extract:

> We are having major programmes like the Reimagining INGO (RINGO) project of which WACSI is part [...] We want to work together with INGOs and partners in the Global South to take a critical look at transforming the way we do development to shift the power [...] Even in the technology space, we have organizations like TechSoup and WACSI that are part of the network pushing the agenda to get the big technology companies to invest more in supporting smaller organizations in the Global South, which all contributes to 'shift the power'.

Implementing the 'shift the power' narrative in projects and programmes

The analysis of the interview data suggests that some African CSOs have played a role in enhancing the 'shift the power' movement by incorporating it into their projects and programmes. For instance, some representatives of philanthropic organizations interviewed said that they had incorporated elements of 'shift the power', such as providing flexibility in funding arrangements (e.g. offering core funding or overhead) and the co-creation of project ideas with community members, into their programmes and projects. They argued that this had enhanced the operationalization of 'shift the power' at the local level. For instance, according to some interviewees, organizations such as the STAR-Ghana Foundation and the Newmont Ahafo Development Foundation have incorporated 'participatory grant-making processes' into their funding arrangements, meaning that they discuss needs and priorities with local actors, which feeds into their grant-making arrangements.

A similar sentiment was shared by a representative of the Kenyan Community Development Fund, who argued that their organization gives its grantees some flexibility with regard to funding arrangements and reporting requirements. More importantly, the interviewees reported that such organizations continue to develop relationships with their grantees and partners beyond their project cycles, as part of their efforts to learn and incorporate innovative mechanisms in grant making. This, the interviewees believed, has helped in shifting the power from the organization to their partners or grantees. An interviewee described how their organization had promoted or enhanced the 'shift the power' movement through grant making as follows:

> We have always adopted a participatory grant-making process as a foundation [...] We have been working with our partners in a modality I would call co-creation, where we sit down to discuss what their needs are and what the priorities should be. And so, you wouldn't see [us] as the usual grant maker, where the relationship ends with grants. We've been with our partners in the field and have used lessons from the field to revise our

grant-making cycle. So, it has been one of our responses of making grants more participatory, community-tailored, and responsive in nature, which contributes to shifting the power.

Challenges and opportunities around localization and 'shift the power' for African CSOs

Despite the contribution of African CSOs to promoting localization and 'shift the power', several constraints or challenges were found to hinder the ability of local actors to effectively drive change. In particular, engendering structural transformation in the aid sector requires CSOs in the Global South to become more transparent and accountable to their intended beneficiaries. According to many interviewees, the CSO sector in the Global South is a haven for embezzlement of donor funds, and many CSOs lack credibility, transparency, and accountability.

Additionally, the current North–South system has long been a financial safety net for CSOs in the Global South, often keeping organizations and staff afloat. This, in effect, has made Southern CSOs overly dependent on organizations in the Global North, limiting their leadership and capacity to be self-reliant, including the capacity to mobilize domestic resources. Many CSOs in the Global South have a long history of investing in building their capacities to access funding from INGOs and donors from the Global North, in the form of proposal writing and pitching. However, little effort from organizations in the Global South has been dedicated towards strengthening their organizational capacity to mobilize resources from their community using local fundraising tools and models. For instance, when asked about enhancing domestic resource mobilization efforts, an interviewee replied, 'We also have to grow our capacities to mobilize local resources'. According to this interviewee and many others, most CSOs have failed to make conscious efforts to invest in their capacity to mobilize domestic resources.

In addition, the political, legal, economic, and social environment within which African CSOs operate influences their ability to mobilize domestic resources. For example, an interviewee explained that an organization's geographical location determines how it can mobilize domestic resources. Compared with organizations with smaller networks, national organizations and organizations operating within a broader network have greater capacity and opportunity to reach and mobilize support and resources from larger stakeholders. Similarly, the legal and regulatory environment for giving and philanthropy in a country also affects organizations' opportunities to mobilize local resources towards shifting power to actors in the Global South.

Finally, African philanthropic organizations, including private foundations established by high-net-worth individuals and corporate organizations from the Global South, face numerous constraints and barriers that prevent them from fully realizing their potential to promote localization and 'shift the power'. These constraints include limited engagement between African philanthropic organizations and CSOs, insufficient resources for African philanthropic organizations to support many local organizations in promoting 'shift the power' narratives, and a lack of an enabling environment that fosters or promotes a local giving culture.

Despite these challenges identified by the interviewees as limiting their capacity to shift power and localize, key informants highlighted domestic resource mobilization as an avenue and opportunity for African CSOs to promote localization and to 'shift the power' to local actors. In the views of the interviewees, the potential contributions of domestic resource mobilization include the following:

Creating flexibility and autonomy for Southern-based organizations

Most of the interviewees asserted that the mobilization of domestic or local resources will create opportunities to diversify funding streams. In addition, it can help organizations address challenges associated with being overly dependent on external donor funding, such as revenue volatility and financial vulnerability. The interviewees argued that the flexibility created through mobilizing domestic resources will allow African organizations to become autonomous and independent in their relationships with donors. They will be able to use their domestic resources to implement projects and programmes that international donors are unwilling to fund. For instance, an interviewee explained that mobilizing domestic resources increases the ability of organizations to pay for their administrative expenses, overhead, and programmes that donors are unwilling to support. Another interviewee described this by stating that

> If Southern-based organizations mobilize domestic resources, I think it will show some diversity in their funding, meaning there are things you can do with some of the resources you have, and it gives them the flexibility to do some of the things they would like to do.

This helps organizations to focus on, and achieve, their institutional goals and their mission. In the words of one interviewee, 'Creating alternative resources gives you more leverage in achieving your objectives as an organization'.

Changing the power dynamic between the Global North and the Global South

The analysis of the interview data suggests that domestic resource mobilization has an enormous potential in terms of promoting 'shift the power' and localization by changing the power dynamics between the Global South and the Global North. The interviewees explained that the relationship has been unequal over the years mainly because of Southern-based organizations' resource dependency on their Northern counterparts. However, the mobilization of local resources by African CSOs creates opportunities for an equal or mutually interdependent relationship by reducing their resource dependence. Thus, mobilizing local resources in this way will help change the narrative because 'he who pays the piper dictates the tune', as an interviewee stated. In explaining how the mobilization of domestic resources will help 'shift the power', especially in terms of agenda-setting and decision-making processes, some interviewees expressed views similar to the following:

> Local resource mobilization by Southern-based organizations would help change the power dynamics because we would have equal partnerships. When you have a partner in the Global North coming to work with a partner in the Global South who is also coming not only with their knowledge, and their capacity, but also money, there will be more of an interdependent relationship than we currently have.

Promoting downward accountability and legitimacy

A recurrent theme across the interviews was that the mobilization of domestic resources has the potential to promote downward accountability, as Southern-based organizations will become more responsive to the needs of their constituents. Many interviewees explained that mobilizing domestic resources thus facilitates the development of stronger relationships between CSOs and their intended beneficiaries. For this reason, CSOs prioritize and become very responsive to the needs of their intended beneficiaries from whom they have mobilized resources, making the CSOs more accountable to these groups.

Our study also identified evidence suggesting a positive relationship between the mobilization of domestic resources and an organization's credibility and pragmatic legitimacy. For instance, interviewees mentioned that, given the challenges and difficulties associated with the mobilization of domestic resources, such as community apathy and lack of trust, if an organization can achieve this, it is an indication that the community values their contributions and that they can command 'local power'. Furthermore, some interviewees emphasized that an organization's legitimacy and worthiness with grassroots communities determine the extent to which the organization can mobilize domestic resources. These interviewees further maintained that legitimacy helps build trust with intended beneficiaries, which is crucial for organizational sustainability. In explaining how the mobilization of domestic resources leads to downward accountability and legitimacy, an interviewee stated,

> Local giving is not just a question about money. It is a question of increasing organizational credibility and legitimacy in the areas in which you are working and increasing a sense of loyalty within the groups [with which]

you are working. If someone is paying you to do something, that means they really value you, even if it is a small contribution.

Promoting community ownership

A more important theme that emerged from the interview data is that the mobilization of domestic resources such as volunteer support promotes community ownership through civic engagement and participation in CSOs' activities. Such engagement helps to give power to the grassroots, allowing community members to participate in decision-making processes, especially those of local CSOs, including community-based organizations. The mobilization of domestic resources therefore creates opportunities for community members to become co-investors rather than beneficiaries of CSOs' interventions, as explained by an interviewee: 'So, it [domestic resources] has a tendency to balance the power in the aid architecture, where citizens move from being recipients of CSOs' interventions [to] become co-investors in any initiative'. The effect is that it creates a sense of ownership and gives power over decision making and resource allocation to the community member supporters and volunteers.

Conclusion

This chapter set out to refocus the narrative around localization and 'shift the power' away from the Global North and towards the Global South by presenting African CSOs' perspectives, roles, challenges, and opportunities around the desired shift of power. The findings presented in this chapter have shown that, in the African context, the narratives of localization and 'shift the power' are framed and understood as building positive relationships among organizations, communities, other CSOs, and international partners, including INGOs. In addition, the findings highlight the significant roles played by African CSOs and the opportunities presented by domestic resources in terms of shifting power. The findings suggest that African CSOs have been active players in efforts to promote localization and 'shift the power' at the local level. CSOs in the Global South have been actively advocating for localization and 'shift the power' by incorporating elements of the 'shift the power' movement (e.g. providing flexibility in funding arrangements) into their project and programme implementation; we found this to be the case especially for African philanthropic organizations. Nonetheless, there is no enabling legal environment for African CSOs to drive and sustain these changes. Additionally, organizations in the Global South contend with internal limitations, such as the embezzlement of funds and a lack of credibility, transparency, and accountability, which restricts their capacity to shift power to the Global South. The current North–South system has long provided a financial safety net for many CSOs in the Global South, making them less self-reliant and limiting their capacity to invest in leadership and the mobilization of domestic resources.

On the basis of our findings, we conclude that global actors need to not only concentrate, discuss, and drive the agenda from the Global North; rather, these actors should direct their efforts towards facilitating organizations in the Global South to lead the charge for localization and shifting the power. Such an approach is required to avoid these notions leading to nothing more than 'a lot of nice aspirational language, but no real action and substantive systems change' (Cornish, 2020). Southern CSOs themselves also need to take more action to address the situation that keeps power with Northern NGOs/donors. This includes investing in capacity building to increase sustainability and mobilizing domestic resources.

For African CSOs to drive localization and 'shift the power', they must develop a clear understanding of the two concepts, join advocacy efforts around these ideas, and engage in movement building to propose concrete pathways for action. African philanthropic organizations should support local organizations by providing financial and non-financial resources for advocacy and social justice initiatives that seek to challenge existing power structures and invest in the local philanthropy infrastructure and capacity strengthening for local CSOs.

In shifting the conversation, there is also a need for African CSOs to create new kinds of inclusive and collaborative mechanisms based on solidarity, collaboration, and giving. This requires local CSOs to identify themselves and form umbrella organizations or coalitions to deliver development programmes and interventions. Finally, to enhance localization and the 'shift the power' movement, CSOs also need to strengthen their voices as key collaborators, innovators, and thought leaders. This revolves around the need for CSOs in the Global South to become more articulate and honest about the added value of their partnerships with donors.

References

Al-Abdeh, M., & Patel, C. (2019). 'Localising' humanitarian action: Reflections on delivering women's rights-based and feminist services in an ongoing crisis. *Gender & Development*, *27*(2), 237–252. https://doi.org/10.1080/13552074.2019.1615280.

Austin, L., Barreiro, J. L., Eshete, A. T., O'Neil, G., Shashaa, H., & Volynets, D. (2019). *Country-level financing solutions for local actors*. International Federation of Red Cross and Red Crescent Societies. Retrieved from: https://gblocalisation.ifrc. org/wp-content/uploads/2019/12/Humanitarian-Financing-for-Local-Actors-IFRC-Case-Studies-Final.pdf.

Barbelet, V., Davies, G., Flint, J., & Davey, E. (2021) *Interrogating the evidence base on humanitarian localisation: A literature study. HPG literature review*. London: ODI. Retrieved from: https://odi.org/en/publications/interrogating-the-evidence-base-on-humanitarian-localisation-a-literature-study.

BOND. (2021). *Catalysing locally-led development in the UK aid system*. London: Bond. Retrievedfrom: https://www.bond.org.uk/wp-content/uploads/2022/03/catalysing_locally-led_development_in_the_uk_aid_system.pdf

Brabant, V. K., & Patel, S. (2018). *Localisation in practice: Emerging indicators and practical recommendations*. Global Mentoring Initiative. Retrieved from: https://reliefweb.int/sites/reliefweb.int/files/resources/Localisation-In-Practice-Full-Report-v4.pdf.

Centre for Humanitarian Leadership & RINGO. (2022). *Transformation in the aid and development sector? Localisation*. Retrieved from: https://centreforhumanitarianleadership.org/wp-content/uploads/2021/12/Localisation45.pdf.

Charter 4 Change. (2015). *Charter for change: Localisation of humanitarian aid*. Retrieved from: https://charter4change.files.wordpress. com/2016/02/charter-for-change-july-20152.pdf.

Cornish, L. (2020). *Is it finally time for the localisation agenda to take off?* Retrieved from: https://www.devex.com/news/is-it-finally-time-for-the-localization-agenda-to-take-off-97323.

Emmens, B., & Clayton, M. (2017). *Localisation of aid: Are INGOs walking the talk?* START Network. Retrieved from: https://startnetwork.org/resource/localisation-aid-are-ingos-walking-talk.

Fellow, S., Paige, S., & Kotsiras, D. (2020). *Time to decolonise aid: Insights and lessons from a global consultation*. London, Peace Direct. Retrieved from: https://www.peacedirect.org/publications/timetodecoloniseaid/.

Hodgson, J. (2018). *#ShiftThePower: How are we doing? Reflections on two years of a hash-tag*. Retrieved from: https://globalfundcommunityfoundations.org/blog/shiftthepower-how-are-we-doing-reflections-on-two-years-of-a/.

Hodgson, J. (2020). Disrupting and democratising development: Community philanthropy as theory and practice. *Gender & Development*, *28*(1), 99–116. https://doi.org/10.1080/13552074.2020.1717214.

Honig, D., & Gulrajani, N. (2018). Making good on donors' desire to do development differently. *Third World Quarterly*, *39*(1), 68–84. https://doi.org/10.1080/01436597.2017.1369030.

Knight, B. (2019). *Systems to #ShiftThePower*. Johannesburg: GFCF. Retrieved from: https://globalfundcommunityfoundations.org/wp-content/uploads/2019/11/SystemsToShiftThePower.pdf

Pincock, K., Betts, A., & Easton-Calabria, E. (2021). The rhetoric and reality of localisation: Refugee-led organisations in humanitarian governance. *The Journal of Development Studies*, *57*(5), 719–734. https://doi.org/10.1080/00220388.2020.1802010.

RINGO. (2020). *The RINGO project. Re-imagining the INGO and the role of global civil society*. London: Rights CoLab. Retrieved from: https://rightscolab.org/ringo/.

Roepstorff, K. (2020). A call for critical reflection on the localisation agenda in humanitarian action. *Third World Quarterly*, *41*(2), 284–301. https://doi.org/10.1080/01436597.2019.1644160.

WACSI. (2021). *Localisation agenda, shift the power and African philanthropic models in Burkina Faso, Ghana, Nigeria and Senegal*. Accra: West Africa Civil Society Institute. Retrieved from: https://wacsi.org/localisation-agenda-shift-the-power-and-african-philanthropic-models-in-burkina-faso-ghana-nigeria-and-senegal/.

14

CONTRASTING GIFTING POSTURES IN A LOCAL GHANAIAN COMMUNITY

Are there lessons about African philanthropy?

Esi Eduafowa Sey and Justice Nyigmah Bawole

Introduction

The concept of African philanthropy is being explored in scholarly discourse as the future paradigm for financing development in African nations. Inherent in this discourse is the assumption that the philosophical ideals and values that underlie poor-to-poor gifting can be harnessed to finance development on the continent (Moyo & Ramsamy, 2014). It has been argued that gifting practices in African societies are an untapped resource for financing development (Moyo, 2011; Moyo & Ramsamy, 2014). Examples of cases in which Africans have pulled together to support each other have been cited to back this argument and highlight the untapped potential of African philanthropy. These examples include three from Kenya: the Westgate Mall attack, the 2007 election violence, and famine in some parts of the country; in each of these cases, Kenyans came together to raise resources, respond, and help those in need. Studies have established how African gifting practices are situated in a socio-cultural context in which 'it is assumed that acts of generosity among kinsfolk will be reciprocated in the short or long run' (Cobbah, 1987, p. 322).

Inherent in the discourse on African philanthropy as a model for financing development is the underlying assumption that poor-to-poor gifting practices can be transferred from their original context as informal, socio-cultural systems of support to a more formal, professionalized development-sector context. This assumption has not yet been fully explored and requires further research, especially in light of findings suggesting that, in the more formal context of non-governmental organization (NGO) projects and initiatives intended to harness local resources for local development, community members may be reluctant to give time, materials, or money and may adopt a posture of dependency and learned helplessness (Atibil, 2014; Fowler, 2000; Mati, 2017). The discourse

DOI: 10.4324/9781003241003-17

on using African philanthropy for Africa's development has not yet included a deep engagement with this possibility and its potential implications for efforts to use this approach to development in Africa.

To contribute to this body of literature, this chapter shares lessons from a largely unsuccessful effort in the Western Region of Ghana that attempted to transfer the gifting practices of pre-existing, community-based self-help associations to the context of a civic union where members would contribute to local development through more formalized structures. We begin by revisiting the conceptualization of African philanthropy. We then present the case, followed by the methods used in this study. Next, we present and discuss our findings. Finally, we share our concluding thoughts.

Conceptualizing African philanthropy for development

Several studies form the foundation of the discourse on the possibilities African gifting practices offer for financing development in Africa. These studies have revisited the notion of philanthropy as charity, arguing that depicting philanthropy as a top-down, altruistic phenomenon presents a limited and skewed perspective on philanthropy that excludes African gifting practices (Fowler & Mati, 2019; Mati, 2017; Moyo & Ramsamy, 2014; Osella et al., 2015; Rusega, 2011). This work suggests that African gifting practices, though not typically characterized by altruism, benevolence, and charity, also count as philanthropy.

Fowler and Mati (2019) have identified bias and incomplete comprehension in the dominant perspective of philanthropy as 'giving back' by elites, and Rusega (2011, p. 10) challenged the archetype of a philanthropic act as 'a donor, motivated by altruism and generosity, bestowing his or her largesse on a grateful supplicant'. The poor, Rusega (2011, p. 10) posited, 'are very active givers', whose help given to one another is not motivated by benevolence or even free choice, but by a sense of duty and recognition of the interdependency between themselves and their social networks. According to Mati (2017), African philanthropy includes a broad range of practices in which both the wealthy and the poor are equally involved. In line with this argument, researchers have posited that indigenous African giving could be a powerful force to alleviate poverty (Helly, 2013; Manji & O'Coill, 2002).

The above scholarly work has argued that, in African societies, gifting is normal and commonplace because of its rootedness in identity and relationships. Gifting is not simply an act; it is an expression of the values of community, interdependence, self-reliance, and solidarity, which are at the heart of societal life in these contexts. Further, gifting is not confined to the wealthy (Everatt et al., 2005); rather, it is a reciprocal exchange between peers, in which today's giver becomes tomorrow's receiver (Cobbah, 1987). In African society, 'at any one given time, one is either a philanthropist or a recipient of one kind or another of benevolence' (Moyo, 2011, p. 1).

However, other studies have reported cases where African communities have not shown active giving, a sense of community, or self-reliance. Mati (2017) found community members in South Africa giving their time and resources to each other but presenting themselves as helpless when relating to the NGOs and development actors that had come in to support community development. Likewise, Atibil (2014), observed that poor communities in sub-Saharan Africa gave their time, skills, money, and material goods to each other but simultaneously developed relationships of dependency with development actors.

In this chapter, we argue that the scholarly discussion on the potential of African philanthropy for funding development has not resolved the contrasting postures related to giving that are observable in African societies. We posit that, with the growing expectations about African philanthropy in the development of the continent, it is important for research to explore these contrasting postures and answer the question of why communities may be vibrant in their giving in informal socio-cultural contexts while simultaneously exhibiting dependency and apathy towards giving in more formalized contexts. In this chapter, we explore a case study that offers some answers to this question.

The case: the Stronger Together Civic Union

The lead author was introduced to the case we investigate here when she was contracted as a consultant by a civil society support organization, tasked with facilitating the strategic reflection processes of a civic union that was struggling to raise funds for its activities. For presentation in this chapter, we refer to this civic union as the 'Stronger Together Civic Union' (STCU), which is a pseudonym.

STCU was formed when, at the request of and with funding from an international NGO (INGO), a community member, Mr. Mensah (a pseudonym), brought together pre-existing, community-based self-help associations in a district in the Western Region of Ghana to form a civic union. The self-help associations comprised associations of market women, farmer-based organizations, students and youth, Christian mothers, distillers, bakers, fishmongers, hairdressers, tailors, dressmakers, commercial drivers, physically challenged persons, and teachers. These associations had been functioning vibrantly as self-help solidarity groups. They routinely supported each other through welfare contributions and small loans. They further initiated, resourced, and carried out activities to solve social problems, providing communal labour and financial and material contributions when needed. The values that motivated them to give their labour and resources were socio-cultural – notably, mutual dependency, self-help, and reciprocity. These self-help associations therefore appeared to be ideal actors for the role of a civic union.

A civic union is a voluntary group of local community leaders and residents who work together to improve the community and the lives of the civic union's members. Civic unions are motivated by patriotism and the values of public participation, accountability, and inclusion. In Ghana, civic unions may be registered as non-profit organizations by the Registrar General's Department and the Department of Social Welfare.

The INGO driving the establishment of STCU, which will be referred to as 'Helping Local Communities' (HLC) in this chapter, also provided funding for about 60 other civic unions to be formed across the region. The expectation was that the civic unions would provide their members with a formal mechanism to continue their self-help initiatives, participate in local governance, and engage with duty-bearers in their local assemblies. Members of the civic unions were expected to contribute their labour, as well as material and financial resources, to the activities of the civic union.

For the first few years of STCU's activities, HLC contributed to financing the civic union by providing funding for administrative costs and giving STCU members lunch packages and money to cover their transportation fares when they attended meetings. This support stopped when HLC's project came to an end after about five years. With the end of the HLC project, STCU began to experience funding challenges. Members were reluctant to pay their dues. They expected to still be given money or food when they attended meetings. This contrasted with the gifting posture maintained in their self-help associations, where they continued to actively give to meet each other's needs.

Mr. Mensah eventually decided to turn STCU into an NGO whose primary source of funding would be donors and INGOs rather than the membership of the civic union. The effort to transfer the giving practices of the self-help associations from their informal setting to the context of more formal development structures had proved unsuccessful. Community members had, it seemed, not transferred the values driving giving in their informal contexts to a more formal, professionalized development context.

Methods

We purposively selected this case because it provides an excellent example of the contrasting postures of community members in terms of giving in an informal setting and in a more formalized setting. We sought to understand why the effort to transfer giving practices from an informal context to a more formal one had been unsuccessful, with a particular focus on why community members were vibrant in their giving in their informal setting but not in the formalized setting that was provided to them. We did not approach the study with a theoretical framework, seeking instead to discover what would emerge from our findings. However, our initial questions were driven by our thinking that context was a key factor at play here. Our research question asked why community members displayed their values regarding giving in one context but not in another context, despite the fact that both contexts related to their welfare and development.

Our key informant was Mr. Mensah, with whom we conducted a semi-structured in-depth interview. We then returned to him to share our findings and validate them. We also held 18 interviews with randomly selected community members, comprising 10 men and 8 women. We approached this as an initial exploratory study, with the expectation that further, more in-depth research will follow. All persons interviewed provided informed consent.

Findings and discussion

As mentioned above, we began the interviews with the assumption that context was a key determinant of the contrasting gifting postures observed. We wanted to understand why STCU members had acted differently in the two contexts mentioned above. Specifically, we were interested in learning why they had acted in accordance with their values in one context but not in the other. However, the analysis of our discussions with Mr. Mensah and other community members shifted our attention away from context as the central issue and instead positioned trust at the centre of the community members' contrasting postures. By placing trust at the centre of our analysis, we found that STCU members were not acting inconsistently in giving vibrantly in one context but not in the other. They were, in fact, behaving consistently with their values, which, we discovered, revolve around trust.

We first explored the question of why STCU members had been reluctant to give their resources to their own civic union's activities. Mr. Mensah's immediate response seemed to suggest that the spirit of voluntarism had been eroded by HLC's provision of food and money when STCU members came for meetings. Mr. Mensah explained that HLC began by offering incentives when civic union members came for meetings; when the incentives stopped, the members no longer attended the meetings, which caused the collapse of several of the civic unions HLC had set up:

> The donors didn't start the process well. You see, they started by giving the community members food and T&T [travel and transportation from their homes to meeting points] when they came for meetings. So, of the 61 civic unions that they started, almost all collapsed when they left.
>
> *[Mr. Mensah]*

However, Mr. Mensah's response to a direct question on whether the spirit of voluntarism was dead among the community members suggested that the civic union's collapse following the withdrawal of HLC's incentives was not because of the erosion of a sense of voluntarism but rather because of the loss of trust. In response to our probing questions, Mr. Mensah emphasized that community members had truly been interested in and committed to the notion of the civic union. They had been energized by the idea of contributing their time and resources to the development of their communities. He emphasized that this interest and commitment still existed. He first drew examples from the past that pointed to community members' belief in the ideals of community and self-help and then explained that community members still held onto those beliefs:

> Look, in those days, there was no road from the communities to the district hospital. If a woman was in labour, community members would line up along the route from her house all the way to the hospital, and they would physically lift her from community to community till they got her to the hospital. There was a time, in 2005, [when] we wanted to build a school. We put up the school ourselves. We contributed money, got local building materials, and contributed our labour. So, as for the self-help spirit, it is still there.
>
> *[Mr. Mensah]*

He continued,

> It is very possible for community members to contribute to community development. In fact, it is a very fine idea. When we built the school, we got masons, electricians, and other technical people from the community. They did not take part in the manual labour, because they were bringing expertise. The rest of us brought our labour, some brought materials. Everybody was happy to help.
>
> *[Mr. Mensah]*

Mr. Mensah explained that these ideals were evident in the STCU experience:

> Community members were ready to give their time. They would come for meetings. They would work, share their time. But they were getting the T&T and so on, and they were expecting it to continue. It was like a contract – the project was bringing food and transport, and community members were bringing their time and energy.
>
> *[Mr. Mensah]*

The STCU members had not understood that these incentives were temporary. As a result, when HLC pulled out of the programme and the flow of these incentives ceased, an unspoken contract was broken, and the members experienced a betrayal of trust.

> When [HLC] exited, people noticed that there was no more T&T, so they stopped attending meetings. I blame the project managers – the INGO. They used those packages to attract people to their meetings. They got the large numbers for their meetings, forgetting that they were creating expectations in the people.
>
> *[Mr. Mensah]*

Again, although this relationship was never referred to as a 'contract', STCU members had entered into an implied contractual relationship of trust with HLC, in which the community members gifted their time and resources, and HLC reciprocated by providing these incentives. In this contract, following the norms of their socio-cultural gifting practices, the obligation to reciprocate was an unspoken agreement between giver and receiver. Ceasing the supply of the incentives was perceived by the STCU members as HLC reneging on their obligation to reciprocate in the relationship.

This raises questions about ownership and the extent to which STCU members saw the civic union's activities as their own. Why would the members expect to receive incentives for projects that were their own? Probing with this question led back to the issue of broken trust, but, this time, Mr. Mensah spoke of STCU members' experiences of broken trust in their relationships with traditional authorities, local-level government functionaries, and political leaders, as well as the impact of these experiences on their relationships with other external actors, such as INGOs.

In a statement that appeared to contradict his earlier comments, Mr. Mensah pointed out that, in spite of the continued existence of the spirit of voluntarism and self-help among community members, they would now be unlikely to give their time and resources to build a community project school, if asked. He explained that, since 1992, when Ghana shifted to democratic rule, community members' experiences with both political and traditional leaders had led to a deep distrust of these leaders. Mr. Mensah gave a number of examples of community members implementing projects with their own resources, only for political leaders to claim that they had carried out those projects.

He returned to an example we introduced earlier in this chapter – that of the school that community members had built – sharing an experience of broken trust that had followed. A politician (the District Chief Executive, the equivalent of the mayor) had approached Mr. Mensah after the community had built the school, attempting to persuade him to credit the school construction to the politician's personal efforts:

> When we finished the work, the DCE [District Chief Executive] sent someone to see me. He came and said, 'You spent 2,500 cedis to put up the school. Let's make it 150 million cedis, and I will give you something [a bribe or a 'cut']. Then we will indicate in the newspapers that the district assembly has put up a school at 150 million cedis'.
>
> *[Mr. Mensah]*

Mr. Mensah turned the offer down. However, he had later read in the national newspapers that the DCE had built that school for 150 million cedis. The DCE had gone ahead and informed the press that he had built the school that had actually been constructed by the local community with their own resources.

Mr. Mensah explained that, in those days, there was no social media and there was little access to the national media houses. As a result, he had been unable to refute the claim in the newspapers.

Instances like this one had left community members with a deep distrust of all external development actors, including INGOs, and of local government officials. Although they still valued self-help and mutual assistance, they refused to express or apply these values in relation to such actors, as they could not trust that their efforts would not be exploited. This was confirmed by an artisan man interviewed as part of the study:

> When you do the work, the politicians will say that they did it. If a community will work and a politician will come and say he did the work with his own money, why will we worry ourselves to do anything?
>
> *[artisan man]*

Community members had also lost trust in the traditional authorities. A woman fish processor observed that this distrust resulted from a perception of their chiefs as politically aligned:

> Apathy is a huge thing here. Previously, when you beat the gong-gong,[1] everyone would come out. But now, the communities are polarized. If they see a chief as belonging to political party X, those of the opposition party will not support what he wants us to do, so they will not come out.
>
> *[woman fish processor]*

Community members did not feel they could trust the leaders of their local assemblies. A woman vegetable seller explained that there was poor accountability in community projects carried out by the assembly and that planned projects were often not implemented:

> They are not rendering proper accounts. We want them to report to us how the monies have been spent, but this is not happening. In the former days, the traditional authorities did not account[2] to us, but at least we could see the evidence of the use of our money. The assembly doesn't account to us, and also the projects we contribute to are not carried out.
>
> *[woman vegetable seller]*

Mr. Mensah explained that, in the face of their distrust of politicians, duty-bearers, and traditional leaders, community members had adopted a business transaction approach to local development projects. Because they could not trust that they would be acknowledged for their contributions to community projects, they demanded immediate compensation for their efforts. An element of economic challenge was also evident, causing community members to demand to be compensated for services they would have offered for free in the past. The end result was that, although community members would previously have offered their time and resources based on trust, now they were replacing that trust with a business transaction mindset in which resources that they would formerly have offered for free were being packaged transactionally and costed accordingly.

The combination of the above experiences became evident in STCU members' posturing. Their past experiences had caused them to distrust politicians, duty-bearers (local assemblies), and traditional leaders. They now extended that distrust to HLC, the INGO that came in to support them by introducing the civic union structure. Thus, although the civic union belonged to them in principle, they still held the fear that their efforts could someday be claimed by HLC as its own, or that they would be let down in other ways. They adopted a business transaction approach to their interactions with HLC and required compensation for their participation in the civic union in the form of meals and money.

Conversely, STCU members continued to give freely within their self-help associations, where they felt they could trust each other. A community member indicated that, in her relationships in her social networks, she could trust that the recipients of her gifts would hold themselves accountable to her. This is because members of her social network all follow the same norms.

> If I help my neighbour to send her son to school, from time to time, she will come back and tell me how he is doing. She will always remind everyone that I was the one who helped to send her son to school. I don't have to force her; she knows she has to do it.
>
> *[woman community member]*

Reciprocity, accountability, and trust mark relationships between givers and recipients in the community setting. This stands in sharp contrast to the local government system, which was intended to provide mechanisms for accountability to community members. Community members have found that this system cannot be trusted to provide them with accountability, and they are thus reluctant to contribute their resources to this system.

Thus, in their simultaneous active giving and seeming apathy, depending on the context, STCU members were reflecting the centrality of trust to the values of community, interdependence, self-reliance, and solidarity, on which local society is built. On the face of it, STCU members appeared to be displaying two different sets of values in the two different contexts – their self-help associations and the civic union. However, they were actually consistently expressing the centrality of trust in their giving practices. For these people, trust is related to reciprocity. In their self-help groups, the members were assured of reciprocity and could therefore freely give to each other. In the civic union, however, their experience of the absence of reciprocity had led to broken trust and caused them to adopt a transactional approach to their giving, or not to give at all.

Conclusion: lessons learned about African philanthropy

As African philanthropy is explored as a paradigm for financing development in Africa, the scholarly discourse must also engage with the contrasting postures that may be observed in the gifting practices of local communities – notably, vibrant giving in socio-cultural support systems and apathy in the more formal, professionalized settings of donor and NGO development projects. The STCU case suggests that this apathy may not be due to an erosion of the spirit of voluntarism and self-help in local communities and that it is not a contradictory or paradoxical phenomenon. Instead, it is reflective of the centrality of trust to the gifting practices of local communities.

Our analysis of this case has shown that trust is central to the values that drive gifting in the socio-cultural support systems of local communities. When local communities do not trust the organizations that seek to support them socioeconomically, they may adopt a posture of apathy and dependency that contrasts with the vibrant giving in their socio-cultural support systems. Past experiences with local assemblies, traditional authorities, politicians, and INGOs have not provided community members with the assurance that they can trust these individuals and entities with their time, money, and labour. The values of mutual dependency and self-help that underlie giving in local communities are grounded in trust. When trust is absent, giving may be withheld. To successfully harness the values behind African philanthropy for financing development projects and programmes, trust-building mechanisms must be explored and built into the design of these initiatives.

Notes

1 A gong-gong can be described as a local loudspeaker. It comprises two pieces of metal that are struck together by a gong-gong beater to attract the attention of community members when a public/community announcement is about to be made. In the past, the gong-gong was a rallying cry for community members to join community labour activities.

2 This participant spoke in her local language, Nzema, and we translated her statements into English. Regarding the word 'account', terms such as 'accountability', 'transparency', and 'governance' have become part of the local parlance.

References

Atibil, C. L. (2014). Philanthropic foundations and civil society in Sub-Saharan Africa. In E. Obadare (Ed.), *The handbook of civil society in Africa* (pp. 457–475). New York, NY: Springer. https://doi.org/10.1007/978-1-4614-8262-8_25.

Cobbah, J. A. M. (1987). African values and the human rights debate: An African perspective. *Human Rights Quarterly*, *9*(3), 309–331.

Everatt, D., Habib, A., Maharaj, B., & Nyar, A. (2005). Patterns of gifting in South Africa. *Voluntas: International Journal of Voluntary and Nonprofit Organizations*, *16*(3), 275–291. https://doi.org/10.1007/s11266-005-7725-z.

Fowler, A. (2000). *Civil society, NGDOs and social development: Changing the rules of the game* (Occasional Paper, No. 1). Geneva, Switzerland: UNRISD. Retrieved from: http://hdl.handle.net/10419/148834.

Fowler, A., & Mati, J. M. (2019). African gifting: Pluralising the concept of philanthropy. *VOLUNTAS: International Journal of Voluntary and Nonprofit Organizations, 30*(4), 724–737. https://doi.org/10.1007/s11266-018-00079-z

Helly, D. (2013). *Philanthropy in Africa and the future of EU's development policies: Useful synergies?* (RSCAS policy paper 2013/05). Fiesole, Italy: European University Institute. Retrieved from: https://cadmus.eui.eu/bitstream/handle/1814/28978/RSCASPP_2013_05.pdf?sequence.

Manji, F., & O'Coill, C. (2002). The missionary position: NGOs and development in Africa. *International Affairs, 78*(3), 567–584. https://doi.org/10.1111/1468-2346.00267.

Mati, J. M. (2017). Philanthropy in contemporary Africa: A review. *Voluntaristics Review, 1*(6), 1–100. https://doi.org/10.1163/24054933-12340014.

Moyo, B. (2011). Transformative innovations in African philanthropy. *The Bellagio Initiative on the Future of Philanthropy and Development in the Pursuit of Human Wellbeing, Commissioned Paper.* Retrieved from: https://opendocs.ids.ac.uk/opendocs/bitstream/handle/20.500.12413/3718/Bellagio-Moyo.pdf?sequence=1.

Moyo, B., & Ramsamy, K. (2014). African philanthropy, pan-Africanism, and Africa's development. *Development in Practice, 24*(5–6), 656–671. https://doi.org/10.1080/09614524.2014.937399.

Rusega, G. A. (2011). Civil society and grassroots philanthropy. In M. Edwards (Ed.), *The Oxford handbook of civil society* (pp. 1–13). New York, NY: Oxford University Press. https://doi.org/10.1093/oxfordhb/9780195398571.013.0036.

PART 4

Learning new roles for the North

15

LOCALIZING HUMANITARIAN KNOWLEDGE MANAGEMENT

A call for pragmatic robust action

Femke Mulder

Introduction: localizing humanitarian knowledge management

There are growing calls in the humanitarian sector for greater localization and more participation in aid (Barbelet, 2018). In response, Northern humanitarian organizations are increasingly collaborating with Southern ones in an attempt to deliver aid that is localized, participatory, and inclusive. This chapter looks at knowledge management (KM) for humanitarian aid in the context of such joint efforts, focusing on 'Local Knowledge' as an artefact constructed for the purpose of aid project management. On the basis of three case studies, the chapter shows how the construction of 'Local Knowledge' is shaped by the power imbalances that characterize North–South collaborations. These power imbalances manifest, for example, as KM guidance only being issued 'top down' and KM accountability only being enforced 'bottom up'. The chapter shows how power operates through KM metrics, spaces, and artefacts during the KM process to filter and transform local knowledges into 'Local Knowledge'. What this means in practice is that 'Local Knowledge' is an artefact tailored to the priorities and perspectives of those in positions of power (Northern organizations). The chapter argues that, as a result, North–South collaborations tend to organize aid around local action *but not local knowledges*, in spite of intentions and appearances. In each case study, the chapter shows why this is a problem and what the implications are for the effectiveness and social justice outcomes of aid.

In terms of effectiveness, arguments for localization and participation broadly hold that aid that is co-designed and delivered by local actors through local networks *and on the basis of local knowledges* is faster, better targeted to local needs, and more sustainable, compared with aid that is primarily designed and led by 'outsiders'. In terms of social justice, arguments tend to centre on the emancipatory or 'empowering' effects of localization and participation, such as their potential

DOI: 10.4324/9781003241003-19

to platform the voices of marginalized groups in aid (Mulder, 2020a). This chapter argues that, because North–South collaborations organize aid around 'Local Knowledge' as opposed to *local knowledges*, these envisioned gains in effectiveness tend not to materialize. Furthermore, because 'Local Knowledge' is the product of established power relationships, its potential to improve the social justice outcomes of aid is limited. Instead, as shown in this chapter, 'Local Knowledge' often plays an important role in legitimizing and reproducing the unequal status quo.

Here, this phenomenon is explored through the lens of *structuration* (Giddens, 1979). Structuration is the process through which individual actions and the wider social structure interconnect to reproduce – or change – the status quo. The chapter explores how the power hierarchies, norms, and institutions that characterize North–South collaborations (social structure) shape KM metrics, spaces, and artefacts. It then examines how these, in turn, influence individual KM actions and decisions in the construction and use of 'Local Knowledge'. Structuration is shaped by power (e.g. Stones, 2009) and greatly affects the social justice implications of KM (or *data justice*, described below). On the basis of this analysis, the chapter suggests an alternative approach to organizing humanitarian KM, recommending three complementary KM strategies based on pragmatic robust action to foster more horizontal North–South aid relationships. This approach has the potential to achieve the goal of localization – the centring of local action informed by local knowledges in aid.

This chapter contributes to this volume's aim of 'starting from the South' by providing direction on how to reimagine and reshape roles and relationships between Northern and Southern aid organizations and redress problematic power structures in aid. More specifically, the chapter offers (1) an analysis of why KM processes in North–South collaborations often decentre local knowledges; (2) an overview of how this decentring affects the effectiveness, efficiency, and social justice outcomes of aid; and (3) an outline for an alternative approach to organizing KM. The remainder of this chapter is structured as follows: It starts by unpacking three core constructs that underpin the case studies, before moving on to outline the research methods used, followed by a description of the cases on which this chapter is based. Then, the chapter presents a discussion section, which describes pragmatic robust action strategies for KM as a potential way forward.

Background: unpacking three core constructs

This section presents the theoretical background for the case studies introduced below. It unpacks three core constructs that are important to understanding humanitarian KM, especially in the context of aid initiatives intended to be localized, participatory, and inclusive.

'Local Knowledge' versus local knowledges

As outlined above, one of the central constructs in humanitarian KM is 'Local Knowledge'. 'Local Knowledge' is an artefact constructed by aid workers for the purpose of informing and justifying humanitarian decisions and actions. However, 'Local Knowledge' differs from what local people actually know and think about things such as local hazards or local needs. What local people actually know and think depends on their context-specific learning over time. Given that differently situated local people will have undergone different learning trajectories, they will 'know' the local situation differently and, as a result, have different local priorities and political views. This paper, therefore, uses the term 'local knowledges' (plural) to refer to these multiple – and often conflicting – local ways of knowing. Furthermore, local knowledges are not set in stone but instead evolve over time as a result of local debates and learning through trial and error. 'Local Knowledge', by contrast, generally denotes a knowledge base that is static and internally coherent. It obscures how different local social realities lead to different ways of knowing and conceals the plural, ever-changing, and conflict-laden nature of local knowledges.

The knowledges that shape knowledge management

The previous section already hints at the fact that KM is integral to the power dynamics that shape North–South collaborations, as this chapter aims to show. KM refers to the process of selecting data and turning it into information to inform decision making in the context of a project, initiative, or issue. The outcomes of such decisions inform learning, which, in turn, shapes knowledge (see Figure 15.1). Although they are often used interchangeably in daily speech, 'knowledge', 'information', and 'data' are distinct. The term 'data' refers to basic facts, whereas 'information' refers to data put into context. 'Knowledge', in turn, refers to the understanding and skill needed to strategically use information. Knowledge is necessary for making decisions based on information, but also for identifying which data are relevant and valuable to the issue at hand, as well as for organizing and contextualizing these data into information (Mulder et al., 2016). Thus, *the knowledge that is the input to KM shapes the knowledge that is the output of KM*. The case studies described in this chapter show how the design and use of KM metrics, spaces, and artefacts in North–South collaborations are primarily shaped by Northern knowledges and how, as a result, 'Local Knowledge' (as a KM artefact) gets tailored to Northern perspectives and priorities. This has social justice implications.

Knowledge management through the lens of data justice

'Data justice' is a useful construct for analysing how KM affects the social justice outcomes of aid. A data justice lens can be used to evaluate KM initiatives (post hoc or during the design phase) to identify negative implications for social justice so as to prevent or address them (Mulder, 2020a). Heeks (2017) identifies five dimensions of data justice, which have been plotted against the KM process in Figure 15.1. At a meta level, *structural data justice* looks at how structuration in the context of KM affects the social justice outcomes of an intervention. This

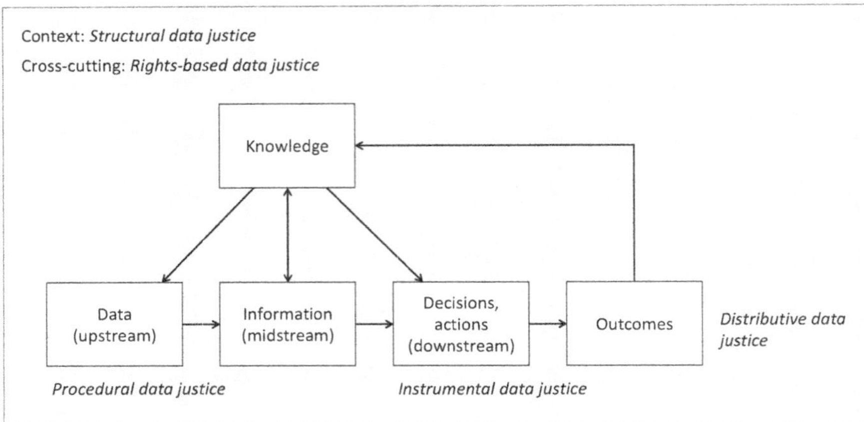

FIGURE 15.1 The process of knowledge management and the five dimensions of data justice (Heeks, 2017; Mulder, 2020a).

is the main focus of the case studies presented in this chapter, although they also touch on the other dimensions of data justice: *rights-based data justice*, which looks at how KM processes interlink with data and information rights; *procedural data justice*, which looks at fairness in how data are selected and turned into information; *instrumental data justice*, which looks at fairness in how information is used in decision making; and finally, *distributive data justice*, which looks at fairness in the overall outcomes of KM.

Case studies: knowledge management in North–South collaborations

As outlined above, this chapter is based on case study research, which entails analysing a real-life phenomenon (e.g. humanitarian KM) in depth and within its real-world context on the basis of one or more cases (Eisenhardt, 1989; Yin, 1981). The case studies presented in this chapter are based on four months of fieldwork in Nepal conducted from 2015 to 2017 and three months of fieldwork in Ethiopia conducted in 2018. The primary research method used during the fieldwork was organizational ethnography, which is a form of qualitative social research that focuses on organizations and their processes of organizing (Ybema et al., 2009). This methodological approach entailed developing data and information using observation, field notes, unstructured and structured interviews, and document and media reviews. The data and information were later analysed thematically (Attride-Stirling, 2001). To facilitate cross-case analysis, the cases were chosen from very different humanitarian contexts: a sudden-onset disaster (earthquakes), a slow-burning crisis (drought), and a conflict setting. The three cases were selected as typical examples of North–South collaborations that aim for localization and participation in aid. In all three cases, aid that was intended to be localized, participatory, and inclusive was delivered through relationships that were marked by stark power hierarchies. The following sections present the three cases to illustrate how this set-up affected the effectiveness and efficiency of KM and to discuss the implications of this for social justice.

Why knowledge management for local aid is often not localized: a focus on hierarchies and knowledge management metrics

The first case study looks at KM for a locally led humanitarian aid project in the context of a slow-burning crisis: the ongoing drought in Ethiopia (2016 to present) and the resulting food crisis. This case study illustrates the role aid hierarchies and KM metrics play in the construction of 'Local Knowledge' as an artefact for project management. The humanitarian project ran from 2016 to 2020 and facilitated the community-based management of acute malnutrition. The project was initiated by a global non-governmental organization (NGO) and funded by a Northern donor. It was designed in close partnership with the federal government of Ethiopia and district-level government bodies. The project was managed by the NGO's country headquarters in Ethiopia, but actual day-to-day implementation was led by the NGO's district-level field offices. All Ethiopia-based NGO staff (except for the executive director) were Ethiopian, as were all government officials involved in the project. Although this structure was described as a 'partnership', the relationships were strictly vertical: Community mobilizers reported to the NGO field staff, who, in turn, reported to the country headquarters, who reported to the Northern headquarters, who reported to the donor. Thus, accountability within the project ran in only one direction. This meant that project data and information were primarily directed upwards and tailored to Northern audiences. For example, all written project documentation was in English (rather than in Amharic or local languages).

Furthermore, although the project materials had been designed in a participatory manner with local government actors, power imbalances (and local strategic interests) meant that these local actors had often reflected back to NGO staff what they thought these external actors wanted to hear. The global NGO involved was well known for its focus on gender. The local officials also knew that the federal government of Ethiopia wanted to mainstream gender in national nutrition strategies. Thus, keen to be part of the project, local government actors made sure to stress the link between household-level gender inequalities and malnutrition in the target areas for the envisioned project. They did not suggest factors that fell outside the NGO's remit. For example, they did not mention the ongoing threat to food security posed by intercommunal tensions, occasional violence, the political situation, or climate change. Discussions with local people during the fieldwork for this case study showed that local power struggles over access to water disproportionately affected more marginalized hamlets. However, this highly contentious local political issue was also not raised in consultations with the NGO. During focus group discussions, local officials tailored the local knowledge they put forward to the interests of the external actors on whom they depended for the project to go ahead. To be clear, gender *did* play an important role in shaping nutritional inequalities at the household level. The problem was not that the 'Local Knowledge' constructed for project management was 'wrong', but rather that it was partial and incomplete.

Despite the incomplete nature of this KM artefact, it informed the design of project materials, which codified the criteria and metrics for KM. After these metrics had been established (before the start of the project), they were set in stone. Because of power imbalances, community mobilizers and field staff had limited scope to amend the criteria during the project. The role of these actors was merely to deliver and report based on the criteria – not to change them. This affected the effectiveness and efficiency of KM. Both the 'problem' and the 'solution' had already been determined in advance – and largely from the outside. As a result, local NGO staff could not accommodate new local insight or evolving local debates in KM. Furthermore, there was little scope for local trial-and-error experimentation. As a consequence, KM's potential to foster local learning and knowledge exchange – between different project field offices, for instance – was severely constrained.

The way 'Local Knowledge' was constructed and used in this project also had implications for the social justice outcomes of KM. It obscured the role power inequalities played in the creation of food insecurity, other than those related to gender at the household level. Thus, important root causes of malnutrition were not officially recognized or addressed. This meant, for example, that more marginalized hamlets continued to struggle disproportionately with water shortages. In this project, KM did not lead to aid management decisions that benefitted those who were most in need (*instrumental data justice*). Instead, it obscured the structural inequalities that the project did not address and legitimized these decisions on the basis that they were informed by 'Local Knowledge'. Thus, KM did little to change the harmful status quo (*structural data justice*).

Why knowledge management for local aid is often not participatory: a focus on hierarchies and knowledge management spaces

The second case study looks at KM at a district-level Emergency Operations Centre (EOC) in the south of Ethiopia during the humanitarian response to the 2018 Guji-Gedeo displacement crisis. This case study illustrates how hierarchies can lead to the marginalization of vital local knowledges in KM spaces, resulting in a breakdown in trust and collaboration. In 2018, over 800,000 people had become internally displaced in Gedeo and West Guji as a result of intercommunal violence (Mulder, 2020b). To coordinate the humanitarian response, the National Disaster Risk Management Commission of the federal government of Ethiopia rolled out two field-level EOCs – one in Gedeo and one in West Guji. It did so in partnership with the United Nations (UN) Office for the Coordination of Humanitarian Affairs. The purpose of the EOCs was to facilitate coordination between local bureaucrats and the national/global humanitarian response. The external responders depended on local bureaucrats for both humanitarian access and official information about the internally displaced people (IDPs). Therefore, the participation of local bureaucrats in the EOC knowledge spaces was essential to the success of the humanitarian mission. However, hierarchies inadvertently got in the way of creating a genuinely participatory KM space.

The federal risk managers and humanitarians at the EOC were all on short-term assignments lasting from one to four months. They were thus largely disconnected from the local people, the local language, the local media, and local knowledges. Even the majority of Ethiopian humanitarians had been flown in temporarily from elsewhere in the country. As was the case in the aid project described in the first case study, the EOCs were embedded in a set of deeply hierarchical structures. The federal National Disaster Risk Management Commission and the humanitarian agencies were vertical organizations that operated with (or through) the UN's Humanitarian Cluster System. This system organizes aid at global, national, and local levels by thematic focus (e.g. food, shelter, and health care). The federal risk managers and humanitarians at the EOC received their guidance, standards, and instructions through this system and from the federal government – not from 'the field'. Reporting and accountability, by contrast, ran in the opposite direction (from 'the field' to national/global headquarters). This meant that global/national standards determined the priorities, criteria, and processes for KM at the EOC. This had the unintended effect of marginalizing local knowledges. For example, all communication and reporting at the EOC was in English, which excluded representatives of the IDPs and host populations. It also disadvantaged local bureaucrats for whom English was their third or fourth language (*procedural data justice*).

The local bureaucrats were the only participants present at the EOC who were not embedded in federal or humanitarian hierarchies. Both federal risk managers and humanitarians had been operating through these interconnected vertical structures for a significant part of their professional lives and shared years of context-specific learning. Therefore, in spite of their obvious differences and disagreements, they broadly shared the same professional way of 'knowing' humanitarian crises, which informed their approach to KM. The local bureaucrats did not share this way of 'knowing' disasters and, as a result, did not present 'the right take' or focus on 'the correct priorities' in their contributions. For example, the issue of whether IDPs should be returned to their villages of origin was approached by the federal risk managers and humanitarians through the lens of global/national standards, which centre on the importance of the voluntariness, safety, and dignity of return. Local bureaucrats, by contrast, approached this issue through the lens of local livelihoods and sustainability, stressing the pressure on the local economy and the need for agricultural work to resume. Because it was not possible to make space for alternative criteria or framings, this clash between knowledges could not be accommodated. The bureaucrats' local knowledge was translated and filtered during KM to fit what a leading coordinator called 'the correct narrative from the field' to inform decision makers. Confidentially, participants from both sides expressed the view that their counterparts were operating in bad faith. The local bureaucrats increasingly disengaged from the EOCs. They began to organize the IDPs' return to their home areas without informing the humanitarians or federal risk managers. They also started to slow-walk the creation and sharing of official information on local IDP numbers on which the EOCs depended. The end result was a complete breakdown of trust and collaboration. KM rendered invisible the power struggle that increasingly undermined the effectiveness of the intervention, hiding (and therefore reproducing) the problems with the status quo in aid relationships (*structural data justice*).

Why knowledge management for local aid is often not inclusive: a focus on hierarchies and knowledge management artefacts

In 2015, Nepal was struck by two major earthquakes occurring in rapid succession. As a result, nearly 9,000 people lost their lives, and 3.5 million people became homeless (Mulder, 2020a). This third case study looks at two initiatives led by local civil society organizations (CSOs) that supported the global/national humanitarian response through KM. The goal of these initiatives was to ensure that the response was informed by local knowledges. This case illustrates how hierarchies can affect local aid workers' ability to include the perspectives of more marginalized groups in these efforts, focusing specifically on the design and use of KM artefacts.

The first initiative was a participatory technology project that was designed by Nepali developers in Kathmandu and rolled out within days of the first earthquake. The project was an interactive online map showing crisis reports for different affected areas in the country. The map was populated and kept up to date through crowdsourcing – local disaster-affected people could report local needs through a webform or using a toll-free telephone number. The CSO leading the initiative processed this information to make it accessible to local volunteers, global humanitarian organizations (e.g. UN agencies), and national government actors (e.g. the military). The second initiative was a participatory KM project led by two Nepali CSOs that specialized in accountability and local interventions. This initiative set out to close the feedback loop between disaster-affected people, humanitarian responders, and government officials. To this end, the project recruited local focal contacts, organized community meetings, and produced interactive radio shows. Later, it also conducted large-*n* surveys in disaster-affected areas. Global NGOs and the national government of Nepal quickly became interested in this initiative. To increase the impact of their efforts (and obtain funding) the CSOs leading the initiative agreed to have it incorporated into an inter-agency common feedback project funded by a major Northern government donor.

Both initiatives relied on standardized templates for selecting, recording, and processing data and information. Given that Northern and Nepali government bodies were important funders and end-users of the KM outputs, the templates were designed with these audiences in mind. This meant that what data mattered – and how it should be transformed into information – was determined a priori and on the basis of external perspectives and priorities. Local perspectives and priorities that did not fit the template were filed away as 'miscellaneous' or not recorded at all. During the KM processes, local knowledges were filtered (to select 'relevant' data), transformed (to fit a template), translated (into Nepali and English), and interpreted (by non-local people) to become 'Local Knowledge' for use in informing decision making.

The most intense filtering occurred at the first stage of the KM processes. The first initiative was only accessible to people who (1) knew of the initiative and (2) had the skills, hardware, and connectivity needed to contribute. This automatically excluded digitally and informationally marginalized groups, such as those living in remote rural areas. The second initiative proactively tried to reach these groups. However, a lack of funds meant that they did not reach people without radios or those living far from the village centres, where community meetings were held. Northern partners did nothing to help or support efforts to be more inclusive and participatory. In fact, they (inadvertently) disincentivized such efforts by pushing for large-*n* surveys and 'big data' approaches, which they regarded as more objective and therefore more valuable compared with small-*n* interpretative approaches to KM. In spite of the CSOs' best efforts, the result was that only relatively privileged people could use these KM initiatives to share their needs and perspectives or push for accountability. Furthermore, people in a digitally and/or informationally underprivileged position had no access or control over the 'Local Knowledge' that was created for their regions (i.e. about them), nor did they have any control over how their needs and priorities were represented in this information (*rights-based data justice*). As a result, the KM initiatives did not help humanitarian responders target those who were most in need or hear their voices. This meant that the outcomes of aid were not as effective or equitable as they could have been (*distributive data justice*).

Indeed, an important problem for humanitarian KM is that Northern actors are sometimes (genuinely or strategically) oblivious to local inequalities and related vulnerabilities (Hilhorst, 2018) and are happy to accept the voices of local privileged people as those of the community. Because of power imbalances, they then incentivize KM that renders local inequalities invisible, hiding (and therefore reproducing) existing patterns of vulnerability (*structural data justice*).

A potential way forward

What is needed

Each of these three case studies has provided an example of how 'Local Knowledge' is, to a significant extent, the product of the power hierarchies that characterize North–South collaborations. The case studies have illustrated how power inequalities influence the design and use of KM metrics, spaces, and artefacts and shown how, as a consequence, local knowledges get filtered and transformed during the KM process to become 'Local Knowledge'. This 'Local Knowledge' is an important artefact for aid project management, as it both informs and legitimizes decision making. However, it is an artefact that is tailored to Northern knowledges. As a result, it encompasses Northern 'blind spots' related to the local inequalities and broader power imbalances that mark the status quo in aid. What this means is that, when 'Local Knowledge' is used in project management (e.g. in decision making or evaluation), it renders invisible key problems with this status quo, thereby effectively validating existing hierarchies (*structural data justice*). The case studies presented above have shown that this is unhelpful because it hinders the organization of KM in a manner that is genuinely localized, participatory, and inclusive. The case studies have also illustrated how a failure to make space for a plurality of competing perspectives and evolving debates makes KM less effective – and can even lead to a complete breakdown in collaboration. The remainder of this chapter focuses on a potential way forward, suggesting pragmatic robust action strategies as an alternative way of organizing humanitarian KM and facilitating more horizontal ways of working.

The rationale for pragmatic robust knowledge management

A pragmatist perspective is based on the idea that there are no 'one-size-fits-all' solutions in humanitarian aid. Instead, pragmatist KM values context-specific experimentation for identifying approaches that work locally. The perspective centres on debate and the exchange of ideas as core methods for evaluating local strategies and experiments. A pragmatist perspective sees KM first and foremost as a process for learning, problem solving, and action. This perspective is underpinned by the notion that knowledges are not fixed, but rather evolve over time as people try out new approaches and evaluate their usefulness through debate. Pragmatist KM aims to capture and build on these evolving knowledges. For that reason, it rejects developing KM metrics and criteria a priori and then setting them in stone. It also rejects siloed problem solving or driving KM in a centralized, top-down manner. Instead, the approach aims to create KM spaces for local trial-and-error learning and to foster debates among actors in different contexts. Therefore, pragmatist KM values *decentralized, multi-sited, and horizontal* ways of working.

This chapter recommends an approach to KM that is not just pragmatic, but also robust. A robust approach to KM prioritizes *openness* and *flexibility*. Its focus is on achieving short-term humanitarian KM goals while preserving the ability to change KM criteria and metrics in the long term. The approach is also robust in that it draws on – *and contributes to* – multiple (conflicting) knowledges, as opposed to a single coherent knowledge base. This means that it adds value to different evaluatory frameworks. The implication of this is that KM can – *and should* – be assessed on the basis of multiple different metrics and criteria for success. Indeed, the approach rejects evaluating KM on the basis of one common standard or one common set of metrics. As a result, with pragmatic robust KM, participants do not need to tailor their KM efforts to Northern audiences or the national government. The goal of pragmatic robust KM is to work in a manner that is not directive, prescriptive, or driven towards consensus.

However, the extent to which the approach is able to foster horizontal exchanges between different knowledges depends on its implementation. The following paragraphs outline three complementary pragmatic robust action strategies for fostering more localized, participatory, and inclusive forms of KM. Given the mutually constitutive nature of KM, aid relationships, and outcomes (*structural data justice*), these pragmatic robust KM strategies have the potential to lead to more egalitarian North–South aid relationships.

Pragmatic robust knowledge management in practice

The main purpose of this chapter is to explore new roles for Northern humanitarian actors wishing to support the centring of local knowledges in local aid. Having outlined why pragmatic robust KM would facilitate this, the focus now shifts to what strategies Northern actors could follow to make this happen. This section builds on the work of Ferraro et al. (2015), who have recommended three interconnected strategies for pragmatic robust action: (1) practice-based strategies, (2) structural strategies, and (3) interpretative strategies.

Practice-based strategies: localization

Zooming out maximally, practice-based strategies look at the localities involved around the world in humanitarian KM and how they should connect to each other. As discussed above, pragmatic robust KM does not involve working in siloes or implementing KM in a top-down manner. At this meta level, the approach would organize KM on the basis of a network formed by linking up a series of local KM spaces (or events), both geographically and across time. The result would be the *netcentric localization* of KM. The reasons for organizing KM in this manner are twofold. First, localized, horizontal KM has the potential to be more innovative, flexible, and responsive to changing local preferences and circumstances, compared with centralized, vertical KM. Second, in highly complex settings, such as humanitarian disasters, it is impossible to know in advance or from a distance exactly which knowledge, information, and data will be needed. Organizing KM in a localized, netcentric manner would support local actors to simultaneously try different approaches in different settings. This approach would drive learning and context-specific problem solving across the network by fostering debates and knowledge exchanges among these settings (e.g. South–South and South–North). However, the effectiveness of this approach hinges on whether KM metrics, spaces, and artefacts can facilitate genuine inclusion and participation. If they can, fruitful exchanges between dispersed knowledges will drive horizontal netcentric learning. However, if they cannot, there is a risk that the KM processes will deepen and reproduce the power inequalities within these networks, as shown in the case studies. To address this, the sections below outline structural and interpretative strategies for enhancing participation and inclusion in KM.

Structural strategies: participation

Zooming in halfway, structural strategies look at the social structure of KM. Specifically, they consider how the power hierarchies, norms, and institutions that characterize North–South collaborations shape interactions in KM spaces. They also look at the design and use of KM artefacts and metrics, as discussed below. Again, pragmatic robust KM is based on the idea that a top-down or solo-action approach is unhelpful when it comes to fostering learning and problem solving in the face of complex issues. Pragmatic robust KM holds that KM should be organized around *participation*. Indeed, structural strategies aim to set *rules for KM* that enable diverse actors, whose priorities and worldviews do not necessarily align, to collaborate constructively together over long periods of time. A data justice lens is useful for designing these rules for a specific KM network, as it helps assess their likely impact on the effectiveness and social justice outcomes of KM in a particular context. One very important issue for pragmatic robust KM is that participation is organized horizontally to stop power imbalances from prioritizing one perspective over others. To facilitate this, the rules for KM should ensure that KM spaces are designed and managed to accommodate a range of actors with different knowledges and priorities. These rules should not only cover basic issues such as skilled facilitation and shared leadership, but also more transformational matters such as horizontal accountability, distributed authority, and diverse success metrics (e.g. Ansell & Gash, 2008). The purpose of the rules is to safeguard against power imbalances, foster trust, and establish legitimacy for the KM processes.

Interpretative strategies: inclusivity and flexibility

Zooming in maximally, interpretative strategies look at the KM artefacts and metrics that shape actions and decisions in aid. These include, for example, reports, scripts, templates, stories, datasets, guidelines, and formats. Complex situations such as disasters can be meaningfully understood through different lenses. Interpretative strategies aim to create KM artefacts that support these different plausible interpretations, as opposed to enforcing one 'correct' perspective or imposing a consensus. Interpretative strategies focus on the design and discursive aspects of KM artefacts. Their aim is to deliver artefacts that are accessible, acceptable, fair, and useful for diverse participants in humanitarian aid. A data justice lens can help assess this during the design phase, as well as the strategies' likely impact on the effectiveness and social justice outcomes of aid. A design that allows for inclusivity and flexibility can facilitate collaboration and exchange among a range of actors with different perspectives and priorities.

When used in tandem, the practice-based, structural, and interpretative strategies of pragmatic robust action described in this section have the potential to radically restructure – and improve – humanitarian KM.

Conclusion

This chapter has investigated KM in the context of North–South collaborations. Its focus has been on humanitarian interventions that aim to be localized, participatory, and inclusive. On the basis of three case studies, the chapter has shown how the vertical way in which KM is often organized in these collaborations obstructs genuinely localized KM. As a result, KM processes end up being centred on Northern knowledges. Even the 'Local Knowledge' that is constructed through KM processes to inform and validate humanitarian decision making is often tailored to Northern perspectives and priorities. The result is that KM processes frequently end up legitimizing the unhelpful hierarchical status quo. This chapter has analysed this situation through the lenses of structuration and data justice, showing its adverse impact on social justice and on the efficiency and effectiveness of aid. The chapter has proposed pragmatic robust action strategies as an alternative way of organizing KM in North–South collaborations. This approach relies on practice-based, structural, and interpretative strategies towards greater *localization, participation, and inclusion* in KM.

Thus, this chapter contributes to this volume's aim of 'starting from the South' by outlining new roles for Northern humanitarian actors in KM. When KM is organized on the basis of pragmatic robust action, at the level of practice, Northern actors are each one local node in a KM network – equal to all other nodes. At a structural level, Northern actors are held accountable and share authority over KM equally with all other network members. At an interpretative level, 'information objects' (e.g. survey templates, guidelines, metrics, and websites) are not tailored to Northern knowledges, but are instead kept open and flexible enough to accommodate all plausible interpretations. This setup would help centre local debates and local solutions in humanitarian aid. It would also help drive learning across the KM network through horizontal knowledge sharing and debate. Given that individual action and social arrangements interlink, the approach has the potential to redress the power imbalances that mark North–South collaborations within and beyond the realm of KM. The end result would be that local actors could centre local action *and local knowledges* in aid, which, ultimately, is the goal of the ongoing sectoral drive for localization and participation.

References

Ansell, C., & Gash, A. (2008). Collaborative governance in theory and practice. *Journal of Public Administration Research and Theory, 18*(4), 543–571. http://dx.doi.org/10.1093/jopart/mum032.

Attride-Stirling, J. (2001). Thematic networks: An analytic tool for qualitative research. *Qualitative Research, 1*(3), 385–405. http://dx.doi.org/10.1177/146879410100100307.

Barbelet, V. (2018). As local as possible, as international as necessary: Understanding capacity and complementarity in humanitarian action *Humanitarian Policy Group Working Paper*. London, UK: Overseas Development Institute. Retrieved from: https://odi.org/en/publications/as-local-as-possible-as-international-as-necessary-understanding-capacity-and-complementarity-in-humanitarian-action.

Eisenhardt, K. M. (1989). Building theories from case study research. *Academy of Management Review, 14*(4), 532–550. http://dx.doi.org/10.2307/258557.

Ferraro, F., Etzion, D., & Gehman, J. (2015). Tackling grand challenges pragmatically: Robust action revisited. *Organization Studies, 36*(3), 363–390. http://dx.doi.org/10.1177/0170840614563742.

Giddens, A. (1979). *Central problems in Social Theory: Action, Structure and Contradiction in Social Theory*. Berkeley: University of California Press.

Heeks, R. (2017). *A structural model and Manifesto for data justice for international development* (Working Paper No.69). University of Manchester, GDI Development Informatics Working Papers. Retrieved from: https://papers.ssrn.com/sol3/papers.cfm?abstract_id=3431729.

Hilhorst, D. (2018). Classical humanitarianism and resilience humanitarianism: Making sense of two brands of humanitarian action. *Journal of International Humanitarian Action, 3*(1), 1–12. http://dx.doi.org/10.1186/s41018-018-0043-6.

Mulder, F. (2020a). Humanitarian data justice: A structural data justice lens on civic technologies in post-earthquake Nepal. *Journal of Contingencies and Crisis Management, 28*(4), 432–445. http://dx.doi.org/10.1111/1468-5973.12335.

Mulder, F. (2020b). Governing the humanitarian knowledge commons. *Politics and Governance, 8*(4), 407–420. http://dx.doi.org/10.17645/pag.v8i4.3138.

Mulder, F., Ferguson, J., Groenewegen, P., Boersma, K., & Wolbers, J. (2016). Questioning Big Data: Crowdsourcing crisis data towards an inclusive humanitarian response. *Big Data & Society, 3*(2), 1–13. http://dx.doi.org/10.1177/2053951716662054.

Stones, R. (2009). Power and structuration theory. In S. Clegg & M. Haugaard (Eds.), *The SAGE handbook of power* (pp. 89–107). London, UK: Sage Publications Ltd.

Ybema, S., Yanow, D., Wels, H., & Kamsteeg, F. H. (Eds.). (2009). *Organizational ethnography: Studying the complexity of everyday life*. London, UK: Sage Publications Ltd.

Yin, R. K. (1981). The case study as a serious research strategy. *Knowledge, 3*(1), 97–114. http://dx.doi.org/10.1177/107554708100300106.

16

THE JOURNEY TO SOUTHERN LEADERSHIP IN PROGRAMMING

The story of a decade-long Ghanaian–Dutch partnership

Mohammed Awal Alhassan and Marijke Priester

Introduction

Learning is often said to be central in international development. As two practitioners in the field, we are very familiar with evaluations and operational research used for learning. However, if you ask what has given us the best insight into the promotion or hindrance of Southern leadership, we would not refer to evaluations; rather, we would tell you about conversations in which we both explained our thoughts and concerns, gave honest answers, and inspired each other. We engaged in the kind of in-depth learning dialogue that is often missing between practitioners from the Global South and those from the Global North. We are not suggesting that the learning from external research is irrelevant; however, we are convinced that the value of self-reflective dialogue on sensitive issues like Southern leadership is underestimated. Such dialogue not only provides insight into how to promote and realize Southern leadership; it can also have a direct actional effect for realizing the change.

Here, we refer to this dialogue as a journey we took while participating in two successive international development programmes. In these programmes, the first author participated as the executive director of a participating civil society organization (CSO) in Ghana and chair of the Steering Committee (SC) of the newly formed CSO alliance in Ghana. The second author worked for a Dutch CSO, first as the programme manager for the programmes' global consortium secretariat (explained in Figure 16.1) and later as a senior advisor.

The CSOs on both sides are national non-governmental organizations that are largely dependent on funding from governments and foundations in the Global North. Their activities include service provision (education and training), awareness raising, and policy influencing in the field of sexual and reproductive health and rights (SRHR), youth, and gender.

DOI: 10.4324/9781003241003-20

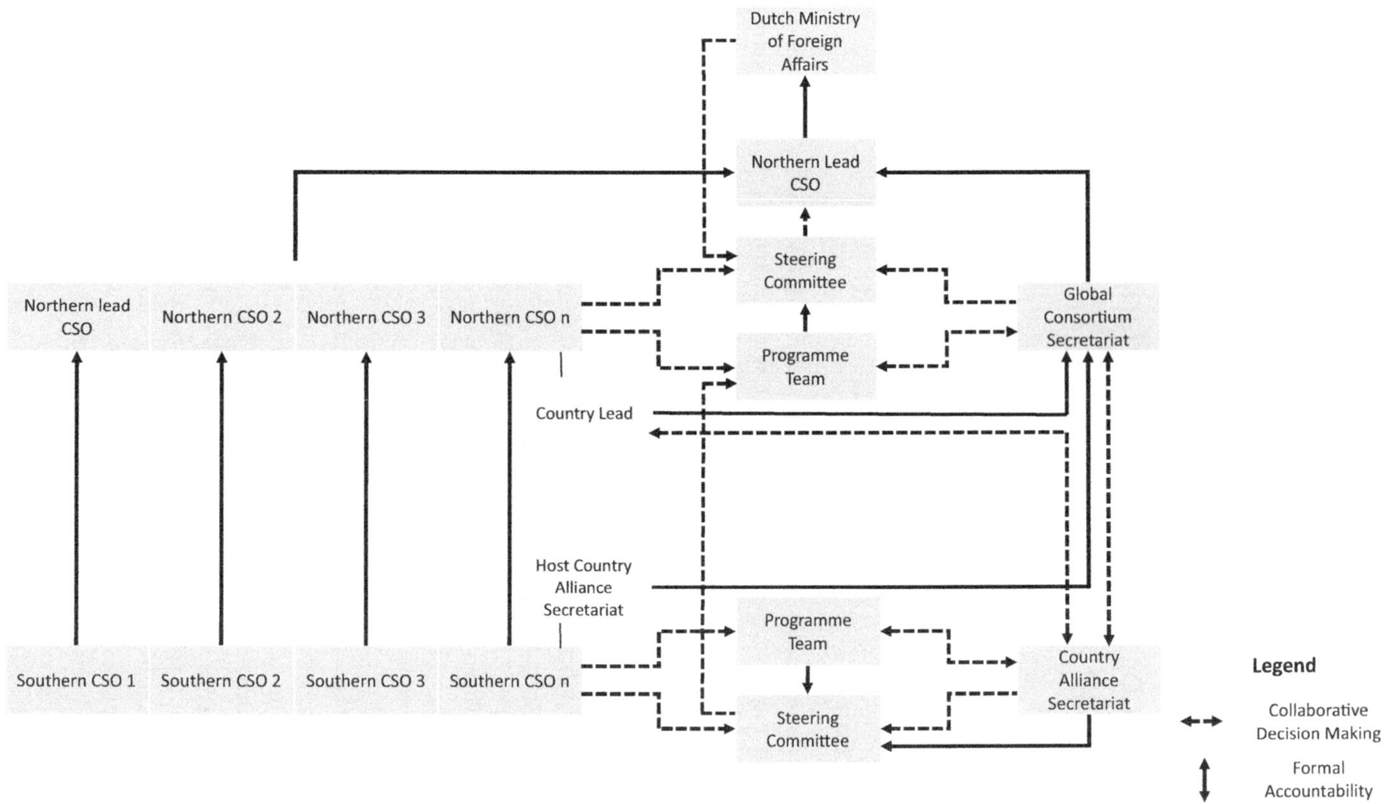

FIGURE 16.1 Formal accountability and collaboration structure in the programmes – ASK (2013–2015) and GUSO (2016–2020).

The development programmes, ASK (2013–2015) and GUSO (2016–2020), were funded by the Dutch Ministry of Foreign Affairs. They were executed in Ghana and other countries in Africa and Asia, with the main goal of improving SRHR among young people (Sawyer & de Mars, 2021; van Ewijk et al., 2016). In Ghana, implementation was carried out by a Dutch–British consortium of CSOs and a country alliance of Ghanaian partner CSOs. The programmes' governance regulated the CSOs' roles and responsibilities as individual CSOs and as consortium/alliance members (see Figure 16.1).

The programmes offered us insight into the long road to Southern leadership, which we understand as CSOs in the Global South shaping programming and influencing roles and collaborations in international development – on their own terms. With Southern leadership, instead of being considered 'partners' of Northern CSOs, Southern CSOs are seen as independent organizations in their own right, embedded in the social and political contexts they navigate.

The journey described in this chapter represents a personal account of how the Ghanaian–Dutch relationship hindered or facilitated Southern-led programming. We also refer to a theoretical framework of power that supports our reimagining of relations, roles, and processes in creating and sustaining Southern leadership. The concept of power and arguments for Southern leadership have long been part of discussions on civil society support in international aid (Buckley & Ward, 2015; Elbers & Arts, 2011). However, although Northern CSOs generally use a vocabulary that shows an intention to work in an equitable way, daily practice in international programming often demonstrates power differences between CSOs from the Global South and those from the Global North. In this chapter, we draw on Pansardi and Bindi's extensive review of the discourse on power. They propose a differentiation of 'power-over', 'power-to', and 'power-with'. Generally, 'power-over' refers to an asymmetrical relation between two or more actors or groups of actors, 'power-to' is an actor's ability to achieve certain outcomes, and 'power-with' is a group's ability to act together in view of collective outcomes or goals (Pansardi & Bindi, 2021). We use these three conceptualizations of power to interpret certain events happening over the span of the two programmes. For instance, there were processes where the Northern CSOs intended to create more space for a 'power-to' context, whereas the Ghanaian CSOs still experienced this as 'power-over'. While some of these processes are shaped by the structure of the aid system, others seem to be rooted in longstanding – often unconscious – patterns of power relationships in programming (Pailey, 2020).

Through reflection on our own experience and using this framework of power, we seek to answer the following questions: (1) Why does it take so long to include 'Southern leadership' in the practice of international development programming? (2) What will it take from the key actors involved to accelerate this process? The story of our journey starts with an understanding of the civil society contexts in Ghana and in the Netherlands. We then discuss key moments or processes during the programmes from the perspective of Southern leadership and suggest some thoughts on action for change. The journey is thus the destination. A conclusive note summarizes our thoughts on the questions of why Southern leadership is so difficult to realize and how reimagining relations and roles can support and speed up the process.

Embedding the journey

The Ghanaian setting

Although the Ghanaian CSO sector is well developed, civil society actions in Ghana are predominantly financed by aid funding, mostly from the Global North (Quantson et al., 2015). After Ghana attained lower-middle-income status in 2011, many Northern countries, including the Netherlands, began to review their partnership relationships with the country. In 2020, Dutch funding for civil society programmes began to decline – replaced by trade and investment support. The Ghanaian government has not yet committed resources to the sector or provided strategic frameworks to support sustainability and ownership of civil society development interventions. In 2019, the government embarked on consultations with CSOs as part of efforts to broaden discussions on the effective implementation of the 'Ghana Beyond Aid' charter (Senior Minister holds consultations with CSOs on 'Ghana Beyond Aid', 2019). The government and civil society in Ghana are critically considering donor dependency, and CSOs are starting domestic resource mobilization initiatives. Still, progress is rather slow, with little support from the government or the private sector. During the two programmes discussed here, Ghana was still eligible for Dutch CSO funding.

In 2013, a Northern consortium of seven CSOs selected Ghana and several other countries to implement a pioneering youth programme called ASK. Under ASK, the consortium members assigned an individual from one organizational member as Northern country lead in each country to guide and supervise the programme design and implementation (see Figure 16.1).

The country leads determined with the global consortium secretariat which Ghanaian partner organization was best qualified to host the country alliance secretariat and administer alliance-related budgets. This was a major programme implementation decision, which the Northern consortium saw as a way of handing financial and operational power to Ghana. It can thus be characterized as a 'power-to' action; the consortium enabled the Ghanaian CSOs to carry out certain goals themselves. However, the Ghanaian CSOs were not involved in the process leading to this decision, which was carried out rather asymmetrically. The Ghanaian CSOs therefore experienced it predominantly as a 'power-over' action in which they had no say. It could be argued that the Northern consortium acted in the interests of the Ghanaian CSOs, working to avoid conflicts. Later, however, the consortium left the in-country budget distribution, which could also potentially lead to conflicts, in the hands of the Ghanaian CSOs. In hindsight, the Northern fear of failing the tough financial requirements of the Dutch

Ministry prevailed, preventing a 'power-with' approach, with the Global South and North acting together for the collective goal in selecting a host.

The Ghanaian partners were then encouraged to select a national coordinator to head the alliance secretariat. A national recruitment team was formed to conduct a competitive selection, which was predominantly led by the Ghanaian CSOs. However, later, the coordinator who was recruited often felt more accountable to the Northern country lead than to the Ghanaian SC who recruited him and to whom he was functionally accountable.

GUSO, ASK's successor programme, built on ASK but with a review of the CSOs involved in both the North and the South. Under GUSO, the Northern consortium redefined the position of the Northern country leads as 'sparring partners' for the national coordinator, highlighting growing autonomy of the national coordinators. The positions were filled by Northern staff on the basis of competencies instead of delegation by a consortium member.

Considering the different concepts of power introduced above, 'power-over' elements were undoubtedly present in the preparatory phase of the programmes.

The Dutch setting

Since 2000, attention for Southern leadership has increased internationally (OECD, 2008). In the Netherlands, this has been reflected in policy notes on international development (Netherlands Ministry of Foreign Affairs, 2001, 2019). The Dutch government has also addressed the fragmentation of the Dutch CSO landscape, introducing a revised CSO grant system in 2011. Under this system, Dutch CSOs, many of which are highly dependent on government funding, were encouraged to apply as alliances. The emphasis on CSOs working together coincided with an increasingly controlling managerial approach at the Ministry. Southern CSO ownership also received attention (IOB, 2017), although Southern CSOs were not eligible to be the lead organization. This situation would last until 2015 when this was allowed in the main 2016–2020 CSO grant scheme and effectively realized by one Southern CSO (Netherlands Ministry of Foreign Affairs, 2015).

In this context, the ASK programme in Ghana was funded. Not all Dutch CSOs were eager to join forces as requested by the Ministry, but this Northern consortium embraced the concept of alliances as necessary for successful implementation. Specialized CSOs with a diverse reach were needed to cooperate for integrated change. In the Global South, the Northern consortium created alliances composed of their bilateral partners, who were tasked with working together.

The 2016–2020 GUSO programme was funded as a strategic partnership with the Ministry of Foreign Affairs (Netherlands Ministry of Foreign Affairs, 2013). In these partnerships, besides being a grant maker, the Ministry became a strategic partner of the Dutch CSOs (IOB, 2019). The accountability requirements of the Ministry remained high, specifically for Northern lead organizations.

In 2019, embarking on the 2021–2025 grant cycle, the Ministry explicitly mentioned the relevance of Southern leadership (Netherlands Ministry of Foreign Affairs, 2019). Still, the number of Southern-led partnerships in the 2021–2025 main scheme is low: two out of 20 (Netherlands Ministry of Foreign Affairs, 2020).

During our journey, we learned that the Dutch grant system influenced the space for 'power-to' and 'power-with' approaches that nurture Southern leadership.

Undertaking the journey: key moments in capturing or missing the turn towards Southern leadership

In searching for an answer to why it takes so long to realize Southern leadership, we focus mainly on hindrances in the North. Although there are also impediments in the South, we believe Southern leadership will only be realized when the Global North actively collaborates in this process – on Southern terms.

We extracted four sets of key moments or processes where Southern leadership should be present:

- Strategic decision making in programme design and strategic positioning in programme governance
- CSO selection and capacity building
- Collaboration and stakeholder processes
- Processes of accountability

We explain their relevance for Southern leadership, their relationship to power concepts, and how Southern leadership could be accelerated, within the context of the Dutch-funded programme system in which we worked.

Strategic decision making in programme design

At the core of the two programmes was a Theory of Change (ToC), a comprehensive description of how and why desired change is expected to happen. It is crucial for Southern leadership that a ToC and the accompanying envisaged results are developed together with the Southern partners.

In retrospect, there were several moments when this was not the case and when 'power-over' predominated. The Northern CSOs jointly established the allocation of the programme budget to their organizations and to the global consortium secretariat. They individually decided in which of the countries each of them would work with their partners. They jointly established the budget ratio between the Southern countries and the Northern consortium, as well as the country budget categories. The Ghanaian CSOs were only approached after the overall programme ToC and outcomes had been designed in the North and approved by the Dutch Ministry. The Northern CSOs' argument was that they did not want to risk making commitments to countries and organizations until they were sure of the Ministry's budget approval. All the Ghanaian partners saw the ToC for the first time during a kick-off workshop for the ASK programme, and, although contextualization of the ToC for Ghana was on the agenda, the Ghanaian CSOs perceived this as superficial because no significant change could happen. The 'what' (indicators) and 'how' (intervention strategies) were already set. The Northern CSOs allowed no changes in the overall ToC but attached value to adding Ghana-specific elements within the general frame. Without this contextualization, the ToC would lead to ineffective programming. From a Ghanaian point of view, the Ghanaian context should have been the starting point for a ToC rather than being of secondary importance. During the workshop, a Ghanaian CSO director noted,

> We are discussing the Theory of Change today and how it fits our context, and we are discussing the strategies to achieve results. Why this discussion at all? We must accept it because the Dutch Ministry has approved it. It affects ownership. It is imposed on us.

In a reflection on the abovementioned power framework with Ghanaian actors, one person suggested refining the concept of 'power-to' by adding 'power-within'. 'Power-within describes a person's sense of self-worth and self-knowledge' (VeneKlasen & Miller, 2002, p. 39). Put differently, it is the confidence of recognizing one's power to take ownership over one's situation and to call for change. During the workshop, why did the Ghanaian CSOs not insist that they needed more space? Confidence could have made a difference here. We use the idea of 'power-within' in discussing the processes of collaboration and accountability below.

In any case, the Ghanaian partners were conspicuously missing at the design stage.

In terms of contextualization, the Northern CSOs introduced a 'power-with' element in allocating the country budget to the foreseen programme outcomes. Responsibility for assessing competence and leading the budget allocation to the outcomes was left to the Ghanaian CSOs, who could act collectively in view of a common goal – a turn towards Southern leadership. This was in sharp contrast to the programme targets, which were pre-determined without the Ghanaian partners' involvement. Proposed targets sent to the Dutch Ministry were shared with the Ghanaian partners for the first time at the workshop, and the feasibility of these targets was discussed for contextualization. At that time, the figures were considered fixed because they had received Ministry approval. The Ghanaian CSOs perceived it as an expression of 'power-over' by the Northern CSOs, who were uncomfortable that the Ministry, expressing its previously mentioned controlling managerial style, had forced them to detail targets in advance.

Compared with the ASK grant scheme, the Ministry allowed more Southern involvement in the first phase of GUSO. During an inception phase from the initial approval to the start of the programme, the Ghanaian CSOs were invited to write a country programme proposal for approval by the Northern consortium. The Ghana proposal was approved only after substantial adaptation was requested. At this point, there was no in-depth dialogue. Communication was limited to annotations requesting changes sent to the Ghanaian CSOs, an updated proposal from the Ghanaian CSOs, and final approval by the Northern consortium. Later, those on the Ghanaian side expressed deep regret about the absence of an in-depth dialogue about the required changes.

Finally, it is important to note that the Ghanaian CSOs involved had already worked for a long time on the issues dealt with in the programme. The new programme should therefore not have begun from scratch; rather, it should have strategically built upon what the Ghanaian CSOs had already achieved. The Ghanaian CSOs had longstanding expertise and good results in SRHR programming and in building youth networks for common action and effective interventions. Although this expertise was recognized by the North, it was not translated upwards through a common dialogue to strategically design the ToC. Instead, the Ghanaian CSOs were asked to colour the ready-made ToC boxes with a Ghanaian touch.

Strategic positioning in programme governance

Southern leadership includes strategic decision making, but this element was missing from the Ghanaian alliance mandate. All country alliances copied the Northern consortium's model of an SC of directors and a technical programme team comprising staff members from the involved organizations. The Ghanaian SC led the programme implementation, which was executed by the Ghanaian programme team and facilitated by the national coordinator, who also headed the country alliance secretariat (see Figure 16.1). The Ghanaian SC focused on in-country issues and was not represented in the global structure. The Northern consortium's decisions were mostly communicated via consortium members and the national coordinator.

In the programme governance, the Southern SCs and the Northern SC – which should have had a relationship on an equal footing – did not communicate; rather, the Southern SCs worked with the Northern programme team (see Figure 16.1), revealing a power imbalance. Southern SCs requested communication with the Northern SC on strategic issues. As CSO directors, they were interested in country-transcending strategic discussions, as they often participated in international fora themselves. However, with the exception of a strategic learning meeting in 2018, their connection with the Northern SC was limited to informative meetings organized by the Northern lead organization.

The Northern country lead and the consortium organizations' programme officers were the main Northern faces known in Ghana. The distinction between the donor (the Dutch government) and the grant-receiving Dutch CSOs, which was clearly felt in the North, was quite blurred in the eyes of the Ghanaian CSOs. The Dutch lead organization of the Northern consortium, especially, was often perceived more as a 'delegated donor' than a fellow CSO.

The model, which crossed vertical bilateral contractual relations between Ghanaian and Northern CSOs with horizontal consortium–alliance relations (see Figure 16.1), complicated strategic action. The contractual relationship between the Ghanaian CSO and the Northern CSO superseded relationships with their Ghanaian fellow CSOs in the alliance.

Overall, strategic decision making for the programmes was limited to the Dutch side. As a CSO director mentioned, 'We are the steering committee, but we have nothing to steer'. The Ghana programme was framed to meet the programme requirements. Opportunities for strategic dialogue based on a common CSO identity, which could have promoted Southern leadership, were insufficiently exploited.

CSO selection and capacity building

Southern leadership involves actively discussing and deciding with whom to partner in a programme. In the two examined programmes, however, the Northern CSOs selected the partners.

Reimagining the process from a Ghanaian perspective involves exploring how the selection mechanisms could be reversed. With Ghanaian CSOs in the lead, they could select the Dutch CSOs on the basis of the expertise and roles needed from the North.

Concerning expertise, the programmes dedicated ample attention to learning and capacity building – potentially a good 'power-to' strategy for supporting Southern leadership. GUSO included alliance-building as an outcome, but there were more opportunities for thematic capacity building than for organizational strengthening because the Northern CSOs had strong thematic expertise and were the main providers.

The Ghanaian CSOs could obtain support from other organizations, but capacity building through the Northern CSOs was generally included in the budgets. From the Southern leadership's perspective, it would be interesting to see what would happen without these 'tied budgets'. If the Southern CSOs would approach other organizations instead of the Northern CSOs under such circumstances, that might indicate that the capacity building is more supply- than demand-driven, because of asymmetrical 'power over' relations.

A final remark on capacity building concerns the Northern CSOs' 'power-to' abilities to support Southern leadership. In retrospect, attention to capacity building in the North was missing, as if the Global North had no gaps in need of filling. This reflects longstanding patterns of white supremacy that have led to stifled progress on Southern leadership (Saad, 2020).

Capacity gaps should be identified on both sides, although the operationalization may be different. For example, Northern CSOs may need more guidance on overall country knowledge and on practical issues beyond academic literature on programme areas.

Reimagining a 'power-with' scenario, involving the ability to act together as Global South and North, capacity building could then become capacity sharing.

Collaboration and stakeholder processes

Southern leadership of individual CSOs can grow wider when CSOs join forces with like-minded organizations and aligned government institutions. The GUSO programme included an organizational outcome of strengthening the country alliances and making them sustainable. The Northern vision behind this was that the alliances could autonomously continue their work after the end of the programme in 2020. The Northern consortium perceived this as an opportunity to contribute to Southern leadership. Securing country sustainability and ownership by strengthening alliances was positively received by the Dutch Ministry. GUSO included Northern support for alliance building, funding for joint activities to strengthen cooperation, and space to formulate a transition plan.

Although the Ghanaian CSOs recorded impressive results through their collaborative approach, alliance building was an outcome predetermined at the programme's design stage, and the Ghanaian organizations' role was to accept it and tick their progress on a tracking template. This was a 'forced marriage', as some would have said. However, these limitations did not stop the Ghanaian alliance from agreeing on an ambitious strategic plan through 2023, attracting new funding from the Dutch embassy, and being included in one of the Dutch-funded strategic partnerships through 2025.

In retrospect, the Northern consortium's positive intentions were based on a shift of power – from 'power-over' to 'power-to' – moving in the direction of a comprehensive and autonomous coalition able to raise funding independently. However, a 'power-with' approach was lacking, with no genuine strategic-level dialogue between the Ghanaian and Northern CSOs. The Northern CSOs were hesitant to engage with the country alliances because they regarded this as a country alliance-owned process and because they were afraid to raise false expectations.

The Ghanaian CSOs had mixed feelings. They had obtained good programme results by working together, and they had worked successfully on positioning the Ghanaian alliance. However, they also felt abandoned by the Northern consortium. It was difficult for them to understand why the Northern consortium had decided to dissolve itself after 2020, whereas the Ghanaian CSOs were expected to take up new activities. Earlier, when the Northern CSOs discontinued their relationships with some of the Ghanaian organizations at the start of GUSO, they appeared to undermine their own concept of alliance building: the alliance membership was apparently motivated by the existence of the programme, which outweighed the intention to build a strong, sustainable alliance. The Ghanaian SC sometimes felt an issue needed to be prioritized but was overruled by the Northern country lead through the national coordinator. Consequently, the Ghanaian CSOs prioritized their relationships with the Northern CSOs over those with other Ghanaian CSOs. Such asymmetrical 'power-over' decisions affect the core of the Global South–North dialogue.

What would have happened if their 'power-within' had been stronger? What if the Southern CSOs had stood together on common ground for their common interests? How would the Northern consortium have answered? This would at least have led to an interesting dialogue. However, the opportunity for a 'power-with' dynamic fostering Southern leadership was hampered by the programme governance model and the 'divide-and-rule' effect of bilateral contractual relations with the Northern CSOs.

An in-depth dialogue between the Ghanaian and Northern CSOs about expectations and hesitancies on both sides could have been highly beneficial. Such a 'power-with' approach, with committed Northern support, without a precondition of being tied to each other, could have fostered a new dimension of Southern leadership among the Ghanaian CSOs and would certainly have increased trust towards the Northern consortium and within the Ghanaian alliance.

Regarding stakeholder processes with other societal actors, we believe that Southern CSO leadership will grow stronger when it is supported by these other actors. The response of the Ghanaian government and its agencies, which showed massive interest in both programmes, played a crucial role. Government and district staff participated in the programmes at multiple levels. At the programme closure summit, national and district government agencies commended the programmes and the alliance for inclusive planning and execution. Overall, because the programmes were aligned with government priorities and because the Ghanaian CSOs engaged in inclusive planning and implementation, the programmes had high acceptance rates and offered opportunities for a prolonged, broad, Southern-led effort.

Given the Dutch source of the programmes' funding, we include the Dutch embassy in our stakeholder reflection. Embassy staff played a convening role for the Dutch-sponsored programmes in Ghana. At the start of GUSO, on a few occasions, embassy staff members expressed some dissatisfaction with their level of involvement in the programme and noted a preference for the alliance to submit mandatory reports to the embassy. The embassy's role as a strategic partner to the Ghanaian alliance, like that of the Ministry to the Northern consortium, was taken up later when the embassy supported strategic engagement with key community groups and government institutions. By the end of 2020, the embassy's dialogue with the alliance was impressive, resulting in a new project where the alliance was involved, with new, though related, priority areas.

In the reimagining of international development, it might be interesting for the embassy and the Ghanaian government to explore a 'power-with' approach of strategically discussing scaling up the excellent GUSO results to other parts of Ghana, given the enthusiasm among community members and the national and district governments. This approach could initiate a transition from a Northern-led strategic partnership between the Ministry and the consortium to a Southern-based strategic partnership among the embassy, the Ghanaian government, and the alliance.

Accountability processes

Regarding upward accountability, in the two programmes considered here, the Global North (notably the Ministry and the lead CSO organization) decided what was required in reporting templates, when and how to report, and conditions to meet for budget transfers. The Ghanaian partners received direct transfers from consortium members and reported to these Northern CSOs for approval. The accountability of the Ghanaian CSOs to their own SC was secondary. The Northern consortium members had to approve the Ghanaian CSO reports before the Ghanaian SC could endorse them and prepare a joint country report.

In the process of alliance building, the Ghanaian CSOs encountered new accountability issues. The Ghanaian alliance's ambitious strategic plan went beyond programme implementation and included the development of a West African knowledge hub on SRHR and young people. New resources had to be mobilized and administered by the alliance secretariat, which required the secretariat to have legal status, meaning, among other things, that the alliance had to formally register to be credible and incorporated in Ghana's laws. Some CSOs in the Ghanaian alliance were initially against registering the alliance because it would then have the same status as its members and could compete with them for resources. Eventually, the Ghanaian CSOs acted together as a group to realize their common goal – 'power-with' dynamics prevailed, and registration took place.

After this registration, the global consortium secretariat hesitated to channel funds to the alliance because of the absence of a track record of the newly established alliance and continued to deal with the country host (see Figure 16.1). The Ghanaian CSOs had previously felt the decision for the Ghanaian alliance secretariat to receive grants for joint activities directly from the global consortium secretariat demonstrated commitment to a power shift. Thus, the lack of Northern commitment to gradually shifting full budget control from the North to the Ghanaian secretariat, as the programme was coming to an end, was experienced as a betrayal. As a result of this situation, some CSOs in the Ghanaian alliance asked for the alliance's dissolution because the North had indicated they could not transfer funds directly to the alliance even after it was registered.

In retrospect, as the alliance evolved, there should have been conscious efforts to channel resources through the alliance, with the Ghanaian CSOs receiving grants directly from the Ghanaian secretariat. Testing the systems of the alliance together and having in-depth discussions on this would have strengthened the alliance building and trust among the Ghanaian alliance members – a 'power-with' approach.

Downward accountability was mainly discussed in the fourth and fifth programme years. Engagement with key state institutions and district and community leaders improved, ensuring accountability to young people and other actors for the use of resources. The Ghanaian CSOs considered local-level engagement with community leaders and young people key for successful programming (see also Chanase, 2021). At this point, the Ghanaian SC decided to strategically involve the Dutch embassy to deepen key state institutions' confidence in the programme. This resulted in a successful monitoring visit by the embassy, leading to positive key state actor engagement.

What about the accountability of the Global North to the Global South? In the programmes, the Northern CSOs had considerable freedom to use the programme budget in their organizations. They had important roles in allocating capacity building, doing research, and developing interventions, but there was no accountability mechanism to the South to assess whether the Northern choices were the most needed in the country programmes.

Accountability demands for the programmes were one-sided as if the North had nothing for which to account to the South. The Ghanaian CSOs did not ask for accountability from the North, but this does not mean that there was no demand for it or that the Northern CSOs should be absolved. Here, dedicating more attention by the Ghanaian CSOs to their 'power-within' could make a difference in terms of attaining a more equal relationship with Northern CSOs. Simultaneously, Northern CSOs should consciously hold themselves accountable for supporting true Southern leadership in programming.

As mentioned above, until 2016, Southern organizations were not eligible to be the lead organizations in Dutch major grant schemes, and the Ministry's narrowly defined managerial accountability conditions played a role here. There is certainly a need for in-depth dialogue if effective accountability that benefits Southern leadership is to be achieved. Such an achievement requires a new way of thinking about accountability, going beyond rigid managerial control.

Conclusive note

Returning to the question of why it takes so long to achieve Southern leadership in international programming, we conclude that changes are required in both mindsets and systems, which are embedded in complex power dynamics. Pansardi and Bindi's (2021) article on differentiating conceptualizations of power provides insight into these dynamics. Such a major transformation takes time. It requires personal growth and political will to adopt a 'power-to' approach and embark on collective 'power-with' action. To achieve this, new relations, processes, and roles will be required in international development. In this conclusive note, we would like to share some thoughts on what this will look like.

New relations

Building Southern leadership affects the power dynamics between the Global South and the Global North. Southern leadership cannot be established when Southern involvement comes in after the core parameters have already been set by the Global North, which was the case in these programmes. When Northern CSOs give space for 'power-to' strategies, they should be aware that Southern CSOs, approaching these strategies from a Southern perspective, may change the priorities. Northern 'power-to' strategies were not always perceived as such by the Ghanaian organizations, and 'power-with' strategies were absent.

There is fear from both the Global North and the Global South, which stifles progress towards Southern leadership. The Global North, as seen in the Northern CSOs, dwells on the capacity of the Global South to lead and is anxious about losing their influence. The Global South, as manifested in the Ghanaian CSOs, fears that the Southern leadership process will lead to more burden in terms of programming and reduced Northern funding support.

It is notable that the issue of Southern leadership in the programmes came from the North, with strong rhetoric but weak commitment for achieving true Southern leadership. This observation, briefly summarized as 'the positive intentions were recognized in you and others, as persons from the Global North, not in the Northern structures', marked one of the most painful moments in the reflective dialogue between the two authors.

New processes

There is a need to allay fears of both sides, which can only happen with a spirit of openness, commitment, mutual accountability, and clear common understanding of implications. Confidence and self-esteem matter when discussing programme design, in dealing with governance and contractual relations, and in requesting accountability from the Global North. Southern CSOs should challenge themselves to catalyze their 'power-within' towards Northern CSOs so they can mobilize and make demands in a genuine dialogue. It is also important to focus on building mutual trust among fellow Southern CSOs from a 'power-with' perspective instead of allowing competition for donor funding to pit them against each other.

Another finding emerging from our journey is that the commitment of Dutch CSOs to Southern leadership can only work if the Dutch government changes its grant mechanism. The call for 'upside-down' thinking, starting from the priorities in Ghana and other Southern countries instead of establishing policy priorities in the Netherlands, is timely. Without the involvement of Southern CSOs in developing programme focus areas, programme design, and selection of Southern and Northern organizations, Southern leadership will remain elusive. In the same spirit, a memorandum of understanding regarding power balance should be standard prior to submitting a funding application.

New roles

It is crucial that the North does not withdraw but rather commits to sustained cooperation and support – on Southern terms. Too often, Southern leadership is understood as a process carried out only by Southern actors. However, Southern leadership in international programming is impossible without reimagining the role of the Global North, which still pulls the strings. Achieving Southern leadership thus requires the Global North's commitment to let go of Northern perspectives, provide investments of time and funding, share its networks, work on breaking down barriers in the Global North, and, especially, have the boldness to undergo the journey of a genuine dialogue, stepping into unknown territory.

Acknowledgements

The authors deeply appreciate the close and critical reading by a group of (former) colleagues in Ghana, the Netherlands, and the United Kingdom. Their comments and suggestions helped to unfold the complexity of 'Southern leadership programming' in current systems.

References

Buckley, L., & Ward, H. (2015). *Getting good at disruption in an uncertain world: Insights from Southern NGO leaders* (IIED Working Paper, December). London: IIED. Retrieved from: https://pubs.iied.org/sites/default/files/pdfs/migrate/11505IIED.pdf.

Chanase, G. (2021). *Shift the power – Ghanaian NGOs at the crossroads of relinquishing power to local communities* [WACSeries, Issue Paper, 7(9)]. Accra: West Africa Civil Society Institute. Retrieved from: https://globalfundcommunityfoundations.org/wp-content/uploads/2021/10/Shift-the-Power-Ghanaian-NGOs-at-the-Crossroads-of-Relinquishing-Power-to-Local-Communities.pdf.

Elbers, W., & Arts, B. J. M. (2011). Keeping body and soul together: Southern NGOs' strategic responses to donor constraints. *International Review of Administrative Sciences*, 77(4), 713–732. https://doi.org/10.1177/0020852311419388.

IOB (Policy and Operations Evaluation Department of Netherlands Ministry of Foreign Affairs). (2017). *Shifting interests, changing relations, support under pressure: Policy review of Dutch support to Southern civil society development*. Retrieved from: https://english.iob-evaluatie.nl/publications/policy-review/2017/04/01/416-%E2%80%93-iob-%E2%80%93-policy-review-of-dutch-support-to-civil-society-development-%E2%80%93-shifting-interests-changing-relations-support-under-pressure.

IOB (Policy and Operations Evaluation Department of Netherlands Ministry of Foreign Affairs). (2019). *Strategies for partners: Balancing complementarity and autonomy: Evaluation of the functioning of strategic partnerships between the Ministry of Foreign Affairs and civil society organizations*. Retrieved from: https://english.iob-evaluatie.nl/publications/publications/2019/08/01/431-%E2%80%93-iob-%E2%80%93-evaluation-of-the-functioning-of-strategic-partnerships-between-the-ministry-of-foreign-affairs-and-civil-society-organisations-%E2%80%93-summary-with-recommendations-and-findings-%E2%80%93-strategies-for-partners-balancing-complementarity-and-autonomy.

Netherlands Ministry of Foreign Affairs. (2001). Brief van de Minister voor Ontwikkelingssamenwerking. Kamerstuk 27433, nr. 3. Retrieved from: https://zoek.officielebekendmakingen.nl/kst-27433-3.pdf.

Netherlands Ministry of Foreign Affairs. (2013). *Brief van de Minister voor Buitenlandse Handel en Ontwikkelingssamenwerking*. Kamerstuk 33625, nr. 39. Retrieved from: https://zoek.officielebekendmakingen.nl/kst-33625-39.html.

Netherlands Ministry of Foreign Affairs. (2015). *Samenspraak en tegenspraak: selectie van de strategische partnerschappen in alfabetische volgorde*. Annex to Kamerstuk 33625–150. Retrieved from: https://zoek.officielebekendmakingen.nl/blg-474161.pdf.
Netherlands Ministry of Foreign Affairs. (2019). *Executive summary strengthening civil society theory of change: Supporting civil society's political role*. Annex 5 to Policy framework for Strengthening Civil Society: Power of voices partnerships. Retrieved from: https://www.government.nl/documents/policy-notes/2019/11/28/policy-framework-strengthening-civil-society.
Netherlands Ministry of Foreign Affairs. (2020). *Overzicht geselecteerde allianties, gesorteerd op thema, inclusief budget*. Annex to Kamerstuk 34952–117. Retrieved from: https://open.overheid.nl/repository/ronl-037d971c-18db-4ab7-8c0f-db852fbc33ad/1/pdf/overzicht-versterking-maatschappelijk-middenveld.pdf.
OECD (2008). *The Accra Agenda for Action (AAA)*. Retrieved from: https://www.oecd.org/dac/effectiveness/45827311.pdf.
Pailey, R. N. (2020). De-centring the 'White Gaze' of development. *Development and Change*, *51*(3), 729–745. https://doi.org/10.1111/dech.12550.
Pansardi, P., & Bindi, M. (2021). The new concepts of power? Power-over, power-to and power-with. *Journal of Political Power*, *14*(1), 51–71. https://doi.org/10.1080/2158379X.2021.1877001.
Quantson, R., Afadzinu, N., Balogun, O., & Arthur, I. H. (2015). *The state of civil society organisations' sustainability in Ghana: Striving, surviving or thriving?* Accra, Ghana: WACSI. Retrieved from: https://wacsi.org/wp-content/uploads/2015/03/The-State-of-Civil-Society-Organisations-Sustainability-in-Ghana.pdf.
Saad, L. (2020). *Me and white supremacy: How to recognise your privilege, combat racism and change the world*. London: Quercus.
Sawyer, J., & de Mars, J. (2021, January 6). Get up speak out for youth rights: Get up, speak out! Celebrating five years of youth-powered sexual and reproductive health and rights. *GUSO Magazine*. Beyond Borders Media & Rutgers. Retrieved from: https://issuu.com/jerrydemars/docs/210104-guso-all-def.
Senior Minister holds consultations with CSOs on 'Ghana Beyond Aid'. (2019, September 10). *Graphic online*. Retrieved from: https://www.graphic.com.gh/news/politics/senior-minister-holds-consultations-with-csos-on-ghana-beyond-aid.html.
van Ewijk, E., van Gent, M., Michielsen, K., & Ogbe, E. (2016). *Access, services, knowledge (ASK) – Youth Empowerment Alliance (YEA): End-of-programme evaluation, synthesis report*. Amsterdam, The Netherlands: Kaleidos Research and ICRH. Retrieved from: http://kaleidosresearch.nl/publication/ask-evaluation/.
VeneKlasen, L., & Miller, V. (2002). Power and empowerment. *PLA Notes*, *43*, 39–41.

17

STARTING ADVOCACY PROGRAMMES FROM THE SOUTH

Rethinking multi-country programming

Margit van Wessel

Introduction: multi-country programming as a missing factor shaping civil society organization collaborations

Over the past ten years, I have been involved with multiple research, consultancy, and evaluation projects on advocacy programmes administered by civil society organizations (CSOs) in the Netherlands, their partners in the Global South, and the Netherlands Ministry of Foreign Affairs, the main donor for these programmes. I have also been closely involved in the debate on relations within the sector, seeking to contribute to the transformations that so many think are needed. As a researcher, I observe a major lacuna in the debate: Multi-country programming is not being discussed as a factor shaping collaborations among CSOs. In this chapter, I discuss why I think this is an important factor and how it could be addressed. Here, I speak from my experience, which is rooted in the Dutch context, especially related to advocacy programming. My focus in this chapter is on what I call 'advocacy for development', defined as 'a wide range of activities conducted to influence decision makers at different levels with the overall aim of combatting the structural causes of poverty and injustice' (drawing on Morariu & Brennan, 2009, p. 100). This can include activities such as lobbying or demonstrations, awareness raising, legal action, and public education, as well as capacity building, constructing networks and relationships, and articulating views and interests through these networks and relationships.

In this chapter, I address the role of what I call 'Northern CSOs', which includes non-governmental organizations (NGOs) based in the North and international NGOs (INGOs) that have multiple offices worldwide but have programmes that may be led from the office in a single country, such as the Netherlands. The key feature to be addressed is the *role from a distance* of managing multi-country programmes, which is a typical role for a Northern CSO office. Below, I introduce

DOI: 10.4324/9781003241003-21

the practice of multi-country CSO advocacy programming by the Netherlands government and explain how the roles of Northern and Southern CSOs are constituted through such programmes. I then point out important limits in how power in CSO programming in development is presently discussed using the concept of 'shifting the power'. Finally, I propose an alternative approach that starts out from Southern agency in specific contexts, turning programming upside down while also capitalizing on Northern CSOs' power.

The case of the Netherlands' support to CSOs

The Netherlands Ministry of Foreign Affairs places high importance on advocacy as a means of achieving inclusive development, as civil society advocacy can help articulate and advance the voices of societal groups – especially those who are marginalized. To provide support (and also partnership; see van Wessel et al., 2020), the Ministry has published calls for proposals that encourage large submissions to be sent in by consortia of CSOs, taking this approach in 2010, 2015, and 2020. Each time, support was offered for five years. Commonly, programmes costing 40 million euros or more over the five years are funded. In the present policy programme, Strengthening Civil Society, for example, 42 consortia are supported from 2021 to 2025 at a total cost of 1.364 billion euros. Typically, three to six highly professionalized CSOs, including many INGOs, form a consortium. In the current programme, it is mandatory to have at least one Southern-based CSO partner in the consortium. Many have more. Typically, the consortium develops and manages a programme that is in large part carried out by 'local partners' contracted by one of the consortium members at country level. The funded programmes typically cover multiple countries in the Global South – sometimes straddling different continents – and are based on a programme-level Theory of Change centred on a single theme, such as climate change, food security, or women's rights. The Ministry's policies provide space for contextualization and adaptation over time. The current funding programme seeks to advance local ownership: Consortia must have policies to ensure control is shared with local partners. However, generically formulated, decontextualized advocacy programmes produced by the CSO consortia are initially approved as the starting points for programmes. Country selection is done by the CSOs, but the Ministry has increasingly sought to set conditions to align programming with its own priorities regarding themes, policy objectives, and countries. Importantly, at this stage, the 'local partners', who are to carry out much of the programmes, are commonly not yet part of the process.

It is after a programme has been approved by the Ministry that the 'consortium member' CSOs select their country-level 'local' partners. This selection can be based on multiple criteria, such as ideological alignment, sound financial management, and other requirements set by the back donor, as well as capacities and existing relations. Fit with the programme's basic objectives, understandings of issues, and strategies is also a requirement. Country offices of Northern CSOs have a leading role here and are often given significant space to decide which partners to contract, provided they fit the programme. Although this contracting mostly happens on an individual basis, in some cases, groups of in-country organizations can apply to be funded. Such groups could be a country-level CSO and its partners or the informal groups it supports, for example. Sometimes, programmes seek to capitalize on existing CSO networks in a country, but, in many cases, direct relations between a consortium member organization and its country-level CSO partners are the most important, as these are the entities between which contracts are made. The CSO consortia leading the programme do often seek to build coherence between global and country-level work, stimulating exchange, alignment, and collaboration among country-level partners. In some cases, this works (see e.g. a story about a Nigerian coalition in van Wessel et al., 2021). A programme can also provide opportunities to develop relations, shared objectives, and coordinated strategy. However, collaboration is not necessarily sought by partners, who may primarily seek funding to advance their organizational interests and objectives, which may only partly match the programme. Moreover, partners may feel placed in what some might call an arranged marriage with CSOs that are not their natural partners.

In line with principles of adaptive management (see Gutheil, 2021), the CSO policy programmes funded by the Netherlands Ministry of Foreign Affairs were designed to be context-sensitive. Early in the process, these programmes have 'inception periods' during which programme-level Theories of Change are to be adapted at country level by the country-level CSOs involved (see e.g. Ho et al., 2020). The programmes are also expected to learn and adapt their Theories of Change over time. This contextualization and adaptation do not necessarily happen to the same degree across different CSO consortia or their different subprogrammes. The roles of Theories of Change are also diverse across different consortia, and these tools are not necessarily prominent in the programmes' everyday running. Additionally, at country level, CSOs may make various choices in terms of how they shape their work, but this will not necessarily show up in reports. Given that interaction with country-level actors is limited, consortium member CSOs working from the Netherlands may have limited information on what actually happens at the country level. Their attention is necessarily divided over multiple countries and sometimes more than one programme. Although some staff members have the chance to focus on programme content, for many, other aspects take up much of the attention: managerial tasks (such as drawing up agreements, making sure financial management is in order and that reports are produced and of the right quality, making sure the programme criteria are met in terms of focus and addressing required elements such as gender, supporting learning processes, and making sure everything is set up and reported according to donor requirements).

From control to contribution

The power of Northern CSOs leading development programmes has been heavily criticized. Specifically, this critique focuses on their power as exercised through managerialism, understood as administrative control, constricting the actions of others. In the current debate on decolonizing development, anti-racism, and #shiftthepower, Northern CSOs are often taken to be the main culprit. However, often working with large institutional donors, Northern CSOs are given responsibility for multi-million-euro programmes, with predefined understandings of issues, objectives, and other key elements. As they are a main channel for donors to distribute funding and carry out donor policies, Northern CSOs are often in a position where they appear to have little choice but to force their partners to comply with conditions that have been predefined in interaction with the donors holding them responsible for their assigned tasks. This form of control is a system feature rather than a feature of just the Northern CSOs involved, and it deserves to be addressed as such.

Researchers have also advanced more complex notions of power that move beyond control. Gaventa's power cube, for example, conceptualizes power as multidimensional, having different forms, showing up at different levels, and existing in different types of spaces (Gaventa, 2019, 2021). Scholars (e.g. Gaventa, 2021; Haugaard, 2012; Pansardi & Bindi, 2021) have also conceptualized power as 'power over', 'power to', 'power with', and 'power within'. While these ideas have been taken up and even become popular in some discussions on power in international development, engagement with power in the production of solutions for civil society collaborations has been limited to addressing 'power over' – much in line with the constricted approach to administrative control discussed above. This is the form of power that is about domination – the ability to constrain the choices of another actor. In this context, 'power over' is typically associated with negative terms: domination, coercion, and disempowerment. How to end this 'power over' is the central question addressed in the current search for solutions regarding power in CSO collaborations. The resultant calls for more direct funding of Southern CSOs aim to take 'power over' away from Northern CSOs and put Southern CSOs in control (Saldinger, 2021). Community philanthropy likewise aims to take 'power over' away from Northern CSOs and put Southern CSOs in control, integrating the aim of enabling Southern CSOs to have closer relations and interactions with their own constituencies. New governance structures/partnership setups aim to share/mitigate the 'power over' of Northern CSOs over their Southern partners and thereby make development more locally led. The wider debate on decolonizing aid addresses assumptions and practices underlying and reproducing 'power over', calling for more acknowledgement and recognition of Southern-based expertise and agency, the end of racism, and a reshaping of the language of development, which helps define and reproduce inequalities (see e.g. Paige et al., 2021).

The approaches to reimagining CSO relations begin from the starting point that the necessary transformation centres on power and thus conclude that addressing inequalities will open up a world of possibilities for Southern CSOs to flourish. Northern CSOs, then, are placed in a position where they must hand over power. Power is a zero-sum game – a set quantity that is moved from one side to another. Northern CSOs must give up their power, privilege, and prejudice to decolonize their relations and focus on the empowerment of CSOs in the Global South. In publications on the topic, it appears to be self-evident that the role of Northern CSOs will decrease as this happens. Their role is to be supportive, but they are primarily to make way (see e.g. Bond, 2021; Paige et al., 2021). While I applaud these important efforts, I note that there is little discussion of possible futures for Northern CSOs, which is surprising given the other forms of power held by Northern CSOs (power to, power with), which could help development efforts with Southern actors in leading roles. Further, among the Northern CSOs I have worked with, I have thus far not seen a fundamental rethinking of the future of Northern CSOs that looks beyond the shifts in 'power over' that are presently being called for. There is thus also not much of an energizing alternative vision for the future, it seems, when it comes to the question facing Northern CSOs – how to collaborate with Southern CSOs, beyond power shifting.

In the academic literature, some works do provide alternative perspectives. A rare discussion of INGO roles provided by Mitchell et al. (2020) described 'transnational NGOs' as declining in relevance and in need of fundamental transformation to remain relevant. They portrayed INGOs as defined by legacy architecture, collectivizing and redistributing resources, and based on a charity model that is not properly geared towards achieving the societal transformations the organizations want. These organizations are at risk of 'successful irrelevance', meaning they will likely be able to continue to exist and administer programmes as they have done before, satisfying the demands of the aid system, but that they will not be in a position to address the root causes of inequality and injustice. According to Mitchell et al. (2020, pp. 230–266), fundamental changes are needed from within INGOs; these authors call for new organizational models, leadership, and structures that address the standards and regulations that are currently geared towards legality and accountability rather than facilitating the changes and transformations to which these organizations want to contribute. Other scholars have pointed to alternative ways of conceptualizing Northern CSO roles in CSO collaborations in development that relativize these roles. For instance, Shipton and Dauvergne's (2021) analysis of South–BRICS–North collaborations centred on CSO collaboration in the Global South and showed Northern CSOs in complementary roles. Roepstorff (2020), analysing localization of humanitarian action, problematized the conceptualization of localization in North–South binary terms, given how local actors are enmeshed in international networks. Although I concur with these insights, they do not yet address the centrality of Northern CSOs administering multi-country programmes in development or advance alternatives that break the constraints that this practice imposes on all parties involved. Below, I offer such an alternative, proposing that programming be turned upside down by centring it on Southern agency, while simultaneously capitalizing on the ability of Northern CSOs' power to support action led by Southern CSOs. From these starting points, avenues for building new roles for Northern CSOs are presented.

Turning programming upside down

It is widely accepted that development programming needs to be context-sensitive. Adaptive management is prominent in development discourse, but this process is as yet poorly institutionalized (Gutheil, 2021). However, even if it were taken up more broadly, adaptive management is a Northern-based paradigm (Gutheil, 2021) that maintains the idea that development can be initiated from outside a particular context and subsequently be adapted to that context. This implies that starting points in terms of understandings, interventions, and objectives are already set. It is thus not a paradigm that allows for local leadership, but one that allows for local leeway. In recent years, a team of researchers with whom I have worked have studied how CSOs in India give shape to their roles (Katyaini et al., 2021; Rajeshwari et al., 2020; Syal et al., 2021; van Wessel et al., 2020). Across the board, it struck me how the CSOs we spoke with, while in 'partnership' programmes with Northern CSOs, were in a universe far removed from the programme context in which their work was supposed to fit. Without exception, they were seeking to fulfil their potential by relating to the possibilities and constraints of their context, as they interpreted them, based on their contextual expertise. Crucially, the capacity to engage with their own contexts defined the nature of the action and change they envisaged. International collaborations or influences were seen as complementary rather than leading and, ideally, as supportive. These CSOs shaped their roles while embedded in relations with their constituencies, other CSOs, and the state. Engaging their contexts from their own perspectives, the CSOs constructed the nature of their work and their way of relating. Contexts and relations both offered possibilities and imposed constraints for the organizations, as was the case, for example, with relations with funders or the state, which would offer avenues for action or constrain the space for action, imposing understandings and ambitions and forcing the CSOs to reorient, at least publicly. Their roles were thus relationally defined in reflexive interplay between the organizations and their relations and contexts, rather than being simply a matter of 'traits' such as organizational type, capacities, and preferred strategy.

Acknowledging the contextualized nature of agency

The studied CSOs often shaped their roles as part of existing networks, with key roles played by domestic actors of various kinds, engaging in ongoing change processes that were nationally or sub-nationally specific in important ways. To the extent that Northern CSOs were important, they appeared to be seen as funders and actors that could play complementary roles to contribute to reaching the Southern organizations' objectives, as understood by the Southern CSOs themselves, taking their own organizations' understandings, capacities, and objectives as starting points. Agency emerged in how the actors related to the possibilities and constraints of their own contextual setting, as interpreted by the actors involved. Our findings reflect agency as conceptualized in Emirbayer and Mische's (1998, p. 970) seminal paper on agency, where agency is defined as

> the temporally constructed engagement by actors of different structural environments—the temporal-relational contexts of action—which, through the interplay of habit, imagination, and judgment, both reproduces and transforms those structures in interactive response to the problems posed by changing historical situations.

This definition encompasses three constitutive elements of agency. One, iteration, refers to 'the selective reactivation by actors of past patterns of thought and action, as routinely incorporated in practical activity, thereby giving stability and order to social universes and helping to sustain identities, interactions, and institutions over time' (Emirbayer & Mische, 1998, p. 971). The second element, projectivity, refers to actors' 'imaginative generation [...] of possible future trajectories of action, in which received structures of thought and action may be creatively reconfigured in relation to actors' hopes, fears, and desires for the future' (p. 971). Third, the practical-evaluative element of agency involves 'the capacity of actors to make practical and normative judgments among alternative possible trajectories of action, in response to the emerging demands, dilemmas, and ambiguities of presently evolving situations' (p. 971). The CSOs in our research were indeed seen to act as agents in the sense that they built their perspectives on what they could be and how they could act on the basis of their engagements with their contexts over time, building understandings about what was possible, right, and desirable for them to be and do within these contexts.

I propose this temporal-contextualized understanding of agency as an important new angle from which to approach CSOs' roles and collaborations. With this understanding, reshaping CSO collaborations is not primarily a question of shifting power, but of acknowledging and starting from the agency that can transform CSOs into change agents, with 'outsiders' to country-based processes playing supportive and complementary roles *of necessity*.

Re-understanding the roles of Northern CSOs

Here, I relate to two small but important existing lines of research. The first line has long stressed the need to approach CSOs' roles as contextual (Lewis & Opoku-Mensah, 2006). Some of this work has focused on identifying contextual factors to explain CSOs' roles (e.g. Marchetti, 2018). Other work has explored how CSOs relate to elements of their context (e.g. Kamstra et al., 2013) or how elements of the context shape CSOs' roles (e.g. Kamstra et al., 2016).

A second, still smaller line of research has shown that CSOs should be seen as agents who negotiate their roles within their contexts, manoeuvring possibilities (e.g. Aarts & Cavatorta, 2013; Hunt, 2008). These two lines of research show, respectively, the importance of context for roles and the importance of seeing CSOs as agents. Neither line of research yet goes to the deeper level of understanding how the embeddedness in context, over time, shapes CSOs' imaginings of what development could be and what they, as actors in that context, could be and do as *naturally privileged* interpreters of the situation – a position that could never be taken over by outsiders.

It follows from this that it has also remained elusive in the literature and in practice what Northern CSOs seeking to support civil society in the Global South should do about context – how relating to context and accepting the leadership of Southern CSOs within their own contexts can help shape Northern CSOs' roles, beyond the constantly repeated pleas for shifting or sharing power and addressing the ills of domination. Over the years, people working for Southern CSOs whom I encountered through diverse projects have shed light on this, consistently referring to specific forms of added value that Northern CSOs had for them, based on their contextually defined perspectives on their own roles.

These CSOs defined the added value of Northern CSOs based on complementarity with their own organization's needs. The Indian CSO representatives we spoke with valued collaboration with international CSOs to the extent that these organizations could help them attain their own established objectives. There was very little discussion of complementarity in terms of collective action on 'global' issues or the grand need for 'common ground' and collective endeavour, challenges that are commonly the focus of discussions on collaboration in CSO consortia and alliances. Although the interviewees were aware of the global nature of issues and were open to internationally developed approaches, the conceptualization of their role and of complementarity with international CSOs in executing that role was largely domestically oriented. A first complementarity they identified was enhanced reputation through association. Indian CSO staff valued being associated with international CSOs, stating that collaboration with international CSOs increased their visibility, credibility, and prestige in domestic CSO and government circles, stating, for example, that meetings with policymakers could be organized more easily when foreign names were attached. Similarly, participation in international fora could be helpful at the domestic level. As one CSO staff member explained, 'if your work is showcased in an international forum through partnerships and collaborations, the state might think of taking up some of your ideas in their policy'. Association with international CSOs thus appears to expand Indian CSOs' mandate in their domestic context in the eyes of important stakeholders, including the state. In the view of some interviewees, association with international CSOs also helped them to gain recognition internationally (e.g. with foreign funders that may classify a CSO in terms of traits such as capacity and values because of its association with international CSOs or networks) (cf. Kumi & Elbers, 2022). A second complementarity lies in the exposure to international frameworks and ideas offered by engagement with international CSOs. Through international collaboration, the Indian CSOs were exposed to new and globally current ideas and developments. This, again, helped the CSOs domestically, given the high status of such frameworks and the ambition of (and related pressure from) the Indian state to relate to such frameworks. As one interviewee explained, 'Global partnerships really help. A global mandate is necessary to highlight an issue. With a global mandate and global events, you can do anything you want – with its backing'. Relatedly, interviewees mentioned the added value of international CSOs' knowledge and expertise, which exposed them to new knowledge, approaches, and professional practices.

According to the Indian CSO representatives, a third type of complementarity offered by international CSOs involves international CSOs' ability to provide funding with a longer-term vision, in contrast to the short-term, visible results often demanded by domestic funders (van Wessel et al., 2020).

Similarly, a research project with Cordaid on linkages between civil society advocacy at international and domestic levels brought out that the interviewees (staff of diverse CSOs working in a Cordaid-administered advocacy programme in diverse Southern countries) approached this question from domestically defined perspectives. They articulated different forms of relevance for linking national and international advocacy. However, this relevance was consistently articulated from the perspective of national-level advocacy. For example, international-level advocacy was seen to strengthen national-level advocacy in diverse ways. Collaboration between international- and national-level advocates could support national advocacy by drawing attention and mobilizing support for country-level issues and efforts, strengthening national-level capacity, raising profiles of national-level advocates, and demonstrating that the national-level advocacy was part of a global effort (van Wessel, 2021). Roles for international-level advocates in the programme were also systematically framed in terms of their capacity to strengthen the national advocacy led by national-level advocates. International advocates could strengthen the capacity of the national-level staff members through, for example, coaching, training, translating, helping with connecting, and learning by doing together. International advocates could also support national-level advocacy by, for instance, helping with analysis and stepping in to conduct joint advocacy targeting international institutions. They could put their international advocacy expertise to work by sharing strategic information, analysing how developments and possibilities at different levels are linked, and broadening national-level advocates' perspectives. At the international level, international advocates could build support for national-level issues to influence national-level processes internationally, as well as drawing on national-level results for this international advocacy.

Another theme observed in previous work with CSOs in various contexts is that of handling constricting civic space. Here, too, my colleagues and I found that domestic-level CSOs spoke from the same position when they defined the added value of Northern CSOs. Staff from some Southern CSOs working in conflict prevention and peacebuilding spoke of the protection they sensed came from being embedded in the Global Partnership for the Prevention of Armed Conflict (GPPAC), an international network of CSOs working on conflict prevention and peacebuilding. They mentioned the enhanced legitimacy they felt they obtained through their engagement with GPPAC, improving their image by association. In other cases, they reported being granted enhanced space because GPPAC provided the legitimizing umbrella of a global network (Arensman et al., 2015, p. 520). Notably, in other contexts, such associations may be detrimental, contributing to the delegitimization of domestic CSOs as foreign agents, bringing alien values into society, and lacking the legitimacy of an obvious domestic constituency. As Fransen et al. (2021) have reported, INGOs, then, may continue to provide support – but from behind the scenes, with domestic CSOs acting more publicly. Alternatively, in some situations, INGOs are able to speak out in ways that domestic CSOs cannot without risking reprisal (Fransen et al., 2021). An interviewee from a CSO in Uganda explained this, discussing the role of Cordaid in advocacy within Africa and referring to an international advocate working with Cordaid's Global Office (in Cordaid, those in this role are commonly referred to as 'experts'):

> It provides protection for those who are speaking, and we're trying to provide the voices. In this work that we do, governments sometimes are not happy when you speak the truth... You can be attacked then [...] But if Cordaid talks about it, there's nothing anybody is going to do. Cordaid is not based in Africa. [Expert] does not work there. And they don't know where [expert] is getting [the] information. That would be a kind of protection.
>
> *(van Wessel, 2021)*

These insights indicate a range of ways in which Northern-based NGOs and INGOs can contribute to the transformative efforts of Southern-based CSOs, centred on specific forms of added value associated with their status and capacities. This can form a basis for stepping away from multi-country programming and for reimagining roles. The idea may seem far-fetched, given how established the practice of multi-country programming is as what makes collaboration possible, with its coherent formulation, contractual accountabilities on the shoulders of the CSOs who administer these programmes, and 'partners' perhaps adapting within limits. However, the foundations underlying current practices continue to be undermined, and various innovative structures of collaboration are being developed and experimented with; this approach could be attached to these attempts at innovation.

Reshaping Northern CSOs' roles

A Northern CSO staff member once wondered, when speaking with me, referring to their Southern partners, 'Would they work with us if we didn't have the money?' Given how many Southern CSOs see multiple forms of added value in Northern CSOs, there is reason to think that many would. Focusing on an organization's 'power to' – its capacity for action – would mean capitalizing on its complementary added value in collaborations, whereas focusing on its 'power with' would mean capitalizing on the collective ability/empowerment that could emerge through collaborations. This would imply a shift from creating and managing interventions to contributing to change processes with others in the lead, while still making the most of Northern CSOs' power, rather than delegitimizing and discarding it. Key elements of Northern CSOs' roles in advocacy programmes that 'start from the South' would include the following.

Rethinking identity

To establish how and to what to contribute, organizations need an agenda, an understanding of the strengths they have and want to invest in further, and a vision on how these strengths can contribute to their agenda when they assume a contributing rather than leading role. Northern CSOs should ask themselves several identity-centred questions: What can our understanding of who we are, our role, and our legitimacy be when we don't set the parameters for programmes but, instead, contribute? What do we bring to the table that is true to our understandings of realities and issues and how to address them, while respecting that we are contributing to the work of people whose understandings may be different? Organizations indeed would need to reflect on how to relate, as organizations, to the diverse understandings they confront in settings where they wish to contribute, as they would need to do more than simply accommodate diversity – They would need to accept that perspectives of others must be understood and accepted to build a contribution in interaction with these. Linking up in this way may require Northern CSOs to reconsider how, and to what extent, some of their driving values may lose their shine of universality in honest interaction with the diversity of values with which they find themselves faced in the Global South.

Linking up with what is already there

Related to the above, to be able to contribute to existing and emerging agendas of CSOs in the Global South, and to link up with these, Northern CSOs would need to identify locally salient agendas in the Global South around which people are organizing and then relate to these agendas without flattening diversities or rejecting unexpected approaches and priorities.

In addition, if it is accepted that Southern CSOs are to be in the lead and that collaboration is to be based on that leadership rather than on a Southern CSO's fit with the starting points and requirements of an externally predefined programme, the legitimacy of Southern CSOs as partners would have to be defined on the basis of the approach and quality of their representation of local constituencies or locally recognized needs and values. This challenge has hardly been addressed thus far, and it is one of the most important gaps in the debate on reimagining civil society collaborations. It is also one not easily resolved, given its magnitude and complexity (see Katyaini et al., 2021; van Wessel et al., 2020).

Collaboration can involve individual Southern CSOs, but, given questions of scale and the complexity of the issues, it is important to support existing, emergent and potential networks and movements and to engage with those that are working on an issue without the need for funding as a driver. This can help Northern CSOs to link up with advocacy processes in the South that are already underway and facilitate building on already flowing local energies, while also making programmes more process-oriented and contextually embedded. This approach moves advocacy programming away from an intervention orientation, which tends to overestimate the impact of individual programmes or interventions and to discount the efforts of other actors and processes involved. Networks and movements may be sub-national, national, regional, and/or international. Engaging with these to strengthen and contribute to them on the basis of the assessment of fit and added value may also help address the unhelpful tendency to think in terms of local/international and North/South binaries (cf. Roepstorff, 2020). Further, building collaboration on the basis of collective purpose and mutuality may help address the sensitive topic of the role of the Northern CSO 'country office', which is at once local and a foreign outpost competing with what some see as the 'truly local'.

Northern CSOs can explore how already-existing CSO advocacy on an issue in a Southern context involves diverse civil society actors and complementarities among them. This involves answering fundamental questions regarding CSOs' agency, as conceptualized above: What, exactly, are the different CSOs working on an issue trying to achieve? From what understandings rooted in past experiences do these CSOs work, and what future vision and capacities to work towards that vision are present? Through what kinds of relating to the context and other actors? What forms of support from the Northern side can best strengthen the ongoing efforts? Northern CSOs engaging with such questions can maintain an openness to working with actors that are meaningfully contributing to change but that would not normally be considered eligible as partners. This may include, for example, of social movements, platforms, and individual activists.

Such an approach could fit well with current tendencies to focus on strengthening voices in the Global South, but it would be good to be specific regarding what is meant by that. Starting from the South in strengthening voices can mean supporting exchange and integration of perspectives, knowledge, and scale in cases of complex, multi-dimensional issues. It can also mean facilitating the articulation and organization of the voices of societal groups that are relatively less heard, or whose understandings and agendas strengthen those who are not well represented in existing civil society or who are commonly left without needed support. Further, it could mean helping to make sure that the full diversity of voices in a context is covered – 'discursive representation' (Dryzek & Niemeyer, 2008). Finally, it could also mean interacting with Southern CSOs and publics on issues and perspectives that are new to them or on which new opportunities or threats are emerging.

Working with opportunities

From the social movement literature, we know that social movement coalition formation depends on multiple conditions, including social ties and the interactions necessary to build and sustain these, conducive institutional structures, fit in terms of culture and ideology, and resources. But also of central importance is what to come together *on* – that is, opportunities and threats that can energize and focus collective strategic action (Van Dyke & Amos, 2017). However, within the aid system, opportunities to work on something depend on opportunities to obtain funding. An organization's agency, grounded in its past engagement with its context, in which its visioning of possibilities is rooted, can become muddled with the burden of meeting outsiders' expectations, disrupting their engagement with the opportunities and threats that their agency enables them to identify and act on. Working with existing, emergent, or potential coalitions in a particular context can help make sure that Northern CSOs are working with the opportunities and threats identified by Southern CSOs as starting points for a programme.

Complementarity

On the basis of the above points, organizations can offer added value of various kinds to contextually embedded CSOs, networks, and movements, supporting their efforts to contribute to change processes in which they are involved. This would mean exploring where agendas can meet and uncovering how different approaches and strengths can complement each other in a Southern-centred change process. For Northern CSOs, this would require articulating and contributing specific forms of added value that capitalize on their power as Northern CSOs. This can bring out and strengthen Northern CSOs' roles in new ways, highlighting and advancing the importance of their specific capacities and contributions. This can include, for example, mobilizing public opinion in the Global North, engaging Northern institutions, raising funds, bringing in international frameworks and international dimensions of issues, engaging in convening, linking, and brokering, contributing technical expertise, coaching, and providing services. Building complementary roles and relations rooted in solidarity with what is already there or emerging in a context (Deveaux, 2021; Garbe, 2022, see also Chapter 2) can help avoid reproducing Northern dominance.

Conclusion

Moving away from multi-country programming and towards context-specific contributions to change would be transformative for Northern CSOs. To contribute meaningfully to Southern-centred processes working with the elements delineated above, Northern CSOs would need to be highly knowledgeable about the contexts and the makeup of civil society in these contexts. Based on this knowledge, they could establish how to contribute to the ongoing work of CSOs, networks, and movements in a particular context in meaningful ways. They could build mutuality rooted in understanding, trust, and acceptance of a contributing rather than a leading role, while still working towards their own agendas and sustaining and growing their specific forms of added value. Given these requirements, it would make sense for individual Northern CSOs to limit their work to a select set of countries or regions and a well-demarcated set of themes.

The proposed approach would require establishing funding and governance structures to fit, enabling fundraising, agenda setting, strategizing, and execution of programmes, as well as their governance. Given how control over funding creates power inequalities, the transformations imagined above can likely only come about when supported by the changes in 'power over' on which so many are working. Innovative upcoming models for the structure and governance of CSO collaborations might be able to provide solutions here, offering alternative ways of handling fundamental questions of control and accountability. Approaches of donors also require transformation to facilitate turning programming upside down. This would change or even leave behind the central 'fundermediary' role of Northern CSOs and raise new questions of control and accountability from donors' perspectives, which would need to be addressed. This may all seem far-fetched now, but, soon, it may not.

References

Aarts, P., & Cavatorta, F. (2013). *Civil society in Syria and Iran: Activism in authoritarian contexts*. Boulder, CO: Lynne Rienner Publishers.

Arensman, B., Barrett, J B., Hilhorst, D, Klaver, D. C., Rasch, E., Richert, W, van Bodegom, A. J., Wagemakers, A., & van Wessel, M. (2015). *MFS II Joint Evaluation of international lobbying and advocacy. Endline Report*. Wageningen: Wageningen University/SGE. Retrieved from: https://library.wur.nl/WebQuery/wurpubs/fulltext/526487.

Bond. (2021). *Catalysing locally-led development in the UK aid system*. London: Bond. Retrieved from: https://www.bond.org.uk/resources/catalysing-locally-led-development-in-the-uk-aid-system.

Deveaux, M. (2021). *Poverty, solidarity, and poor-led social movements*. New York: Oxford University Press.

Dryzek, J. S., & Niemeyer, S. (2008). Discursive representation. *American Political Science Review, 102*(4), 481–493. https://doi.org/10.1017/S0003055408080325.

Emirbayer, M., & Mische, A. (1998). What is agency? *American Journal of Sociology, 103*(4), 962–1023.

Fransen, L., Dupuy, K., Hinfelaar, M., & Zakaria Mazumder, S. M. (2021). Tempering transnational advocacy? The effect of repression and regulatory restriction on transnational NGO collaborations. *Global Policy, 12*, 11–22. https://doi.org/10.1111/1758-5899.12972.

Garbe, S. (2022). *Weaving solidarity: Decolonial perspectives on transnational advocacy of and with the Mapuche*. Bielefeld: transcript Verlag.

Gaventa, J. (2019). Applying power analysis: Using the 'Powercube' to explore forms, levels and spaces. In R. McGee, R., & J. Pettit (Eds.), *Power, Empowerment and Social Change* (pp. 117-138). Abingdon: Routledge.

Gaventa, J. (2021). Linking the prepositions: using power analysis to inform strategies for social action. *Journal of Political Power, 14*(1), 109–130. https://doi.org/10.1080/2158379X.2021.1878409.

Gutheil, L. (2021). Adaptive project management for the civil society sector: Towards an academic research agenda. *International Development Planning Review, 43*(3), 393–418. https://doi.org/10.3828/idpr.2020.17.

Haugaard, M. (2012). Rethinking the four dimensions of power: Domination and empowerment. *Journal of Political Power, 5*(1), 33–54. https://doi.org/10.1080/2158379X.2012.660810.

Ho, W., van Wessel, M., & Tamas, P. A. (2020). *The hidden life of theories of change*. The Hague/Wageningen: Hivos/Wageningen University & Research. Retrieved from: https://library.wur.nl/WebQuery/wurpubs/fulltext/533885.

Hunt, J. (2008). *Local NGOs in national development: The case of East Timor*. PhD thesis RMIT University.

Kamstra, J., Knippenberg, L., & Schulpen, L. (2013). Cut from a different cloth? Comparing democracy-promoting NGOs in Ghana and Indonesia. *Journal of Civil Society, 9*(1), 1–20. https://doi.org/10.1080/17448689.2013.771078.

Kamstra, J., Pelzer, B., Elbers, W., & Ruben, R. (2016). Constraining is enabling? Exploring the influence of national context on civil society strength. *VOLUNTAS: International Journal of Voluntary and Nonprofit Organizations, 27*(3), 1023–1044. https://doi.org/10.1007/s11266-016-9697-0.

Katyaini, S., Wessel, M. V., & Sahoo, S. (2021). Representation by development organizations: Evidence from India and implications for inclusive development. *The Journal of Environment & Development, 30*(1), 98–123. https://doi.org/10.1177/1070496520983599.

Kumi, E., & Elbers, W. (2022). How internationally funded NGOs promote gender equality in horticulture value chains in Kenya. *Third World Quarterly*, 1–17. https://doi.org/10.1080/01436597.2022.2081543.

Lewis, D., & Opoku-Mensah, P. (2006). Moving forward research agendas on international NGOs: Theory, agency and context. *Journal of International Development, 18*(5), 665–675. https://doi.org/10.1002/jid.1306.

Marchetti, R. (Ed.). (2018). *Government–NGO relationships in Africa, Asia, Europe and MENA*. London: Routledge.

Mitchell, G. E., Schmitz, H. P., & Bruno-van Vijfeijken, T. (2020). *Between power and irrelevance: The future of transnational NGOs*. New York: Oxford University Press.

Morariu, J., & Brennan, K. (2009). Effective advocacy evaluation: The role of funders. *The Foundation Review, 1*(3), 100–108.

Pansardi, P., & Bindi, M. (2021). The new concepts of power? Power-over, power-to and power-with. *Journal of Political Power, 14*(1), 51–71. https://doi.org/10.1080/2158379X.2021.1877001.

Paige, S., with Kotsiras, D., & Peace Direct. (2021). *Time to Decolonize Aid. Insights and lessons from global consultation*. Retrieved from: https://www.peacedirect.org/publications/timetodecoloniseaid/.

Rajeshwari, B., Deo, N., & van Wessel, M. (2020). Negotiating autonomy in capacity development: Addressing the inherent tension. *World Development, 134*, 105046. https://doi.org/10.1016/j.worlddev.2020.105046.

Roepstorff, K. (2020). A call for critical reflection on the localisation agenda in humanitarian action. *Third World Quarterly, 41*(2), 284–301. https://doi.org/10.1080/01436597.2019.1644160.

Saldinger, A. (2021). *USAID chief Samantha Power details localization push*. December 8. Retrieved from: https://www.devex.com/news/usaid-chief-samantha-power-details-localization-push-102256#:~:text=U.S.%20Agency%20for%20International%20Development%20Administrator%20Samantha%20Power%20made%20the,and%20organizations%20in%20the%20effort.

Shipton, L., & Dauvergne, P. (2021). The politics of transnational advocacy against Chinese, Indian, and Brazilian extractive projects in the Global South. *The Journal of Environment & Development*, 10704965211019083. https://doi.org/10.1177/10704965211019083.

Syal, R., van Wessel, M., & Sahoo, S. (2021). Collaboration, co-optation or navigation? The role of civil society in disaster governance in India. *VOLUNTAS: International Journal of Voluntary and Nonprofit Organizations*, 1–14. https://doi.org/10.1007/s11266-021-00344-8.

Van Dyke, N., & Amos, B. (2017). Social movement coalitions: Formation, longevity, and success. *Sociology Compass, 11*(7), e12489. https://doi.org/10.1111/soc4.12489.

van Wessel, M. (2021). *Linking and localizing in multi-level advocacy, lessons from the Capacitating Change Programme*. Wageningen University & Research/Cordaid. Retrieved from: https://www.civil-society-research-collective.org/repository/blogs/linking-and-localizing-in-multi-level-advocacy.

van Wessel, M., Hilhorst, D., Schulpen, L., & Biekart, K. (2020). Government and civil society organizations: Close but comfortable? Lessons from creating the Dutch "Strategic Partnerships for Lobby and Advocacy." *Development Policy Review, 38*(6), 728–746.

van Wessel, M., Ho, W., Marty, E., & Tamas, P. A. (2021). *Advocacy in context: Stories from South Sudan, Nigeria, Burundi, Central African Republic and Afghanistan*. Cordaid. Retrieved from: https://edepot.wur.nl/543871.

van Wessel, M., Naz, F., & Sahoo, S. (2020). Complementarities in CSO collaborations: How working with diversity produces advantages. *VOLUNTAS: International Journal of Voluntary and Nonprofit Organizations*, 1–14. https://doi.org/10.1007/s11266-020-00227-4.

PART 5

Choosing new starting points for collaboration

18

A FEMINIST APPROACH TO COLLABORATION

A sex workers' network in India

B. Rajeshwari, Margit van Wessel and Nandini Deo

Introduction

Research on civil society partnerships and their power dynamics largely focuses on North–South relations, often emphasizing funding relations, including implications for who gets funded, as well as how funding relations constrain civil society organizations (CSOs) and force them to change their agendas and ways of working (Banks et al., 2015; Deo & McDuie-Ra, 2011; Jalali, 2013). Efforts to equalize power relations (e.g. the #Shiftthepower movement[1] and the Grand Bargain's call to allocate more funds to Southern CSOs)[2] have mainly sought to address these constraining factors. Debates and experiments concerning reshaping these power relations are also taking place, as seen with, for example, the RINGO project (RINGO, n.d.) and efforts towards 'localization' (van Brabant & Patel, 2018) and more equal partnerships (O'Brien & Evans, 2017). However, limited attention has been directed to the development of localized and more equal collaboration 'from the ground up' through direct engagement among organizations.

In this chapter, we focus on a case of CSO collaboration in India, where feminist collaboration provided space for narrowing resource gaps through a shared commitment to the rights of the represented groups. We illustrate how feminist engagement with intersectionality, positionality, and agency can shape how sex workers' advocacy emerges from lived experience while harnessing the power of a country-based feminist CSO acting as a donor and partner. This example of the bottom-up management of power differentials in pursuit of shared goals through mutual support involves a collaboration between a sex workers' network in India and a Delhi-based feminist human rights CSO working on issues related to sexuality and women's reproductive rights. The network brought together organizations throughout India (16 states) to advocate for respect, reliance, and

DOI: 10.4324/9781003241003-23

recognition for sex workers. The network and the feminist CSO worked with a shared commitment to sex workers' rights in feminist rights-based discourse. Building on their reflections on internal and external challenges to equal partnership, the partners drew on joint feminist principles of sharing, learning, and critiquing with a non-patronizing approach to narrow the power differential between the sex workers' network and the other organizations involved.

We begin by presenting the case context and methods, followed by a discussion of the feminist theory and practice influencing how the feminist CSO shaped their collaboration with the network. Then we present our findings (the application of the feminist principles and how they shaped the network), concluding with lessons learned for CSO collaboration more broadly.

Case context

Advocacy around sex work and sex workers' rights in India was in a significant phase when we started our research on this subject in 2018. The sex workers' network in India was focusing its advocacy on responding to the 'Trafficking in Persons (Prevention, Protection, and Rehabilitation) Bill, 2018'. This bill, which is commonly known as the anti-trafficking bill, garnered attention from sex workers' groups. In 2021, organizations in the sex workers' movement again came together to respond to a draft anti-trafficking bill put forward by the Ministry of Women and Child Development.

There are two sex work narratives in India. The dominant narrative portrays sex work as immoral, forced, and a consequence of trafficking. According to National Crime Records Bureau data, 95% of victims of trafficking in India are forced into prostitution (Divya, 2020). Sex work perspectives rooted in this narrative centre on how to prevent trafficking and rescue and rehabilitate those who are "trapped" in this immoral trade (Misra et al., 2000). This view is popular in policymaking circles in India, and the 2021 anti-trafficking bill reflects this discourse. The secondary narrative situates sex workers and their marginalization within a human rights discourse, approaching sex work as work chosen by people whose choice should be respected. Organizations working in this vein advocate for better health facilities, educational opportunities for sex workers' children, and social security[3] for sex workers. These organizations, largely led by sex workers, advocate for reducing the stigma around sex work to allow sex workers to live with dignity and respect.

The feminist CSO in this study, a human rights organization based in the Global South and led by women from the Global South, partnered with a network of community-based organizations (CBOs) primarily led by sex workers. The feminist CSO had worked to expand sexual and reproductive freedoms and advance the human rights of all people for over 20 years. The network advocated for the recognition of sex work so that sex workers would be provided with access to social and health security. The Delhi office of the feminist CSO worked with the network from a human rights-based approach, aiming to strengthen organizations and social movements while playing a supportive role, aiding local partners in achieving their goals. The feminist organization's principles of sharing, learning, and critiquing with a non-patronizing approach allowed the sex workers to take the lead in determining their advocacy goals and methods. This approach created space for conversation and dialogue on sex work with international organizations, national collectives, and diverse types of sex workers (brothel-, street-, and home-based). Despite the feminist organization's privileged position (e.g. as the donor and resource creator), they consciously worked to make the partnership more equal through their channels of communication.

Methods

The first author (based in India) conducted 14 semi-structured interviews with the key network leadership, CBO members from six different states, feminist CSO staff members, and activists associated with the network. The data include interviews with brothel-based and home-based sex workers. The first author also visited the office of the sex workers' network on the outskirts of Delhi and interviewed members in their own space, where they could communicate more openly. Additionally, she attended a dialogue session that included a conversation among different stakeholders on how to articulate sex workers' rights. We also analysed documentation including public and internal documents such as reports from several dialogue sessions and discussions between the network and other organizations. The three authors analysed the data as a team, seeking to identify how feminist principles addressing power in collaborations were expressed in the collaboration, drawing out the related implications and challenges.

Feminist theory and practice

The concept of intersectionality was developed in 1989 by American legal theorist Kimberlé Crenshaw (1989), who used this framework to understand how the courts and police failed to 'see' how women of different racial and class backgrounds experienced domestic violence. She argued that identity is not additive – each person exists at the intersection of multiple dimensions of identity. Each individual's location within the matrix of identity shapes their experiences. In the Indian context, Menon (2015) has rejected the term 'intersectionality', arguing that Indian social activists learned how to think about identity in this nuanced way on their own in the course of their struggle for freedom. Other Indian feminists have responded that intersectionality continues to be useful in pushing activism to be more cognizant of the dangers of exclusion and marginalization within a movement (Gopal, 2015; John, 2015).[4] In this chapter, we find that an intersectional feminist approach to collaboration led the examined feminist CSO to create space for multiple voices and agendas within the sex workers' network, understanding that class, region, religion, caste, ability, and other dimensions of identity create a variety of experiences of sex work. Rather than trying to force one dominant narrative, the network actively included multiple voices and goals.

Standpoint theory, developed by feminist theorists, draws attention to the positionality of individuals in a dialogue, arguing that knowledge is socially situated (Hartsock, 1983)[5] and that those on the margins are better able than those in powerful positions to see and deconstruct power structures (hooks, 2000). These ideas offer a check on power differentials in collaborative networks. By arguing that each person or organization has only partial and situated knowledge and that those who are in dominant positions have less knowledge, a feminist approach to collaboration has the explicit goal of addressing power relations. Work by theorists such as Mohanty (1988) and Rege (2003) has substantiated these ideas in the Indian context. Others have applied these ideas specifically to civil society networks in India (Chandhoke, 2005; Deo & McDuie-Ra, 2011). In addition to making explicit how resources lead to power imbalances, feminists also work to mitigate these imbalances. In the case examined here, the feminist CSO, powerful because of its access to funding and expertise, takes active steps to reduce the possibility that its access to resources will lead it to become dominant within the network.

Feminists have also increasingly embraced the importance of individuals' 'own voices'. This phrase refers to the idea that, in addition to needing diverse stories, these stories must be told by the individuals involved (Duyvis, 2015[6]). This allows marginalized groups to articulate their own personal experiences – no one needs to speak for them. This is the most recent moment in a powerful current in feminism emphasizing the importance of women finding their own voices, allies amplifying those voices, and these voices directly articulating women's political demands (Ahmed, 2018). The construction of a narrative about oneself is a powerful feminist moment (Rajeshwari et al., 2020), and the studied sex workers' network is committed to empowering sex workers to speak for themselves in this way. Below, we make the following three central claims and analyse how the feminist concepts of intersectionality, positionality, and voice shaped the collaboration:

1 The network's collaboration with the feminist CSO created a space for dialogue and engagement to make intersectional identities visible in the sex workers' network.
2 Power differentials in the collaboration were addressed through the CSO taking a self-reflective approach with consciousness of positionality. Despite this approach, the feminist CSO sometimes struggled because of complex power differentials.
3 The sex workers' diverse lived experiences and perspectives were translated by the network with the help of the feminist CSO and others, supporting the sex workers' agency to make decisions for their own movement.

Practicing intersectionality

One core aspect of the partnership was the creation of space for the sex workers to fully express their intersectional identities, which shaped their varying experiences of sex work. Beginning with an acknowledgement of difference, the central need for respect and dignity when facing multiple forms of subordination was articulated in the collaboration.

The network aimed to bring sex workers from different parts of India together in a single platform where they could address problems they encountered. This goal faced two main challenges: First, the network did not have sufficient resources to bring the sex workers from different parts of India to participate in a single platform. Second, it was challenging to engage sex workers with diverse backgrounds (brothel-, home-, and street-based) in dialogue. Both challenges were addressed in the feminist CSO's collaboration with the network. The partnership provided access to physical space and resources (monetary and intellectual) and to other networks and organizations to facilitate dialogue among network members. Intellectual resources generally took the form of important information on international and national laws that could impact sex workers and their rights.

The feminist CSO helped the network to engage with sex workers with diverse identities because the CSO's intersectional lens allowed them to identify and counter exclusionary analyses of oppression where one form of oppression is prioritized over others. Indeed, in recent years, the recognition of intersectionality – driven partly by the work of the feminist CSO – has made the sex workers' movement in India more inclusive and flexible by giving space to the voices of diverse marginalized groups and trying to address underlying injustices. Its feminist background and intersectional approach allowed the feminist CSO to exhibit sensitivity to multiple identities in its collaboration with the diverse sex workers' network. The feminist CSO opened platforms for sex workers to speak about their experiences when they felt comfortable and safe sharing them. For example, the president of the network was included as a resource person speaking in feminist leadership training programmes offered by the feminist CSO for community-building organizations. A significant way the feminist CSO facilitated an intersectional approach in the sex workers' movement (where the sex workers were largely ciswomen but also included transgender women) was through making space for diverse network members to engage with other women's movement activists and university students, speaking to them about their experiences. This was important because other feminist organizations were not readily accepting of the network's narrative that sex work is a choice and were uncomfortable sharing a platform with sex workers. The network was able to engage with this feminist organization because it practiced feminist principles by acknowledging the diverse sex workers' agency to define themselves.

As the sex workers had different backgrounds and engaged in sex work in diverse ways, their struggles were not all the same. For instance, some sex workers wanted to engage with the network without being identified. One reason to avoid being publicly identified as a sex worker was to protect their other identities as wives, mothers, or providers for their families. The sex workers struggled with the complexity resulting from their multiple identities and sharing their experiences with others put them in a vulnerable position. Therefore, trust needed to develop between the feminist CSO and the network members before the latter could share their stories on common issues. Working from an intersectional feminist approach, the feminist CSO understood these differences and imagined the possibility of a dialogue that gave space to multiple voices. As a feminist organization, it was also sensitive to the complex realities of the sex workers' lives, which helped the CSO to respect these women's boundaries and to engage with the network. The CSO's understanding of intersectional identities let them to reject activism based on a 'single, exclusionary identity or single-issue politics'.[7] For example, the collaboration addressed the following challenge, expressed by a CBO office bearer from Ahmedabad, who explained the importance of bringing in the voices of sex workers who do not want to join open protests or public demonstrations:

> Most of the sex workers [here] work from home, and there are no brothels as in the case of West Bengal and other parts of India. This makes it difficult for them to get organized, as not everyone wants to come out in the open and acknowledge their status as a sex worker. Many sex workers want to hide their identity and do the work, and this makes it difficult to bring them within the group. Even before the organization was made, everyone was doing their own individual work, and whenever any sex worker would roam around on the streets with condoms, then the police would harass them. This problem was mainly because we were not organized, but we did not know that this was the main issue 'til I and a few more sex workers were sent for an exposure visit to Kolkata.

Exposure visits, aim to introduce sex workers from diverse backgrounds, through practical and real-life situations, so that they can exchange views, build trust, and develop a common language of advocacy as a network. Through these interactions, the sex workers recognized their shared challenges, learned that they faced similar harassment, and saw the necessity of an organized effort to address their concerns.

A diverse set of organizations and groups participated in the agenda-setting meetings,[8] which were primarily coordinated by the network and facilitated by the feminist CSO. These meetings gave space to different types of sex workers (brothel-based, home-based, street-based, and traditional sex workers[9]) to voice their views, creating a point of intersection for the different types of sex workers. Prior to this collaboration, only brothel-based sex workers had access to spaces for expressing their views and interacting with different stakeholders (e.g. Durbar Mahila in Bengal).[10] The network, in partnership with the feminist CSO, extended this space to other types of sex workers. In this forum, cross-cutting themes such as labour laws, legal options for sex workers, and access to welfare schemes were discussed, which created space for positioning sex workers in a labour framework, thus widening the scope for claiming sex workers' rights.

Convergences between the struggles of sex workers and those of other marginalized groups, such as cleaners (*Safai Karamcharis*) and differently abled people, were also discussed. These meetings thus broadened the sex workers' horizon and helped them find common links between their own and others' struggles. The sex workers came to understand that the struggles related to their sexuality were not just about being sex workers but also about being women (and in some cases transgender) and reflected on how this impinged on their right to survive with basic social security.

Positionality and self-consciousness

In taking the role of a facilitating partner, the feminist CSO was conscious of its position of power in its relationship with the network. The feminist CSO engaged in continuous self-reflection on its positionality in this partnership and accepted that power differentials cannot be completely overcome but can be addressed openly. The feminist CSO also struggled with the tension between positioning itself as an organization based completely in the South and as an organization with connections to other international organizations in the North, Asia, and Africa, bringing global understanding and the 'privilege' that comes with this status.

The feminist CSO was conscious of its own positionality, which involved not only power but also the need for constant self-reflection. The need to question their position was articulated by a key CSO staff member:

> There has been a huge amount of work to never co-opt the ability of that community to self-lead, which is very tricky. If it's a self-led movement, then we would not like to just come in between and co-opt their space.

The feminist CSO and the network maintained a working relationship based on mutual respect. Before deciding how to proceed with advocacy, a consultation between the feminist CSO and key members of the network was always held. The feminist CSO understood that it had privileged access to information and understanding of the global context, which could be helpful for the network. The feminist CSO could influence other women's rights organizations in India and globally, countering the narrative that sex work is never a choice or that sex work is violence. This CSO had long engaged on sex workers' issues from this stance, building trust with the group.

The CSO staff sought to ensure that asymmetrical access to resources (which drives power asymmetry) did not lead to the domination/imposition of one view over others. The feminist CSO viewed its privileged position as a strength that could bring global perspectives and experiences to the network. However, such global experience could also be a limitation if the CSO felt compelled to lead, which might result in co-option of the movement. Thus, the path was not always straightforward for the feminist CSO, and they struggled internally in dealing with their position. The network embraced the feminist CSO's role as a partner bringing global perspectives on sex work, but such set roles in a collaboration suggest unequal relationships. Discussing the feminist CSO's role in the partnership, a central office bearer of the network noted that,

> Better use of words is something that the [feminist CSO] helps the network with. We do not understand many times what exactly the donor wants. The feminist CSO has the organizational strength of skilled and educated staff along with the language skills to be able to guide them and help them in all this. They are able to package things well for reports. It is important to package, and even advertisement of the work is very important, and [the feminist CSO] helps us with all this. Yet, in doing so, the feminist CSO has never asked us to change our activities within a programme. They have asked us how we want to shape a programme rather than telling us how they want things to be done.

The network and the feminist CSO built collaboration-seeking common ground, respecting each other's requirements and expectations and remaining conscious of their positions. This was articulated by a central office bearer of the network as follows:

> When we started working with [the feminist CSO], we wanted the sex workers' rights to be discussed at different levels all over the country. Beyond this, we realized that it was a feminist organization that believes that 'sex work is work' and that it should be decriminalized. We never felt these issues getting in the way while working with the feminist CSO, whose philosophy matches with ours, unlike a few other feminist organizations whose members privately agree with our core values but cannot support [them] as an organization. In the case of this feminist CSO, they support our core value – 'sex work is work' – as an organization; that is vital to us.

The collaboration was built on the common ground of regarding sex work as work. The network located its narrative around choice, respect, and recognition for sex work. This understanding emerged from viewing sex workers as having the agency to select their profession instead of viewing them as victims. Network members found it easier to work with organizations that also viewed sex work within this framework. The feminist CSO, despite being aware that many would call this false consciousness and stress the need for rescue and rehabilitation, respected sex workers' agency to choose. The sex workers' network saw rescue and rehabilitation as a forced solution – not one they would choose. Recognizing this ultimately provided a basis for supporting the sex workers in voicing their issues and advocating for their rights. Subsequently, the lived experiences of the sex workers in the network shaped the language articulating and advocating for sex workers' rights, with the feminist CSO and the network working together on these efforts.

Acknowledging 'own voices'

The feminist CSO supported and acknowledged sex workers' 'own voices' by facilitating dialogue with sex workers, offering different starting points, and providing a platform for finding common ground for advocacy. The network's main objective was to build advocacy for sex workers' rights. For organized advocacy, they needed some common ground, while acknowledging their diversity. However, the diversity among the different types of sex workers (brothel-based, home-based, street-based, and traditional sex workers) made it challenging to determine common core principles for their demands. Each type of sex worker struggled with unique challenges, as mentioned above. The feminist CSO responded by facilitating dialogue among the diverse sex workers. The methods applied were simple – create space for dialogue and make the movement about sex workers' voices and not about the feminist CSO. The creation of such a space does not mean differences were dissolved but that the various types of sex workers were able to voice their views, be heard, and exercise agency to decide their path in the movement. These conversations were used to determine the demands and strategies for representing the sex workers at the national level. As the network grew to include additional types of sex workers, this challenge remained an issue. The feminist CSO realized that some CBOs working with sex workers did not want to join the network because they had other priorities such as everyday survival or the functioning of their own organizations. Even when sex workers are not formal network members, the network still engaged with them for larger advocacy goals and sought their support on issues such as the response to the anti-trafficking bill.

The opportunity and space created for the sex workers to speak for themselves and voice their concerns acknowledged and facilitated their agency to decide the future of their movement. The sex workers themselves determined with whom to engage, how their movement should proceed, and what shared ground they wanted to highlight. In this journey, the sex workers needed allies and collaborations with organizations that would give them space to exercise their agency to decide their own path. This supportive role was played by the feminist CSO in its collaboration with the sex workers' network.

The dialogue and space for conversation gradually led to the identification of points of convergence among the sex workers. Most of them wanted the right to live with dignity and respect and as people who had chosen to engage in sex work to support their families or themselves. An organized effort on this issue was important, given the everyday harassment by local gang leaders and police and the need for legal measures and norm changes to protect sex workers' rights. In the interviews, the sex workers described their experiences. As a sex worker from Tamil Nadu explained,

> When a sex worker goes to file a report, the police say that they deserve it, as they are doing this kind of work. We also want to be treated with respect and dignity. We are doing sex work, but that does not mean that we are open to abuse or sexual favours without consent. This is something which becomes very difficult to make the others understand, who just assume that our work leads to abuse. We are told that we are sex workers, and, because of our work, we should be ready to face such situations as physical abuse. This is not the sort of response that we expect from the police. It means that we have no respect or dignity.

The president of the network suggested that all sex workers need to come together and build a sense of reliance on each other, as they often face multiple levels of exploitation:

> We find many of the sex workers, particularly those working from home, reluctant to come out in the open and identify themselves. We tell them that they can engage in the network by choosing to not reveal their identities. This is how we can build support for each other by recognizing their difficulties in identifying themselves. This support will be important for the movement, in the long run – more than any outside aid or help. We have to fight for our own cause.

Such sex workers shared their lived experiences individually with the central office bearer and sometimes in open discussions organized by the network and facilitated by the feminist CSO.

The collaboration with the feminist CSO was important to the network, but, over the years, they also relied on support in shaping their advocacy from individuals and other partner organizations. For example, they worked closely with professionals such as doctors and lawyers in the struggle for their rights. A doctor who had worked with the network since its inception and who was revered by them as an inspiration described what the sex workers wanted while forming a network:

> 'Respect, reliance, and recognition'[11] – the three Rs – are what the sex workers are looking for at the national level. I came to this conclusion after my constant interaction and conversations with the sex workers. I also feel that they do not share this reality with everyone – that they come to this profession by making an informed choice. They often project themselves as victims for an easy way out. They do not want to be judged and are scared of being stigmatized.

The three Rs were a result of conversations between those who worked with the sex workers in different capacities (as health practitioners, target interventionists, and the feminist CSO) and the sex workers themselves. In this dialogue, the sex workers spoke about their work and arrived at common ground, and shared core principles. Respect was interpreted from the sex workers' constant use of '*izzat*', and recognition was taken from '*pehchaan*', another word the sex workers often used. Reliance emerged from an understanding among the sex workers that they must build trust ('*bharosa*') among each other and construct a network. With help from the feminist CSO and other partner organizations, the network was able to build this trust by providing space for the open discussion of grievances, dialogue bringing out disagreements, and an atmosphere where sex workers realized that these disagreements and differences would not stop them from engaging with each other. Everyone could speak and every voice counted.

These views were translated by the feminist CSO for national-level advocacy for the rights of sex workers. It would not have been possible for the feminist CSO and the network to formulate these three core principles (the three Rs) if the sex workers had not been able to construct them in their own voices. The sex workers voiced their issues, fears, and insecurities. The network's role was prioritizing these three rights for national-level advocacy, creating consensus through dialogue with different types of CBOs and other groups struggling for their rights. These groups included trade/labour unions, pension unions, and unorganized sector workers.[12] The language of advocacy focusing on 'respect, reliance, and recognition' resulted from internal conversations among the sex workers. In collaborating and engaging with the other groups, the sex workers broadened their demands, wanting to be recognized as workers like the other groups. This, they believed, would strengthen their movement and advocacy for access to the social security schemes available to other workers. As suggested by a network member,

> The idea was to make the struggle for the rights of the sex workers more and more inclusive. They wanted to build a consensus among several groups for the rights of sex workers. They wanted to build the Delhi-based CSO's understanding as well on this – that not only sex workers are talking for their rights, but there are others also who are talking about their rights. They also wanted to make those who represented the rights of the sex workers understand that the sex workers were not just talking about their rights but also about the rights of the other groups who were marginalized and not included.

Lessons for addressing power differentials in civil society collaborations

The feminist approach to collaboration described in this chapter shows how one organization addressed power differentials among organizations by recognizing the diversity in their partner network of sex workers, showing how a completely

Southern-led initiative addressed this issue. The chapter demonstrates that, even in this Southern context involving significant efforts to address inequalities, there are inequalities in terms of resources and access to power that impact how partnerships work. Our exploration of inequalities and how to address them can yield lessons for similar contexts across the Global South. A feminist approach to collaboration embedded in the recognition of intersectionality, diversity, positionality, and agency through facilitating people's 'own voices' offers the following three lessons for addressing power differentials in CSO collaborations.

First, CSOs that acknowledge intersectionality must enable multiple identities to be expressed, addressed, and incorporated into their collaboration, creating an inclusive space with similar conditions for everyone, where everyone can feel safe interacting. In the examined collaboration, inclusive space and shared understanding of intersectionality were not just symbolic; they were practiced through building an environment where different voices were heard. This is possible only when the feminist principles mentioned above are brought into everyday practice in partnerships among organizations with different strengths and positions. It is necessary to recognize the diversity of lived experience and see it as an asset rather than a problem.

Second, CSOs in powerful positions can begin by exploring and accepting their own positionality within collaborations. They must take a self-reflective approach, cultivating mutual respect, recognizing partner agency, and adopting a facilitating stance. Then, power can become a resource contributing to marginalized people making themselves heard, rather than a means to achieve compliance. The chapter shows that reflecting on positionality does not come easily or automatically and that CSOs sometimes struggle with positioning themselves. CSOs' continuous exploration of their own positions within partnerships is needed as the partnership evolves.

Third, CSOs can recognize the agency and voice of the groups they work with, accepting their choices and their ability to decide. CSOs can adopt this principle in forming collaborations, facilitating the expression of constituent voices, and taking these as starting points for further development of their vision and action.

These lessons suggest mechanisms through which power differentials can be addressed, if not entirely overcome. When adopted in partnerships, these principles can help community-led organizations make decisions for their movements, with more powerful partners taking a facilitating role rather than a leading role. Such pathways in partnerships can further strengthen the voices of grassroots Southern organizations in advocacy, supporting their movements.

Acknowledgements

The authors of the chapter are grateful to the organizations and their members who agreed to participate in this research, gave their valuable time, and shared their insights. Without their generous support, this research would not have been possible.

Notes

1 https://globalfundcommunityfoundations.org/what-we-stand-for/shiftthepower/
2 https://interagencystandingcommittee.org/grand-bargain
3 Social security would mean having a ration card, the Aadhar card, which is necessary to, for example, get a bank account or register to vote.
4 The feminist concept of intersectionality was coined in the West. As is the case with other concepts, Indian feminists have had their own take on intersectionality, creating space for a debate and allowing CSOs in India to use intersectionality as a way forward to address the rights of diverse marginalized groups.
5 Hartsock (1983) and later hooks (1984) and Mohanty (1988) are important reference points and add value as foundational standpoint theorists.
6 The hashtag 'own voices' was initially used by Corrine Duyvis, a novelist and the founder of the website 'Disability in Kidlit', trying to centre the voices of marginalized groups.
7 See Runyan (2018). Here, Runyan argues that those informed by intersectionality reject a monolithic movement based on a single, exclusionary identity or single-issue politics.
8 The network periodically convenes meetings where network members from different parts of India come together to decide their goals, agenda, and next steps.
9 Traditional sex workers come from families that have engaged in sex work for generations and consider this trade to be passed from one generation to another. During the interviews, they called themselves 'traditional sex workers'.
10 The Durbar Mahila in Kolkata (India) was one of the first organized attempts by sex workers in India to advocate for their rights.
11 This is a slogan used by sex workers and not a translation by the authors. The translation emerged internally in the movement on the basis of conversations among the sex workers and collaborating CSOs.
12 In India, a large number of workers are in the unorganized sector. These workers do not fall under any government labour act and therefore cannot access the welfare schemes and benefits the government provides for the organized labour force.

References

Ahmed, S. (2018). Feminist hurt/feminism hurts. In A. Koivunen, K. Kyrölä, & I. Ryberg (Eds.), *The power of vulnerability: Mobilising affect in feminist, queer and anti-racist media cultures* (pp. 59–68). Manchester: Manchester University Press.

Banks, N., Hulme, D., & Edwards, M. (2015). NGOs, states, and donors revisited: Still too close for comfort? *World Development, 66*, 707–718. https://doi.org/10.1016/j.worlddev.2014.09.028.

Chandhoke, N. (2005). How global is global civil society? *Journal of World-Systems Research*, 355–371. https://doi.org/10.5195/jwsr.2005.388.

Crenshaw, K. (1989). Demarginalizing the intersection of race and sex: A black feminist critique of antidiscrimination doctrine, feminist theory and antiracist politics. *University of Chicago Legal Forum, 1*, 139–167.

Deo, N., & McDuie-Ra, D. (2011). *The politics of collective advocacy in India: Tools and traps.* Sterling, VA: Kumarian Press.

Divya, A. (2020) Sex workers in India on the verge of debt bondage and slavery, says a study. *The Indian Express*, December 24. Retrieved from: https://indianexpress.com/article/lifestyle/life-style/sex-workers-in-india-on-the-verge-of-debt-bondage-and-slavery-says-a-study-7117938/.

Duyvis, C. (2015, September 6) #ownvoices, to recommend kidlit about diverse characters written by authors from that same diverse group. [Tweet]. Retrieved from: https://twitter.com/corinneduyvis/status/640584099208503296?ref_src=twsrc%5Etfw%7Ctwcamp%5Etweetembed%7Ctwterm%5E640584099208503296&ref_url=http%3A%2F%2Fwww.corinneduyvis.net%2Fownvoices%2F.

Gopal, M. (2015). Struggles around gender: Some clarifications. *Economic and Political Weekly, 50*(33), 76–77.

Hartsock, N. (1983). *Money, sex, and power.* Boston, MA: North-eastern University Press.

hooks, b. (2000). *Feminist theory: From margin to center.* London: Pluto Press.

Jalali, R. (2013). Financing empowerment? How foreign aid to Southern NGOs and social movements undermines grass-roots mobilization. *Sociology Compass*, 7(1), 55–73. https://doi.org/10.1111/soc4.12007.

John, M. E. (2015). Intersectionality: Rejection or critical dialogue? *Economic and Political Weekly, 50*(33): 72–76.

Menon, N. (2015). Is Feminism about 'Women'? A critical view on intersectionality from India. *Economic and Political Weekly, 50*(17), 37–44.

Misra, G., Mahal, A., & Shah, R. (2000). Protecting the rights of sex workers: The Indian experience. *Health & Human Rights, 5*(1), 88–115.

Mohanty, C. (1988). Under Western eyes: Feminist scholarship and colonial discourses. *Feminist Review, 30*(1), 61–88. https://doi.org/10.1057%2Ffr.1988.42.

O'Brien, N. F., & Evans, S. K. (2017). Civil society partnerships: Power imbalance and mutual dependence in NGO partnerships. *VOLUNTAS: International Journal of Voluntary and Nonprofit Organizations, 28*(4), 1399–1421. https://doi.org/10.1007/s11266-016-9721-4.

Rajeshwari, B., Deo, N., & van Wessel, M. (2020). Negotiating autonomy in capacity development: Addressing the inherent tension. *World Development, 134*, 105046. https://doi.org/10.1016/j.worlddev.2020.105046.

Rege, S. (2003). More than just tacking women on to the 'macropicture': Feminist contributions to globalisation discourses. *Economic and Political Weekly, 38*(43), 4555–4563.

RINGO. (n.d.). *The RINGO project. Re-imagining the INGO and the role of global civil society.* London: Rights CoLab. Retrieved from: https://rightscolab.org/ringo/.

Runyan, A. (2018). What is intersectionality and why is it important. *Academe, 104*(6), 10–14.

van Brabant, K., & Patel, S. (2018). *Localisation in practice. Emerging indicators & practical recommendations.* Retrieved from: https://www.alnap.org/help-library/localisation-in-practice-emerging-indicators-and-practical-recommendations.

19

PRACTISING ORGANIZATIONAL AUTONOMY AT THE COMMUNITY LEVEL

Evidence from advocacy projects in Uganda and Vietnam

Lena Gutheil

Introduction

Organizational autonomy is often assumed to be a prerequisite for organizations' successful policy and advocacy work, as well as a precondition for 'starting from the South'. This line of thinking relies on a liberal, Western conceptualization of civil society that assumes that organized civil society is inherently good and acts fully autonomously (i.e. independently) of the state and other actors (Mercer, 2002). This chapter renounces such a view and aligns instead with those authors who showcase the fluidity among states, civil society organizations (CSOs), and other actors (Bernal & Grewal, 2014, p. 8; Sampson, 2017, p. 13). Making use of a case study of two donor-funded organizations in Vietnam and Uganda, the chapter engages with the notion of organizational autonomy in a relational manner and examines how organizations at the sub-national level negotiate organizational autonomy by navigating relationships with the state and with the intermediary organizations that fund them. It thereby answers the following research question: *How is organizational autonomy negotiated in development projects at the community level in the context of restricted civic space?* Here, organizational autonomy is defined as the degree of discretion an organization performs in relation to other stakeholders and in multiple domains (Bach, 2014, p. 344). The chapter thus contributes to the further theorizing of a relational perspective on civil society activities in hybrid and autocratic regimes, as called for by Wischermann et al. (2018), which goes beyond a dichotomous analysis of CSOs as either enemies of the state or co-opted by state authorities.

While many studies focus solely on the restrictions that CSOs face because of repressive states (e.g. van der Borgh & Terwindt, 2012) or on the constraints international donors impose on CSOs (e.g. Banks et al., 2015) this chapter aligns instead with studies examining the day-to-day engagement of CSOs with state

DOI: 10.4324/9781003241003-24

and non-state actors (Syal et al., 2021, p. 2; Toepler et al., 2020). It specifically moves the attention away from international donors and towards domestic funding relationships.

Data for the case study were collected as part of a larger research project by means of interviews, participant observation, and document analysis. This chapter focuses on one CSO based at the sub-national level in Uganda and one provincial chapter of the Women's Union (WU; a mass organization) in Vietnam. Even though mass organizations are state-based, the WU is known to assume a number of civil society functions such as awareness raising, lobbying and advocacy, and service delivery. Among the mass organizations in Vietnam, the WU is known for having the strongest civil society orientation. Some analysts classify mass organizations as CSOs, with others at least stressing their hybrid character (Wells-Dang, 2014, p. 165). Both organizations that are part of the case study implement the same donor-funded programme, which is aimed at enabling village community groups to participate in budget-monitoring processes, in the context of restricted civic space. The comparison of the two organizations demonstrates the different ways in which a supposedly independent CSO and a chapter of a mass organization navigate relationships with the intermediary CSOs that are funding them and with state authorities. Thus, the chapter shows how organizational autonomy is negotiated in specific civil society contexts.

In this study, the degree of organizational autonomy was assessed using Verhoest et al.'s (2004) taxonomy for measuring autonomy in different domains. Using this taxonomy to analyse practices instead of documents reflects the fact that, rather than the formal level of decision-making competencies, it is their actual use in practice that is important for implementation. Although the CSO appeared to be more autonomous than the mass organization on paper, this did not result in more discretion in practice. The findings showed that the WU was enabled to conduct political and even oppositional work at the community level – not in spite of but rather because of their incorporation in state structures. The Ugandan example illustrates how dependency relationships can change over time. Dependency relationships are not necessarily constraining and can also be important assets for organizations. Thus, I argue that autonomy does not have a set value in itself but instead reveals its meaning in the evolving and context-dependent practice of organizational relationships.

The chapter starts by summarizing the body of knowledge dealing with CSO autonomy, before presenting Verhoest et al.'s taxonomy for measuring autonomy. Next, I describe the methods used in the study and introduce the participating organizations. Subsequently, the two organizations' practices are analysed using Verhoest et al.'s framework. The chapter closes with a discussion of the findings and the presentation of my concluding statements.

CSO autonomy revisited

CSOs have to navigate complex relationships with their funders, constituents, and the local government. These relationships have often been found to limit their autonomy. The development studies literature especially problematizes the relationships between CSOs and their international donors: CSOs are said to suffer from mission drift, estrangement from their constituents, and depoliticization, weakening their legitimacy as autonomous actors (Banks et al., 2015, p. 709). In addition, governments increasingly constrain CSOs' autonomy. Van der Borgh and Terwindt (2012) named five different actions and policies that restrict CSO operations: physical harassment and intimidation, criminalization, administrative restrictions, stigmatization, and shrinking spaces for dialogue.[1]

Whereas there is a great deal of research on comparatively large, professional CSOs operating from capital cities, there is considerably less research on smaller, more informal organizations. Van Stapele et al. (2020, p. 6) contend that there are significant differences between the organizations collectively referred to as CSOs. Larger CSOs are contracted directly by donors, whereas more informal organizations, which often work directly with the beneficiaries of an intervention, are contracted by domestic intermediaries. These intermediary organizations are usually based in the capital of a country and provide a link to the international donor. Many intermediaries pass on the donors' accountability requirements to sub-national actors to minimize risks. For sub-national organizations, the resulting sub-contractor role often means that there is little funding available for administrative overhead, salaries, and other running costs such as utilities, which hampers organizational consolidation and autonomy (Kelly & Birdsall, 2010, p. 1583).

Clearly, the specific situation for relatively small and informal organizations depends on the country context and on the kind of work they are doing. However, one characteristic feature may be the undervaluing of sub-national organizations' strengths with regard to liaising with communities and understanding the local context. In the academic literature, these organizations are frequently portrayed as lacking the financial and management skills required by the aid industry (Kelly & Birdsall, 2010, p. 1585). Aveling (2010, p. 1593) found that the staff of an organization based in the countryside felt that they were less respected by the government and had less representation in regional fora, compared with organizations based in the capital, reducing their chances of participating in decision-making processes. The close proximity of sub-national organizations to local leaders and authorities in rural settings may be another characteristic feature. Whereas relationships between CSO and government staff members may not be very close in urban settings, in rural areas, these actors may know each other very well or even be related.

The effects of registration requirements may also be different for smaller organizations with lower capacities. In Uganda, sub-national CSOs must register with the district local government (Maru, 2017, p. 68), which some organizations participating in the present study described as a demanding process. In Vietnam, the preconditions for registration are so extensive that most rural organizations are not registered; as a consequence, many international organizations prefer to work with the mass organizations (Pallas & Nguyen, 2018, p. 8). Interestingly, in Vietnam, community participation is supported by the 'grassroots decree', which (at least on paper) allows villagers to actively take part in village decision-making processes and authorizes them to form committees to monitor the local government.

Assessing organizational autonomy

To analyse development organizations' degree of autonomy in a relational manner, I used Verhoest et al.'s (2004, p. 104) theoretical dimensions. The notion of autonomy should not be confounded with independence: 'Autonomy refers to a dependency relationship between several actors' and establishes the degree of discretion an organization exercises in multiple domains (Bach, 2014, p. 344). Verhoest et al. (2004, p. 109) argued that the degree of autonomy cannot be determined by looking only at decision-making competencies; the government's (or other actors') ability to constrain the use of these competencies through various means must also be considered. Thus, Verhoest et al.'s framework offers a perspective on organizational autonomy that is both multidimensional and relational. However, it does not include a processual, temporal dimension. Therefore, I propose to enhance the rather static framework by looking at organizational practices as processes unfolding as dependency relationships evolve over time.

Verhoest et al.'s six dimensions for measuring autonomy are generally subsumed under the two categories of 'autonomy as the level of decision-making competencies of the agency (concerning management on the one hand and concerning agency policy on the other hand)' and 'autonomy as the exemption of constraints on the actual use of decision-making competencies of the agency (referring to structural, financial, legal and interventional constraints on the agency's decision-making competencies)' (Verhoest et al., 2004, p. 104; see Figure 19.1).

Autonomy as the level of decision-making competencies refers to two dimensions. Managerial autonomy, the most intuitive category, corresponds to the choice and use of inputs of an organization. For instance, managerial autonomy could relate to financial management, human resource management, or the planning of everyday tasks. The second dimension is policy autonomy, which indicates decision-making competency with regard to the organization's broader outcomes and goals; policy autonomy is thus a higher-order category than managerial autonomy and refers to the procedures and policy instruments (Verhoest et al., 2004, p. 105).

Autonomy as the exemption of constraints on the use of decision-making competencies looks specifically at four dimensions assessing how other actors can withdraw or constrain an organization's decision-making competencies. Structural autonomy points to an accountability relationship with a superior institution, such as a board of directors, a government institution, or an institute's council. This concerns questions of hierarchical supervision and oversight by external bodies (Verhoest et al., 2004, p. 105). Financial autonomy assesses the degree of financial

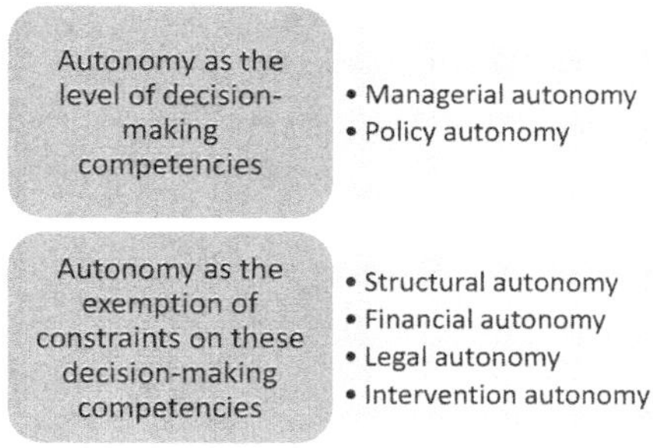

FIGURE 19.1 Verhoest et al.'s (2004) dimensions of organizational autonomy.

dependence on other bodies. Legal autonomy measures to what extent the legal personality of an organization prevents its competencies from being withdrawn by its superior (Verhoest et al., 2004, p. 106). The last dimension is intervention autonomy, which spells out to what extent an organization is bound to engage in reporting, evaluations, and audits according to standards defined before implementation. If these controls are tied to sanctions in case of deviations, it is assumed that an organization will act more conservatively and less autonomously (Verhoest et al., 2004, p. 106).

While Verhoest et al. define both dimensions of autonomy vis-à-vis the government, the analysis here also takes into account autonomy vis-à-vis intermediary organizations acting as funding agencies for the sub-national organizations.

Methods

The case study

This chapter is based on a larger research project on the Strategic Partnerships for Dialogue and Dissent Programme, funded by the Ministry of Foreign Affairs of the Netherlands and implemented through Oxfam Novib. The underlying policy framework of the programme acknowledges that, to fulfil their political role, CSOs in aid recipient countries need 'to be locally rooted, strong, legitimate and autonomous' (Kamstra, 2017, p. 17). The research data were drawn from interviews, participant observation, and document analysis, covering actors at all levels of the programme. This chapter focuses on a Ugandan sub-national CSO and a provincial chapter of the WU in Vietnam, focusing on their relationships with intermediary CSOs and with state authorities.

In Uganda, the research focused on a CSO, Citizen Action and Change (CAC).[2] CAC is based in a small town in one of Uganda's three poorest districts, which is a six-to-seven-hour ride from the capital city of Kampala. The organization had nine staff positions, three of which worked primarily on the Strategic Partnership Programme. The organization started as a group of friends and was formally registered in 2006 as part of a project funded through the

Oxfam Country Office and Hivos. CAC aims to work for the improvement of public policy, services, and governance, as well as to build civic competence among citizen alliances. In the Strategic Partnership Programme, CAC's responsibilities revolved around work with neighbourhood assemblies – local voluntary groups founded to foster community participation and to monitor the local government's spending decisions. CAC generally facilitated and monitored the neighbourhood assemblies' activities, facilitated trainings, organized events, and established links with sub-county and district government officials.

In Vietnam, the studied organization is a provincial chapter of the state-run WU, which is one of five mass organizations in Vietnam. These mass organizations are membership organizations that are hierarchically organized from the central level down to the community level. While civic space in Vietnam has been slowly opening up since the reforms of the 1980s, the official registration of domestic CSOs is a challenge, with registration remaining a privilege reserved for only a few well-connected, professional, and mostly urban organizations that largely work in a non-confrontational manner (Pallas & Nguyen, 2018). Because of its organizational capacities, its track record of outreach at the community level, and its good relations with the local government, the WU[3] has emerged as a key partner for development activities. Although mass organizations are tightly controlled by the Communist Party at the central level, the community level is much more independent.

The provincial WU examined here is located an 11-hour drive away from Vietnam's capital city, Hanoi. The province where this organization is located is among the poorest third of all Vietnamese provinces. The WU has 20 paid staff members and coordinates the work of the district, ward, and village chapters of the WU. The work on the Strategic Partnership Programme is led by one coordinator, who works closely with the lower-level chapters of the WU. Similar to the situation in Uganda, programme efforts in Vietnam revolve around the mobilization of community groups who are empowered and trained to monitor local budget processes and organize public dialogues.

Data collection and analysis

The chapter focuses on data collected at the sub-national level from the WU in Vietnam and from CAC in Uganda, their intermediaries, and the community groups with which they work. The responsible project managers at CAC and the WU were interviewed, as were the project managers at their intermediary organizations. Group interviews were held with community groups (six in Vietnam and two in Uganda). I engaged in field visits, which provided me with opportunities for participant observation of practices such as activity planning and coordination while taking part in project activities and meetings. Specifically, I visited each country twice to follow up on project developments. Data in Uganda were collected in December 2018 and September 2019, and Vietnam was visited in May 2019 and February 2020. Data on the sub-national level in Vietnam were collected in collaboration with a Vietnamese research assistant because of the language barrier and accessibility issues. The interviews were transcribed and coded using MaxQDA software. The data were coded using a coding scheme based on project practices. Subsequently, major codes were summarized and used for organizing the findings along the dimensions proposed by Verhoest et al. (2004).

The data have several limitations. Participant observation was only possible to a very limited extent at the sub-national level in Vietnam because of the outbreak of the COVID-19 virus and also because of government constraints. Because I could not enter Vietnam again because of the pandemic, data collection was continued by the research assistant alone. However, the two researchers were in close contact during the research process to ensure that the research was conducted in a comparable manner in both countries.

Findings

A summary of the findings can be found in Table 19.1.

Autonomy as the level of decision-making competencies

Managerial autonomy

At the beginning of the project implementation within the Strategic Partnership Programme, CAC was only hired on a fee-for-service basis, which means they were paid per activity and did not receive a contract. In the last two years of project implementation they were promoted to the status of a sub-granting organization, receiving a contract and gaining additional managerial responsibilities. CAC designed their own work plan in accordance with the overall programme goals and the budget provided, in collaboration with the Oxfam country office (intermediary). The way the work plan was implemented (i.e. which staff members were responsible for conducting the activities and when) was up to CAC. Activities and budget lines could be shifted to a limited extent. CAC did the work with the neighbourhood assemblies and local government officers completely independently.

The WU received an activity plan and budget for this project from their intermediary CSO based in Hanoi, and there were few changes during project implementation. For instance, instead of organizing ten seminars on budget oversight experience among community groups, the WU proposed to hold a knowledge transfer workshop for WU staff members. In Vietnam, the authorities' approval was needed to change project activities, making this possibility arduous, and it was thus mostly avoided. The WU could decide independently who would work on the programme; however, training sessions were always conducted together with the intermediary CSO. The WU's work with community groups and the local government was conducted independently.

Policy autonomy

CAC was free to set its own vision and mission. Although they were not the initiators of the programme studied in this case, they were invited for a co-creation session by the country office, allowing them to participate in the design of the programme goals. They did not have a say in determining the budget size, outcome indicators, or financial management system, however.

As a mass organization subject to the state's authority, the provincial WU is subordinate to the central WU and thus follows national guidelines and five-year priorities. There is leeway in implementing activities with volunteers at the local level, provided that they remain in line with the WU's overall mission. In terms of the project under investigation here, the situation was similar to that of CAC. After the project had been conceived, the WU provided their input with regard to project activities; however, in the implementation phase, they were subject to their intermediary's accounting and reporting procedures. Before the project began, the intermediary CSO also submitted the project dossier to the Provincial Department of Planning and Investment, which was in charge of reviewing it and submitting it to the People's Committee[4] for approval. After the People's Committee approved, the project was proposed to the WU.

Autonomy as the exemption of constraints on decision-making competencies

Structural autonomy

CAC is not dependent on a board or other supervising body, and donor staff members are not formally part of the organization. However, in reality, CAC was in close contact with the project coordinator at the country office and was accountable to this intermediary organization. Because CAC was founded as part of another Oxfam project, they were especially closely connected to the country office. Further, although CAC is structurally independent from the local government, they asked the district chairpersons for permission to start neighbourhood assemblies, and their monitoring work was greatly facilitated by the inclusion of district and sub-country officials in their capacity-building measures.

The WU, in addition to being accountable to the central WU, is also accountable to the authorities and can therefore be considered structurally dependent. WU staff members are elected every five years by the provincial conference, which consists of staff and members of the WU. As most WU staff are also party members, the lines between the WU and the state are blurred. In the examined project, the WU closely followed suggestions made by the intermediary.

Financial autonomy

Although CAC is free to apply for funding, at the time of the data collection, the organization was implementing only the examined project. Thus, in practice, they can be seen as highly dependent on the Oxfam country office and, more generally, on donor money. The project support did not cover all the administrative costs and staff positions for CAC. When they were paid per activity, they could not cover overhead costs such as office rent, utilities, and administration at all and had to rely on private loans to survive. When they became a coordinating and sub-granting organization, they received a contract that included some overhead.

The WU is not dependent on projects, as its full-time staff are civil servants. The organization relies almost exclusively on government funding and does not raise its own revenue apart from membership fees and occasional donor projects. Most activities rely heavily on volunteers, and, because of budget constraints, it is not always possible to conduct all the activities they envision. Acquiring additional funding through donor projects is welcome, as long as it contributes to fulfilling national plans.

Legal autonomy

Legally speaking, CAC is an autonomous organization, and neither the donors nor the government can alter its mission or decision-making competencies; nonetheless, the possibility of being accused of financial mismanagement or partisan politics poses a risk to the organization. In the past, one of CAC's donor-funded projects was stopped because its approach was deemed too political by the authorities. The Ugandan Non-Governmental Organization Bureau and its sub-national committees monitor non-governmental organization (NGO) operations and may revoke an organization's permit, blacklist an organization, or make an organization's shortcomings public (Kelly, 2019, p. 14). For this reason, the current project examined in this study opted for a non-confrontational approach, including government officials in capacity-building measures and dialogue.

The WU is not legally autonomous. As a state-based organization, the WU's rights and responsibilities are regulated by the Vietnamese Constitution and Vietnamese law. Their legal status is tied to the state's administrative units, and they follow the legal guidelines established by the central WU. While their vision and mission are not likely to be altered, the guidelines on membership, voting procedures, disciplinary measures are frequently adapted – the latest version is from 2017, and the version before that was from 2012. The budget-monitoring activities carried out through the examined project are legally supported by the grassroots decree.

Intervention autonomy

For both organizations, compliance with the project work plan and budget were strictly monitored. Financial compliance was especially emphasized by the contracting organizations. If there were any irregularities, the organization would face sanctions and, in the worst case, contract termination. Apart from

TABLE 19.1 Summary of different dimensions of autonomy in Citizen Action and Change (CAC) in Uganda and in the Women's Union (WU) in Vietnam

Dimension of autonomy	*CAC Uganda*	*WU Vietnam*
Managerial autonomy	Designed their own work plan; designed activities in line with a given budget, in collaboration with the country office	Received work plan and budget from their intermediary
	CAC was in charge of implementation	The WU was in charge of implementation
	Adaptation was possible	Adaptation was mostly avoided
Policy autonomy	Free to set their own mission and vision	Must follow national guidelines and priorities; project approval from authorities required
	CAC was not included in determining the budget size, outcome indicators, or accounting system, but they were invited for a co-creation session for the entire programme	The WU was not included in determining the budget size, outcome indicators, or accounting system
Structural autonomy	Formally independent; informally, they were dependent on the intermediary, as they only relied on one grant at the time	The WU is accountable to the central WU and the authorities; the line between the WU and the Communist Party is blurred
	CAC followed suggestions made by the intermediary	The WU followed suggestions made by the intermediary
Financial autonomy	Formally independent to apply for funding	The only revenue raised apart from projects is through membership fees; projects are welcome if they are in line with national plans
	CAC was dependent on the intermediary, as this was their only project; CAC was first hired on a fee-for-service basis and later received a contract	Staff receive salaries from the state; they are not dependent on projects
Legal autonomy	Legally independent; however, government interference is possible	The WU's legal status is based on the Vietnamese Constitution and Vietnamese law, as well as legal guidelines from the central WU
Intervention autonomy	Compliance is monitored by the country office; if irregularities with regard to operations or financial management are detected, sanctions will be applied, and the contract can be terminated	Compliance is monitored by the intermediary and the authorities; if irregularities with regard to operations or financial management are detected, sanctions will be applied, and the contract can be terminated

monitoring, there was also an independent financial audit, which was tied to sanctions. However, monitoring was mostly carried out via written accounts and telephone conversations. Field visits occurred only a few times per year.

Summary of the findings

While both organizations exercise a fair amount of managerial autonomy, they have less discretion with regard to policy autonomy. Neither organization was part of the programme application phase; however, CAC was invited for a co-creation session in the inception phase, whereas the WU was not consulted at all. The finding from the literature that community-level organizations are mainly excluded from programme development (Aveling, 2010, p. 1595) is thus partly confirmed.

With regard to legal, financial, and structural autonomy, the WU faces substantially more constraints on the use of decision-making competencies, compared with CAC. This can be explained by the WU's status as a mass organization that is integrated in the Communist Party system. Technically, CAC is legally, financially, and structurally independent; however, the organization's exclusive reliance on one grant at the time of the data collection, in effect, created a financial dependency. Thus, the relatively high level of autonomy that CAC could exercise could not be fully realized. CAC is an organization that used to be hired only on a fee-for-service basis, which hampers organizational consolidation and financial diversification. While CAC's level of decision-making competencies is fairly high, the actual discretion they exercise is low. The organization's situation changed when they received a contract and grant-giving responsibilities towards the end of the programme period. This may become an important stepping stone for advancing their organization.

In contrast, the WU, as a government-funded mass organization that is structurally, legally, and financially dependent, benefited from having their overhead covered and from working in an enabling political environment. Having the official legal mandate to monitor public expenditure conveyed legitimacy and protection to the community groups and resulted in pressure for the local authorities to join dialogues and react to requests. Thus, in this case, the lack of structural autonomy was a prerequisite for implementing such a sensitive project in the Vietnamese context. Similarly, in Uganda, the approach of including the local authorities from the beginning, even though this was not a legal necessity, facilitated budget monitoring and community participation.

With regard to intervention autonomy, both organizations showed a very low amount of discretion. Compliance with work plans and financial plans was strictly monitored, and there was little room for adaptation.

Discussion and conclusion

Verhoest et al.'s (2004) framework has proven useful for this relational analysis of organizational autonomy, as this framework does not solely rely on an organization's formal level of autonomy but also takes into account how autonomy is practised. Although the organizations' relationships with the authorities and with intermediaries constrained or had the potential to constrain the organizations' decision-making competencies, these relationships were still evaluated positively by the interviewees, who noted that these relationships provided their interventions with legitimacy and also expertise. The Vietnamese case, in particular, shows that the incorporation of the WU within state structures made budget-monitoring activities possible. Vietnamese CSOs are known for refraining from oppositional projects (Wells-Dang, 2014, p. 169), but the data analysed here indicate that, if mass organizations are included as assuming civil society functions, there is space for political work at the local level in the Vietnamese context. The embeddedness of the WU in the villages, their political mandate, and the enabling legal environment (i.e. the grassroots decree) made the approach a good local fit. Although civic space seems to be shifting more towards granting mostly apolitical service providers room to operate (Toepler et al., 2020, p. 650), the case study presented in this chapter shows that, even in restrictive settings such as Vietnam, there is still room for interventions that engage with politics. The proximity of social relations in the studied communities strongly contributed to providing an enabling environment for civil society–state collaboration. Further research should systematically examine to what extent sensitive projects in smaller communities differ from those in urban areas, in the context of hybrid and autocratic regimes.

Adopting a relational perspective on autonomy, combined with a focus on analysing the day-to-day engagement of stakeholders, has the potential to reveal how organizations manage to implement politically sensitive projects in hybrid and autocratic regimes. The application of Verhoest et al.'s framework has shown that autonomy should not be seen as inherently of value – that is, more autonomy does not necessarily result in better project implementation. Furthermore, adding a temporal, processual dimension to Verhoest et al.'s rather static framework allowed me to show that practising autonomy is an ongoing process that changes over time and that the meaning of autonomy is also bound to change. When CAC became a sub-granting organization, they finally received a contract, which, in the long run, may also strengthen their grant management capacities and result in more intervention autonomy. Their relative dependency on the intermediary (i.e. a lack of structural autonomy) thus acquired another meaning and became an asset when CAC was promoted in this way.

This chapter proposes that, instead of postulating that organizational relationships are beneficial for CSOs if they provide more autonomy, it would be useful for scholars and practitioners to evaluate organizational relationships in terms of their emancipatory effects. Although CAC benefited from being promoted to the role of sub-granting organization, it remains to be seen whether their embeddedness in the existing programme relationships will enable the organization to proactively grasp new project opportunities. The meaning of organizational autonomy is not fixed; rather, it is primarily revealed in the practice of organizational relationships, which is an open-ended and context-dependent process without guaranteed results.

Apart from the processual dimension, I also found a consideration of the intermediary's dependency on the implementing organization to be missing in Verhoest et al.'s framework. It is striking that, in both cases examined here, the intermediaries had few alternatives in terms of collaborating with a different organization. In Vietnam, the WU offers a unique network of volunteers that reach down to the village level and also has government support. In Uganda, the intermediary needed a sub-national partner who spoke the local languages and who knew and had built trusting relationships with the local leaders and villagers. The success of an intervention depends heavily on collaboration at the sub-national level, which results in high relative bargaining power for community-level organizations. For instance, in Uganda, CSO staff members were not always available for project activities or meetings because they were only working part-time on the project, which was tolerated.

Analysing relationships between intermediaries and organizations at the sub-national level can be seen as one way of 'starting from the South'. While the academic focus to date lies mostly on dependency relationships between international donors and domestic CSOs in the Global South, the analytical framework in this chapter offers one way of approaching questions of organizational autonomy in the South without reproducing the 'bad donor/good CSO' narrative. There is certainly a tension between the managerial pressure intermediary organizations are often subject to and are prone to hand down on the one hand and the rather informal nature and community orientation of many sub-national organizations on the other. While this tension cannot easily be resolved, a first step would be to take a closer look at and invest more in modes of collaboration at the intermediary–sub-national nexus. Adaptive management approaches (see Gutheil, 2021 for an overview) could be interesting 'starting points for collaboration' in this regard. These approaches rest on the idea that domestic actors know best how to respond to the specific project context. Although the WU might not fit with Western donors' ideals about civil society, local actors can make a more informed decision about which organizations are a good fit for certain interventions. At the same time, the adaptive management agenda suggests involving local actors in agenda setting (policy autonomy) and offering flexibility in implementation (intervention autonomy), which is often withheld from sub-national-level organizations. When international donors trust local partners, and intermediaries and sub-national organizations start investing in their modes of collaboration, dependency relationships can turn into assets for all parties involved.

Acknowledgements

The author would like to thank all participating organizations and individuals for their time and patience. A special thanks must be extended to Quang

Minh Pham, who collected some of the data in Vietnam and provided invaluable support throughout the fieldwork period and beyond.

Notes

1 It should be noted, however, that civil society can only emerge and thrive in the context of a strong state with political institutions that allow for participation and accountability and protect civil society actors. Ideally, the state and civil society are mutually reinforcing.
2 Because the interviewees wished to remain anonymous, a pseudonym is used for the organization in Uganda, and the exact locations of the organizations, including the provincial Women's Union, are not disclosed. For the same reason, the name of the Vietnamese intermediary is not provided.
3 Generally, the Women's Union offers training, social and financial support schemes, counselling, and mass education. For more information, see Waibel and Glück (2013).
4 The People's Committee is the local executive branch of the local authority (the People's Council). The People's Council is elected by the population, and the People's Committee is appointed by the People's Council. For more information on local governance in Vietnam, see Nguyen et al. (2013, p. 42).

References

Aveling, E. L. (2010). The impact of aid chains: Relations of dependence or supportive partnerships for community-led responses to HIV/AIDS? *AIDS Care, 22*(Sup 2), 1588–1597. https://doi.org/10.1080/09540121.2010.507954.

Bach, T. (2014). The autonomy of government agencies in Germany and Norway: Explaining variation in management autonomy across countries and agencies. *International Review of Administrative Sciences, 80*(2), 341–361. https://doi.org/10.1177/0020852313514527.

Banks, N., Hulme, D., & Edwards, M. (2015). NGOs, states, and donors revisited: Still too close for comfort? *World Development, 66*, 707–718. https://doi.org/10.1016/j.worlddev.2014.09.028.

Bernal, V., & Grewal, I. (2014). Introduction: The NGO form: Feminist struggles, states, and neoliberalism In I. Grewal & V. Bernal (Eds.), *Theorizing NGOs: States, feminisms, and neoliberalism* (pp. 1–18). Durham, NC: Duke University Press. https://doi.org/10.1215/9780822377191-001.

Gutheil, L. (2021). Adaptive project management for the civil society sector: Towards an academic research agenda. *International Development Planning Review, 43*(3), 393–418. https://doi.org/10.3828/idpr.2020.17.

Kamstra, J. (2017). *Dialogue and dissent theory of change 2.0: Supporting civil society's political role*. The Hague, The Netherlands: Ministry of Foreign Affairs of the Netherlands. Retrieved from: https://includeplatform.net/wp-content/uploads/2020/07/Annex1_DialogueandDissentTheoryofChange-June2017.pdf.

Kelly, K. J., & Birdsall, K. (2010). The effects of national and international HIV/AIDS funding and governance mechanisms on the development of civil-society responses to HIV/AIDS in East and Southern Africa. *AIDS Care, 22*(Sup 2), 1580–1587. https://doi.org/10.1080/09540121.2010.524191.

Kelly, L. (2019). *Legislation on non-governmental organisations (NGOs) in Tanzania, Kenya, Uganda, Ethiopia, Rwanda and England and Wales* (K4D Helpdesk Report). Brighton, UK: Institute of Development Studies. Retrieved from: https://assets.publishing.

service.gov.uk/media/5d9b558ded915d354c1af0ff/656_NGO_Legislation_East_Africa.pdf.

Maru, M. T. (2017). *Shrinking civil society space in the Horn of Africa: The legal context.* Pax for Peace & KACE. Retrieved from: https://www.kacesudan.org/wp-content/uploads/2017/09/PAX_REPORT_KACE_FINAL_digi_single_page.pdf.

Mercer, C. (2002). NGOs, civil society and democratization: A critical review of the literature. *Progress in Development Studies, 2*(1), 5–22. https://doi.org/10.1191/1464993402ps027ra.

Nguyen, T. C., Nguyen, N. D., Do, P. T. T., & Nguyen, T. P. (2013). *Municipal government in Vietnam: Case studies of Ho Chi Minh City and Da Nang.* Hanoi, Vietnam: University of Economics and Law &The Asia Foundation.

Pallas, C. L., & Nguyen, L. (2018). Transnational advocacy without Northern NGO partners: Vietnamese NGOs in the HIV/AIDS sector. *Nonprofit and Voluntary Sector Quarterly, 47*(4S), 159S–176S. https://doi.org/10.1177/0899764018758462.

Sampson, S. (2017). Introduction: Engagements and entanglements in the anthropology of NGOs. In A. Lashaw, C. Vannier, & S. Sampson (Eds.), *Cultures of doing good: Anthropologists and NGOs* (pp. 1–18). Tuscaloosa: University of Alabama Press.

Syal, R., van Wessel, M., & Sahoo, S. (2021). Collaboration, co-optation or navigation? The role of civil society in disaster governance in India. *Voluntas: International Journal of Voluntary and Nonprofit Organizations, 32*, 795–808. https://doi.org/10.1007/s11266-021-00344-8.

Toepler, S., Zimmer, A., Fröhlich, C., & Obuch, K. (2020). The changing space for NGOs: Civil society in authoritarian and hybrid regimes. *Voluntas: International Journal of Voluntary and Nonprofit Organizations, 31*(4), 649–662. https://doi.org/10.1007/s11266-020-00240-7.

van der Borgh, C., & Terwindt, C. (2012). Shrinking operational space of NGOs – A framework of analysis. *Development in Practice, 22*(8), 1065–1081. https://doi.org/10.1080/09614524.2012.714745.

van Stapele, N., Woensdregt, L., Nencel, L., & Rwigi, E. K. (2020, January). *Towards inclusive partnerships: The political role of community based organizations (CBOs) and the official development aid system (ODA) in Nairobi, Kenya.* NWO. Retrieved from: https://includeplatform.net/wp-content/uploads/2020/01/Nencel_Research_report.pdf.

Verhoest, K., Peters, B. G., Bouckaert, G., & Verschuere, B. (2004). The study of organisational autonomy: A conceptual review. *Public Administration and Development, 24*(2), 101–118. https://doi.org/10.1002/pad.316.

Waibel, G., & Glück, S. (2013). More than 13 million: Mass mobilisation and gender politics in the Vietnam Women's Union. *Gender & Development, 21*(2), 343–361. https://doi.org/10.1080/13552074.2013.802148.

Wells-Dang, A. (2014). The political influence of civil society in Vietnam. In J. D. London (Ed.), *Politics in contemporary Vietnam: Party, state, and authority relations* (pp. 162–183). Hampshire, England: Palgrave Macmillan.

Wischermann, J., Bunk, B., Köllner, P., & Lorch, J. (2018). Do associations support authoritarian rule? Evidence from Algeria, Mozambique, and Vietnam. *Journal of Civil Society, 14*(2), 95–115. https://doi.org/10.1080/17448689.2018.1464707.

20

BEYOND THE NORTH–SOUTH DICHOTOMY

A case study on tackling global problems starting from the South

Runa Khan, Dorothee ter Kulve and Sarah Haaij

> Instead of working in two units – the implementers and funders – we aim to work as one global unit that properly understands the needs of the community.
>
> Runa Khan

Introduction

This chapter presents a case study of a Southern-led organization. The example of FRIENDSHIP, a Bangladesh-based social purpose organization (SPO), shows new starting points for collaboration between Northern and Southern development partners in today's world. We explore a collaboration that is not imbalanced by the interplay between 'recipient' and 'benefactor' or the dichotomy between 'weak' and 'strong' partners; here, instead, a collaborative spirit is central to impact and outcomes.

In 2002, when localization of funding was still far from the norm and international politics and norms still presented a 'donor–donee' mindset rather than one of partnership driven by mutual work to fill gaps, FRIENDSHIP began navigating the power imbalances of North–South relations and establishing itself as a legitimate player in the field, aiming to remain free from donor dominance and true to the organization's values, which subsequently shaped FRIENDSHIP over the next 20 years.

Today, FRIENDSHIP, which identifies as an organization working for a social purpose, is headquartered in Bangladesh and has 4,300 employees, with registered offices in five European countries as part of the FRIENDSHIP International network. The organization provides direct services to millions of the most climate-impacted people in Bangladesh.

This chapter invites organizations to imagine development cooperation differently, moving towards a new model of mutual cooperation – a model where

DOI: 10.4324/9781003241003-25

Southern-led civil society organizations (CSOs) can lead on policy and impact and where donor organizations are stimulated to contribute to development by providing the necessary funding, knowledge, and network resources.

Because it analyses real practices rather than only formal documents, this chapter will be useful for practitioners navigating development power imbalances. For academics, the chapter opens research areas on identifying the characteristics needed for Southern-led CSOs to establish strong boundaries, take the lead on policy and impact, and remain independent. How can it be ensured that development truly starts from the region where there is need?

The heart of the model

For this chapter, FRIENDSHIP journeyed inwards, reflecting on 20 years of development and attempting to distil some of the core elements that contribute to what we refer to here as the FRIENDSHIP model.

FRIENDSHIP started in 2002 with a floating hospital and has developed into an SPO with a yearly budget of 17 million euros that works on all pressing issues faced by the communities of Bangladesh, where climate change determines daily life. Today's programmes are holistic, spanning access to health care, disaster relief, capacity building and climate resilience, education, inclusion, access to rights, and cultural preservation.

At the heart of this holistic model are the needs of the communities the organization serves. The focus is on addressing needs identified by the community as a whole. In the words of Runa Khan, the founder and executive director of FRIENDSHIP,

> The trust and legitimacy of the work are achieved because of the pursuit to ensure that the right needs are fulfilled at the right time, in the right amount, in the right way, and these needs and policies are not something that can be determined by external financial givers or partners.

In addition to the needs-based approach, several other interconnected elements, to a greater or lesser extent, contribute to the FRIENDSHIP model. This chapter explores the following elements: the role of community involvement, the international network, balancing partnerships, and the organization's focus on Southern-led programming and the power relations that evolve from this approach. We begin by providing background and context on the origins and the overall journey of the organization.

FRIENDSHIP

The organization's origins and journey

FRIENDSHIP's journey started in Bangladesh, a country where 65% of the land area is underwater at different times of the year and where, in 2000, 48.9% of the people lived in poverty (World Bank, 2022). When Khan looked around at the start of the millennium, she saw a country leaning heavily on aid and bilateral loans, with millions of citizens with poor access to basic services. 'How is it possible that, in a country where millions of dollars are spent on addressing the poor's needs, so many are left unvoiced and unaddressed?', she asked. It was in search of an answer to this question that the FRIENDSHIP concept sprouted.

Since 2000, Bangladesh has made remarkable progress in terms of reducing poverty. Poverty declined from 44.2% in 1991 to 20.5% in 2019 (Asian Development Bank, 2022). In parallel, life expectancy and literacy rates have increased significantly. The country's United Nations Human Development Index increased from 0.34 in 1980 to 0.632 in 2020 (The Global Economy, 2022). However, despite this 'Bangladesh miracle', millions continue to be left behind with unaddressed needs, mostly on the river islands in the North and the coastal belt in the South. The extreme difficulty of access has made nongovernmental organizations (NGOs), government bodies, and businesses avoid working in these areas. Thus, services that could have enabled the communities to develop were not established.

Today, with 170 million people and an annual budget of US$71 billion, US$13 billion of which is expected to come from aid and bilateral loans, funds are still not reaching the most vulnerable communities (NewsNext, 2021). There are over 50,000 registered national humanitarian and development organizations and 265 active international NGOs (INGOs) in Bangladesh, but inaccessible, migratory communities are still left behind.

Simultaneously, the question of community resilience among the 7 million people served annually by FRIENDSHIP has become crucial. According to a report by Climate Central (2019), by 2050, 42 million people in Bangladesh may be displaced because of climate change (Climate Central, 2019), especially in isolated riverine islands, which are particularly exposed to climate change effects like riverbank erosion, cyclones, and annual floods.

Turbulent beginnings

To reach out to communities in need, in 2000, Khan determined that a platform was needed:

> I addressed a fundamental first need of a remote, unaddressed community: health care – proper, dependable care, through a mobile medical unit using the community itself as primary caregivers. So I tried to get funds for this idea of a mobile hospital ship.

However, not a single organization, government, aid agency, or INGO agreed to fund the project proposal, arguing that it did not fit into their budget lines, was very high risk because of its innovative nature, and was not an accepted system of working.

In the end, it was the multinational company Unilever that decided to fund the project. The company trusted that the FRIENDSHIP initiators had the commitment and ability to realize the project. Personal relationships and the ability to establish connections reaching beyond the 'usual suspects' in development contributed to the start of project activities.

Since that first floating hospital, FRIENDSHIP has developed a health care system to provide quality health services and information to remote communities. The focus is on filling gaps, with the organization working only on services that are not yet provided by formal structures.

Starting in 2005, a three-tier health system was developed to ensure nobody is left behind. This three-tier health delivery service consists of (1) hospital ships and land hospitals; (2) mobile satellite clinics going to the communities on a regular basis, as well as static clinics; and (3) community health workers living in the communities – all to serve at the grassroots level.

Currently, five more hospital ships have been commissioned from FRIENDSHIP by a bilateral donor on behalf of the Government of Bangladesh, with this model becoming dominant in health care for providing care to migratory communities in the country.

Thus, filling in gaps has evolved into systemic change through FRIENDSHIP's unique approach to pressing development issues.

A mission of needs

> I may not always know how, but I've always known what I wanted to reach.
>
> *Runa Khan*

Establishing the first NGO mobile ship-hospital touches upon one of the principles that underpin the FRIENDSHIP model: its clear mission to engage in action that corresponds to the needs of the people the organization is serving. From the start, the organization's focus has been taking a needs-based and mission-based approach to developing the community as a whole to build self-reliance. When seeking external support, FRIENDSHIP holds firm to solutions that stem from grassroots understanding and local expertise. Ownership by the local communities not only facilitates effective collaboration to deliver services but also ensures efficient use of resources and long-term sustainability. Over the years, many interventions that the organization started in response to community needs have become integrated into public service structures. Examples include the vaccination programme, family planning, and cervical cancer screenings. With the uptake of the vaccination programme, for instance, vaccination coverage in the focus areas has increased from far less than 57% in 2000 (the national rural area average at the time) to 92% in 2021 (personal communication Civil Surgeon Kurigram, 2022; MIS Team, 2022).

Indisputably, the idea of working in a needs-based way is not unique to FRIENDSHIP. Worldwide, CSOs often work with the needs of their communities in mind. The suggestion being advanced here is that it is not only desirable but also very much possible to remain true to this approach, with CSOs not compromising to fit with a preconceived project design in relationships with international donor partners but instead ensuring the best possible design within the limitations of their particular context.

Community is key

On building legitimacy through quality

> What we do, we want to do it so well that people would want to pay for it if they could.
>
> *Runa Khan*

The poor cannot afford poor solutions; they need the best solutions possible for them to be willing to continue to use a CSO's services to improve their lives. When aiming to provide high-quality services, strong legitimacy in the community is key; this legitimacy is therefore an important component of the FRIENDSHIP model.

FRIENDSHIP started with the most difficult service to provide, bringing dependable health services to the community doorstep, something most NGOs would steer clear of because of the complexity of starting and sustaining such a programme. From day one, people advised against this choice of programme, arguing that FRIENDSHIP should instead start with less risky health prevention initiatives. By starting with a fully functional hospital, including surgeries, alongside health education and prevention, however, community trust was built, as the organization demonstrated that the people's well-being was the central motivation of their work.

As Khan summarized, 'That the people we address can't pay for the services doesn't mean we don't aim for the highest quality possible'. This idea is reflected in the FRIENDSHIP rainwater-harvesting hospital for disadvantaged communities, which was awarded the prestigious RIBA International Prize for Architecture in 2022, and in the free schools FRIENDSHIP has built, which achieve high scores on national examinations.

Community participation and trust building

FRIENDSHIP also works to ensure community ownership by taking a participatory approach. The organization's field operations team engages with the community before any project is initiated. The team works with local participants – influential people and regular members of the community – to understand community needs before working out solutions the organization might develop with them. This approach is very much in line with the design thinking process that is now popular in the development sector. In all FRIENDSHIP interventions, formal systems are set up to keep the community involved in the evolution of the project; examples of this involve groups formed for disaster risk mapping, legal and social issue resolutions, and income support.

The organization makes it a point to align incentives for new projects in a way that the community has some ownership of the results and to ensure sustainability of the impact of the programme. For example, the schools, weaving centres, and raised villages are all built on land donated by the community; more specifically, this land is often donated by relatively well off, influential members of the community.

The international network

On personal relations and high-profile networking

> Find people who share your vision; that way, you can provide them with a platform through which they can achieve this mission they already feel.
>
> *Runa Khan*

FRIENDSHIP started from the South and developed into a strong global team. FRIENDSHIP International originated in January 2006 in Luxembourg. Currently, the global organization has operations in five European countries: Luxembourg, the Netherlands, the United Kingdom, Belgium, and France. The decision to establish a presence in Europe was very deliberate. It was about setting up a platform in Europe to get as close as possible to European donors and other supporters, thereby avoiding long chains of partnerships that too often dilute donor relationships and projects. Today, about 50% of the development budget of the organization is raised by this international network.

A few months after founding FRIENDSHIP, Khan realized that the modality of the NGO world, 'working from project approval to project approval', was not the way she would make a sustainable difference. Khan started by following up on personal relationships and networking sessions. At the French Embassy in Bangladesh, she met the Grand Duchess of Luxembourg and began to lay the groundwork for a European network. 'It provided me with the opportunity to create FRIENDSHIP as an independent organization, directly linking those who were providing funding to see and feel the impact they were making', Khan said. This network started with a handful of international partners and grew into a global team built on high-level expertise, a shared mission, a strong network, and, according to team members, the overarching core value of verity.

Today, the mission of the European teams includes advancing the agenda of localization and making sure the Bangladesh team can focus on designing and implementing community-based programmes. These European teams, ranging in size from one to six staff members per country, fulfil important functions of

FRIENDSHIP, including fundraising and building new partnerships. Equally important functions are networking and expertise sharing. Each FRIENDSHIP International team is governed by a board of directors or trustees.

The sharing of expertise, which depends on team members' backgrounds, includes activities ranging from providing juridical advice to supporting the organization in research, finance, advocacy, and accounting, to name a few examples. For instance, if advocacy or activism is needed towards governments or United Nations institutions based in Europe, FRIENDSHIP International teams can do that – their international colleagues are not there only to raise funds. The organization has evolved into a group of professionals that all bring something to the table. Design and implementation mechanisms come from the South, and ideas, skills, knowledge, funds, and ability come from the entire global team.

The international teams are all chaired by high-profile professionals with strong expertise in the different fields of activity carried out by the international Southern-led CSO. A background in development is not a prerequisite. Representing fields ranging from law and finance to politics, management, and strategic action planning, all team chairs, and board members have a proven track record and strong network in their field, ensuring the level of quality that the organizational leadership believes is needed to support its programmes. Some international team members are donors themselves, whereas others dedicate time and professional input. This structure, with the centre of gravity in Bangladesh and high-profile but relatively few staff members in the offices in Europe, exemplifies the model.

Making an international network work for you

Some of the global team members entered the network through personal relationships; others, like one of the few development experts on the team, joined because they saw the FRIENDSHIP model as what this board member referred to as 'the future of development aid' that he wanted to be part of. For all positions, carefully selecting the people you want to work with is necessary. 'In practice, you don't need a person specialized in accounting to design a project', Khan noted, reflecting on what she had learned; 'You need him/her helping to strengthen our systems of accounting. That means that sometimes you just have to approach the right person and be brave enough to ask'.

Shared mission

Within FRIENDSHIP, there is an awareness that the people who were committed to the mission, especially in the early days when the organization had no major funding, were willing and able to dedicate their time to the organization without being remunerated for their work. According to Khan, this brought together a group of people who were intrinsically motivated to work for the cause and who had a shared mission. Team members typically had already shared the basic elements of the mission before joining; in Khan's words, 'I only provided the platform and with that helped them to achieve a mission they already felt. Now the teams help us along by opening doors to potential donors and relations in Europe that would have remained closed'. Team members in Europe can help, for example, with approaching certain European-based family foundations that can be considered closed entities with which it would take time to build trust 'on the ground'. In other cases, team member assistance is more practical, as is the case when a Dutch legal entity is required to start a formal partnership.

Strong network

The team members offer their networks and the accompanying access – not only to donors but also to medical volunteers, universities, and other valuable linkages. For example, a former minister brought in information regarding funding possibilities through Luxembourg's development department. Another team member had access to surgeons who wanted to volunteer in Bangladesh hospitals.

Representatives from all teams participate in a monthly meeting to share updates and lessons. This is coordinated by a partnership team in Bangladesh. Irrespective of the conventional distinction between North and South, all the teams work towards an environment that recognizes the value of each partner and trusts local organizations to bring their capacity for understanding community needs and proposing the right solutions. At this point, the concept of verity comes in; we elaborate on this idea in the next section.

Building partnerships

The role of a truthful story when forging strong partnerships

> When I met Khan, I was inspired by her vision. In Bangladesh, I saw how much she had realized in the communities; I knew then that this is the development action I want to support.
>
> *Dorothee ter Kulve*

FRIENDSHIP considers their ability to attract and retain partners over the long term to be a success. In 2002, a multinational business joined the organization as a partner; in 2006, it was a European governing body. Today, there are businesses, families, governments, banks, and institutional donors who are committed to supporting the organization's approach over the long term. FRIENDSHIP's experience shows that an organization can forge trust-based relationships while also making sure to avoid becoming just an implementing partner to donors.

Partner experience from FRIENDSHIP Netherlands

Dorothee ter Kulve, chair of FRIENDSHIP Netherlands, is responsible for some of the organization's major partnerships with European donors. After being introduced to Khan via a shared connection in 2007, ter Kulve, who has a background in business, decided to visit the organization in Bangladesh: 'From the very beginning, I was impressed by the incredible work that was being realized in the communities despite little resources. Then and there, I decided that this is the type of development action I wanted to contribute to'.

Like other members of the international network, ter Kulve stressed that she found Khan to be an inspirational leader with a strong vision on how to improve the lives of the neediest people:

> Her ability to translate this vision into manageable, concrete actions is one of her strengths and one of the reasons I wanted to use my corporate experience for FRIENDSHIP. I figured I could mobilize my network in the Global North, something that can be difficult and costly to do from Bangladesh, and find people who are interested in funding an organization that I can guarantee will make an impact.

Defining your story

When reaching out to possible new partners, it is important to be able to present a story that is truthful. This is facilitated by the European chairs, like ter Kulve, not solely focusing on fundraising but being well versed concerning the programmes in the communities. Ter Kulve noted,

> Within NGOs, fundraising and programming are often separate entities, but the fact that I am in close contact with the Bangladesh team and know the daily situation on the ground – the successes but also the setbacks – makes me able to tell a story that holds truth. Potential partners appreciate that.

The organizational model of FRIENDSHIP is important in this regard. This is the vision on which the South–North model of the global team was developed. The international network works for FRIENDSHIP Bangladesh and thus ultimately for the communities.

This model can be contrasted with what ter Kulve refers to as 'the consultant approach' to development:

> From a desk, on the other side of the world, a problem is identified, and then a solution is designed and funds are raised. When the funds have been raised, the implementing organization is contracted or a local organization is set up from scratch. In my experience, our model – where needs are defined

and solutions designed before connections to possible funders are made – constitutes one of the reasons that not only the members of the team like myself but also the funders want to contribute to FRIENDSHIP's story.

In the Netherlands, the organization has been successful in attracting a few private funders – business and family foundations, mainly from the team's direct network. These relationships are built through the activities of the Dutch team (one staff member and an active board), who prepare a large number of presentations and attend many (informal) networking events, as well as actively pursuing partners considered potential matches with the organization's values. For example, in one area where FRIENDSHIP works, government schools stood empty and school attendance was low because of a lack of qualified teachers. A community solution was designed, where unemployed community members were trained to become the FRIENDSHIP primary school teachers. According to ter Kulve, 'This was a powerful story I could share during meetings and network events in the Netherlands, so I approached foundations and organizations that are open to supporting our educational solution'.

After the first contact has been established, FRIENDSHIP presents the potential partner with a community needs-based solution for which the organization is seeking funding. A conversation then follows, where endorsement of the organization's message ('People develop themselves; the communities are the ones with the power to change, and the funders can contribute to this building of power') is key. After the partners agree on a trajectory and impact, cooperation can start. Ter Kulve noted, 'I think this turned out to be a key choice – that we choose partners open to the idea that our local communities and our local teams design, own, and execute initiatives in their context'.

What makes a partnership?

Vocabulary matters. Within the organization, there is a preference to speak of 'partners' rather than 'donors'. The terms 'donor' and 'recipient' imply a certain power imbalance. In the word 'partners', there is recognition that both parties are of equal importance and willing to listen to each other.

For a partnership to work well, its parameters need to be defined early in the process. Naturally, both partners influence the process and bring experience and working methods to the relationship. In this regard, the organization does not try to avoid donor influence per se. 'The premise is mutual agreement, so the parameters of cooperation presented by the partner need to fit us', Khan asserted; 'If these don't match our values, we cannot cooperate'.

Integrity, dignity, quality, justice, and hope are the five values that guide FRIENDSHIP's work and decisions. The concept of verity – the idea of being truthful – is an overarching value for the organization. Instances where cooperation did not work out occurred when there was incompatibility on one of these key values – for example, if the partner wanted to maintain absolute control of

FRIENDSHIP's way of working. In the case of a dominant partner, there is no space for trust and mutual respect to develop, and basic values like justice and integrity can easily be violated. Khan asserted, 'It is these so-called "organizational soft values" that people tend to underestimate, but to me, they are the core of our work. Even though many find that difficult to believe'.

In this approach, one elementary skill is being able to integrate the organization's value set throughout their work and relations. Considering verity, according to Khan, being truthful is a prerequisite for cooperation with team members and with partners 'because being true, doing what you say and having a track record to show for it, builds trust'. It is this verity and trust that can lay the foundation for FRIENDSHIP's idea of a control-free partnership – where the partner trusts the Southern-led CSO to take the lead in realizing the jointly agreed result.

What is in it for the funders?

In today's development world, where there are thousands of organizations with equally good intentions, building partnerships is not always easy. Working together takes mutual respect, trust, and time. Small-scale, pilot partnerships can be initiated with budgets under US$10,000, creating space to build relationships.

An exemplary case of this is a long-term partnership between FRIENDSHIP and a Dutch multinational company that started with a small project for women's empowerment. Only after two years of working together, when company representatives visited the programme and colleagues in Bangladesh, did this partner come to fully understand FRIENDSHIP's value set and holistic approach to development, which the Dutch team had tried to explain all along. In this case, the partner had to see the work to be able to fully grasp it and to be open to wider cooperation. Today, the company is one of FRIENDSHIP's major strategic partners.

Time and again, a visit to see FRIENDSHIP's work in person has played a key role in getting the final 'yes' and retaining partnerships. A large European bank regularly brings groups of executives to the river islands to discuss the practices they witness being implemented with their support. Additionally, the international teams establish direct connections with the partners and responsible department(s) of the organization in Bangladesh. Ter Kulve described these processes as follows:

> I realized that it is about making your partners understand the impact that you are creating. You have to explain and show that the communities are the ones with the power to change, that the funders can contribute to the building of the power on the ground. So you have to provide them, the partners, with the possibility to become part of and contribute to that impact.

Programming and power relations

On avoiding a donor-driven way of working

> Growth can never be the goal; you cannot grow well if you compromise on essentials.
>
> *Runa Khan*

FRIENDSHIP's approach to programme design is based on the idea that solutions precede finances. The basic programming is done in Bangladesh and is independent of the funders. Thus, the focus is on keeping a flexible budget, with the belief that 30%–40% of the funding should be flexible to make the right decisions in a fast-changing, dynamic context.

The goal here is to act according to the organization's values and objectives, seeking help from intermediaries only when there is a close match of goals and agendas. Not being 'donor-driven' permits the organization to develop its programmes according to the needs of the communities it serves. At the same time, the organization is open to new technology and ideas that can support its mission.

Although the above may read as a natural reflection of the 'shift-the-power' debates shaping the development world, FRIENDSHIP's approach continues to face resistance. Many donors that provide funding for civil society initiatives highlight the importance of local ownership but at the same time continue to emphasize programming by Northern organizations.

In the case of FRIENDSHIP, in 1998, after the organization's initial registration, it took years to get the first funds for a hospital ship; however, this plan was nevertheless not scrapped for an alternative project or accomplished with a donor where there might be a conflict of interest with health. The same remains true for FRIENDSHIP's newly developed programmes today.

Power relations

There is resistance to FRIENDSHIP's method of work from some partners. Institutional donors who are used to calling the shots more often have trouble recognizing an equal partnership and instead prefer to deal with implementing partners, where the donor controls the balance of power. In preliminary dialogue, efforts are made to stress that having FRIENDSHIP as just an implementing partner is not an efficient use of resources. For this message to resonate, the complete team, from the staff in Bangladesh to employees in the European network, needs to fully endorse the organization's needs-based programming capabilities.

An example of this is seen in a Rohingya camp education programme, which started with a small intervention partner of a United Nations organization and eventually grew four times larger in scale. Currently, this intervention partner is in the process of incorporating parts of FRIENDSHIP's intervention model into its own programmes. Courage is sometimes needed to base decision making on more than the amount of funding being offered. At the beginning of the United Nations partnership, the management team on the intervention partner's side was adamant about maintaining some designs that FRIENDSHIP did not want to integrate. The FRIENDSHIP team was confident enough about the solution they wanted to carry forward instead, and high-level bilateral discussions were carried out to get a final 'yes' to FRIENDSHIP's distinct approach to the problem.

There is a challenge in that many international donors always want a deadline or an exit strategy so that the problem can be considered 'solved'. These ideas conflict with the FRIENDSHIP approach, which is long term – investing in people is an ongoing process, especially in the fields of health, education, and climate action. FRIENDSHIP is vocal about this difference, which has led the organization to spend significant effort and time setting up programmes and finding partners who are willing to listen and understand.

Clear expectations

The balance of power in negotiations between FRIENDSHIP and potential partners is handled delicately. To reduce the likelihood of a misunderstanding arising in the future, the programme design and deliverables are all rolled out from the beginning. In their relationships with partners, the European teams find that being clear about core values before going into business enhances FRIENDSHIP's credibility.

As mentioned above, FRIENDSHIP's five core values are integrity, dignity, quality, justice, and hope. Based on a well-defined code of ethics, these values are communicated throughout the organization and applied consistently in all activities and programmes. The 'ethic of the month' is also presented to all employees, discussed at the beginning of all community meetings, and included in the curricula of school programmes. Other executors, like UNICEF and local government entities, are also starting to integrate this code of ethics.

Nevertheless, getting potential partners to buy into the FRIENDSHIP way of working can be a challenge. Ensuring that there is support for a holistic programme rather than only for certain programme parts often takes considerable effort. An important note on this point is that both Southern-led CSOs and their partners need space to make substantial contributions. A balanced relationship is not a one-way street. Therefore, FRIENDSHIP focuses on creating a 'lean' way of working that allows some scope for all stakeholders to contribute to the final output without interfering with the prearranged solution, mission, and values. A partner can offer suggestions, connections, or know-how that advances the impact of the mission; however, the core of the intervention – the community-defined needs and associated community-based solutions – are non-negotiable.

FRIENDSHIP's experience shows that input from long-term partners tends to focus more on strengthening the organization than on controlling interventions. For example, a private donor suggested that the organization establish a Bangladesh-based communication department and then supported this initiative.

Say 'no' and walk away

The trap of Northern compliance starts when an organization focuses more on pleasing and appeasing the funders from the North than on investing in the quality of the aid being delivered. FRIENDSHIP had to navigate this trap carefully by sometimes being willing to fight, understanding when to try to convince a partner and when to say 'no deal'.

The idea of seeking partnerships only when there is a close match of goals and agendas may seem like the approach of an organization in the privileged situation where substantial fundraising is not a precondition for survival. This will not necessarily reflect the experience of many Southern CSOs with power relations in today's development world. However, the conviction put forward here is that, when organizations are working with this model, they have to be able to say 'no' to partnerships that do not advance their mission, even if this results in less organizational growth. In Khan's words, 'Growth can never be the main goal. You cannot grow well if you compromise on essentials'. Describing a case when an INGO invited FRIENDSHIP to run a programme to establish a community group and an accompanying communal fund, with the intention of handing over the group's management to the community itself within a year, Khan explained, 'I said "no" because I think spending money like this does not contribute to communal development. You cannot make people who have nothing share 50,000 dollars among themselves out of the blue; you need to develop structures for that'.

Conclusion

FRIENDSHIP is an example of a Southern-led organization with a global team that has a community needs-based impact. In this chapter, we explored the FRIENDSHIP case to expand our understanding of the possibilities for collaboration between the Northern and Southern partners in today's world. Here, the ideal is moving towards development cooperation where South and North meet halfway based on mutual understanding and respect, creating the ability to face the world's most pressing issues.

For FRIENDSHIP, integrity, dignity, quality, justice, and hope are the five values at the core of their work. These values are communicated systematically, and storytelling about maintaining the core values has been adopted in the organization, leading to an understanding of the organizational culture at every level.

In this chapter, we have argued that the power of a truthful, shared story not only unites FRIENDSHIP's employees but is also key in building trust-based (as opposed to transactional) relationships with international advocates and partners. The outline of this story is written in Bangladesh, and FRIENDSHIP's partners are then presented with the possibility of sharing in its narration and contributing to the story's continuation by supporting the organization's impact in local communities.

At the heart of FRIENDSHIP's evolving story are the needs of the communities the organization serves. To maintain a Southern-led approach in serving these communities, an interplay of elements is at work. The most important elements are the building of legitimacy in the community through high-quality projects; the creation of an international, high-profile network with partners that contribute quality skills, networks, and prestige; the forging of trust-based, long-term partnerships based on verity and with clearly defined parameters that accept Southern leadership and serve the communities' interests; and the courage to lead on programming and to walk away from collaboration when needed.

For Southern-led CSOs around the world, the elements that contribute to navigating new forms of collaboration beyond the North–South dichotomy will differ with place and time. Considered in this light, the FRIENDSHIP model presented here should not be approached as a strict set of rules; rather, it should be seen as framework that can instigate debate and awareness towards a future of collaborative development policies starting from the Global South.

References

Asian Development Bank. (2022). *Poverty data: Bangladesh*. Retrieved from: https://www.adb.org/countries/bangladesh/poverty.

Climate Central. (2019). *Flooded future: Global vulnerability to sea-level rise worse than previously understood*. Retrieved from: www.climatecentral.org/pdfs/2019CoastalDEMReport.pdf.

MIS Team. (2022). Health Quality Indicator (HQI) Report. Dhaka: FRIENDSHIP.

NewsNext. (2021). *Bangladesh unveils over 71-billion-dollar national budget*. Retrieved from: Bangladesh unveils over 71-billion-dollar national budget (newsnextbd.com).

The Global Economy. (2022). *Bangladesh human development*. Retrieved from: https://www.theglobaleconomy.com/Bangladesh/human_development/#:~:text=Bangladesh%3A%20Human%20Development%20Index%20(0,1)%2C%201980%20%2D%202020%3A&text=The%20average%20value%20for%20Bangladesh,of%200.632%20points%20in%202020.

World Bank. (2022). *Poverty headcount ratio at national poverty lines Bangladesh*. Retrieved from: https://data.worldbank.org/indicator/SI.POV.NAHC?locations=BD.

21

SHIFT THE POWER? CONSTRAINTS AND ENABLERS OF MORE EQUITABLE PARTNERSHIPS BETWEEN NON-GOVERNMENTAL ORGANIZATIONS

The case of Dutch small-scale development initiatives in Uganda and India

Sara Kinsbergen, Mieke Molthof, Linda van der Hoek and Anna Vellinga

Introduction

Currently, in the field of international development cooperation, there is a strong renewed call to shift power from civil society organizations (CSOs) from the Global North to those from the Global South. With the launch of the #ShiftThePower campaign in 2016, the Global Fund for Community Foundations gave this longstanding discussion a new push, instigated by the idea that shifting power is 'not only the right thing to do, but also the most effective way to ensure results that will last and that are owned and shaped by the people they are meant to reach' (GFCF, n.d.).

Both in academic and in policy circles, these calls are reflected in discussions about equal or authentic partnerships between Northern and Southern CSOs – partnerships built on equality, trust, mutual respect, and reciprocity. However, the continuation over time of the debate seems to suggest that (unequal) power relations have proven to be remarkably resilient. This could imply that the impediments to change have been stronger than the (expected) drivers of change. Through a case-study exploration of the drivers of and impediments to change in North–South collaboration, in this chapter, we seek to gain a deeper understanding of the mechanisms that explain why change does, or does not, occur – including the effect of personal relations. The study presented here seeks to provide enhanced insight for more effective policymaking aimed at 'doing differently' and shifting power to organizations in the South.

DOI: 10.4324/9781003241003-26

We are doing so by applying the 'private development initiatives' (PDIs) partnership framework (Kinsbergen, 2014; Schnable, 2015). These Northern-based, small-scale, voluntary development organizations are often established in response to what, in hindsight, is often described as a life-changing encounter during a holiday or longer stay in a developing country. It is not only the organizational features of PDIs that distinguish them from more established non-governmental organizations (NGOs); PDIs are also often characterized by their partnerships in the countries where they operate, being strongly personal and informal in nature. The inspiring head teacher a person from the North met and befriended during a trip through Kenya or the doctor a Northern citizen worked with during a volunteer stay in a clinic in the south of India do not only trigger the establishment of foundations but also then become these foundations' 'local partners' with whom they start designing and implementing development projects. With personal encounters and friendship-like relations at the centre of the organizations, PDIs are expected to be particularly suitable for establishing 'true' authentic partnerships. Although some studies have indeed suggested that personal relations can be important in fostering transformative learning and establishing equal and authentic partnerships (see e.g. Lister, 1999), there seems to be a gap in the literature in terms of research on if and how such personal relations actually support more equal North–South collaboration. With this exploratory study that focuses specifically on a type of NGO that holds the personal at its heart, we seek to open up the debate on this issue.

Analytical framework

The search for authentic partnerships

In ideal-typical terms, a partnership can be defined as a dynamic relationship that 'encompasses mutual influence, with a careful balance between synergy and respective autonomy, which incorporates mutual respect, equal participation in decision-making, mutual accountability, and transparency' (Brinkerhoff, 2002, p. 216). In the field of international development, partnerships are often depicted as a way of providing local communities with 'ownership' of the interventions that aim to advance development (Abrahamsen, 2004). Such partnerships are promoted[1] both with idealistic motives as 'the most appropriate relationship as defined by value-laden principles' and by more instrumental rationales, as a means to enhance efficiency and effectiveness (Brinkerhoff, 2002, p. 21). The ideal type of partnership, however, is rarely achieved in reality (Aagaard & Trykker, 2020; Brinkerhoff, 2002; Contu & Girei, 2014; Fowler, 1998, 2015; Lister, 2000; Schaaf, 2015). 'Partnership' has been an aspiration for Northern development organizations since the 1970s, but Fowler (1998, p. 1) observed that they 'have shown little ability to form equitable relations, i.e. true partnership', with development organizations in the South.

In the literature on North–South NGO partnerships, Lister (2000) has specifically drawn attention to the importance of the power dynamics within these relationships, building on the classic work of Dahl (1957), who conceptualized power in terms of influence on decision making. For Dahl (1957, pp. 202–203), 'A has power over B to the extent to which he can get B to do something that B would not otherwise do'. According to this understanding, '[i]nfluence reflects an episodic perspective of power[2] [...] based on the hierarchical ordering of authority grounded in resource control' (Elbers, 2012, p. 29). This conceptualization allows to determine the relative influence of Southern organizations (i.e. the balance of power) and to shed light on the extent to which organizations have been able to develop 'true' authentic partnerships. Following the approach adopted by Lister (2000), we distinguish between structural influence and operational influence, with the former linked to control over resources and the determination of strategy – which we will mainly relate to the design of the partnership – and the latter linked to decisions about the activities undertaken – which we will mainly relate to project implementation.

Impediments to change

By exploring previous studies on the work of NGOs in general and PDIs in particular, we identified a number of recurring drivers of and impediments to change in these organizations and their development interventions (Aagaard & Trykker, 2020; Appe & Schnable, 2019; Banks & Hulme, 2014; Batti, 2017; Brinkerhoff, 2002; Brinkerhoff & Brinkerhoff, 2004; Brown & Kalegaonkar, 2002; Elbers & Schulpen, 2013; Fowler, 1998; Jones & Deitrick, 2020; Kinsbergen et al., 2020; Lister, 2000; Mawdsley et al., 2020; Michael, 2004; Sutton et al., 2010). We expect these factors to also be useful in understanding the changes North–South collaborations are undergoing – changes reflected in the extent of each actor's influence in decision making. Although this list is by no means exhaustive, the factors selected for the current study, presented in Table 21.1, are those that featured most prominently in previous research on the work of PDIs.

We will use this list as an analytical framework to study the central partnerships in this study, as well as the changes observed in them. Although we realize that external and/or contextual factors also influence partnerships and changes in them, in this chapter, we focus on internal and/or behavioural factors – i.e. factors related to the partners themselves and the interactions between them.

TABLE 21.1 Factors influencing change

Impediment to change	*Driver of change*
Resource scarcity	Capacity strengthening
Philanthropic consumerism	Personal relations

Resource scarcity

Control over financial resources has been identified in the literature as one of the most significant obstacles to the realization of authentic partnerships (Aagaard & Trykker, 2020; Lister, 2000). According to Fowler (1998, p. 11), '[a]n abiding problem in building partnerships between northern NGDOs [nongovernmental development organizations] and those elsewhere is the transfer of finance between them'. Power differences based on control over these resources can undermine 'the mutuality needed for effective partnership' (Brinkerhoff & Brinkerhoff, 2004, p. 246). Similarly, Batti (2017, p. 160) has pointed out that 'in practice many partnerships between international and local NGOs remain one-way funding streams', referring to an uneven playing field where the partner in control of the financial resources often determines the partnership terms. Hence, we expected resource scarcity on the part of local organizations to function as an impediment to the development of equal relationships.

Philanthropic consumerism

A second, interlinked factor that could result in funding organizations being in the driver's seat, is what can be termed 'charitable consumerism' (Banks & Hulme, 2014). This refers to the search of donors or volunteers/staff members of organizations for consumable development interventions in return for their contribution of funding or time. Previous studies found that PDI volunteers search for the 'fun factor': To reward their often significant voluntary time investment, they seek to spend their time on the activities that they experience as rewarding, which are often those that directly contribute to the realization of the development interventions (Kinsbergen, 2014). Consequently, PDI members are most often strongly involved in the design and implementation of the development projects they support. This involvement is further strengthened by PDIs' partial reliance on private donors in their personal circles (e.g. friends, family, and colleagues). Because of this, there is a lot at stake for them in terms of guaranteeing that the funding is spent in line with the donors' preferences. Both of these mechanisms are known to result, overall, in a prominent role for PDI members, sometimes at the expense of the roles and positions of their local counterparts, and might thus hinder a shift in power from North to South.

Drivers of change

Capacity-strengthening programmes

Capacity-strengthening programmes have been identified in the literature as a key driver of change. As noted by Batti (2017, p. 166), '[i]t is imperative for a partnership to develop strategies that will focus on enhancing the capacities of local NGOs so that the organizations may gradually undertake partnership governance and management activities as the partnership matures'. Brown and Kalegaonkar (2002, p. 231) have listed various possible effects of the provision of such capacity strengthening, including 'strengthening individual and organizational capacities, mobilizing material resources, providing information and intellectual resources, building alliances for mutual support, and building bridges across sectoral differences'. Indeed, capacity investment has been identified in the literature as a factor that can significantly influence the prerequisites of and success factors for effective partnerships (Brinkerhoff, 2002). Lister (2000, p. 236) has suggested that, although power asymmetries are reinforced by the framework within which interaction takes place, 'the "capacity-building" which is a common element of partnership arrangements strengthens a Southern agency's voice and ability to affect the overall framework'. This also leads to the expectation that changing financial flows will be able to contribute to a power shift by rectifying or at least diminishing the power asymmetries deriving from initial differences in control over financial resources (Michael, 2004). All this suggests that capacity strengthening could be an important way to influence resource flows and might be able to contribute to a power shift in North–South relationships.

One notable example of a capacity-strengthening programme that aims specifically to empower local partners is the 'Change-the-Game' programme of the Dutch Wilde Ganzen Foundation. The programme aims to change the 'rules' of the development game by transferring power to communities and enabling them to shape their own future. The core assumption of the programme's Theory of Change is that a fundamental shift in power can be obtained through diversifying the funding base for local partners, which increases local ownership (Steinhäuser, 2020). Two interrelated pathways are central to the programme's Theory of Change: First, the programme aims at strengthening organizations' (local) fundraising capacity to decrease their dependency on foreign funding to carry out their work. This is also intended to strengthen the organization's local constituency, contributing to the organization's legitimacy. Second, building on this support base, organizations are trained in advocacy that targets government actors. The programme was created in 2016 and was initially set up in collaboration with NGOs in Brazil, Kenya, and India. It is currently offered in 12 countries and in a blended (both online and offline) setup. In this study, we will use the Change-the-Game programme to focus on capacity strengthening as a possible driver of change.

Personal relations

In studies that offer advice for designing more equitable partnerships, one recommendation is to build personal relations rooted in trust (Elbers & Schulpen, 2013; Mawdsley et al., 2002, 2005, 2020). Eyben (2006) has described how the formalization of relations between donors and NGOs increases donors' power, which undermines transformative learning because it hinders the mutual accountability associated with trust-based relations. Personal relations can serve as a counter-force to rigid, top-down, managerial structures. Kumi and Copestake (2021, p. 3) found a positive role of such 'informal networks, connections, personal contacts and friendship [...] in enhancing collaboration between donors and national NGOs'. Likewise, Dichter (1989, p. 10) has suggested that,

> because of the myriad sensitivities which exist between North and South, the partnerships and collaborations which have proven to be successful are usually those where strong personal relationships (even 'bonding') have developed between persons in the North and the South.

Brown (1996) has explained the role of personal relations in the context of the effect of social capital. He reasoned that stronger personal relationships correspond to higher social capital, serving to facilitate cooperative problem solving and the bridging of power differences and knowledge gaps. It can hence be expected that more equitable partnerships might be fostered by informal relations, which have been described as 'a form of interaction among partners engaging in dialogue, the rules of which are not pre-designed, and enjoying relative freedom in the interpretation of their roles' requirements' (Misztal, 2000, p. 46) – elements that characterize the relations of PDIs.

Methods

For the purposes of this study, 16 partnerships (eight Netherlands–Uganda partnerships and eight Netherlands–India partnerships) were selected on the basis of the participation of local organizations in the Change-the-Game programme from 2016 to 2020. Because the Change-the-Game programme is a Dutch programme, partnerships of Dutch PDIs were selected. India and Uganda were chosen because there was a lack of previous research measuring the impact of the programme in these contexts. Data collection took place from November 2020 to April 2021. In total, 41 semi-structured interviews were conducted, mostly online, with the founders, directors, and coordinators of both the Dutch organizations and their Ugandan and Indian counterparts; 21 interviews for the Netherlands–India partnerships and 20 interviews for the Netherlands–Uganda partnerships were conducted. The interviewees were asked to describe the partnerships from the programme initiation until the present, with each participant outlining the life history of their partnership. The main topics included the start of the partnership, the structure of the organization, the structure of the partnership, communication, accountability, decision making, financial flows, the Change-the-Game training, local fundraising, and the future of the partnership. The interviews were recorded and transcribed verbatim. The transcripts were then coded either using qualitative data analysis software (NVivo) or manually.

Findings

The partnership: how it started

Even though the organizations differed from each other in various ways, the PDIs and their partnerships with local organizations in India or Uganda shared the presence of personal relations at the heart of the start of the PDIs and their partnerships. Most of the PDIs participating in this study originated from a travel, internship, or volunteering experience in the Global South, which inspired citizens from the Global North to start their own development initiative. Many of the partnerships hence started as a result of an 'accidental' personal encounter with the living conditions of local communities leaving very deep impressions on travellers. Driven by this personal experience, these people felt compelled to do something, and they set up an initiative. This is well illustrated by the following statement from one of the founders of one of the PDIs:

> When we [...] travelled to India, it soon became clear to us that we had to do much more. We saw the misery of this country pass before our own eyes. Doing nothing was no longer an option for us; we could not ignore this. [...] When we came home, we had to process our experiences. India left a deep impression on us [...], and after deliberation it seemed wise to set up a foundation. We immediately set to work, not knowing what was waiting for us all.

This personal character was also reflected in the institutional design of the partnership, or 'the set of rules which regulate interaction and the way in which outcomes are produced within partnerships' (Elbers & Schulpen, 2013, p. 50). The overall picture that emerged from the interviews is that the rules of the game of the partnership frameworks were determined by the following elements: (1) the personal preferences of the members of the PDI (e.g. starting sewing schools because of a sewing hobby); (2) the vision and beliefs of the Dutch organization (e.g. 'a project should always have a clear beginning and end'); (3) the preconditions and preferences of the PDI's back donors (e.g. a ban on overhead costs); and (4) the organizational limitations of the PDI (e.g. financial limitations). Each of these factors limited the scope of the projects. Hence, charitable consumerism (reflected in elements 1, 2, and 3) was clearly at play in the process of setting the boundaries of the partnership framework. A concrete example that reflects the fourth element and shows how it limits the local organization's room for manoeuvre and therefore the desired impact, is captured by the following statement by a member of a local organization:

> One thing I would propose to change is the budget. [...] Because, ideally, we are budgeting based on the available conditions and maybe what we

> anticipate in the future. But they [the PDI members] say, 'No, this is a very big project. Reduce it'.

In general, the ad hoc origins of the PDIs and the personal character of their partnerships create a situation where the relationship tends to be governed primarily through informal, tacit ways of operating rather than formal rules.[3] In a 'learning by doing manner', PDIs determine the rules of the framework (e.g. finding out the limitations of their own back donors). In a similar way, via a process of 'trial and error', the local counterpart organizations familiarize themselves with the framework. The following extracts from interviews with PDI members are illustrative of this point:

> They have a very clear idea of what they can ask of us.

> Ultimately, we have the last word. We are the ones who give the money. We made the decision to focus mainly on education. [...] That has been a decision, and we have more or less just announced it; we have communicated why we decided it that way, but it was our decision in the end.

Overall, the interviews indicated that many of the PDIs were responsible for the set-up of the partnership framework, with the local organizations having little or no voice.

In addition to the framework being determined mainly by the organizations from the Netherlands, it also became clear through the interviews that, from the start of their cooperation, the local organizations were strongly dependent on the financial contributions of their Dutch counterparts for the implementation and running of the local organizations' projects. These financial flows played an important role in determining the initial balance of power within the partnerships. The findings suggest that the dependence on foreign donors was rather significant for the local organizations within the partnerships, with funds from these donors providing 60%–100% of the local organizations' funding. For many of the partnerships, their partner PDI provided most of the project funds.

Change within the partnership over time

We found that the interviews suggested that, over time, the parameters of the partnership framework continued to be largely determined by the preferences of the PDIs' volunteers and donors. Several interviewees explained how the relationship became stronger, with frequent visits being instrumental in this. Time also played a role in conditioning partners within the partnership framework, as explained by a PDI member:

> [Upon receipt of a project proposal of a local partner] we usually only have a few minor questions, because they clearly know what they can ask from us. We are familiar with one another for such a long time; they do not come with strange requests.

All this results in both sides of the partnership knowing what they can expect and expressing contentment with their partnership overall. Nonetheless, the interviews also revealed some clear wishes among the local organizations for adjustments to the partnership or its preconditions. For example, participants expressed a preference for budgeting based on conditions on the ground instead of the preferences of the Dutch PDI members.

In terms of control over resources, we found that the PDIs tended to remain in control of the finances over time, with many of these organizations continuing to fund the largest part of the project costs. Local fundraising by the organization in the South often represented only a small portion – if any – of the total funding. Additionally, in terms of decision making regarding activities to be undertaken, although the local organizations were often in charge of everyday tasks, this was not without the involvement of the PDIs, and ultimate control remained in the hands of the PDIs. This finding is well reflected in the following statement, made by one of the interviewed representatives of a PDI that was active in Uganda:

> Sometimes, a situation exists where the people there want things done differently or feel we interfere too much. But it is my – our – project and we are involved. [...]. The set-up of the project is in our hands, and decisions are made by our organization.

Importantly, this situation brings risks that may manifest when the time comes for exit strategies and the actual handing over of control, hindering real transformation. One of the interviewees from a PDI noted, for example, 'I do think we are working towards withdrawal. They [the members of the local organization] don't know that yet. We state that a bit in veiled terms'. Whereas more formal development organizations tend to establish a clear plan for any partnership they enter from the start, with explicit objectives and a strategy for their exit, this is not the case with PDIs. Their more ad hoc, informal, and personal character seems to make them less focused on handing over control. Especially when it comes to the end, there is uncertainty on these points. It appears that many PDIs do not develop a clear exit strategy from the start or prepare their local counterparts to assume ownership of the project.

Explaining change (or the lack of change)

Capacity strengthening is not a silver bullet

The local partners of the PDIs explained how partaking in the Change-the-Game capacity-strengthening programme clearly changed their outlook on local fundraising opportunities and strategies. At the time of the study, half of these participants had taken action in response to the programme by organizing fundraising events or collecting in-kind contributions from the communities where they worked. However, so far, these activities have not led to a significant shift in the funding balance between the local organizations and their Dutch counterparts.

Although one might expect the capacity-strengthening programme to be part of an exit strategy, the statements made by the representatives of the PDIs and their local counterparts participating in the Change-the-Game programme suggested that neither group considered the programme as a way to transfer power to the South. Their approach to the programme seemed rather instrumental, with a focus on generating local resources as a way of realizing the project rather than as a method for transforming the partnership. Interestingly, the few organizations that did manage to raise a first substantial amount locally used these funds to set up projects that did not fit within the framework of their existing donor partnerships. Although capacity strengthening cannot currently be seen as a silver bullet, this finding supported the theoretical assumption that the one who pays decides[4] and thus also the idea that a shift in control over financial resources might have the potential to increase local organizations' room for manoeuvre. We hence conclude that, although our data do not show capacity strengthening to be a strong driver of change, there is an indication that it has the potential to play this role in the future. This raises the question of what has prevented these partnerships from realizing genuine change, given the organizations' participation in the capacity-strengthening programme.

Personal relations as a constraint rather than a catalyzer

Contrary to what the literature suggests (Brown, 1996; Kumi & Copestake, 2021; Lister, 2000), we found the personal character of PDIs and their partnerships to be the key factor explaining why no significant power shift occurred in the studied partnerships. Although these friendly relations were helpful at first in instigating partnerships and, later on, in fostering mutual understanding, they could eventually become a hindering factor in two ways.

First, from the interviews, it became clear that many PDIs were set up ad hoc in response to personal motives by individuals without professional backgrounds in international development; even so, the PDIs still determined the framework, thereby essentially disregarding the professionals in the South. Appe and Schnable (2019, p. 13) note that,

> [A]t best, they might not know the context where they are working well enough to make effective decisions, and at worst, may implicitly or explicitly disregard the local knowledge and capacity of their Global South recipient communities when making decisions.

Instead of stimulating local ownership, Haaland and Wallevik (2017, p. 219) found that these accidental aid agents 'do not necessarily have a specific focus on what participation entails in practice'.

Second, although the representative of one organization stated that they were very much capable of separating the friendship side from the business side ('We are friends where we are friends and business where it should be business'), the interviews also indicated that partnerships guided by implicit, unspoken rules can stand in the way of equal relationships. In the interviews, the representatives of various organizations referred to their partners as a sort of 'extended family', with the relationship at times becoming 'too close for comfort', describing hesitancy in confronting the other side. In one of the interviews regarding the partnerships in India, a PDI representative noted,

> I think I have to be careful that it doesn't become too much of a friendship. [...] I was also invited to the wedding of the youngest brother, and then you go out with the whole family. [...] I am actually the "employer" [quotation marks indicated by the interviewee], but somehow also not. That is a bit of a tension.

To overcome the tension between being friendly and being able to be critical, one PDI representative adopted the strategy of hiding behind the organization and its donors:

> I don't say I think this or that, but [that] the donors do or the donors will ask me why, as they are really critical. So, I always bring the donors forward, which is also true of course, but this way I can somewhat avoid having a discussion with them.

At almost all decision-making moments, the rules remain implicit, resulting in a 'learning-by-doing' dynamic, with things being decided by the PDI and little ground for starting a discussion because of the lack of formally established, written rules – a problem that is reinforced by the friendship component and strong personal relations between PDIs and their local counterparts. The difficulty of critiquing one another has been pointed out in the literature on North–South relationships in general and on partnerships with PDIs in particular (Kinsbergen et al., 2017; Kumi & Copestake, 2021).

The strong personal nature of the partnerships appeared to be a key factor inhibiting change. This was generally related to resource scarcity and charitable consumerism, the two impediments to change mentioned in the description of the analytical framework above, making it essentially an overarching or reinforcing impediment. This seems contrary to the notion put forward by Kumi and Copestake (2021, p. 12) that personalized relationships in the form of friendship are 'an important inter-personal relation mechanism that facilitates the emergence of cooperation and collaboration' and Brown's (1996) argument that 'the stronger the personal relationship, the higher the levels of social capital available for co-operative problem-solving and the more easily gaps created by different levels of power and knowledge can be bridged' (in Lister, 2000, p. 229).

The shift in power promoted by a capacity-strengthening programme appears to be hindered by the personal character of the examined PDIs and their partnerships. In the first phase of the partnership, such personal relations may be a driver of change, facilitating cooperation and trust; however, when it comes to real transformation (i.e. exit strategies and the actual handing over of control), these personal relations risk becoming more of a stumbling block. Because of the strong, personal interconnectedness of PDI members with the local organizations, the projects they have supported, and the communities where they work, taking a step back is often a very complicated process. Our findings thus seem to indicate that the potential positive impact of a capacity-strengthening programme such as the Change-the-Game programme, in terms of shifting power, negatively interacts with the effects resulting from partnerships that are strongly personal in nature.

Conclusion and discussion

The personal character of PDIs and their partnerships, which results in friendly and informal relations, turns out to be an important explanatory factor for the lack of change towards more equitable partnerships. Compared with many studies emphasizing the positive impact of personal relations, including various chapters in this book, we find that the picture is more complex with respect to realizing the aspired change towards more equal partnerships and that caution is warranted. Personal relations, resulting in largely implicit partnership frameworks, tend to be a strong factor hindering the drivers of change, such as capacity-building programmes, in realizing their potential in terms of bringing about more equal partnerships. The findings of our study therefore also point to the perhaps unexpected value of formal rules as a facilitator of local ownership. While there has been scepticism about managerialism (i.e. 'knowledges and practices associated with formalized organizational management' [Roberts et al., 2005]) to enhance the effectiveness of development aid (Gulrajani, 2011), our analysis points to the important role that formal rules can fulfil. Although managerial logics have been criticized for 'creating new hierarchies and systems of authority with a powerful managerial elite at its apex [and for …] introducing generic "cookbooks of action" that are not tailored to local circumstances' (Gulrajani, 2011, p. 10), the practice of formalizing may in fact strengthen rather than weaken the voice of the less powerful side by providing the organization with a position from which it can negotiate. In terms of 'doing differently', the challenge is therefore to find the right balance between investing in personal relations that help to foster trust and establishing formal rules that help to provide Southern CSOs with sufficient leverage. To prevent the risks that personal relations can bring about and to ensure that there is a transition of power to the South, organizations – especially those with a people-to-people approach – would do well to set a minimum framework of formal rules to help clarify the roles and expectations and provide a point of reference from which local organizations can start to renegotiate the rules. This concerns discussing the parameters that determine the framework, such as the duration of the partnership, the allocation of funding, and the frequency of reporting (see also Elbers, 2012 for examples of rules that structure the relationship), which would enable everyone to know where they stand and ultimately prepare for a sustainable conclusion of the collaboration. This approach can be used to better integrate local insights and subsequently increase Southern leadership through enhanced local ownership.

Although the study has focused specifically on Dutch small-scale development organizations and their Ugandan and Indian local counterparts, the findings are of relevance to the broader field of international development, especially considering the implications of a potential setback in power asymmetries between the North and the South that these (increasingly prominent) organizations may bring about as a result of their way of approaching partnerships. The findings suggest that PDIs, their local counterparts, and co-funding agencies may wish to consider encouraging or developing some degree of formality to complement their informal relations for the purpose of providing a basis from which the rules of the game can be renegotiated and allowing for a shift of power within the partnership. In further research, it will be of interest to study the impact of the COVID-19 pandemic on power relations between the North and the South. The COVID-19 pandemic may have served as a trigger for local organizations to step up their game and take matters more into their own hands. To date, research has shown that the consequences can be both positive, with donors being forced to take a step back because of travel restrictions, and negative, through the hindering of, for example, local fundraising activities (Kinsbergen et al., 2021).

The study presented in this chapter has demonstrated the analytical value of the set of factors influencing change and the interplay between them in providing better insight into the underlying conditions that are necessary for producing equal partnerships, including the right balance between personal relations and formal rules. This analytical framework may be helpful in guiding further academic research on this topic, exploring the power dynamics within partnerships and the interplay between various drivers of and impediments to change in more depth. The focus of this analysis was on internal and/or behavioural factors; future studies could also analyse the role of external factors that might affect power relations and the desired shift in power. For instance, government policy might serve as a driver of change through regulation or infrastructure that supports CSOs' room for manoeuvre, which could, in combination with other drivers of change such as capacity-strengthening training, help to outweigh the countervailing forces of the impediments to change.

Notes

1 It should be noted that striving for such an ideal type of partnership has also been criticized (see e.g. Fowler, 2000).

2 As explained by Elbers (2012, p. 28),

> Episodic power refers to discrete, strategic acts initiated by self-interested actors to achieve outcomes in interaction with other actors. This mode of power has been the traditional focus of organisational research and theory, with its emphasis on examining which actors are most able to influence organisational decision

making. [...] Episodic power is always exercised in the context of social relations. As such, it is highly situated and contained, in which episodes of power are tied to the deliberate actions of actors.

3 As explained by Elbers and Schulpen (2013), whereas formal rules are set out in legal texts (e.g. contracts and policy documents), informal rules tend not to be spoken, let alone written down.
4 This idea is in line with the saying 'He who pays the piper calls the tune'.

References

Aagaard, P., & Eberhard Trykker, S. (2020). The road to partnerships in practice: Practical wisdom as an alternative to managerialism in NGO partnerships. *Development Policy Review, 38*(2), 266–282. https://doi.org/10.1111/dpr.12427.

Abrahamsen, R. (2004). The power of partnerships in global governance. *Third World Quarterly, 25*(8), 1453–1467. https://doi.org/10.1080/0143659042000308465.

Appe, S., & Schnable, A. (2019). Don't reinvent the wheel: Possibilities for and limits to building capacity of grassroots international NGOs. *Third World Quarterly, 40*(10), 1832–1849. https://doi.org/10.1080/0143 6597.2019.1636226.

Banks, N., & Hulme, D. (2014). New development alternatives or business as usual with a new face? The transformative potential of new actors and alliances in development. *Third World Quarterly, 35*(1), 181–195. https://doi.org/10.1080/01436597.2014.868997.

Batti, R. (2017). Factors influencing effective management of NGO partnerships. *Humanities and Social Sciences, 5*(5), 158–170. https://doi.org/10.11648/j.hss.20170505.11.

Brinkerhoff, D. W., & Brinkerhoff, J. M. (2004). Partnerships between international donors and non-governmental development organizations: opportunities and constraints. *International Review of Administrative Sciences, 70*(2), 253–270. https://doi.org/10.1177%2F0020852304044254.

Brinkerhoff, J. M. (2002). Assessing and improving partnership relationships and outcomes: A proposed framework. *Evaluation and program planning, 25*(3), 215–231. https://doi.org/10.1016/S0149-7189(02)00017-4.

Brown, L. D. (1996). Participation, social capital and intersectoral problem solving: African and Asian cases. *World Development, 24*(9), 1467–1479. https://doi.org/10.1016/0305-750X(96)00053-8.

Brown, L. D., & Kalegaonkar, A. (2002). Support organizations and the evolution of the NGO sector. *Nonprofit and voluntary sector quarterly, 31*(2), 231–258. https://doi.org/10.1177/0899764002312004.

Contu, A., & Girei, E. (2014). NGOs management and the value of 'partnerships' for equality in international development: What's in a name? *Human Relations, 67*(2), 205–232. https://doi.org/10.1177%2F0018726713489999.

Dahl, R. A. (1957). The concept of power. *Behavioral Science, 2*(3), 201–215. https://doi.org/10.1002/bs.3830020303.

Dichter, T. W. (1989). *Issues critical to a shift in responsibilities between U.S. PVOs and Southern NGOs.* Advisory committee on voluntary foreign aid. Retrieved from: https://pdf.usaid.gov/pdf_docs/pnabg227.pdf.

Elbers, W. J. (2012). *The partnership paradox: principles and practice in North-South NGO relations.* Nijmegen: CIDIN.

Elbers, W., & Schulpen, L. (2013). Corridors of power: The institutional design of North–South NGO partnerships. *Voluntas, 24*(1), 48–67. https://doi.org/10.1007/s11266-012-9332-7.

Elbers, W. J. (2012). *The partnership paradox: principles and practice in North-South NGO relations*. Nijmegen: CIDIN. Retrieved from: https://repository.ubn.ru.nl/bitstream/handle/2066/91410/91410.pdf.

Eyben, R. (2006). The power of the gift and the new aid modalities. *IDS Bulletin*, *37*(6), 88–98.

Fowler, A. (2015). International non-governmental organisations and aid: No longer a case of levelling the partner playing field. In Civicus *State of civil society report* (pp. 137– 159). Retrieved from: http://www.civicus.org/documents/reports-and-publications/SOCS/2015/SOCS2015_ESSAY8_NGOsAndAid.pdf.

Fowler, A. F. (1998). Authentic NGDO partnerships in the new policy agenda for international aid: dead end or light ahead? *Development and Change*, *29*(1), 137–159. https://doi.org/10.1111/1467-7660.00073.

Fowler A. F. (2000). Introduction – beyond partnership: Getting real about NGO relationships in the aid system. In: Questioning partnership: The reality of aid and NGO relations. *IDS Bulletin*, *31*(3), 1–13.

GFCF (n.d.). https://globalfundcommunityfoundations.org/about-us/.

Gulrajani, N. (2011). Transcending the Great Foreign Aid Debate: Managerialism, radicalism and the search for aid effectiveness. *Third World Quarterly*, *32*(2), 199–216. https://doi.org/10.1080/01436597.2011.560465.

Haaland, H., & Wallevik, H. (2017). Citizens as actors in the development field: The case of an accidental aid-agent's activities in aid-land. *Forum for Development Studies*, *44*(2), 203–222. https://doi.org/10.1080/08039410.2017.1305444.

Jones, J. A., & Deitrick, L. (2020). Does the theory of voluntary sector failure provide insight into food pantries? A case study of a network of food pantries in San Diego, CA. *Voluntas 31*, 870–880. https://doi.org/10.1007/s11266-018-00047-7.

Kinsbergen, S. (2014). *Behind the pictures: Understanding private development initiatives*. Doctoral dissertation Radboud University Nijmegen. Retrieved from: https://www.narcis.nl/publication/RecordID/oai:repository.ubn.ru.nl:2066%2F126456.

Kinsbergen, S. (2019). The legitimacy of Dutch do-it-yourself initiatives in Kwale County, Kenya. *Third World Quarterly*, *40*(10), 1850–1868. https://doi.org/10.1080/01436597.2019.1644497.

Kinsbergen, S., Koch, D. J., & Troost, J. (2020). *Limits to growth: Explaining the boundaries of financial expansion of small-scale development initiatives*. Unfold Private Development Initiatives – working paper series, number II. Nijmegen: Radboud University Nijmegen.

Kinsbergen, S., Pijnenburg, M. M. G., Merlevede, T., Naus, L. J. L., & Koch, D. J. (2021). Citizen Initiatives for Global Solidarity: Response to and impact of the COVID- 19 crisis. Voluntas, 1–27. Retrieved from: https://www.narcis.nl/publication/RecordID/oai:repository.ubn.ru.nl:2066%2F228650.

Kinsbergen, S., Schulpen, L., & Ruben, R. (2017). Understanding the sustainability of private development initiatives: What kind of difference do they make? *Forum for Development Studies*, *44*(2), 223–248. https://doi.org/10.1080/08039410.2017.1307270.

Kumi, E., & Copestake, J. (2021) Friend or patron? Social relations across the national NGO–donor divide in Ghana. *European Journal for Development Research*. https://doi.org/10.1057/s41287-021-00375-3.

Lister, S. (1999). *Power in partnerships? An analysis of an NGO's relationship with its partners*. London: Centre for Civil Society, London School of Economics. Retrieved from: http://eprints.lse.ac.uk/29093/1/int-work-paper5.pdf.

Lister, S. (2000). Power in partnership? An analysis of an NGO's relationships with its partners. *Journal of international Development*, *12*(2), 227–239. https://doi.org/10.1002/(SICI)1099-1328(200003)12:2%3C227::AID-JID637%3E3.0.CO;2-U.

Mawdsley, E., Townsend, J. G., & Porter, G. (2005). Trust, accountability, and face-to-face interaction in North–South NGO relations. *Development in Practice, 15*(1), 77–82. https://doi.org/10.1080/0961452052000321613.

Mawdsley, E., Townsend, J. G., & Porter, G. (2020). Trust, accountability and face-to-face interaction in North–South NGO relations. In A. Fowler & C. Malunga (Eds.), *NGO management: The Earthscan companion* (pp. 230–235). Abingdon: Earthscan.

Mawdsley, E., Townsend, J. G., Porter, G., & Oakley, P. (2002). *Knowledge, power and development agendas: NGOs North and South*. Oxford: INTRAC.

Michael, S (2004). *Undermining development: the absence of power among local NGOs in Africa*. Oxford: James Currey.

Misztal, B. (2000). *Informality: Social theory and contemporary practice*. London: Routledge.

Roberts, S., Jones, J. P., & Fröhling, O. (2005). NGOs and the globalization of managerialism: A research framework. *World Development, 33*(11), 1845–1864. https://doi.org/10.1016/j.worlddev.2005.07.004.

Schaaf, R. (2015). The rhetoric and reality of partnerships for international development. *Geography Compass, 9*(2), 68–80. https://doi.org/10.1111/gec3.12198.

Schnable A. (2015). New American relief and development organizations. *Social Problems, 62*, 309–329. https://doi.org/10.1093/socpro/spv005.

Schulpen, L., & Huyse, H. (2017). Editorial: Citizen initiatives for global solidarity. The new face of European solidarity. *Forum for Development Studies, 44*(2), 163–169. https://doi.org/10.1080/08039410.2017.1306956.

Steinhäuser, P. (2020). Assumptions underlying development programs, a case study about the assumptions underlying the Change the Game Academy program. Master's thesis. Maastricht: Maastricht University.

Sutton, D., Baskerville, R., & Cordery, C. (2010). A development agenda, the donor dollar and voluntary failure. *Accounting, Business & Financial History, 20*(2), 209–229. https://doi.org/10.1080/09585206.2010.485749.

22

CONCLUSIONS

Margit van Wessel, Tiina Kontinen and Justice Nyigmah Bawole

Introduction

This book seeks to provide significant contributions to the debate on needed changes in North–South collaborations concerning power, control, accountabilities and colonial mindsets, and help catalyze innovation. The book has aimed to provide ideas for reimagining CSO collaborations from the perspective of 'starting from the South', exploring the roles, relations, and processes shaping CSO collaborations in development. First, focusing on roles, who does what in CSO collaborations was reimagined, starting from the perspectives and agency of Southern CSOs. Second, exploring relations, the questions of who matters and how were addressed, with an attempt to move beyond the North–South binary. Third, focusing on processes, the nature of new collaborations if leadership from the South were more prevalent was considered. The five sections of the book have provided reimaginings from different angles: (1) how Southern CSOs could reclaim the lead, (2) how the North–South dyad could be displaced, (3) what Southern-centred questions emerge, (4) what kinds of new roles Northern actors could assume, and (5) what the new starting points for CSO collaborations could be. This chapter returns to the questions posed in the introductory chapter, reflects on the answers to these provided by the individual chapters, and reviews the main insights emerging from the five sections of the book. The chapter also presents overall conclusions and suggestions for research and practice on how to move towards 'starting from the South'.

Reimagining roles, relations, and processes

The chapters of this book touch on widely relevant elements of CSO collaborations in development, broadly conceived, addressing the domains of advocacy, service delivery, and capacity development. Similarly, the chapters consider

DOI: 10.4324/9781003241003-27

broadly relevant aspects of development programmes, such as agenda setting; strategizing; the production and usage of various forms of knowledge, skills, and relations; and the building of legitimacy.

Notwithstanding this broadness, when it comes to roles, the chapters consistently argue that Southern CSOs are positioned to shape development in context-specific ways. The chapters 'start from the South', in that they view, analyse, and reimagine collaboration from within Southern settings and portray Southern CSOs as drivers of development acting from their own contextually relevant knowledge on issues, strategies, legitimacy, relational capital, and perspectives. The situatedness of development in Southern contexts and the capacity of Southern CSOs to relate to these contexts make these CSOs capable of leading development, as the chapters argue. To start with roles then: Southern CSOs' agency in realizing their existing and potential leadership is stressed throughout the book. The chapters also emphasize the relevance of diversity among CSOs and their different roles, including social movements, individual activists, community-based organizations, professional non-governmental organizations (NGOs) at the domestic level, and international NGOs (INGOs). However, typically, the chapters assign leading positions to organizations taking up roles closest to the people they work with and focusing on domestic constituencies. Here, collaboration is also mostly conceived with a domestic focus, drawing attention to the roles of different CSOs within the same country setting, which has thus far received little attention in debates on CSO collaboration. These debates tend to be skewed towards global processes around internationally defined issues, with a prominent role for large INGOs. CSO roles are defined through their interactions with allies, their constituencies, and various other actors including the state and other domestic CSOs, as well as INGOs and Northern CSOs, which constitute only one form of relevant other. The chapters in this book thus relativize the prominent role of INGOs and Northern CSOs in development; some do see the role of such organizations as potentially highly relevant – but on new terms. INGOs and Northern CSOs and INGOs are called on to adjust – following the leadership of Southern CSOs and taking up supporting roles based on that lead, such as facilitating, linking, training, funding, and translating. The capacities, resources, and power of INGOs and Northern CSOs are seen as relevant in many ways. They can bring in much-needed support that otherwise would not come through – for domestically sensitive topics, for example. With their high levels of prestige, these types of organizations can help amplify local voices. By providing funding, they can facilitate the growth and flourishing of Southern CSOs. Given the centrality of contextually embedded CSOs in development, Broadly speaking, most of the chapters in this book call on international CSOs to take more supporting roles, carefully geared towards the agendas defined by Southern CSOs, and to accept Southern CSOs' leadership. It must be acknowledged here that the degree and nature of such support will depend at least partly on civic space – there are many contexts today where international civil society is delegitimized, especially when it comes to advocacy and sensitive topics. In short, reimagined roles involve contextually embedded Southern leadership, diversity in roles, and a repositioning of INGOs and Northern CSOs in supporting roles.

When it comes to relations, the embeddedness of CSOs in relations within their own contexts is shown to be a crucial resource for shaping action and navigating questions of legitimacy and effectiveness, which are largely defined by domestic relations. CSOs' domestic relations with constituencies, state agencies, and other non-state actors of various kinds are thus brought to the fore. The chapters draw attention to these relations, illustrating their prime importance for the survival of organizations and the success of their endeavours. The chapters also indicate the high demand for organizational capacities and resources associated with managing these relations and reimagine relations with INGOs and Northern CSOs as based on recognition of Southern CSOs' resources and capacities and the validity of their perspectives as starting points for collaboration. INGOs, to the extent they will be involved, are asked to act as facilitators and investors, furthering the leadership of Southern CSOs to contribute to development in their own contexts. In a few chapters, interdependence between CSOs is stressed, given their exchange of various resources. In one chapter, independence from INGOs and Northern CSOs is stressed as a viable and logical option, considering the resources that can be mobilized and the heavy price that must be paid without this independence, in terms of pandering to INGOs' and Northern CSOs' requirements and assumptions. The book thus aims to shift attention to how CSOs' relations with various actors at the domestic level shape locally owned development. However, some chapters also show that domestic CSO relations can mimic and reproduce the inequalities and disempowerment frequently associated with North–South CSO collaborations. Connected with the emphasis on starting out from Southern contexts is the message that relations are to be built on new terms. These terms evoke mutuality and include aspects such as recognition, trust, solidarity, connectedness, respect, sharing, transparency, reciprocity, interdependence, networking and acknowledgment of the multiple relations CSOs have.

Processes shaping the reimagined collaborations similarly shift attention away from linear North–South relations defined through contractual relations and towards processes of development influenced by conditions and dynamics in Southern contexts. Collaboration processes need to facilitate relating effectively to these contexts. Processes such as knowledge production and management, strategy development, and building organizational legitimacy are defined within Southern contexts. Collaboration should facilitate such processes and work towards strengthening the role of Southern CSOs in leading these processes within their contexts. Connected with this emphasis on centring process on Southern contexts, identified elements of good collaborative processes again evoke mutuality. They are reimagined to help grow meaningful collaboration together and include aspects such as reflexivity, learning, co-creation, exchange, negotiation, connecting diversities, building assets and linking up with what is there.

Plural vantage points

The main message of this book thus revolves around the notion of starting collaboration from contextually grounded Southern CSO leadership, which can grow with mutuality as a guiding principle. With the five sections approaching this idea from different angles, each offering specific ways in which our thinking on roles, relations, and processes in civil society collaborations in development can be approached. Each section of the book presents analyses of varied aspects and provides practical recommendations rooted in these analyses. The sections all offer opportunities for the fundamental reorientation of CSO collaborations in development.

The first section, 'Reclaiming the lead', emphasizes the basic point that Southern CSO leadership can be reclaimed based on what Southern CSOs offer, with implications for Northern-based actors (e.g. CSOs and researchers), who are asked to relate to Southern CSOs from a more facilitating, supportive stance, rooted in the recognition of Southern CSOs' agency, capacities, and resources. The chapters in this section show how collaborations can be practically rooted in the lived experiences of Southern communities and CSOs, highlighting the key role of acknowledging, mobilizing, and working with contextual knowledge while doing justice to constraining conditions.

The second section, 'Displacing the North–South dyad', shifts attention from this dyad to a wider orientation on CSO collaborations, emphasizing different types of roles, relations, and processes of exchange, interaction, and interdependence. The chapters in this section highlight the multiplicity of CSO relations, legitimacy requirements, and resources being exchanged, thus expanding our understanding of key aspects of CSO collaborations in development.

The third section, 'Southern-centred questions', shifts the attention from international CSO relations to different questions, centring on the dynamics among Southern CSOs and others in their contexts (e.g. other CSOs, constituencies, and the state). The chapters in this section argue for recentring legitimacy relations to focus on communities and constituencies; explore domestic CSO collaborations; present African CSOs' perspectives, roles, challenges, and opportunities around the desired shift of power; conceptualize Southern CSO roles as independent and home-grown; and zoom in on the centrality of trust to the gifting practices of local communities, as something that can be built and harnessed for financing development projects and programmes. These chapters thereby propose a reorientation of what relations matter and relativize the relevance of INGOs and Northern CSOs by viewing their roles in a wider, contextually defined frame.

The fourth section, 'Learning new roles for the North', focuses on what the recentring this book proposes implies for INGOs' and Northern CSOs' roles. While chapters in other sections of this book also discuss this question, here, specific assumptions and starting points commonly shaping these CSOs' roles are brought to light, and alternatives are suggested for knowledge management, power sharing/shifting, and programming. The chapters in this section show what 'starting from the South' will require in practice, emphasizing shifting mindsets and fundamentally reorienting Northern roles, relations, and processes. Openness to different interpretations and priorities while developing more horizontal forms of learning and facilitating rather than leading roles are important here, as is an expanded understanding of power that includes 'power to' and 'power with'.

The fifth section, 'New starting points for collaboration', provides inspiration for imagining new ways of collaborating, offering different principles and approaches that may support making CSO collaborations more oriented towards Southern contexts and more Southern-led. The chapters in this section primarily reconsider the foundations of CSO relations, mostly moving away from formal dimensions and addressing the roles and intricacies of the informal, focusing on elements like recognition of multiple identities, lived experiences and agency, the relational dimensions of autonomy, and the role of personal and trust-based relations.

'Starting from the South': a transformative stance

The chapters and sections of this book recentre the shaping of CSO collaborations, directing attention to the various contexts that we refer to as the Global South. Rather than linking with previous approaches to reimagining civil society collaborations, which have mostly been situated within the aid system, seeking to change it, the chapters in this book take a transformative stance. They relativize international collaboration at a fundamental level, asking INGOs, Northern CSOs, and their donors to follow the lead of Southern CSOs, with their contextually geared perspectives, resources, capacities, and ways of working. INGOs and Northern CSOs are to provide support from a stance of recognition of these elements, while also shifting focus to different, wider sets of relations that are, again, contextually defined.

This book thus addresses the need for reimagining of the roles of INGOs and Northern CSOs. These roles are currently thoroughly shaped by management-centred approaches sustained by control over funding and entrenched mindsets and practices. Thus far, the debate on reimagining CSO collaborations in development is highly concerned with shifting and sharing this control. The question of what is to become of INGOs and Northern CSOs, with a 'fundermediary' role of passing funds to other actors through building and managing multi-country programmes as their main function (Sriskandarajah, 2015), has not previously been directly addressed.

One of the editors of this volume, who regularly interacts with INGOs and Northern CSOs on the subjects of Southern ownership and leadership, often finds staff members struggling for ways to imagine how to transfer leadership to the South. The questions raised often concern management and accountability for funding. How can programmes be managed? How can the funds spent be accounted for? How can the risks involved be managed? Accountabilities associated with the fundermediary role are a main area of attention. Less openly discussed are concerns around the loss of organizational relevance and the loss of jobs, which sometimes come up in more personal conversations. Often, therefore, the questions and concerns are negatively framed, with reference to the existing system. How can a new system fit the requirements we are facing? Fundamental structures and assumptions shaping the aid system set up around the principles of management and control remain firmly in place. How to change roles, relations, and processes in fundamental ways can indeed be hard to imagine. Longstanding starting points that shape these three elements, arguably, are losing their self-evident primacy, but there are no new starting points on which to anchor the imagined transformed system. The new foundations that would be needed are not there yet. Many changes that have been worked on thus far – theoretically, and sometimes also in practice – such as 'giving' ownership to Southern CSOs (Sander, 2021), imagining or working towards adaptive management (Gutheil, 2021), or addressing questions of epistemological justice (Icaza & Vázquez, 2013) do not truly question INGOs' and Northern CSOs' fundermediary role, the programming prerogative that comes with it, or the centrality of the North–South dyad above other types of relations. It is this foundation that is addressed in this book by the different chapters and the book as a whole, with the message that emerges from the collection of chapters together and our situating them in the existing broader debates in practice and theory.

By emphasizing 'starting from the South', the book calls for starting civil society collaborations from the capacities, understandings, resources, and perspectives held by Southern CSOs within their own contexts. It also offers first steps towards reimagining roles for Southern CSOs as leaders, showing how this leadership is contextually rooted for CSOs in the Global South, taking no evident heed of 'capacity development' as administered by INGOs. At the same time, many chapters present INGOs and Northern CSOs as relevant or potentially relevant. The book thus also offers first steps towards reimagining roles for INGOs and Northern CSOs grounded not in their programming prerogative but in their capacity to offer support and to invest, following the lead of the Global South because of recognition of the validity of Southern leadership and the need to offer support that is context-specific and thus flexible and diverse.

We present an imagining of collaborations that works from knowing how different actors matter to a change process in different ways. This imagining is open-ended and rooted in recognition of what each organization stands for and brings to the collaboration. Such collaborations must also be based in meaningful connections linking capacities, perspectives, and goals. This signals a move away from managerial perspectives that may be rooted in the best of intentions and energized by laudable objectives but tend to come with constraints. Managerial approaches are centred on alignment with predefined agendas and understandings. They require that Southern CSOs exhibit a readiness to comply with international frameworks and 'tools' that they must work with to shore up collaborations. With such approaches, Southern CSOs must also ensure that all spending is accounted for and that all activities are in line with what the donors were promised, working towards documenting prespecified outcomes.

Ultimately, then, while the task of reimagining collaboration among CSOs in development may seem enormous, there is also a simplicity to the idea of moving away from complex multi-country programming, at least in the eyes of the authors of the different chapters in this book. 'How can we help?' is the question to be asked by INGOs and Northern CSOs, accepting that Southern CSOs are already agents, whose efforts others may be able to support with various resources, knowledges, relations, and capacities. How to find the freedom to provide these kinds of assistance is a more complicated question, and this may well be where INGOs and Northern CSOs (and maybe also Southern-based CSOs working with institutional donors) will face the most significant challenges. These organizations, too, are enmeshed in a system that keeps them in a constrained position, making them work as managers at the expense of their roles as change agents, even though they are likely much more driven by a will to contribute to change than by a desire to manage funding streams. Indeed, although it is generally Southern CSOs whose enforced mission drift is problematized, others in the development system also appear to suffer under the present system, with so much of their attention going towards procedurally oriented tasks. Donors are a crucial part of this system, and any transformation will have to take shape in close coordination with them.

An agenda for research and practice

Drawing on the analyses presented in the different chapters in this book, as well as our reflections on them, we have identified a range of questions for research and practice that require further exploration, research, design, and experimentation concerning reimagining civil society collaborations in development. Research and the work of practitioners are integrated here, as they will need to feed into each other to advance the fundamental transformations called for in this book. Here, we present these remaining issues as six overarching themes.

Towards Southern-led CSO collaborations

There is a need for further research that focuses on how the changes and transformations CSOs seek could be supported through different types of collaborations. This research should consider more thematic and strategic aspects instead of the management questions that have thus far dominated both research and policy agendas. The insights and recommendations emerging from the various chapters in this volume, and this concluding one, can provide valuable entry points for the needed research pursuits.

However, although this book offers such entry points for further research on 'starting from the South', more should be done to support donors and well-resourced INGOs and Northern CSOs in dealing with the question of how to let go of old practices and adopt new ones. Taking the example of multi-country programming as discussed in Chapter 17, INGOs and Northern CSOs have been encouraged to shift from a project approach to a programme approach to avoid fragmentation of their activities and to achieve greater impact. However, although the adoption of programme approaches has built stronger coherence from the point of view of INGOs and Northern CSO, it has also introduced new challenges to be addressed. Programmes are designed on the basis of principles and understandings of how change comes about that have limited space for contextualization. They are also often developed before 'Southern partners' are brought in to fit the programme goals. How to start collaboration from Southern organizations rather than beginning with predefined, large-scale Northern programming is an open question that will require further research, process design, and experimentation to identify new solutions. The same can be said about the notions of capacity and capacity development. Questions of whose capacities are to be brought in, how this should be done, to strengthen whom, and for what purpose deserve to be rethought and redesigned, exploring these issues from Southern perspectives and with an acknowledgement of existing capacities.

The insights and claims in this book also come with fundamental challenges on other fronts. As the authors in this book claim, other questions, such as what constitutes a 'good' partner and how to assess whether organizations are leaders in their own contexts when determining which Southern CSOs to work with by playing supporting roles, need more scrutiny. While some CSOs may be in a position to lead, the question of how to validate such claims remains unresolved. Questions of who and what they lead, by what (and whose) standards, and towards what goals become urgent when the criteria of fitting into Northern CSO programmes and goals are no longer prioritized.

Similarly, while the book has sought to imagine what 'starting from the South' could look like, it is important to realize that the drivers and motivations of INGOs and Northern CSOs may often not fall in line with these possibilities. The INGOs and Northern CSOs appearing in the chapters in this book mostly have at least some level of interest in more equal collaboration. However, some INGOs and Northern CSOs may have strong economic and ideological reasons for maintaining control over certain issues and areas in the South, to the extent of competing with each other. In such situations, there is not much impetus to change practices to move in the direction of Southern leadership. Moreover, relinquishing their grip on the conception, design, execution, management, and control of development would run counter to the interests and perceptions of good practices held by many, including back donors. This book's theme and goal did not include examining the complex dynamics between INGOs/Northern CSOs and their donors or how these can be addressed in the reimagined collaborations. Answering these questions, however, is crucial to the transformations called for throughout this book. In the complex global power dynamics of building alliances for control and influence in general, INGOs and Northern CSOs may also be part of an agenda seeking to maintain the influence of Northern economic or ideological hegemony over the South.

Questions of what parts of civil society to support and with what risks are also relevant here. In some contexts, INGOs and Northern CSOs supporting certain Southern CSOs as embedded in their own course of development will be highly problematic and deemed undesirable. An example can be seen in the context of the global war on terrorism and the securitization of CSO development. After the 9/11 events, Northern nations took an active interest in shaping advocacy to de-escalate extremism across nations suspected to be providing a nurturing environment for ideas and actions that would eventually pose threats to Northern nations. Under these circumstances, some Northern CSOs aligned their advocacy efforts in certain Southern contexts with Northern states' security aims, as a strategy to increase global security (Howell, 2014). In such situations, supporting the agency of Southern CSOs would likely be questioned on the grounds that Southern CSOs may be influenced by extremist views, potentially contributing to the radicalization of local populations; thus, supporting their agency would be supporting what has been called 'uncivil society' (Glasius, 2010). The broader point here is that questions of how agendas may collide and the implications of this for collaboration may come up regularly for INGOs, Northern CSOs, and donors who are serious about 'starting from the South'. Clearly, this requires careful reflection on whose agendas should be leading and on what grounds this should be decided.

Embeddedness in Southern contexts

Answering the call of the chapters of this book to work with Southern CSOs as leaders in their own contexts requires in-depth knowledge and close engagement from INGOs and Northern CSOs. There are, then, more questions, given that relinquishing multi-country programming on decontextualized terms means working from, and understanding of, diversity. How can INGOs and Northern CSOs identify the diverse organizations with which to work, and how can they justify working with the varied understandings, perspectives, and objectives of these CSOs? How can INGOs and Northern CSOs define their new role as just one node in a wide set of relations rather than a leading organization that 'has a programme'? Addressing these questions will require reflection and a redesign of organizational identities and roles, in close interaction with Southern CSOs.

Considering the wide spectrum of roles and relations in CSO collaborations in development, the diverse types of CSOs that may collaborate productively with each other and with other societal actors (e.g. the media, academia, the private sector, and allies within the government) in a given context also need more attention. Although numerous alliances including a variety of actors exist, they have rarely been documented or evaluated for wider sharing and learning, and research on this is scant. To illustrate: while there is a wide literature on transnational advocacy networks of CSOs, the literature on subnational, national and regional advocacy networks is minimal, making it hard to establish the nature and relevance of such collaborations in specific domains and contexts.

While there should be a shift in focus towards the Southern sides of collaborations, romanticizing the South and the 'local' should be avoided. Instead, a realistic understanding by both Northern and Southern actors should be promoted. For instance, the implications of the prevalent patron–client networks and diverse social obligations emerging in diverse contexts (Lorch, 2017) should be identified and subjected to reflection. CSOs, at any level and in any context, are part and parcel of the existing social fabric. For example, CSOs are sometimes established by local economic and political elites and thus may be used to increase political support (e.g. to drive contestation in general elections). Additionally, some CSOs can function as extensions of authoritarian states, seeking to control the manifestations of citizens' engagement in criticizing the regime in power. Therefore, analyses and understanding of the societal and political constellations are required for research or practice in any context, as 'starting from the South' means departing from the existing social dynamics in each location, which, for diverse reasons, some CSOs seek to maintain, whereas others aim for change and transformation.

Questions of legitimacy

A number of chapters in this book discuss questions of legitimacy. There is a particular need for further analysis and conceptualization of legitimacy in the context of collaborations that start from the South. Questions such as who has legitimacy, based on whose evaluation, and which criteria should be used to determine this, need to be addressed. For example, Southern CSOs have often advocated for legitimacy and the subsidiarity principle (that decisions should be taken at the most local level possible), arguing that they are Southern-embedded and consequently legitimized to act on behalf of local communities. However, the limited research available identifies an important tension here, indicating that Southern CSOs' relations with communities vary in degree, nature, and quality (Katyaini et al., 2021) and suggesting that such CSOs may align with donor demands rather than really representing the people and having the legitimacy among them that they claim to have (Elbers et al., 2021). Several questions have been posed by governments, local communities, and scholars: Are professionalized Southern CSOs 'external agents'? Do they represent local communities? How embedded are they, and how different are they from INGOs and Northern CSOs in terms of strategies of implementation? Who is being represented, and in what sense? Who is excluded? (Katyaini et al., 2021). Despite such questions of legitimacy, Southern CSOs typically demonstrate superior contextual understandings and relations compared with their Northern collaborators and can thus claim a legitimacy rooted in local knowledge and embeddedness. Understanding the issues surrounding how different sources of legitimacy come into play, for whom, and for what will require further research and engagement in practice.

In the current architecture of collaboration, however, the legitimacy of Southern CSOs in the eyes of their potential collaborators is in large part determined by their ability to build strategies and programmes in line with programme needs, their capacity to manage finances, and their competence in monitoring and evaluation – in other words, being professional NGOs. In efforts to address the foundations of CSOs' legitimacy, close attention should be paid to the CSOs' relations and interactions with the people they work with and the constituencies and values they claim to represent. There is a need for new approaches to viewing CSOs and their roles that take relations within a context as the foundation for their place in shaping development. Reflection, research, and design regarding ways to understand, assess, support, and work with these relations through programming can help equip CSOs to build and acknowledge legitimate roles that start from the South. This pursuit can also equip Southern and Northern CSOs, INGOs, and donors to establish understandings and standards for seeking collaboration on this basis (cf. van Wessel et al., 2020).

New starting points for collaboration

If the role of INGOs and Northern CSOs is not first and foremost to manage multi-country programmes, what is their relevance? There is a need for research that helps these powerful organizations with strong capacities in multiple areas to define their added value in different types of domains and arenas and for various types of organizations and objectives, as well as to determine how that added value can best be put to use. Further, it is important to overcome ingrained organizational understandings and practices around knowledge to capitalize more on Southern-based knowledge through incorporating acknowledgement, documentation, sharing, learning, and upscaling in ways that break through the limitations of the North–South dyad. Uncovering how to achieve such outcomes and how diverse Southern knowledges can inform wider civil society learning and practice may be important new research areas.

There is disagreement within this book and beyond on the question of whether the needed transformations are about 'shifting' or 'sharing' power. However, rejecting the power of INGOs and Northern CSOs as coercion would reflect a flat conceptualization of power as a zero-sum game and coercion as its only expression. Other understandings of power allow for more complex approaches, with power potentially supporting and enabling (see e.g. Gaventa, 2021; Haugaard, 2012). Taking this latter type of perspective provides a richer set of futures to explore. Research can help INGOs and Northern CSOs to identify what they bring to the table in collaborations, beyond the prerogative and capacity to manage. These organizations may have valuable strengths that could be used to support Southern CSOs in moving forward with their self-identified needs and goals. Relatedly, as discussed in some of the book's chapters, the power of INGOs and Northern CSOs lies not only or primarily in their control over the Southern CSOs they work with. They can also be seen as important companions or allies who can support and complement using their complementary strengths on various fronts. They can also help promote certain issues, such as human rights in contexts where civic space for local CSOs is restricted or where funding for political roles for specific causes or groups could not otherwise be obtained. More in-depth research is needed on Southern views and experiences regarding new, more complementary, and facilitating roles for INGOs and Northern CSOs in collaborations. Such work will also facilitate the efforts of INGOs and Northern CSOs to reshape their roles in ways that engage CSOs in the Global South on more equal terms or, as the chapters in this book advocate, to take up supporting and facilitating roles while also capitalizing on their own power, motivation, and capacities. The challenge of incorporating and harnessing these varied strengths, however, requires working together with donors, who must be ready to experiment with alternatives.

Although ongoing discussions among INGOs and Northern CSOs consider the necessity of transforming collaborations and addressing the prevalent relations and privileges, including themes such as decolonization and racism, to date, little research examining the premises of such critical theoretical discussions has been carried out on CSO collaborations. Scholarly contributions to the field since the late 1980s largely address a narrow range of issues related to partnership, power, and accountability. More understanding of mechanisms related to race and white privilege within collaborations and more thorough explorations of decolonization are needed. Investigating the new roles mentioned above may open up, diversify, and brighten current critical debates on CSO collaborations by introducing constructive, future-oriented approaches and practices.

Research on and a redesign of accountability questions and mechanisms within the development system are also needed to address the hegemony of a reporting culture focusing on monitoring and evaluation centred on upward accountability on imposed terms. Some INGOs and other actors have experimented with alternative ways of accounting and reporting, especially when it comes to non-financial accountability. More research is needed on these alternative accountability practices and on how financial accountability could function – for instance, in situations where public aid funding is allocated directly to Southern CSOs.

The value of comparative advantage

Another area of interest that requires additional evidence is the supposed comparative advantage of adopting a Southern-led approach in CSO collaboration. While North–South, South–South, and other variants of the relations between and among Northern and Southern CSOs may be emotionally and morally satisfying in a variety of ways, it is important to research whether, when, and how Northern-led and/or Southern-led approaches offer comparative advantages when it comes to the changes and transformations CSOs seek to achieve. This would include research into the comparative advantages of collaborations between CSOs beyond the North–South dyad, including thus far understudied domestic and transnational alliances, such as those involving diasporas, social movements, and other actors not fitting the image of the conventional, professionalized NGO. While there have been many analyses of the successes and failures of Northern-led approaches, more research is needed on the achievements – however defined – of Southern-led initiatives. Identifying what works and uncovering why it works in terms of Southern leadership may inspire many CSO practitioners in the North and the South who are seeking to reimagine how to shape their futures.

Further research is also required to understand the conditions under which a particular approach to CSO collaboration has the greatest impact. Ideally, democratic states provide the critical conditions under which 'starting from the South' can provide comparative advantages and Southern CSOs can act on the basis of their goals and interests. However, CSOs face challenges in both autocratic/hybrid and democratic states, with conditions described as shrinking or squeezing civic space (Buyse, 2018). CSOs are increasingly controlled by states, and burdensome bureaucratic demands with the constant threat of de-registration, the freezing of bank accounts, or direct harassment limit Southern CSOs' agency. While some governments in developing countries crack down on INGOs/Northern CSOs and Southern CSOs receiving support from INGOs/Northern CSOs, others respect or are at least more tolerant of INGOs and Northern CSOs. This may depend both on the regime and on the topic being covered. Therefore, again, a contextual understanding of the conditions under which 'starting from the South' will have the strongest impact and of what kinds of roles INGOs and Northern CSOs can assume in restricted circumstances is needed.

Towards the pluriverse

Opening up CSO collaborations to diversity means being open to a multitude of knowledges and imaginings of how to live and relate in this world – what Escobar (2011, 2018) has called the 'pluriverse'. Moving towards a pluriverse in shaping CSO collaboration would not only mean decolonizing in the sense of abandoning mindsets and practices of domination; it would also mean opening up to the possibilities that may come with the discovery of new knowledges and new ways of coming together. We are presently quite far from such a state. While decolonization has entered the vocabularies of INGOs and Northern CSOs, there is still little research on efforts to decolonize CSO collaborations, let alone on opening up to the pluriverse in shaping these collaborations.

Relatedly, much of the current critical analysis on power in CSO collaborations is still conducted and published by scholars at universities in the Global North. The contributions are often based on longer or shorter periods of 'fieldwork' with CSOs in the Global South for projects often commissioned by INGOs or Northern CSOs and largely conceived outside the research site. We hope this book and the agenda for research and practice we have elaborated here will encourage researchers and CSO practitioners from the Global South to increasingly engage in critical theorizing and empirical analysis. This may help to break the pattern of INGOs and Northern CSOs, accompanied by Northern researchers, being the most vocal and silencing voices from the South.

Exploration and development of new approaches that 'start from the South' will be much helped by research grounded in contextually rooted perspectives, with researchers with deep contextual understandings and relations in leading roles – and recognized as such by others in positions that allow them to provide support. Drawing on the idea of pluriversality, to identify how 'translations' between the multiple worlds in the pluriverse can take place in practice, more research should be done on clashes and dialogues between the diverse epistemologies in the context of civil society collaborations (Escobar, 2018, p. 83).

However, putting forward a pluriversal research agenda will require further fundamental changes in how the world is understood and categorized. Academic researchers, whether they are located in the Global North or in the Global South, typically draw on epistemologies and categorizations that have evolved in Western theory. This is also the case in this book, as most of the chapters draw from theories discussed in mainstream Western social science. Obviously, a foundational concept of the book, 'civil society organization', is itself based on the current 'epistemic table of the modern social sciences' (Escobar, 2018, p. 84), where civil society is one of the main concepts discussed in relation to modernization and the evolution of the modern state. Therefore, drafting an agenda for pluriversal research on civil society collaborations may be an epistemological impossibility. Rather, new research agendas with new conceptualizations of constellations of people in their relations with others, nature, and the spiritual – which acknowledge forms and aspects that have often been ignored in Western epistemologies and hence in Northern approaches to collaborations – are needed to enable both CSO collaborations and academic research to 'start from the South'. This epistemological shift towards Southern theorizing (Connell, 2007) or the de-Westernization of investigations (Mignolo, 2021) will be a challenging future agenda for the authors of this book and others interested in relations and dialogues among peoples, organizations, and worldviews from what we call the Global North and the Global South.

References

Buyse, A. (2018). Squeezing civic space: Restrictions on civil society organizations and the linkages with human rights. *The International Journal of Human Rights*, *22*(8), 966–988. https://doi.org/10.1080/13642987.2018.1492916.

Connell, R. (2007). *Southern theory: The global dynamics of knowledge in social science*. Cambridge: Polity Press.

Elbers, W., Schulpen, L., & Frobisher, E. (2021) Stuck in a "Catch-22": Why donors fail to include grassroots perspectives on CSO legitimacy. *European Journal of Development Research*. https://doi.org/10.1057/s41287-021-00406-z.

Escobar, A. (2011). Sustainability: Design for the pluriverse. *Development*, *54*(2), 137–140. https://doi.org/10.1057/dev.2011.28.

Escobar, A. (2018). Transition discourses and the politics of relationality: Toward designs for the pluriverse. In B. Reiter (Ed.), *Constructing the Pluriverse. The geopolitics of knowledge* (pp. 63–89). New York: Duke University Press.

Gaventa, J. (2021). Linking the prepositions: Using power analysis to inform strategies for social action. *Journal of Political Power, 14*(1), 109–130. https://doi.org/10.1080/2158379X.2021.1878409.

Glasius, M. (2010). Uncivil society. In H. K. Anheier, S. Toepler, & R. List (Eds.), *International Encyclopedia of civil society* (pp. 1583–1588). New York: Springer. https://doi.org/10.1007/978-0-387-93996-4_6.

Gutheil, L. (2021). Adaptive project management for the civil society sector: Towards an academic research agenda. *International Development Planning Review, 43*(3). https://doi.org/10.3828/idpr.2020.17.

Haugaard, M. (2012). Rethinking the four dimensions of power: Domination and empowerment. *Journal of Political Power, 5*(1), 33–54. https://doi.org/10.1080/2158379X.2012.660810.

Howell, J. (2014). The securitisation of NGOs post-9/11. *Conflict, Security & Development, 14*(2), 151–179.

Icaza, R., & Vázquez, R. (2013). Social struggles as epistemic struggles. *Development and Change, 44*(3), 683–704. https://doi.org/10.1111/dech.12039.

Katyaini, S., Wessel, M. V., & Sahoo, S. (2021). Representation by development organizations: Evidence from India and implications for inclusive development. *The Journal of Environment & Development, 30*(1), 98–123.

Lorch, J. (2017). *Civil society and mirror images of weak states*. London: Palgrave Macmillan.

Mignolo, W. D. (2021). *The politics of decolonial investigations*. Durham, NC and London: Duke University Press.

Sander, A. (2021). Reclaiming partnership–'rightful resistance' in a Norths/Souths cooperation. *Third World Quarterly*, 1–14. https://doi.org/10.1080/01436597.2021.1957672.

Sriskandarajah, D. (2015). Five reasons donors give for not funding local NGOs directly. *The Guardian*, November 9.

van Wessel, M., Hilhorst, D., Schulpen, L., & Biekart, K. (2020). Government and civil society organizations: Close but comfortable? Lessons from creating the Dutch "Strategic Partnerships for Lobby and Advocacy." *Development Policy Review, 38*(6), 728–746.

INDEX